Y0-CSE-306

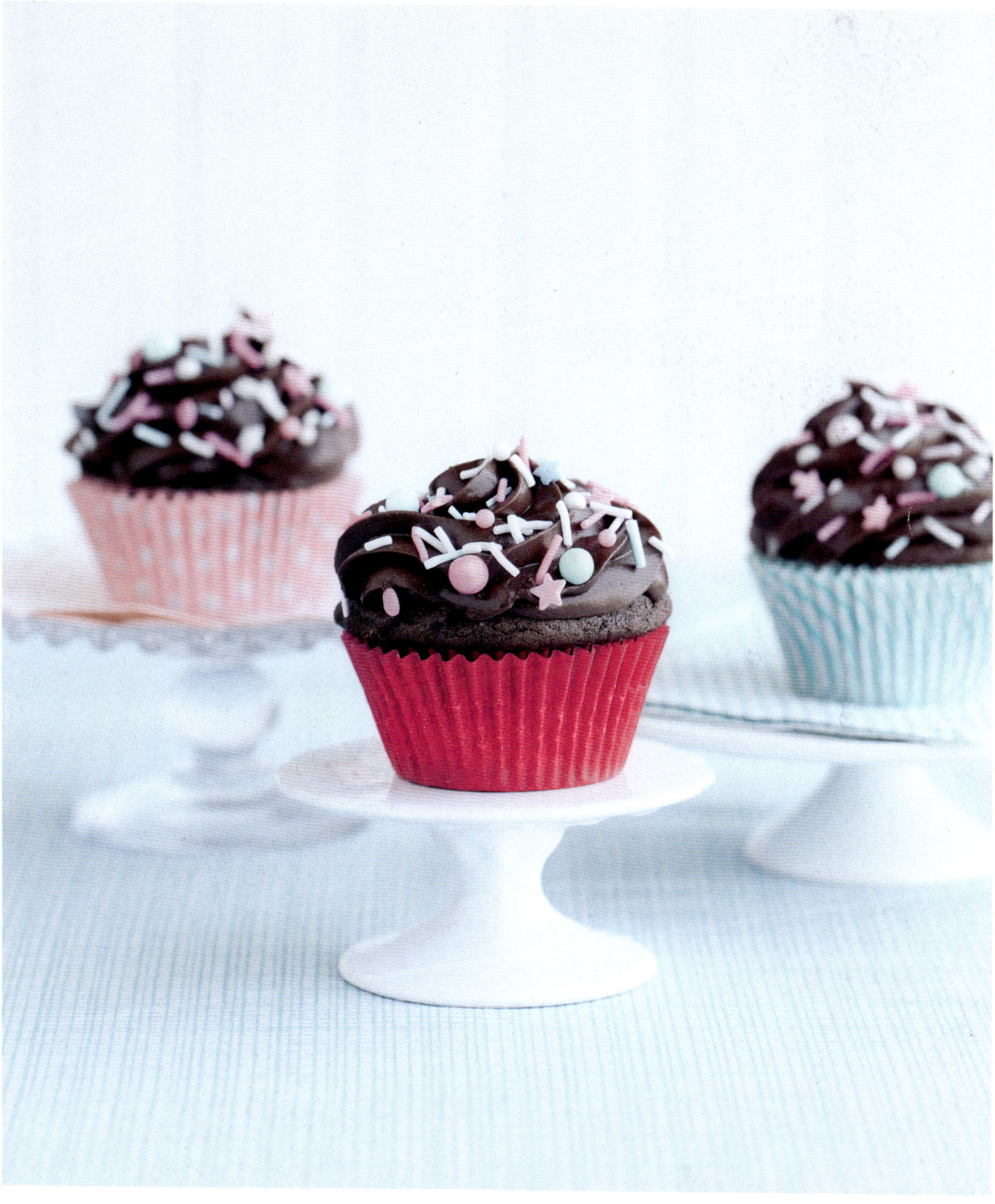

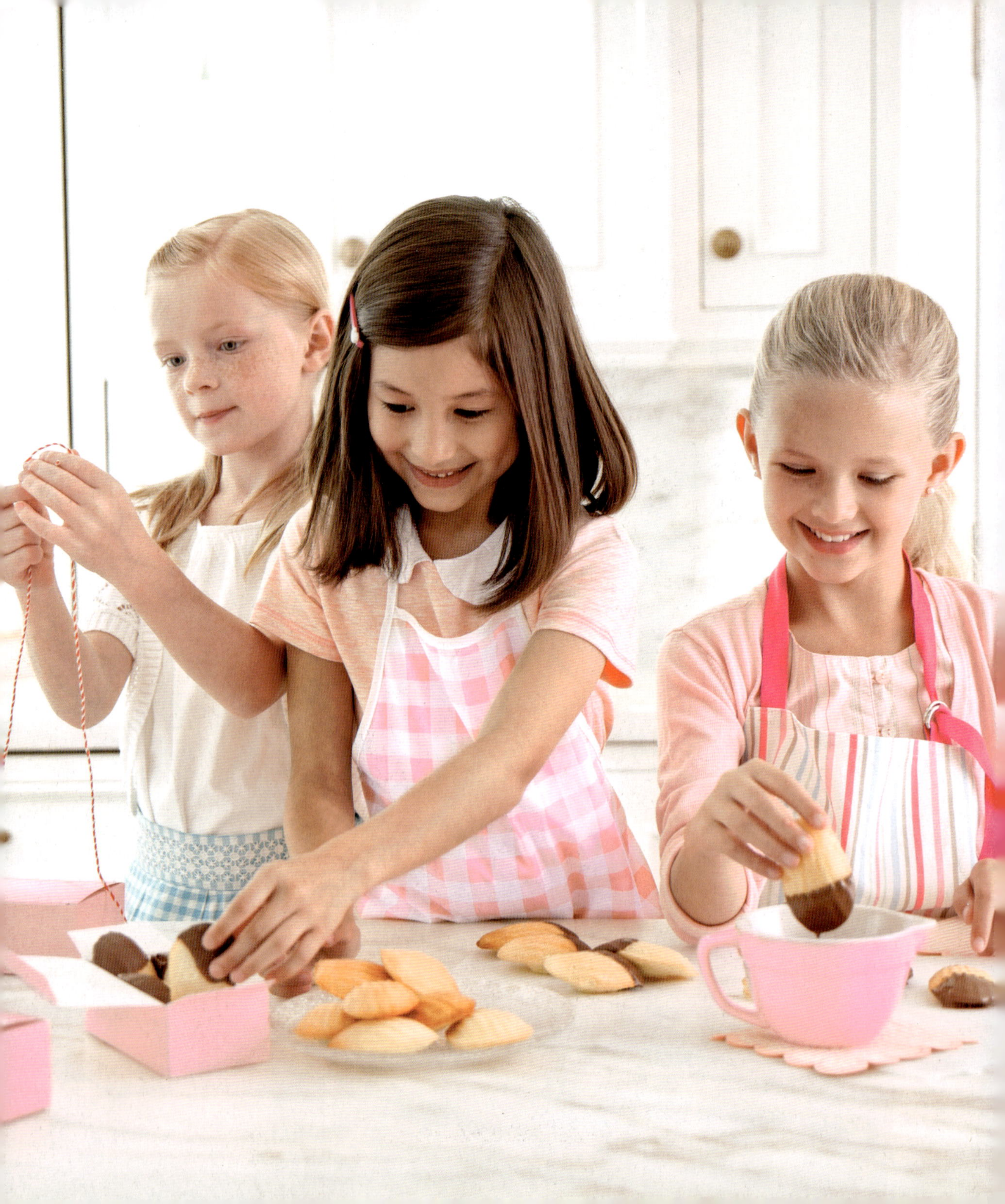

★ American Girl®

The Big Book of Baking for Kids

FAVORITE RECIPES TO MAKE & SHARE

Photography **Nicole Hill Gerulat**

weldon**owen**

TOOLS YOU'LL NEED 9
BAKE LIKE A PRO 10

Cookies

14
Thumbprint Cookies

17
Pinwheel Icebox Cookies

19
Snickerdoodles

20
Elephant Ears

23
Fortune Cookies

26
Chocolate Chip Cookie Sandwiches

29
Chocolate Crinkle Cookies

30
Raspberry Jam Heart Cookies

32
Kitchen Sink Cookies

33
Homemade Oreos

35
Lemon Crinkle Cookies

36
Hot Chocolate Cookies

Contents

39
Galaxy Cookies

42
Triple-Chocolate-Chunk Cookies

45
Chocolate-Dipped Butter Cookie Triangles

46
Confetti Cookies

49
Milk-and-Cookie Cups

53
Chewy White Chocolate Coconut Cookies

54
Chocolate-Covered Mint Wafers

57
Chocolate-Filled Vanilla Sandwich Cookies

59
Sugar Cookie Cutouts

62
Classic Peanut Butter Cookies

63
Chocolate-Drizzled Almond Florentines

64
Donut Cookies

69
Peppermint Swirl Macarons

73
Flower Cookie Pops

75
Colorful Macarons

79
Ice Cream Sandwiches

80
Moon Pies

83
Gingerbread Cookies

Bars, Brownies & Blondies

86
Caramel-Glazed Blondies

89
Sugar Cookie Bars

90
Ooey-Gooey Layer Bars

92
Lemon-Blackberry Crumb Bars

93
Frosted Chocolate Brownies

95
Nut, Seed & Fruit Granola Bars

96
Lemony Berry Bars

99
Chocolate-Peanut Butter Brownies

100
Crispy Rice & Chocolate Layer Bars

Cakes

106
Golden Layer Cake with Chocolate Frosting

110
Black Forest Cake

112
Tres Leches Cakes

115
Chocolate Chip Cookie Birthday Cake

116
Pink Orange Cake

119
Frosted Apple Cake

122
Spiced Apple & Honey Cake

125
Southern Tea Cakes

127
Mixed Berry Shortcake

129
Chocolate Ice Box Cake

133
Cranberry Upside-Down Cake

134
Baked Nectarines with Cinnamon Streusel

136
Honey Madeleines

138
Orange Madeleines

139
Chocolate Madeleines

140
Chocolate-Dipped Vanilla Madeleines

Cupcakes

144
Devil's Food Cupcakes

147
Strawberries & Cream Cupcakes

148
Snowball Cupcakes

151
Sweet Lemony Cupcakes

152
White Chocolate & Raspberry Cupcakes

155
Red Velvet Cupcakes

156
PB&J Cupcakes

157
Yellow Cupcakes

159
S'mores Cupcakes

160
Pumpkin Cupcakes

163
Strawberry Cupcakes

165
Chocolate-Banana Cream Pie Cupcakes

169
Toasted Coconut Cupcakes

170
Pink Velvet Cupcakes

173
Snow White Cupcakes

174
Cookies 'n' Cream Cupcakes

177
Gingerbread Cupcakes

178
Rainbow Cupcakes

180
Triple Chocolate Cupcakes

181
Butterfly Cupcakes

183
Cupcake Cones

184
Iced Lemon Drizzle Cupcakes

Muffins & Pastries

188
Sugar-and-Spice Popovers

191
Cinnamon Rolls with Cream Cheese Icing

193
Vanilla-Glazed "Toaster" Pastries

194
Blueberry Turnovers

196
Apple Galettes

197
Crumpets

199
Jam Twists

200
Bite-Sized Chocolate Chip Scones

203
Cinnamon-Sugar Donut Holes

205
Apricot Puff-Pastry Twists

206
Cosmos Doughnuts

209
Spiced Applesauce Muffins

211
Coffee Cake Muffins

212
Strawberry Jam Muffins

215
Mini Blueberry-Oat Muffins

216
Cranberry-Oat Muffins

217
Pumpkin Spice Muffins

218
Apple Streusel Muffins

Pies & Tarts

222
Blackberry Slab Pie

225
Mini Peach & Cherry Pies

227
Easy Cheesecake Pie

228
Cinnamon-Swirl Apple Pie

232
Sweet Potato Pie

235
Classic Pumpkin Pie

237
Individual Cherry Cobblers

238
Strawberry Hand Pies

239
Maple-Pecan Pie with Shortbread Crust

240
Chocolate-Raspberry Tartlets

243
French Apple Tart

244
Blackberry Tart with Pecan Crust

247
Lemon Tart with Raspberries

248
Lemon Tartlets with Sugared Flowers

251
Cranberry Chess Tart

252
Shortbread Crust

253
Tart Dough

Icings & Frostings

256
Royal Icing

259
White Chocolate Frosting

260
Fluffy Vanilla Frosting

263
Cream Cheese Frosting

264
Chocolate Frosting

266
Peanut Butter Frosting

267
Rich Chocolate Glaze

269
Vanilla Custard

270
Caramel Drizzle

271
Crumb Topping

272
Whipped Honey Frosting

INDEX **274**

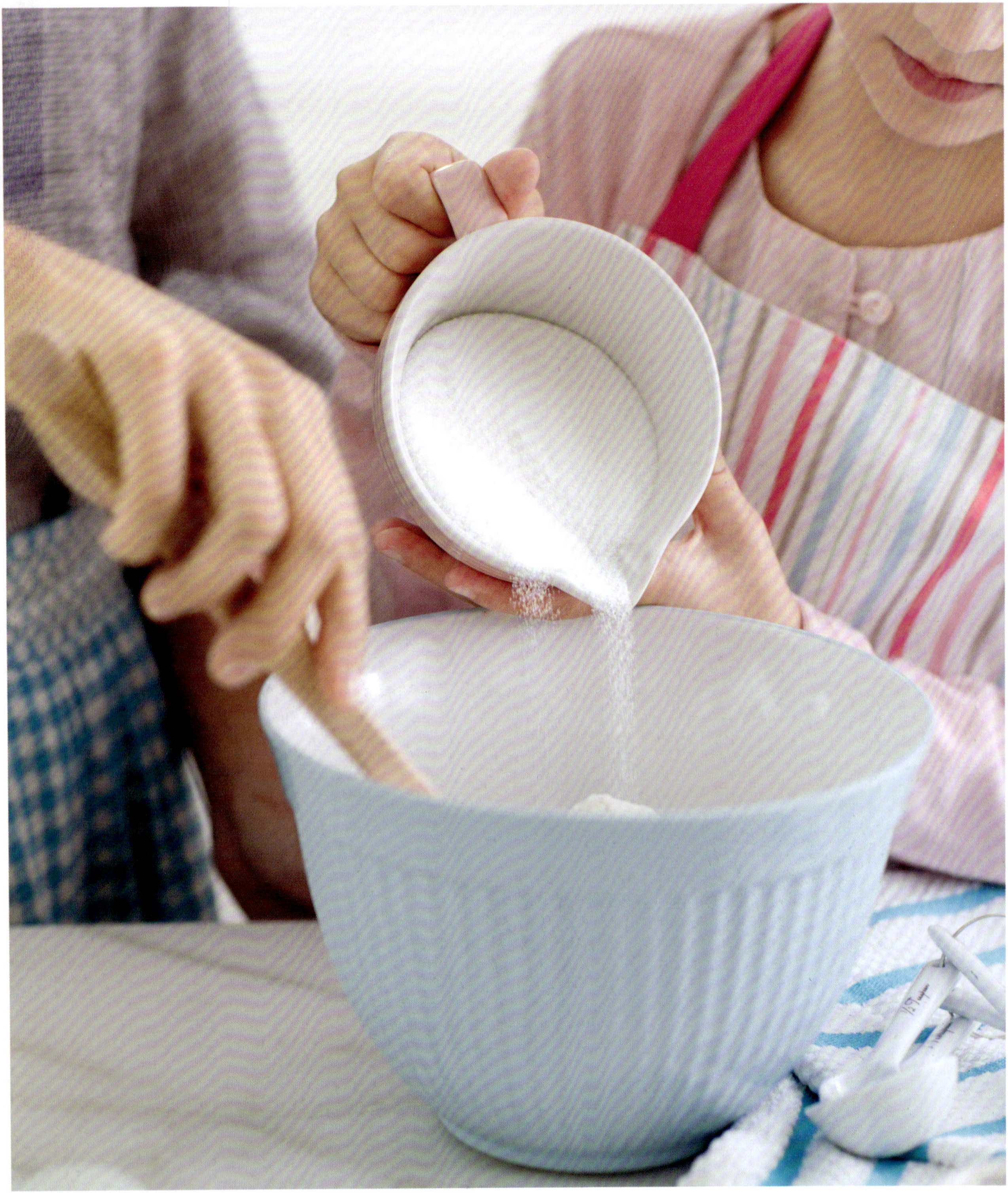

Tools You'll Need

The recipes in this book use a few basic baking tools. There's no need to go out and buy everything all at once—you can collect tools slowly over time, as you try more and more baking recipes.

★ **Aprons** are handy to help keep your clothes tidy when you are baking.

★ **Cookie cutters** come in all shapes. All-time favorites are butterflies, stars, flowers, and hearts, but use any shape you like.

★ **Cookie sheets**, especially think, heavy ones, help cookies bake evenly and won't warp in the oven.

★ **Small metal icing spatulas** are good for spreading frosting on cupcakes and cakes. A piping bag fitted with a pastry tip is another way to add frosting or to write fun messages on top of cookies, cakes, and cupcakes.

★ An **electric mixer** makes quick work of batters and frostings, beating egg whites and cream, and more. Always ask an adult for help when using appliances. Use a mixing bowl and wooden spoon or whisk in a pinch.

★ **Madeleine pans** are charming French molds used to create dainty, shell-shaped cakes in a variety of flavors.

★ A **piping bag** fitted with a pastry tip is another way to ice cookies and also to pipe cookie dough onto cookie sheets.

★ **Measuring cups and spoons** help you measure your ingredients accurately and easily. Choose graduated sets for dry ingredients and a liquid pitcher for wet ingredients.

★ **Oven mitts** or pads protect your hands from hot pans, oven racks, cookie sheets, and baking dishes. Always ask an adult to help when working near a hot oven or stove.

★ An **ice cream scoop** is helpful for dividing batter evenly into muffin pans.

★ **Parchment paper** is paper that's been treated to give it a nonstick surface. It's used to line cookie sheets and pans so that baked goods won't stick. If you don't have parchment paper, butter the pans and dust them with flour.

★ A **rubber spatula** is helpful for mixing batters and scraping them into pans, like when you transfer the last bits of batter from a bowl to a muffin pan.

★ Standard **muffin pans**, with 12 cups, are used for the cupcake recipes in this book; for some recipes, you'll need two muffin pans.

★ **Imagination and a good dose of creativity** are the two most important baker's tools of all. Have fun!

Bake Like a Pro

BE OVEN SMART

Be extra careful when working around a hot oven and hot baking dishes. Always use oven mitts and have an adult help you with taking pans in and out of the oven.

GET HELP WITH APPLIANCES

Electric mixers make mixing batters quick and easy. Always have an adult assist you when using appliances.

STAY ORGANIZED

Staying organized and paying attention are important baking skills. Before you preheat the oven, it's important to read the full recipe and ingredient list. Then it's time to clear a clean surface and lay out all your baking tools and ingredients. Once the food is in the oven, don't forget to set a timer!

MORE TIPS

★ When making dough, turn off the electric mixer periodically to scrape down the bowl with a rubber spatula in between adding ingredients. This will help the ingredients to combine better.

★ If dough is too hard to roll directly from the fridge, let it stand at room temperature for a few minutes before rolling. You can also use your hands to mold the dough into a ball if it starts to crumble.

★ Butter should be at room temperature for most of the recipes in this book, since it is easier to work with in its softened state. Eggs will mix into a batter more evenly if they are at room temperature, but it's not critical for the recipe to work properly.

★ Dust your rolling pin with flour before rolling out dough.

★ To roll dough scraps, gently gather the scraps and press them together with your hands, then roll them out and cut out additional shapes. After a second rolling, discard any remaining dough.

★ Use a metal spatula to transfer dough shapes from your work surface to baking sheets.

★ Be sure to wait for your cupcakes, cookies, cakes, or pastries to cool completely before you frost them, or the frosting might melt and drip off of them.

Baking with Care

Adults have lots of culinary wisdom and can help keep you safe in the kitchen. Always have an adult assist you, especially if your recipe involves high heat, hot ovens, sharp objects, and electric appliances.

This symbol appears throughout the book to remind you that you'll need an adult to help you with all or part of the recipe. Ask for help before continuing.

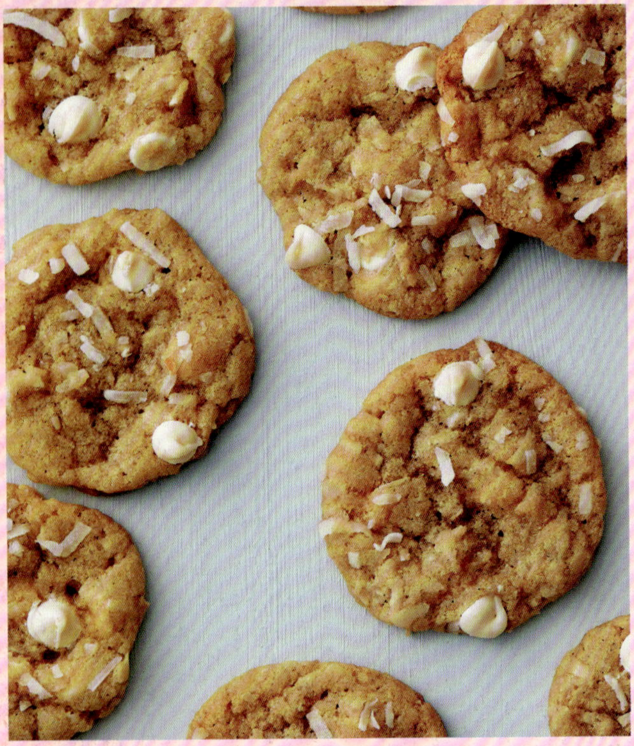

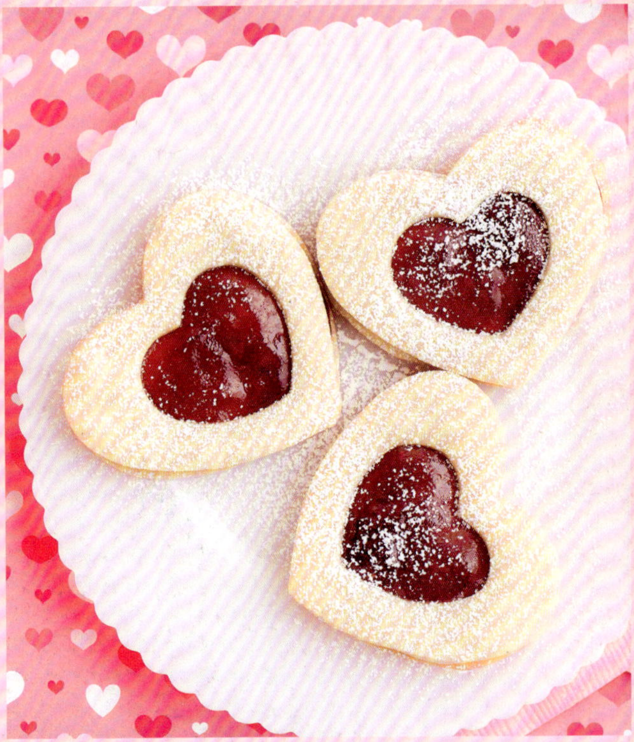

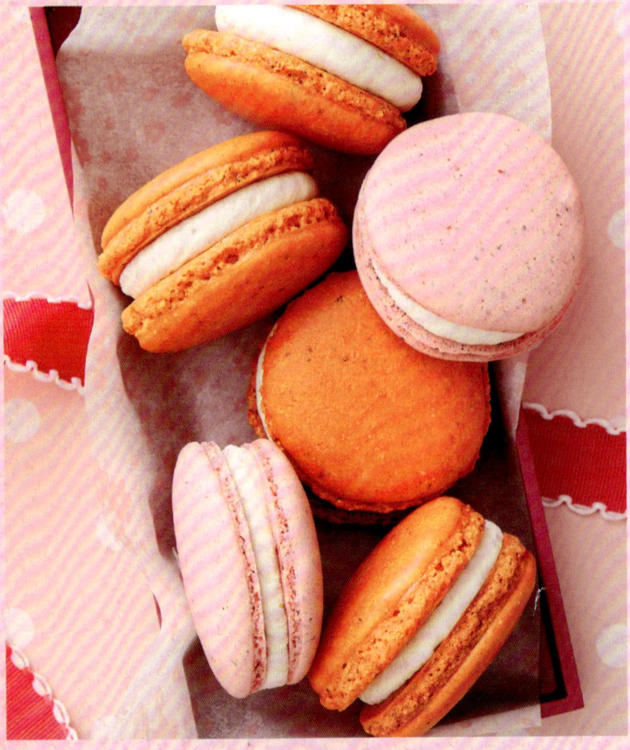

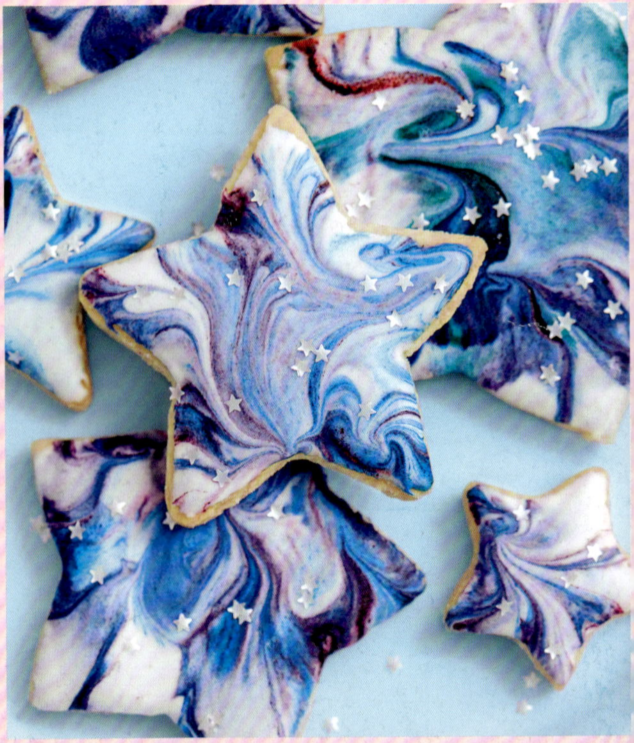

Cookies

Thumbprint Cookies

Use your thumb to create a small indent in the center of these buttery, almond-scented cookies before baking, and fill each one with your favorite fruity, jewel-toned jams, like raspberry, blackberry, or apricot.

MAKES ABOUT 24 COOKIES

2 cups all-purpose flour

½ teaspoon baking powder

¼ teaspoon salt

1 cup (2 sticks) unsalted butter, at room temperature

½ cup sugar

1 teaspoon finely grated orange zest

¾ teaspoon vanilla extract

¼ teaspoon almond extract

½ cup raspberry, apricot, or blackberry jam

Position 2 racks in the oven so that they are evenly spaced and preheat the oven to 350°F. Line 2 cookie sheets with parchment paper.

In a medium bowl, whisk together the flour, baking powder, and salt. In a large bowl, using an electric mixer, beat the butter and sugar on medium speed until fluffy and pale, about 3 minutes. Add the orange zest, vanilla, and almond extract and beat on medium speed until combined. Turn off the mixer and scrape down the bowl with a rubber spatula. Add half of the flour mixture and mix on low speed just until blended. Add the rest of the flour mixture and mix just until blended. Scrape down the bowl.

Scoop up a rounded tablespoonful of dough, then use your finger to push the dough onto 1 of the prepared cookie sheets. Fill both cookie sheets with dough, spacing the mounds 2 inches apart. You should be able to fit 12 cookies on each cookie sheet.

Dip your thumb in a little flour and use it to make a dent in each ball of dough. Spoon a small amount of jam into each dent. You can vary the types of jam you use to make different flavors of cookies.

Bake the cookies until lightly browned, about 18 minutes. Ask an adult to help you remove the cookie sheets from the oven and set them on wire racks. Let cool for 10 minutes, then use a metal spatula to move the cookies directly to the racks. Let the cookies cool completely and serve.

Kissed by chocolate
Instead of using jam, place a chocolate tear-shaped drop into each cookie indent before baking.

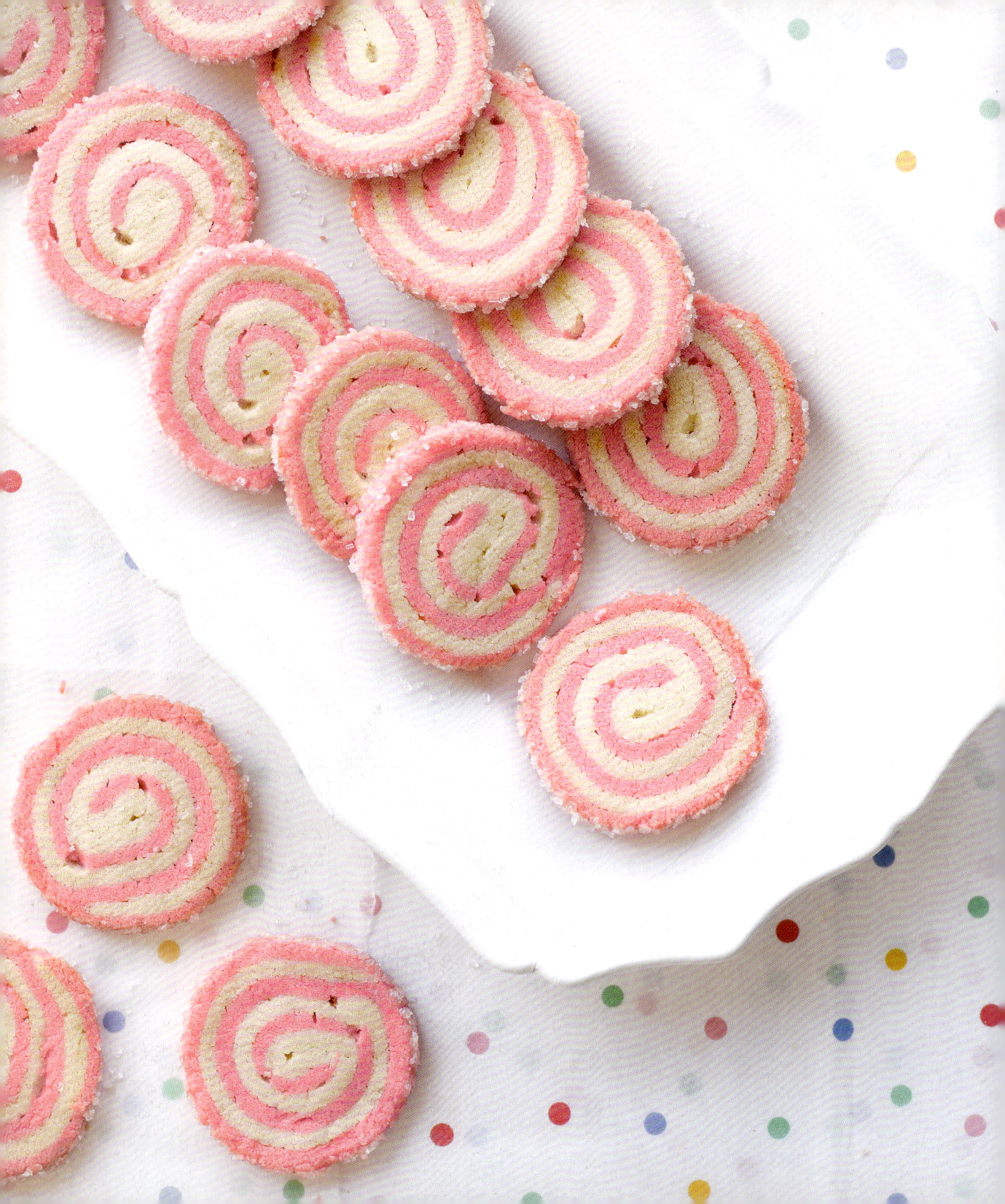

Pinwheel Icebox Cookies

These whimsical cookies are chilled in the refrigerator to help them set into perfect colorful pinwheels. You can make them into cookie pops by inserting ice-pop sticks before baking (follow the directions on page 73).

MAKES ABOUT 48 COOKIES

2 cups all-purpose flour

1 teaspoon baking powder

¼ teaspoon salt

12 tablespoons (1½ sticks) unsalted butter, at room temperature

¾ cup granulated sugar

1 large egg yolk

1½ teaspoons vanilla extract

½ teaspoon red, blue, or green food coloring, plus more as needed

½ teaspoon peppermint extract (optional)

About ½ cup coarse decorating sugar, for rolling (optional)

In a medium bowl, whisk together the flour, baking powder, and salt. In a large bowl, using an electric mixer, beat the butter and granulated sugar on medium speed until fluffy and pale, about 5 minutes. Turn off the mixer and scrape down the bowl with a rubber spatula. Add the egg yolk and vanilla and beat until combined. Add half of the flour mixture and mix on low speed just until blended. Add the rest of the flour mixture and mix just until blended. Scrape down the bowl.

Dump the dough onto a clean work surface and divide it in half. Add one half back to the bowl and sprinkle the food coloring and peppermint extract, if using, over the dough in the bowl, then gently knead until well combined and evenly colored.

Cut 4 sheets of wax paper, each one about 18 inches long. Set each dough half on the center of a wax paper sheet and use your hands to shape the dough into a rectangle. Cover each piece of dough with a second wax paper sheet and, one at a time, using a rolling pin, roll out the dough halves into 16-by-10-inch rectangles. Remove the wax paper from one side of each dough rectangle and place the colored rectangle over the plain one. Starting from a long side and using the wax paper on the bottom piece of the dough to help, tightly roll the dough into a log. If you like, scatter the coarse sugar on a rimmed cookie sheet and roll the log in the sugar to coat the outside. Wrap the log tightly in plastic wrap and refrigerate until firm, at least 1 hour or up to overnight.

~ *Continued on page 18* ~

Colorful swirls

Make these cookies even more swirl-erific by coloring both halves of the dough with your favorite colors.

~ *Continued from page 17* ~

Preheat the oven to 350°F. Line 2 cookie sheets with parchment paper. Unwrap the dough log and set it on a cutting board. Ask an adult to help you use a knife to trim off the ends, then cut the log crosswise into ¼-inch-thick slices. Place the slices on the prepared cookie sheets, spacing them about 2 inches apart.

When both cookie sheets are full, bake only 1 cookie sheet at a time until the cookies are firm to the touch (ask an adult for help!), about 12 minutes. Ask an adult to help you remove the cookie sheet from the oven and set it on a wire rack. Let cool for 5 minutes, then use a metal spatula to move the cookies directly to the rack. While the cookies are cooling, put the second cookie sheet in the oven and bake in the same way. After you have removed the cookies from the first cookie sheet, line the empty cookie sheet with new parchment paper and bake the rest of the cookies in the same way. Let the cookies cool completely and serve.

Snickerdoodles

Toss a ball of sugar cookie dough in cinnamon and sugar before baking, and voilà, you get a snickerdoodle! Not only do they have a super-funny name, these cookies smell amazing while they bake and taste yummy-licious.

MAKES 36 COOKIES

2¾ cups all-purpose flour

1 teaspoon baking powder

¼ teaspoon salt

1 cup (2 sticks) unsalted butter, at room temperature

1¾ cups sugar

2 large eggs

2 teaspoons vanilla extract

1 teaspoon ground cinnamon

Preheat the oven to 350°F. Line 2 cookie sheets with parchment paper.

In a medium bowl, whisk together the flour, baking powder, and salt. In a large bowl, using an electric mixer, beat the butter and 1½ cups of the sugar on medium speed until well blended, about 1 minute. Add the eggs and vanilla and beat on low speed until combined. Turn off the mixer and scrape down the bowl with a rubber spatula. Add the flour mixture and mix just until blended.

In a small bowl, stir together the remaining ¼ cup sugar and the cinnamon. Scoop up a rounded tablespoonful of dough. Scrape the dough off the spoon into the palm of your hand and roll the dough into a ball. Drop the ball in the cinnamon sugar and roll it around to coat it completely. Place the ball on a prepared cookie sheet. Continue scooping, shaping, and rolling the dough in sugar, spacing the balls about 3 inches apart on the cookie sheets. You should be able to fit 12 cookies on each cookie sheet.

When both cookie sheets are full, bake 1 cookie sheet at a time until the edges of the cookies are lightly browned but the tops are barely colored, 10 to 12 minutes. Ask an adult to help you remove the cookie sheet from the oven and set it on a wire rack. Let cool for 5 minutes, then use a metal spatula to move the cookies directly to the rack. While the cookies are cooling, put the second cookie sheet in the oven and bake in the same way. Repeat to bake the rest of the cookies. Let the cookies cool completely and serve.

Elephant Ears

These swirly cookies are made from puff pastry and become sugary-crisp when baked. They're shaped like puffy elephant ears, which is how these treats get their name.

MAKES ABOUT 20 COOKIES

2 tablespoons unsalted butter, melted

½ teaspoon vanilla extract

½ cup granulated sugar

½ cup powdered sugar, sifted

1 sheet frozen puff pastry, thawed

Preheat the oven to 375°F. Line 2 cookie sheets with parchment paper. In a small bowl, stir together the melted butter and vanilla; set aside to cool. In another bowl, using a fork, stir together the granulated and powdered sugars. Measure out ½ cup of the sugar mixture and set aside.

Sprinkle 3 tablespoons of the remaining sugar mixture onto a work surface. Place the puff pastry on top of the sugared surface. Sprinkle more of the sugar mixture on top of the pastry, spreading it evenly with your hands.

Using a rolling pin and beginning at the center of the pastry, roll the pastry into a 10-by-20-inch rectangle, sprinkling a little more sugar mixture underneath and on top of the pastry so the pastry doesn't stick.

Using a pastry brush, brush the butter mixture over the surface of the pastry. Sprinkle evenly with the reserved ½ cup sugar mixture. Starting at one short end, fold a 2-inch-wide band of the pastry over onto itself. Repeat this folding until you reach the center of the pastry (probably 3 folds). Now fold the other end of the rectangle in the same way. Fold one band on top of the other to form a long rectangle. Press to stick it together, then ask an adult to help you cut the rectangle crosswise into ½-inch-thick slices. Place the slices on the prepared cookie sheets, spacing them 2 inches apart.

Bake the pastries 1 cookie sheet at a time until golden, about 15 minutes. Let the cookies cool for 5 minutes, then use a metal spatula to move them directly to a wire rack. Let cool completely and serve.

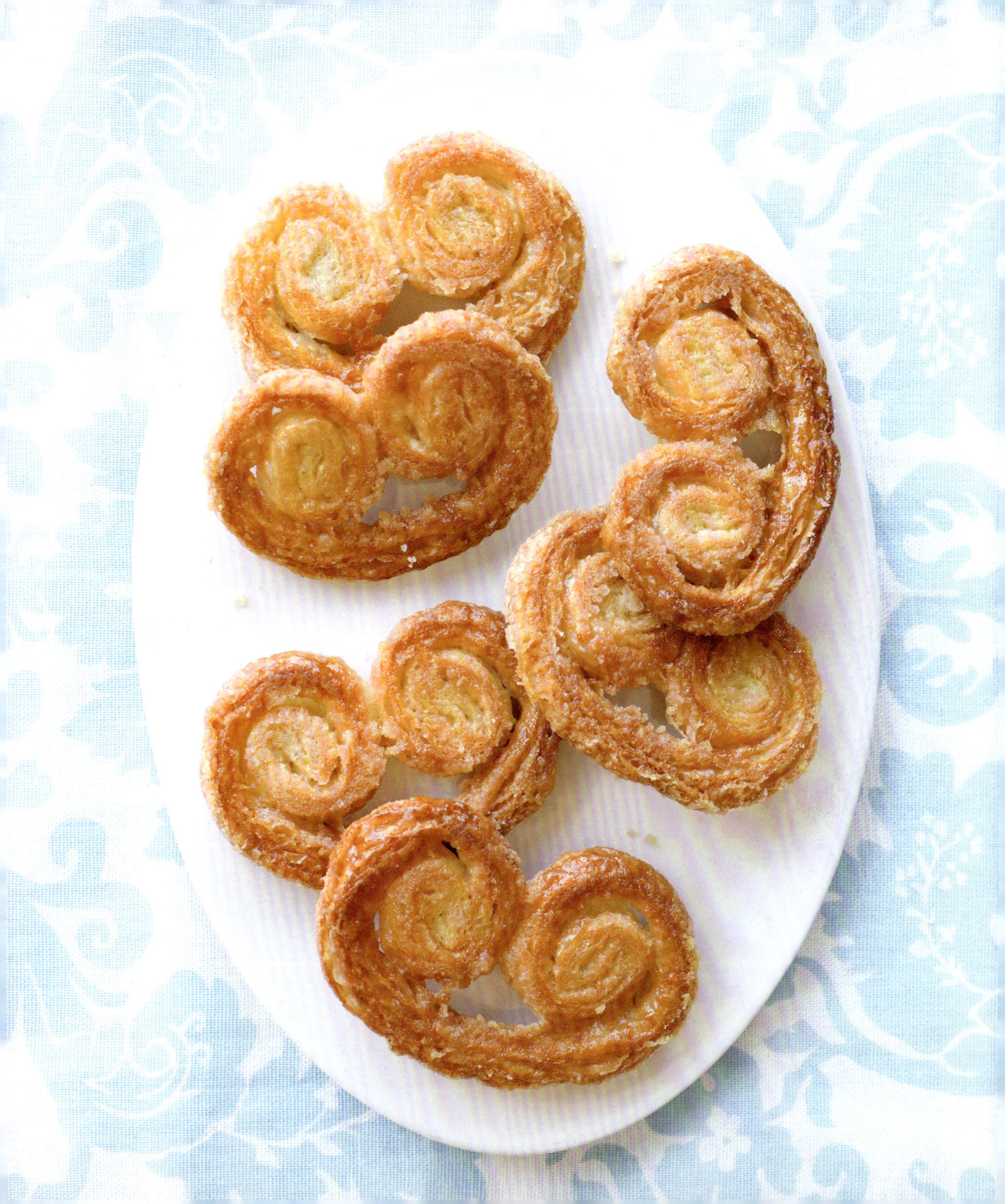

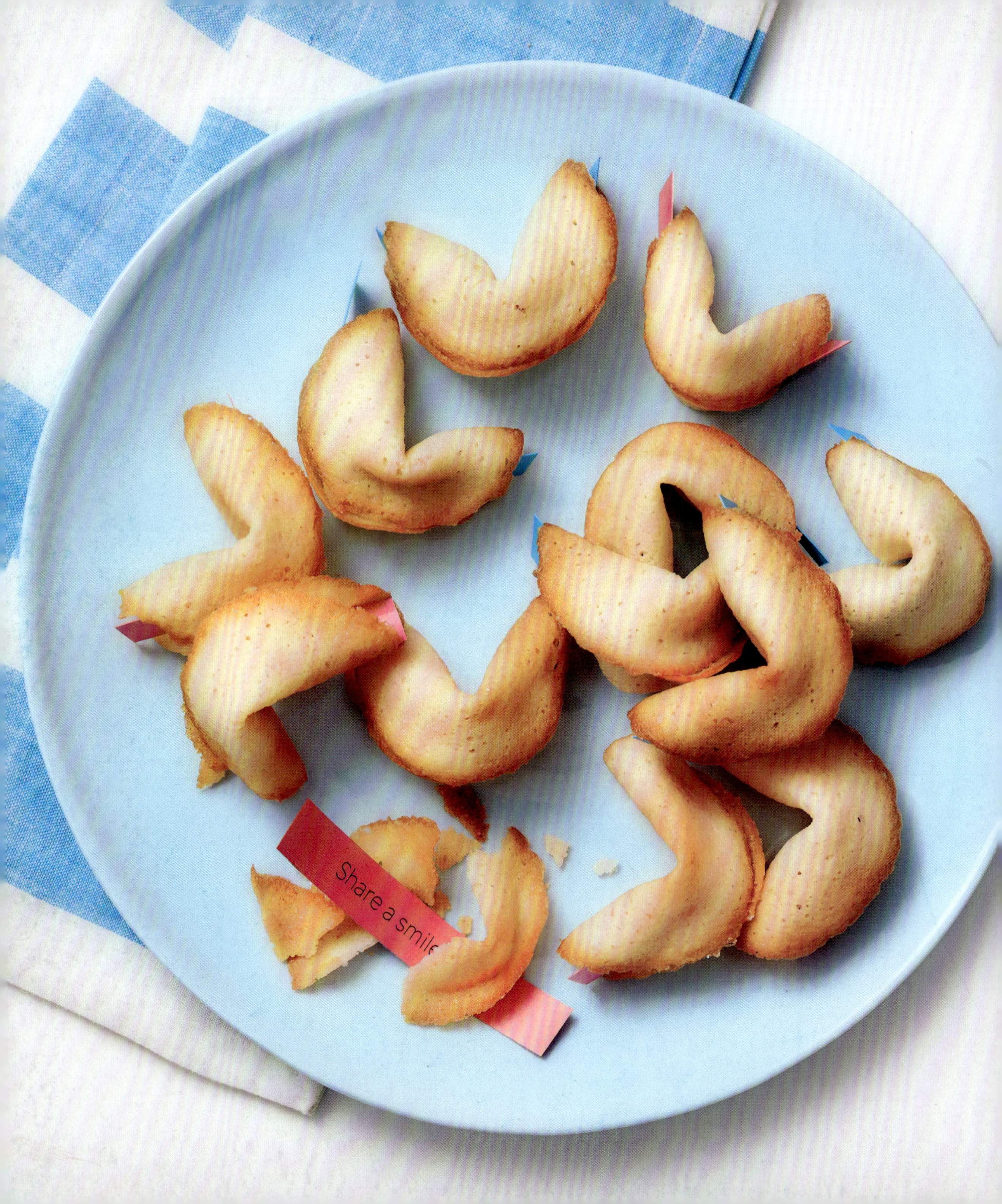
Share a smile

Fortune Cookies

No need to order takeout to enjoy these fun cookies—you can bake your own! Be creative with the messages you write, which is one of the best parts of the process.

MAKES 12 COOKIES

¼ cup all-purpose flour

¼ cup sugar

Pinch of salt

1 large egg white

¼ teaspoon vanilla extract

Preheat the oven to 375°F. Line a cookie sheet with parchment paper, then lightly grease the parchment with nonstick cooking spray.

Cut 12 strips of colored or white paper, each about 4 inches long by ½ inch wide. Write a "fortune" on each strip.

In a medium bowl, whisk together the flour, sugar, and salt. In a small bowl, whisk the egg white and vanilla until light and frothy, about 3 minutes. Add the egg white mixture to the flour mixture and stir with a wooden spoon until well combined. The batter will be thin.

Have ready a liquid measuring cup or mug and a muffin pan for shaping the cookies after baking. Scoop 1 teaspoon of the batter onto a prepared cookie sheet and, using a small icing spatula, spread it evenly into a circle about 3 inches in diameter. Repeat to create 3 more circles. Bake until the edges of the cookies are just starting to turn light brown but the centers are still pale, about 5 minutes. Remove the sheet from the oven and, using a metal spatula, move the cookies to a wire rack, turning them upside down. Working quickly, place a fortune in the center of each cookie. Wearing an oven mitt, fold the hot cookies in half and pinch the edges closed. Press the straight edge of a cookie against the rim of the measuring cup and fold it over the rim to create a center crease. Place the cookie in the muffin pan so it keeps its shape. Repeat with the remaining folded cookies. Bake the remaining batter in 2 more batches and shape the cookies in the same way.

Try something new!

You're a smart cookie!

Share a smile!

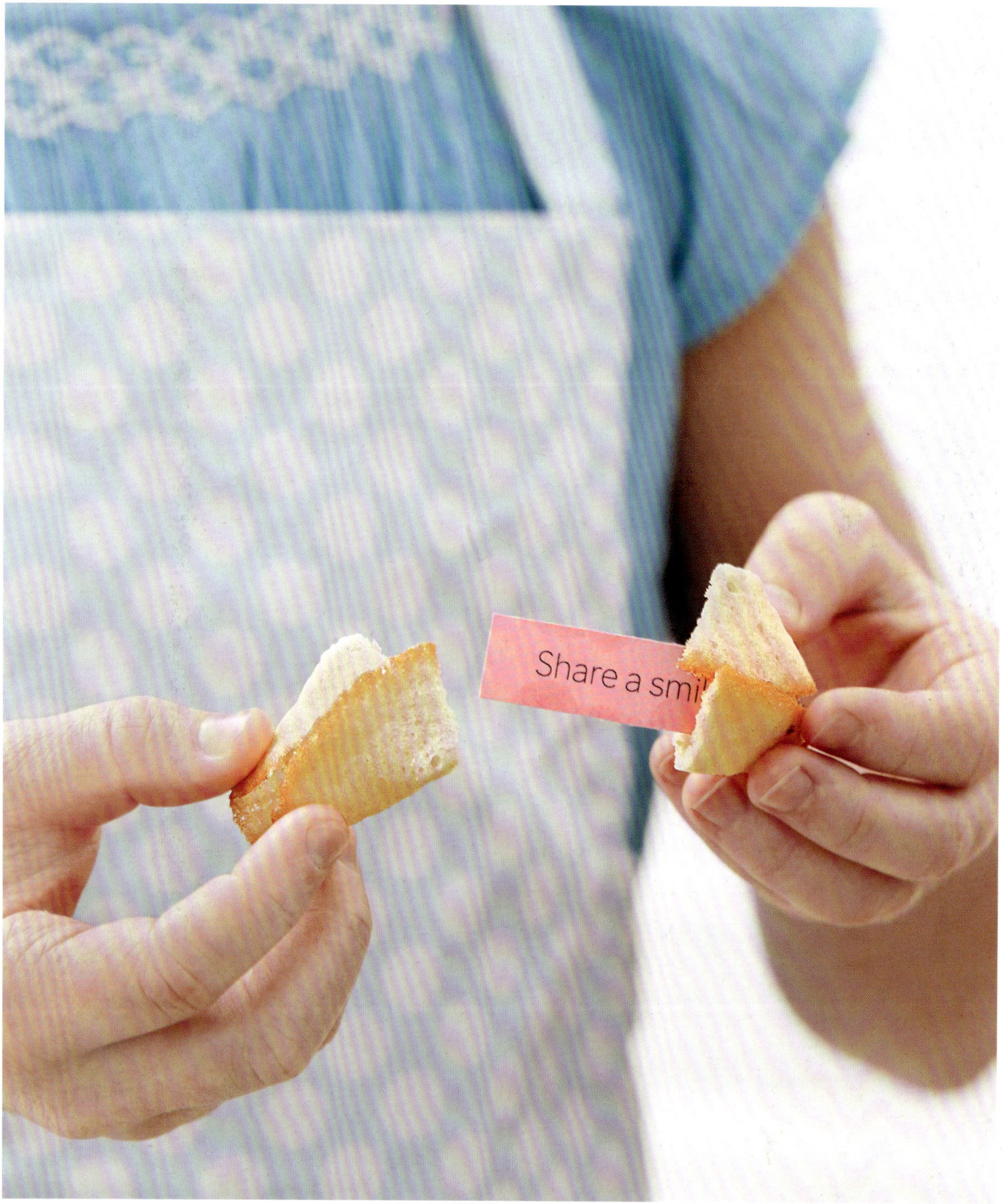
Share a smi

Chocolate Chip Cookie Sandwiches

One of the most scrumptious cookies just got even more irresistible! Take two chocolate chip cookies, put a thick layer of super-chocolaty frosting between them, and you've got a new favorite treat. Don't forget a big glass of cold milk!

MAKES ABOUT 28 SANDWICH COOKIES

2 cups all-purpose flour

1 teaspoon baking soda

½ teaspoon salt

1 cup (2 sticks) unsalted butter, at room temperature

¾ cup firmly packed light brown sugar

¾ cup granulated sugar

2 large eggs

2 teaspoons vanilla extract

2 cups semisweet chocolate chips

Chocolate Frosting (page 264)

Preheat the oven to 350°F. Line 2 cookie sheets with parchment paper.

In a medium bowl, whisk together the flour, baking soda, and salt. In a large bowl, using an electric mixer, beat the butter, brown sugar, and granulated sugar on medium speed until well blended, about 1 minute. Add the eggs and vanilla and beat on low speed until well combined. Turn off the mixer and scrape down the bowl with a rubber spatula. Add half of the flour mixture and mix on low speed just until blended. Add the rest of the flour mixture and mix just until blended. Add the chocolate chips and beat just until the chips are mixed evenly into the dough. Scrape down the bowl.

Scoop up a rounded tablespoonful of dough, then use your finger to push the dough onto 1 of the prepared cookie sheets. Repeat with the rest of the dough, spacing the mounds 3 inches apart on the cookie sheets.

When both cookie sheets are full, bake 1 cookie sheet at a time until the tops of the cookies are lightly golden in the center, 10 to 12 minutes. Ask an adult to help you remove the cookie sheet from the oven and set it on a wire rack. Let cool for 5 minutes, then use a metal spatula to move the cookies directly to the rack. Repeat to bake the rest of the cookies. Let the cookies cool completely.

Turn half of the cookies bottom side up and spread a thick layer of frosting on the surface of each upside-down cookie. Top each with a second cookie, placing the bottom side onto the filling. Serve right away.

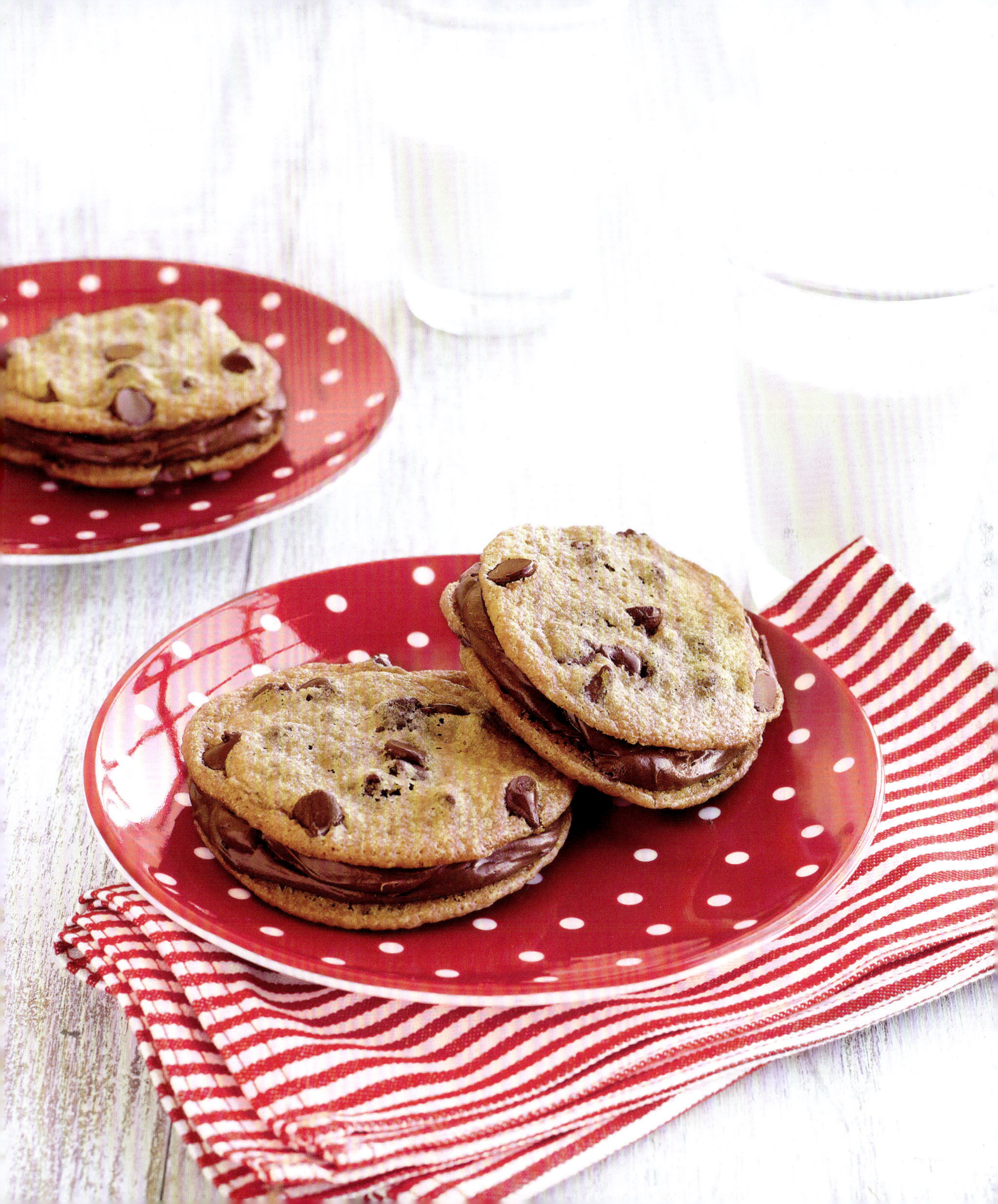

Double choco-rific
Make these brownie-like cookies even more chocolaty by adding ½ cup mini chocolate chips to the batter.

Chocolate Crinkle Cookies

Coated in a flurry of powdered sugar and extra-fudgy inside, these cool-looking cookies will satisfy even the biggest chocolate craving. These treats also go by the name "earthquake cookies" because of their crackly tops.

MAKES ABOUT 24 COOKIES

½ cup powdered sugar, sifted

1⅔ cups all-purpose flour

½ cup unsweetened cocoa powder, sifted

1½ teaspoons baking powder

¼ teaspoon salt

½ cup (1 stick) unsalted butter, at room temperature

1¼ cups granulated sugar

2 large eggs

½ teaspoon vanilla extract

Preheat the oven to 350°F. Line 2 cookie sheets with parchment paper. Put the powdered sugar into a medium bowl and set aside.

In another medium bowl, whisk together the flour, cocoa, baking powder, and salt. In a large bowl, using an electric mixer, beat the butter and granulated sugar on medium speed until fluffy and pale, about 3 minutes. Turn off the mixer and scrape down the bowl with a rubber spatula. Add 1 egg and beat on medium speed until blended. Add the other egg and the vanilla and beat until blended. Turn off the mixer and add the flour mixture. Mix on low speed just until blended. Scrape down the bowl.

Scoop up a rounded tablespoonful of dough. Scrape the dough off the spoon into the palm of your hand. Roll the dough into a ball, set it on a large plate, and shape the rest of the dough into balls in the same way.

When all of the dough has been shaped, roll the balls in the powdered sugar until completely covered. Place the balls on the prepared cookie sheets, spacing them about 2 inches apart.

Bake the cookies 1 cookie sheet at a time until crackled and puffed, 10 to 12 minutes. Ask an adult to help you remove the cookie sheet from the oven and set it on a wire rack. Let cool for 15 minutes, then use a metal spatula to move the cookies directly to the rack. Let cool completely and serve.

Raspberry Jam Heart Cookies

Heart-shaped, jam-filled sandwich cookies with a dusting of powdered sugar are the perfect treat for any celebration, especially a sweetheart party. If you like, bake the cookies a day ahead, store them in an airtight container, and fill them the day of your party.

MAKES ABOUT 16 COOKIES

2 cups all-purpose flour

½ teaspoon salt

1 cup (2 sticks) unsalted butter, at room temperature

¾ cup powdered sugar, plus extra for dusting the cookies

2 teaspoons vanilla extract

6 tablespoons seedless raspberry jam

In a bowl, whisk together the flour and salt. In the bowl of an electric mixer, beat the butter and powdered sugar on medium speed until smooth. Add the vanilla extract and beat until blended. Scrape down the bowl with a rubber spatula. Add the flour mixture and beat on low until the dough comes together in large clumps. Dump the dough onto a work surface, divide it in half, and press each piece into a disk. Wrap each disk in plastic wrap and refrigerate until firm, at least 40 minutes or up to overnight.

Position 2 racks evenly in the oven and preheat the oven to 325°F. Line 2 cookie sheets with parchment paper. Sprinkle a work surface with flour. Using flour as needed, roll out one dough disk to ¼ inch thick. Using a 2½-inch heart-shaped cookie cutter, cut out as many cookies as you can. Using a 1-inch heart-shaped cookie cutter, cut out the center from half of the cookie hearts. Place the hearts on the prepared cookie sheets, spacing them evenly. Repeat with the second dough disk. Press the scraps together and repeat the process.

Bake the cookies until the edges are lightly browned, rotating the pans halfway through, 12 to 15 minutes. Let cool on a wire rack for 5 minutes, then use a metal spatula to move the cookies directly to the rack to cool completely.

Spread 1 teaspoon of raspberry jam on each heart without a cutout, leaving a ¼-inch border. Put a little powdered sugar in a sieve, dust the hearts with cut-out centers, then place on top of the jam-covered cookies. Dust the small heart cookies with powdered sugar. Serve right away or store in an airtight container at room temperature for up to 3 days.

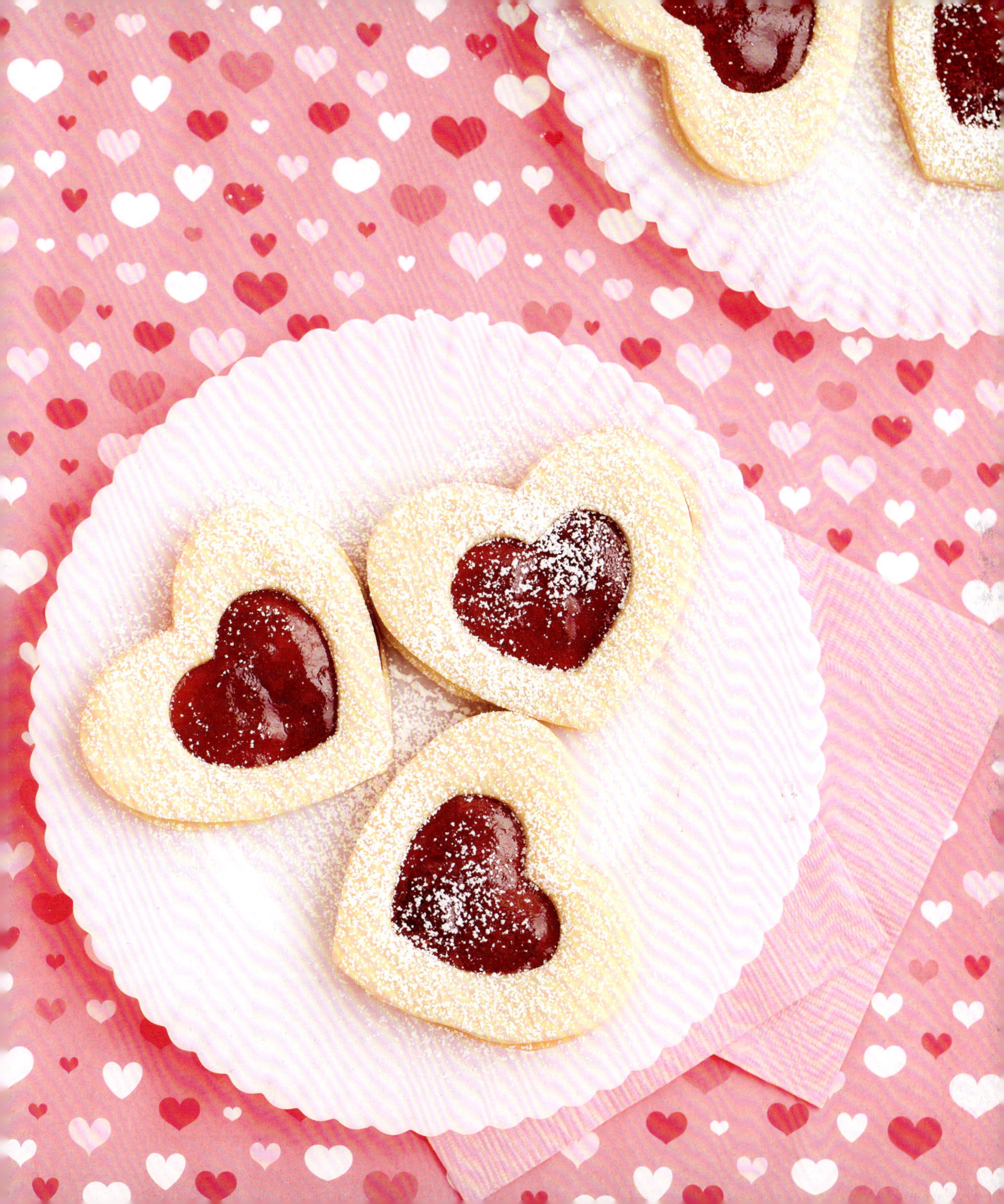

Kitchen Sink Cookies

As you might guess from their name, these cookies have it all. Chock-full of oats, chocolate chips, shredded coconut, and almonds, they offer something for everyone. For crispier cookies, press the mounds flat and bake for an additional 2 minutes.

MAKES ABOUT 3½ DOZEN COOKIES

1 cup slivered almonds

1½ cups all-purpose flour

½ teaspoon baking powder

½ teaspoon baking soda

¼ teaspoon salt

1 cup (2 sticks) unsalted butter, at room temperature

¾ cup firmly packed light brown sugar

½ cup granulated sugar

2 large eggs

1½ teaspoons vanilla extract

2 cups old-fashioned rolled oats

1 cup sweetened shredded coconut

1 (12-ounce) bag semisweet or bittersweet chocolate chips

Position 2 racks evenly in the oven and preheat to 350°F. Spread the almonds on a rimmed baking sheet and toast in the oven, stirring once or twice, until lightly golden, about 8 minutes. Remove the baking sheet from the oven. Let the nuts cool completely.

Increase the oven temperature to 375°F. Line 2 cookie sheets with parchment. In a medium bowl, whisk together the flour, baking powder, baking soda, and salt. In a large bowl, using an electric mixer, beat the butter, brown sugar, and granulated sugar on medium speed until creamy, about 2 minutes. Turn off the mixer and scrape down the bowl with a rubber spatula. Add 1 egg and beat on medium speed until blended. Add the other egg and the vanilla and beat until blended. Turn off the mixer and add the flour mixture. Mix on low speed just until blended. Add the oats and coconut and mix on low speed just until combined. Add the toasted almonds and the chocolate chips and mix just until combined. Scrape down the bowl.

Drop heaping tablespoons of the dough onto the prepared baking sheets, spacing the mounds about 1 inch apart. Bake for 7 minutes, then rotate the cookie sheets. Continue to bake until the edges of the cookies are golden brown, about 6 minutes more. Remove the cookie sheets from the oven and set them on a wire rack. Let cool for 5 minutes, then use a metal spatula to move the cookies directly to the rack. Let the cookies cool completely and serve.

Homemade Oreos

If you don't have a pastry bag for piping the filling onto these iconic sandwich cookies, fill a gallon-size zipper-lock plastic bag halfway with the filling. Push the filling into one corner of the bag, twist the top closed, and snip off about ¼ inch from the corner.

MAKES ABOUT 12 COOKIES

COOKIES

1¼ cups all-purpose flour

¾ cup granulated sugar

¾ cup unsweetened Dutch-process cocoa powder

1 teaspoon baking soda

¼ teaspoon baking powder

¼ teaspoon salt

¾ cup (1½ sticks) unsalted butter, at room temperature

1 large egg, plus 1 large egg yolk

FILLING

½ cup (1 stick) unsalted butter, at room temperature

1½ cups powdered sugar

1 tablespoon whole milk

1 teaspoon vanilla extract

Preheat the oven to 375°F. Line 2 cookie sheets with parchment paper.

To make the cookies, in a large bowl, whisk together the flour, granulated sugar, cocoa powder, baking soda, baking powder, and salt. Add the butter and, using an electric mixer, beat on low speed for 2 minutes. Add the egg and egg yolk and beat on medium speed until it forms a dough, about 2 minutes.

Dust a clean work surface with flour and roll out the dough to an even ¼-inch thickness. Using a 2-inch round cookie cutter, cut out rounds of the dough. Move them to the prepared cookie sheets, spacing them about 1 inch apart. Gather the dough scraps together, then roll them out and cut out additional rounds. If the dough is too sticky to roll, wrap it in plastic wrap and refrigerate until slightly firm, about 15 minutes. You should have about 24 rounds.

Bake 1 cookie sheet at a time until the centers of the cookies are firm to the touch, 8 to 10 minutes. Remove the sheet from the oven and set it on a wire rack. Let cool for 5 minutes, then move the cookies directly to the rack. Let cool completely.

To make the filling, in a large bowl, combine the butter, powdered sugar, milk, and vanilla. Using an electric mixer, beat on medium-high speed until smooth, about 3 minutes. Scrape the filling into a pastry bag fitted with a ½-inch tip. Turn half of the cookies bottom side up. Pipe about 2 teaspoons of the filling onto each overturned cookie. Top with the remaining cookies, bottom side down, and gently press together so the filling runs just to the edges.

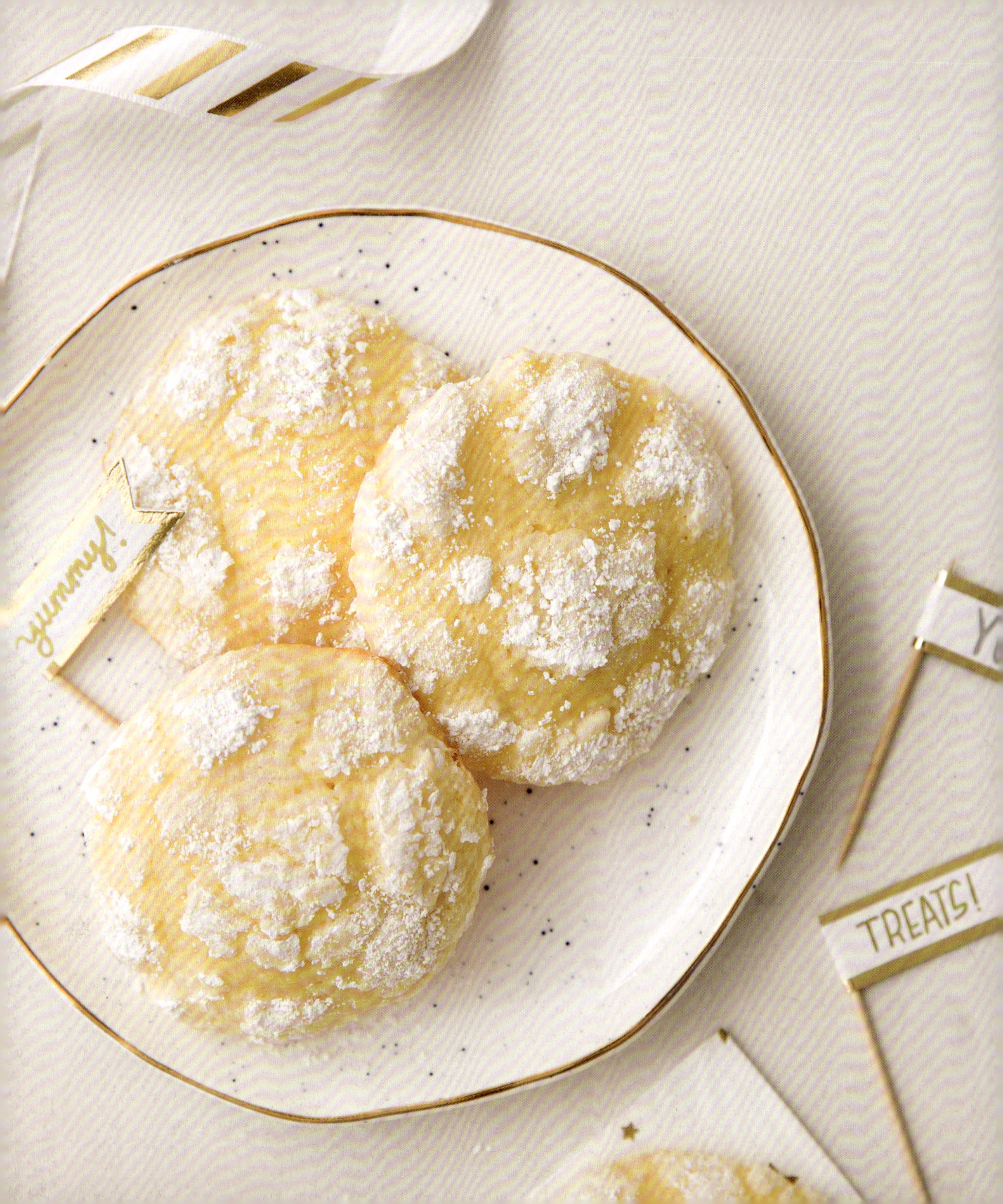

yummy!
TREATS!

Lemon Crinkle Cookies

These pretty cookies—a lemon lover's dream—have thin, crisp shells covered in snowy sugar. Inside is a bright burst of edible sunshine and irresistible chewiness. The dough has to chill, so make it the night before your cookie party.

MAKES ABOUT 28 COOKIES

2 cups all-purpose flour

2 teaspoons baking powder

¼ tsp salt

½ cup (1 stick) unsalted butter, at room temperature

1 cup granulated sugar

1 tablespoon finely grated lemon zest

3 large eggs

3 tablespoons fresh lemon juice

1 teaspoon vanilla extract

½ cup powdered sugar, sifted

In a bowl, whisk together the flour, baking powder, and salt. In a large bowl, using an electric mixer, beat the butter, granulated sugar, and lemon zest on medium speed until creamy, about 2 minutes. Add the eggs one at a time, beating well after adding each one. Turn off the mixer and scrape down the bowl with a rubber spatula. Add the lemon juice and vanilla and beat until blended. Turn off the mixer. Add the flour mixture and mix on low speed just until blended. Cover the bowl with plastic wrap and refrigerate for at least 1 hour or up to overnight.

Position 2 racks evenly in the oven and preheat to 350°F. Line 2 cookie sheets with parchment paper. Put the powdered sugar into a shallow bowl.

Scoop up a tablespoonful of the chilled dough and roll it into a rough ball between the palms of your hands (the dough will be very sticky, so you will need to wash your hands occasionally while you are forming dough balls), then drop it into the powdered sugar and roll until completely covered. Place the balls on the prepared cookie sheets, spacing them about 2 inches apart. Press down on the dough balls to flatten them slightly.

Bake for 7 minutes, then rotate the cookie sheets. Continue to bake until the cookies are cracked and puffed and the edges are just starting to brown, about 6 minutes more. Let cool on a wire rack for 5 minutes, then use a metal spatula to move the cookies directly to the rack. Let cool completely and serve.

Hot Chocolate Cookies

Do you love a big mug of hot chocolate with marshmallows floating on top? Why not try it in cookie form? These chewy chocolate cookies topped with toasty marshmallows are sure to become your new favorite chocolate treat.

MAKES ABOUT 26 COOKIES

1½ cups all-purpose flour

½ cup unsweetened cocoa powder, plus more for dusting

¼ cup hot chocolate mix

1 teaspoon baking powder

¼ teaspoon salt

3 large eggs

1⅔ cups sugar

2 teaspoons vanilla extract

4 tablespoons (½ stick) unsalted butter, melted and cooled slightly

1 bag mini marshmallows or 13 regular-size marshmallows, halved crosswise

In a bowl, whisk together the flour, cocoa powder, hot chocolate mix, baking powder, and salt. In the bowl of an electric mixer, beat the eggs, sugar, and vanilla on high speed until light in color and thick, about 3 minutes. Add the butter and beat on medium speed until blended. Scrape down the bowl with a rubber spatula. Add the flour mixture and mix on low speed just until blended. Cover the bowl with plastic wrap and refrigerate for 1 hour.

Position 2 racks evenly in the oven and preheat to 350°F. Line 2 cookie sheets with parchment paper. Scoop up heaping tablespoonfuls of the chilled dough, roll them into balls between the palms of your hands, and place on the prepared cookie sheets, spacing them 2 inches apart.

Bake for 6 minutes, then rotate the cookie sheets. Continue to bake until the cookies are puffed and look dry, 4–6 minutes more. Let cool on a wire rack for 5 minutes, then move the cookies directly to the rack.

Once they are all baked, arrange the cookies in a single layer on one unlined cookie sheet. Position an oven rack 6 inches below the broiler and preheat the broiler. Place a few mini marshmallows on the center of each cookie (or, if using regular-size, place a marshmallow half cut-side-down on the center of each cookie). Broil until the marshmallows are gooey and golden (watch them carefully!). Let cool on a wire rack. Just before serving, put a spoonful of cocoa powder in a fine-mesh sieve and lightly dust the cookies with cocoa.

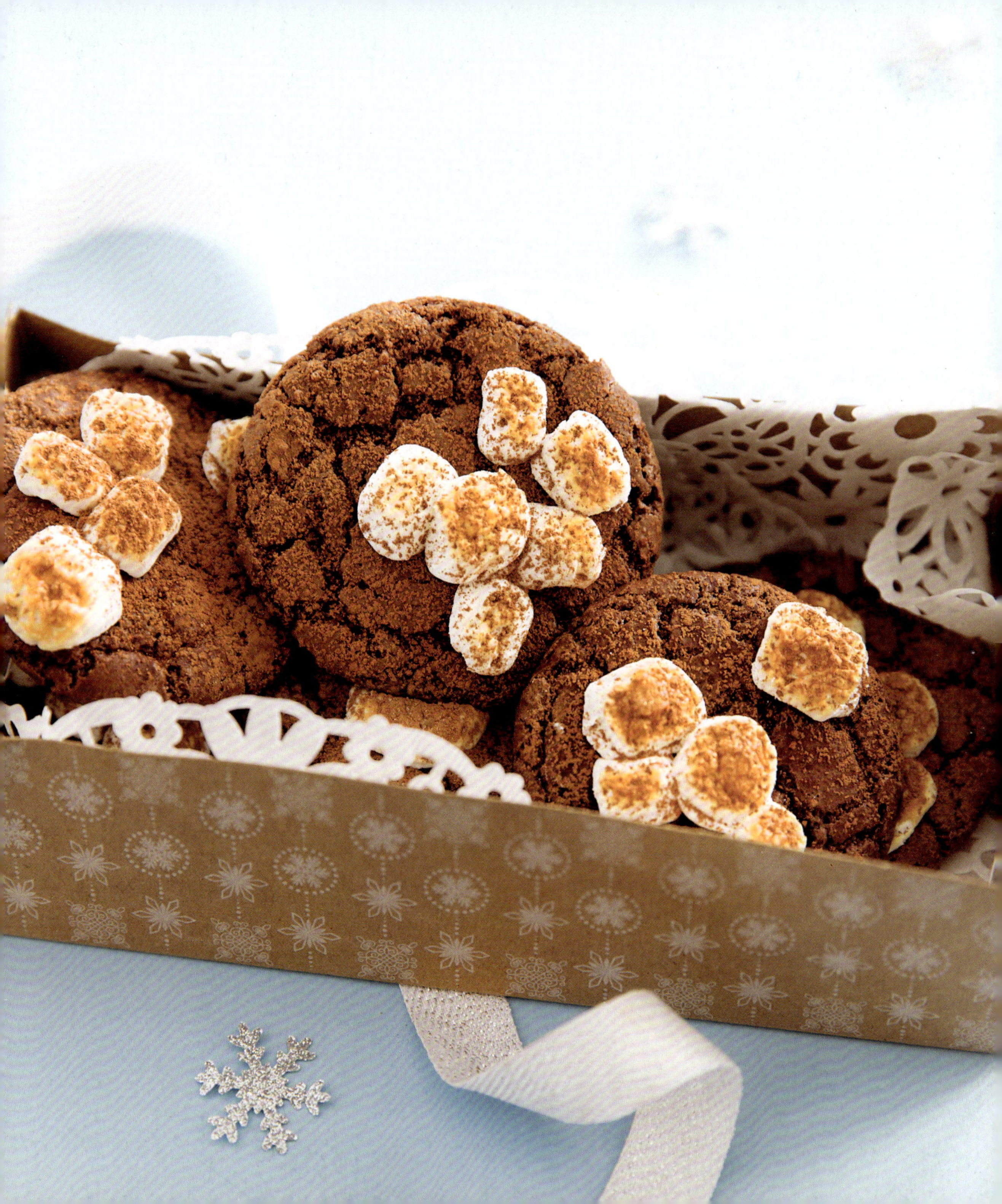

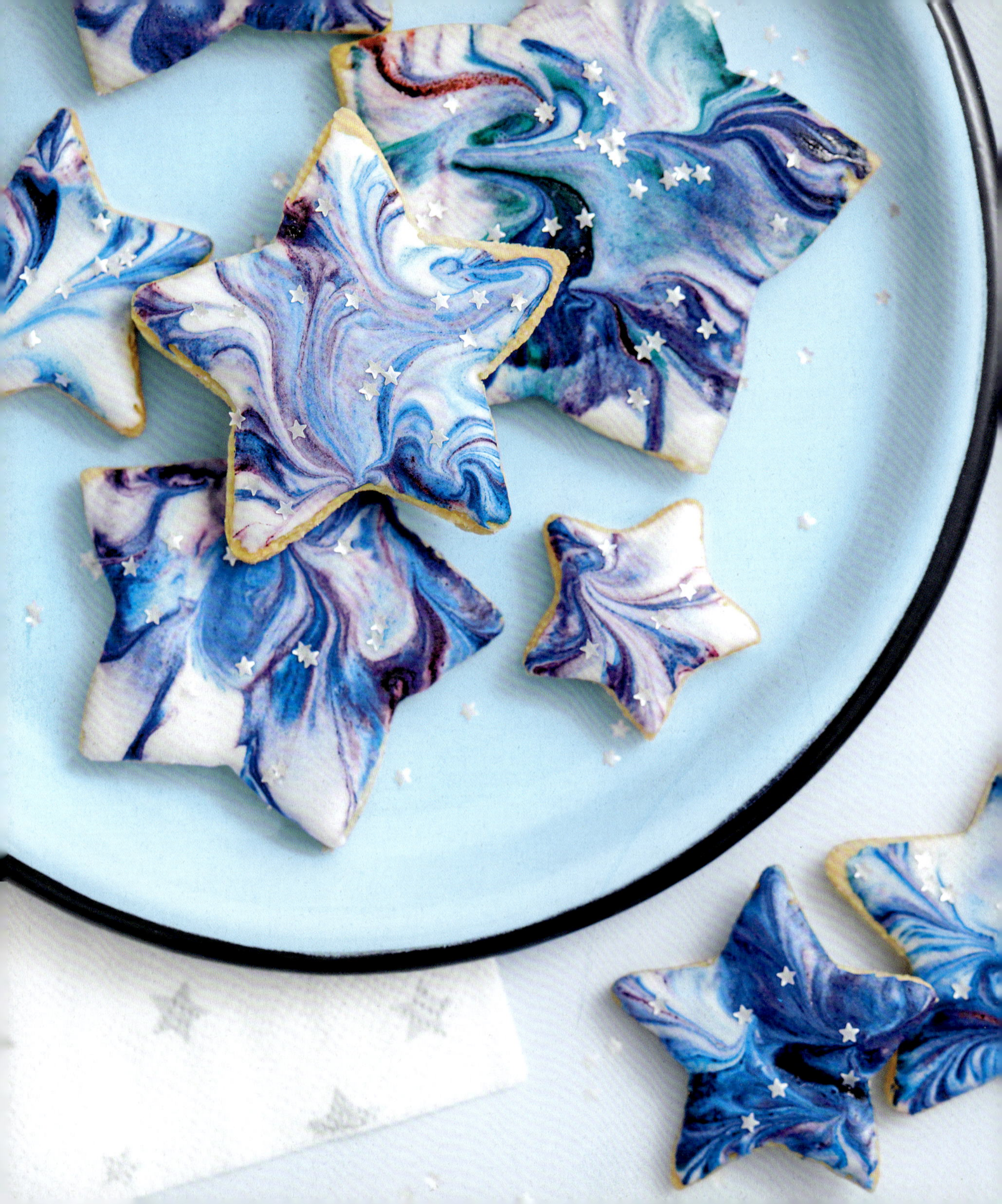

Galaxy Cookies

Reach for the stars with these super cool cosmic cookies. If you like, use different sizes of star cutters and/or different combinations of food colorings in each bowl for a really colorful starry night!

MAKES ABOUT 40 COOKIES

Sugar Cookie Cutouts (page 59), cut into 3-inch stars, baked, and cooled

Vanilla Icing (page 60)

Pink, blue, and purple gel paste food coloring

Edible glitter and/or edible silver star sprinkles, for decorating (optional)

Line 2 cookie sheets with parchment paper.

Divide the icing evenly among 3 bowls. Dip a toothpick into the pink food coloring, then dip the coloring into a bowl of icing. Dip a clean toothpick into the blue food coloring, then dip the coloring into same bowl. Do the same with another clean toothpick and the purple food coloring. Then use the toothpick to gently swirl the food colorings into the icing. Don't overßswirl or the colors will blend together—be sure to leave a good amount of white icing showing through. Repeat this process with the remaining 2 bowls of icing.

Dip the surface of a cookie into the icing and gently twist it to let any excess icing run off. Place the cookie icing-side-up on 1 of the prepared cookie sheets and sprinkle with edible glitter or stars (if using). Repeat with the remaining cookies. When the first bowl of icing no longer has colored swirls or if the colors have started to blend together too much, use the next bowl of icing.

Let the icing on the cookies dry at room temperature until firm, at least 1 hour or up to overnight. (Store the cookies in an airtight container, layered between sheets of parchment paper. They will keep for 3 days at room temperature.)

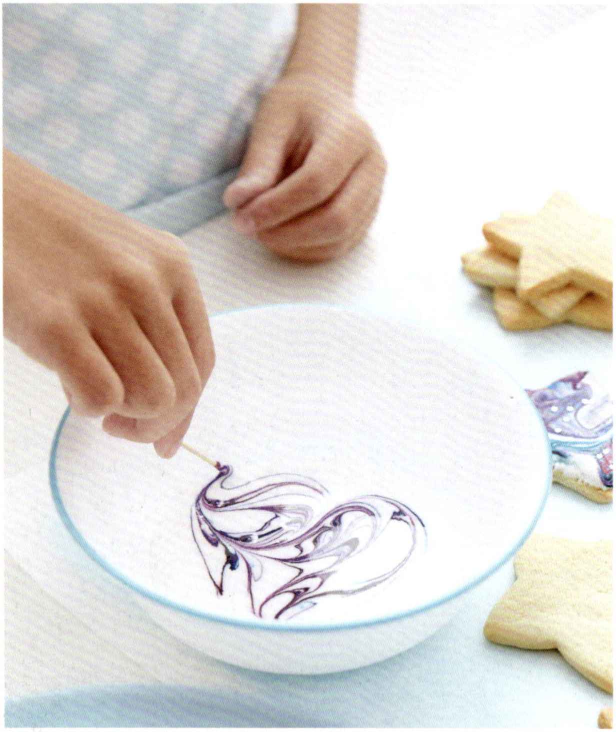
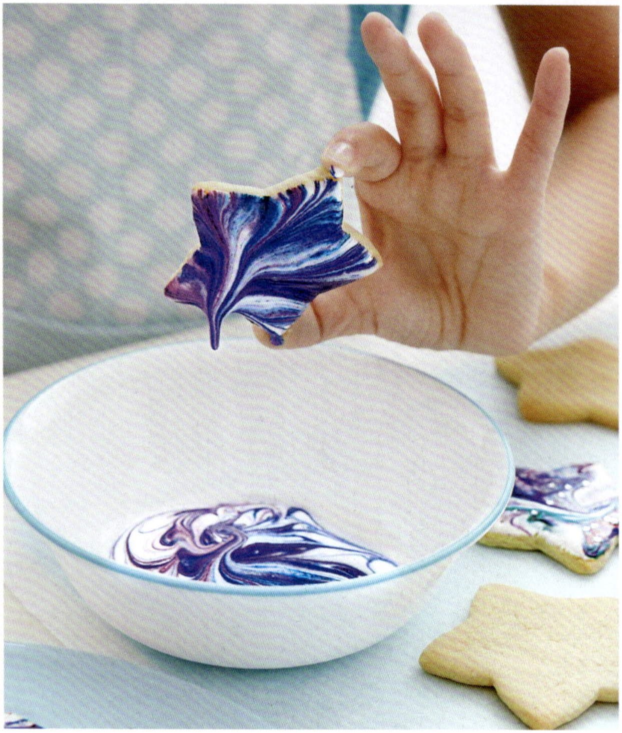
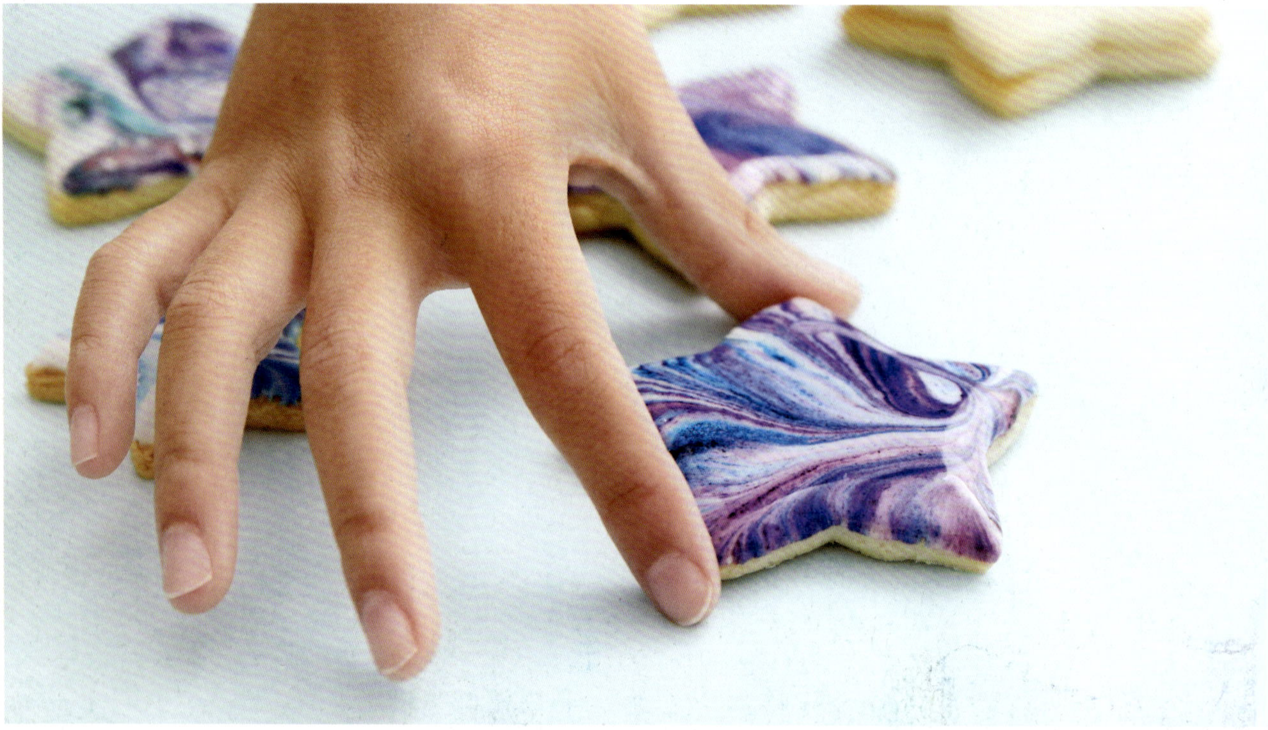

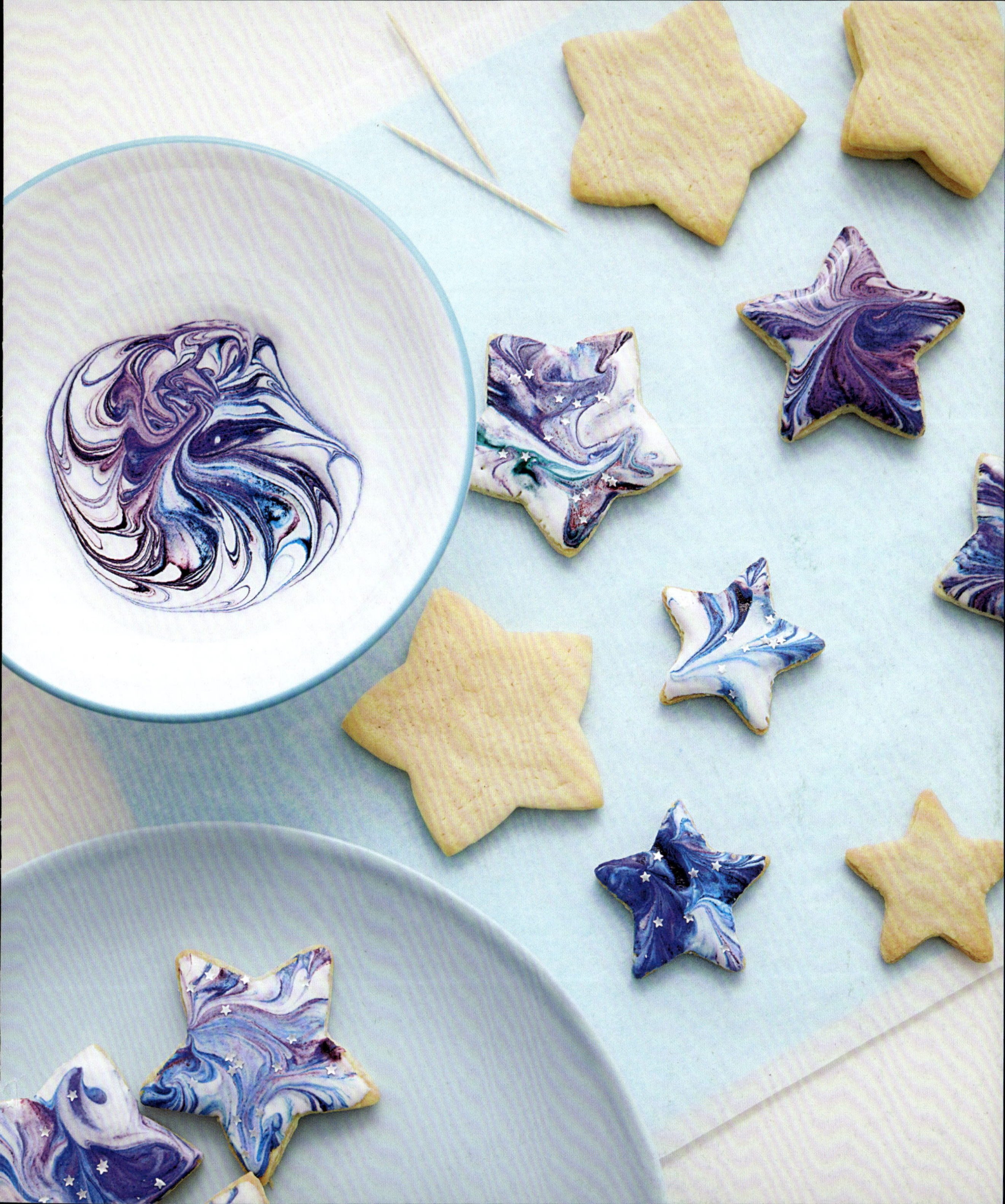

Triple-Chocolate-Chunk Cookies

Packed with chunks of dark, milk, and white chocolate, these cookies are a triple threat. If you like, you can use ⅔ cup each of semisweet, milk chocolate, and white chocolate chips instead of chopping chocolate blocks.

MAKES ABOUT 32 COOKIES

2 cups all-purpose flour

1 teaspoon baking soda

½ teaspoon salt

1 cup (2 sticks) unsalted butter, at room temperature

¾ cup firmly packed light brown sugar

¾ cup granulated sugar

2 large eggs

2 teaspoons vanilla extract

4 ounces (about ⅔ cup) semisweet or bittersweet chocolate, roughly chopped

4 ounces (about ⅔ cup) milk chocolate, roughly chopped

4 ounces (about ⅔ cup) white chocolate, roughly chopped

Preheat the oven to 350°F. Line 2 cookie sheets with parchment paper.

In a medium bowl, whisk together the flour, baking soda, and salt. In a large bowl, using an electric mixer, beat the butter, brown sugar, and granulated sugar on medium speed until well blended, about 2 minutes. Add the eggs and vanilla and beat on low speed until well combined. Turn off the mixer and scrape down the bowl with a rubber spatula. Add about half of the flour mixture and mix on low speed just until blended. Add the rest of the flour mixture and mix again just until blended. Turn off the mixer, add the chopped chocolate, and stir with a wooden spoon until the chocolate is evenly mixed into the dough.

Drop heaping tablespoons of the dough onto the prepared cookie sheets, spacing the mounds about 3 inches apart. Bake 1 cookie sheet at a time until the cookies are light golden brown on top, 10 to 12 minutes. Remove the sheet from the oven and set it on a wire rack. Let cool for 5 minutes, then use a metal spatula to move the cookies directly to the rack. Repeat to bake the rest of the cookies. Let cool completely and serve.

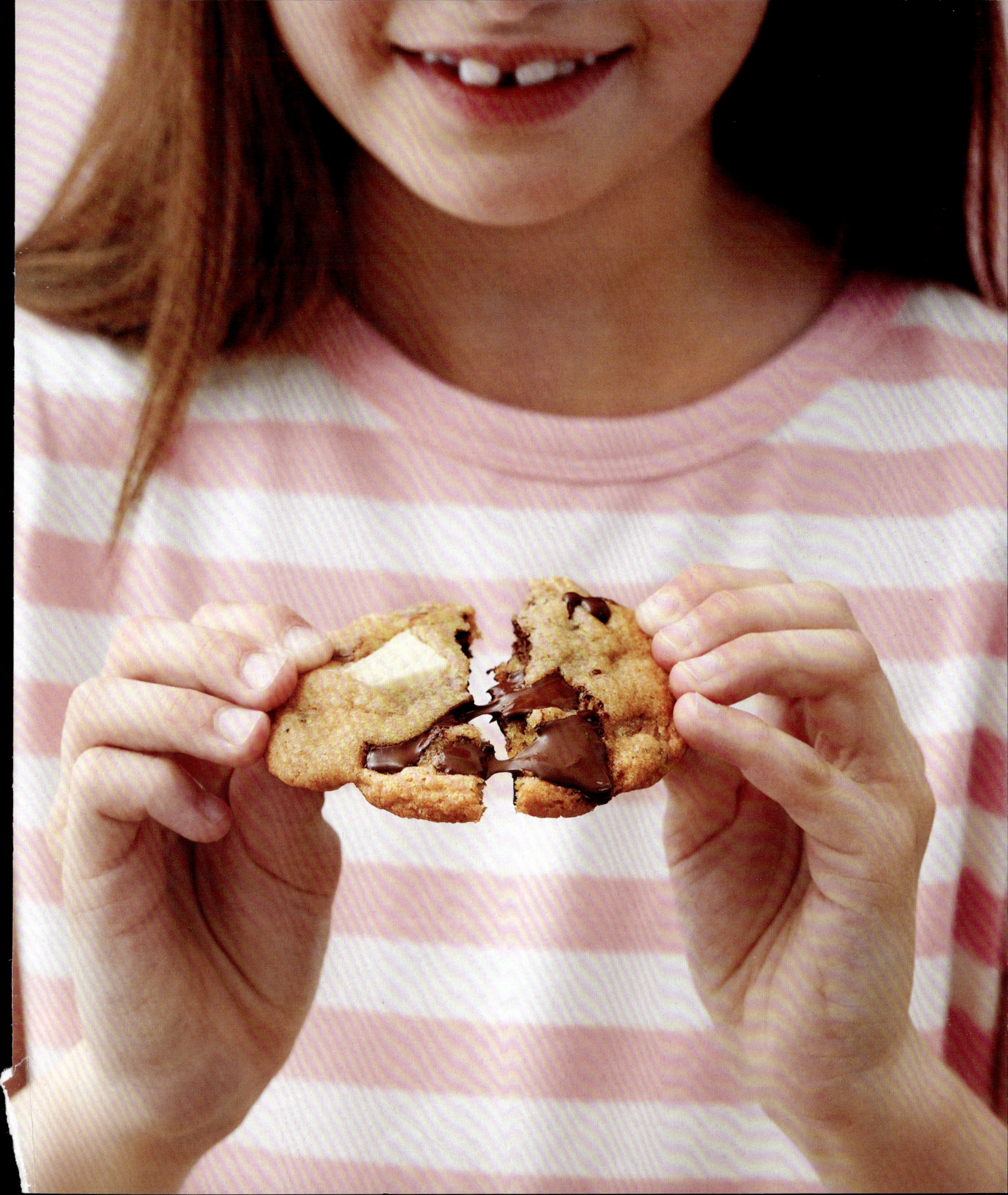

Tasty toppings
Instead of using sprinkles, try topping these cookies with chopped candy canes, toasted nuts, or pretzels.

Chocolate-Dipped Butter Cookie Triangles

Invite a few friends over to make these rich, buttery cookies dipped in chocolate and decorated with festive sprinkles. Make sure to let the chocolate set up before serving the cookies, or else be prepared for messy fingers!

MAKES ABOUT 18 COOKIES

2 cups all-purpose flour

½ teaspoon salt

1 cup (2 sticks) unsalted butter, at room temperature

½ cup sugar

2 teaspoons vanilla extract

1 (12-ounce) bag (2 cups) semisweet or bittersweet chocolate chips

Rainbow sprinkles, for decorating

In a medium bowl, whisk together the flour and salt. In a large bowl, using an electric mixer, beat the butter and sugar on medium speed until light and fluffy, about 3 minutes. Add the vanilla and beat until well combined. Turn off the mixer and scrape down the bowl with a rubber spatula. Add the flour mixture and beat on low speed just until blended.

Lightly dust a clean work surface with flour. Using the rubber spatula, scrape the dough out onto the work surface, then shape it into a disk with your hands. Wrap the disk in plastic wrap and refrigerate for 30 minutes.

Preheat the oven to 350°F. Line a cookie sheet with parchment paper.

Dust your work surface with flour and set the dough on the surface. Roll out the dough to ¼-inch thickness. Using a pizza cutter and a ruler, cut the dough into 4-inch squares, then cut each square in half diagonally into triangles. Transfer to the prepared cookie sheet, spacing them about 1½ inches apart. Bake until the edges of the cookies are golden brown, 12 to 14 minutes. Remove the sheet from the oven and set it on a wire rack. Let the cookies cool.

Place the chocolate chips in a medium microwave-safe bowl. Microwave on high power, stirring every 30 seconds, just until the chips are melted and smooth. Dip each cookie halfway into the melted chocolate, then let the excess chocolate drip back into the bowl. Carefully place the cookie back on the cookie sheet and sprinkle the chocolate-coated side with rainbow sprinkles. Let stand at room temperature until the chocolate has set, then serve.

Confetti Cookies

With colorful sprinkles both inside and out, every bite of these cookies is like a party. You can change the sprinkles to match the occasion or holiday—use red and green for Christmas; red, white, and blue for the Fourth of July; or pink and red for Valentine's Day.

MAKES ABOUT 36 COOKIES

COOKIES

2¾ cups all-purpose flour

1 teaspoon baking powder

¼ teaspoon salt

1 cup (2 sticks) unsalted butter, at room temperature

1½ cups granulated sugar

2 large eggs

2 teaspoons vanilla extract

2 tablespoons rainbow sprinkles, such as nonpareils

ICING

2½ cups powdered sugar

8 teaspoons whole milk

2 teaspoons vanilla extract

Rainbow sprinkles, for decorating

Preheat the oven to 350°F. Line 2 cookie sheets with parchment paper.

To make the cookies, in a medium bowl, whisk together the flour, baking powder, and salt. In a large bowl, using an electric mixer, beat the butter and granulated sugar on medium speed until well blended, about 1 minute. Add the eggs and vanilla and beat on low speed until well combined. Turn off the mixer and scrape down the bowl with a rubber spatula. Add about half of the flour mixture and mix on low speed just until blended. Add the rest of the flour mixture and mix again just until blended. Turn off the mixer, add the sprinkles, and stir with a wooden spoon until the sprinkles are mixed evenly into the dough.

Scoop up 1 rounded tablespoon of dough. Roll the dough into a ball using your palms, and place on a prepared cookie sheet. Repeat with the remaining dough, spacing the balls about 3 inches apart. Bake 1 cookie sheet at a time until the edges of the cookies are light golden brown, about 13 minutes. Remove the sheet from the oven and set it on a wire rack. Let cool for 5 minutes, then use a metal spatula to move the cookies directly to the rack. Repeat to bake the rest of the cookies. Let cool completely.

To make the icing, in a small bowl, whisk the powdered sugar, milk, and vanilla until smooth. Spoon about 1 tablespoon of the icing onto each cookie, letting it drip over the edges a little. Decorate with rainbow sprinkles. Let the icing dry at room temperature until firm, at least 2 hours.

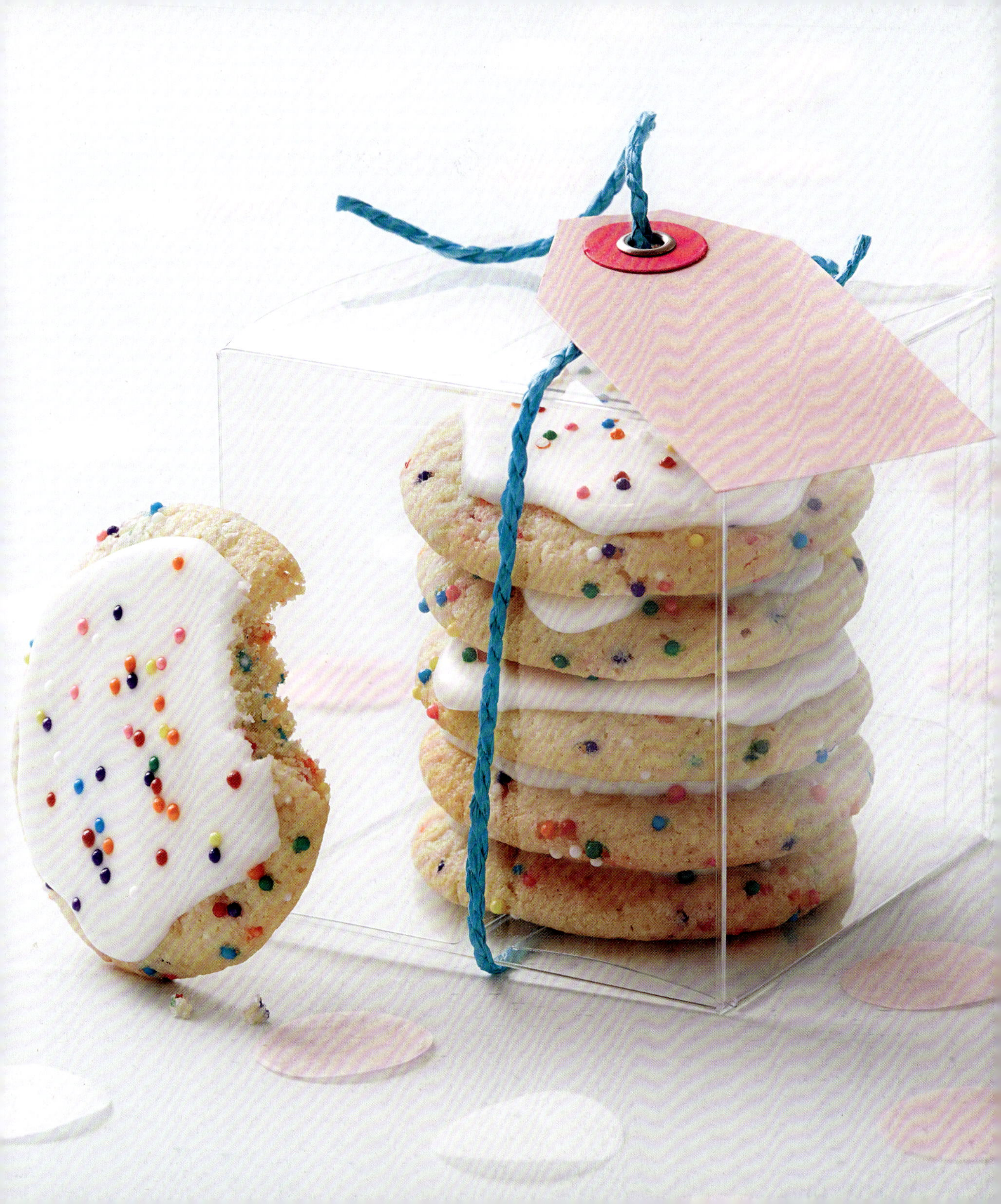

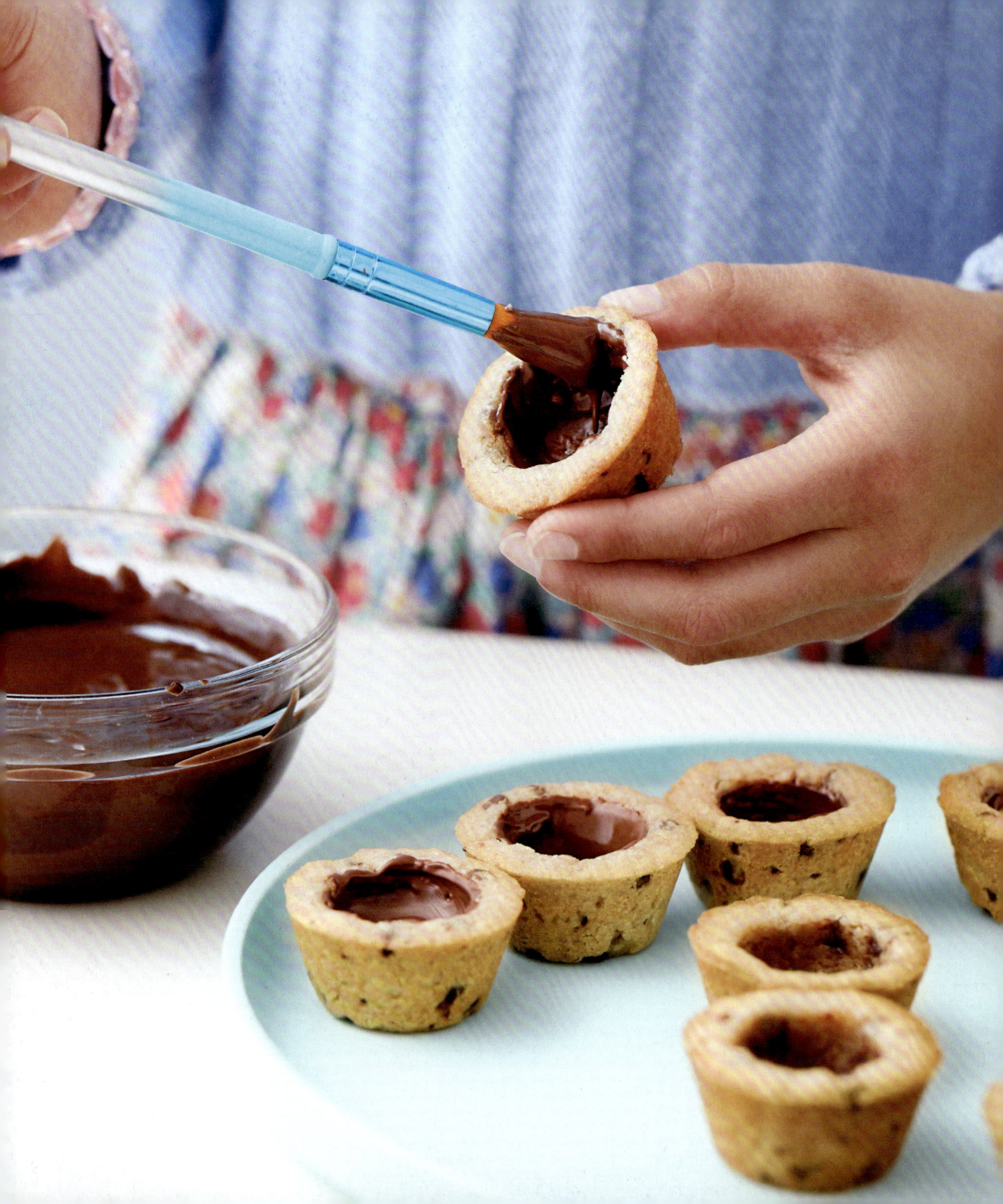

Milk-and-Cookie Cups

Cookies and milk are a perfect pairing, so why not combine them into mini chocolate chip cookie cups coated with chocolate, then filled with cold milk? Make these sweets for a sleepover and watch the reactions when you pour milk right into the cookies!

MAKES 36 COOKIE CUPS

2 cups all-purpose flour

½ teaspoon salt

1 cup (2 sticks) unsalted butter, at room temperature

½ cup firmly packed light brown sugar

½ cup granulated sugar

1 large egg

2 teaspoons vanilla extract

1 (12-ounce) bag mini semisweet chocolate chips

1½ cups cold whole milk, for serving

Grease a 24-cup mini muffin pan with nonstick cooking spray.

In a medium bowl, whisk together the flour and salt. In a large bowl, using an electric mixer, beat the butter, brown sugar, and granulated sugar on medium speed until well blended, about 1 minute. Add the egg and vanilla and beat on low speed until well combined. Turn off the mixer and scrape down the bowl with a rubber spatula. Add about half of the flour mixture and mix on low speed just until blended. Add the rest of the flour mixture and mix again just until blended. Turn off the mixer, add ¾ cup of the chocolate chips, and stir with a wooden spoon until the chips are mixed evenly into the dough.

Spoon 1 tablespoon of dough into each muffin cup, pushing the dough into the bottom and up the sides of each cup so that the dough rises slightly above the rim. Use a ½-teaspoon measuring spoon to smooth the center well. Refrigerate the pan, uncovered, for 30 minutes. Cover the bowl containing the remaining dough with plastic wrap and refrigerate while the first batch chills and bakes.

Continued on page 50

> **Handy measures**
> Use a ½-teaspoon measuring spoon to shape the cookie cups before and after they're baked.

~ *Continued from page 49* ~

Preheat the oven to 350°F.

Bake the cookie cups until the edges begin to brown, about 20 minutes. Remove the pan from the oven and set it on a wire rack. Immediately use the ½-teaspoon measuring spoon to smooth the center wells once again. Let cool for 15 minutes, then carefully remove the cookie cups, using a small icing spatula to help loosen them, and set them directly on the rack. Let the muffin pan cool completely. Remove the remaining dough from the refrigerator and bake the second batch in the same way. Let the cookie cups cool completely.

Add the remaining chocolate chips to a medium microwave-safe bowl. Microwave on high power, stirring every 15 seconds, just until the chips are melted and smooth. Don't let the chocolate get too hot!

Spoon about ½ teaspoon of the melted chocolate into each cookie cup. Tip and rotate the cups so that the chocolate coats the sides. Let the chocolate set for 20 minutes.

Just before serving, fill each cookie cup with milk.

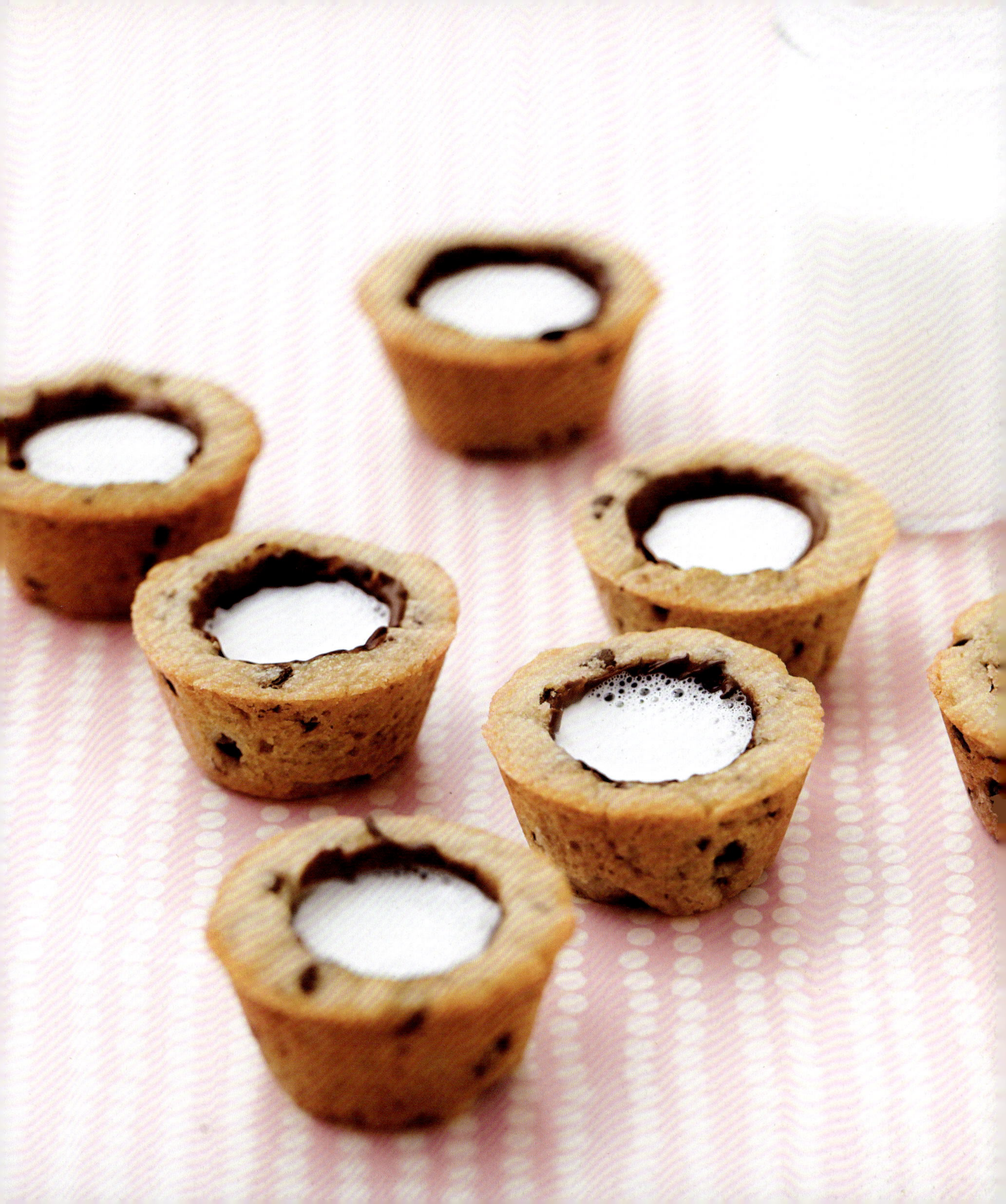

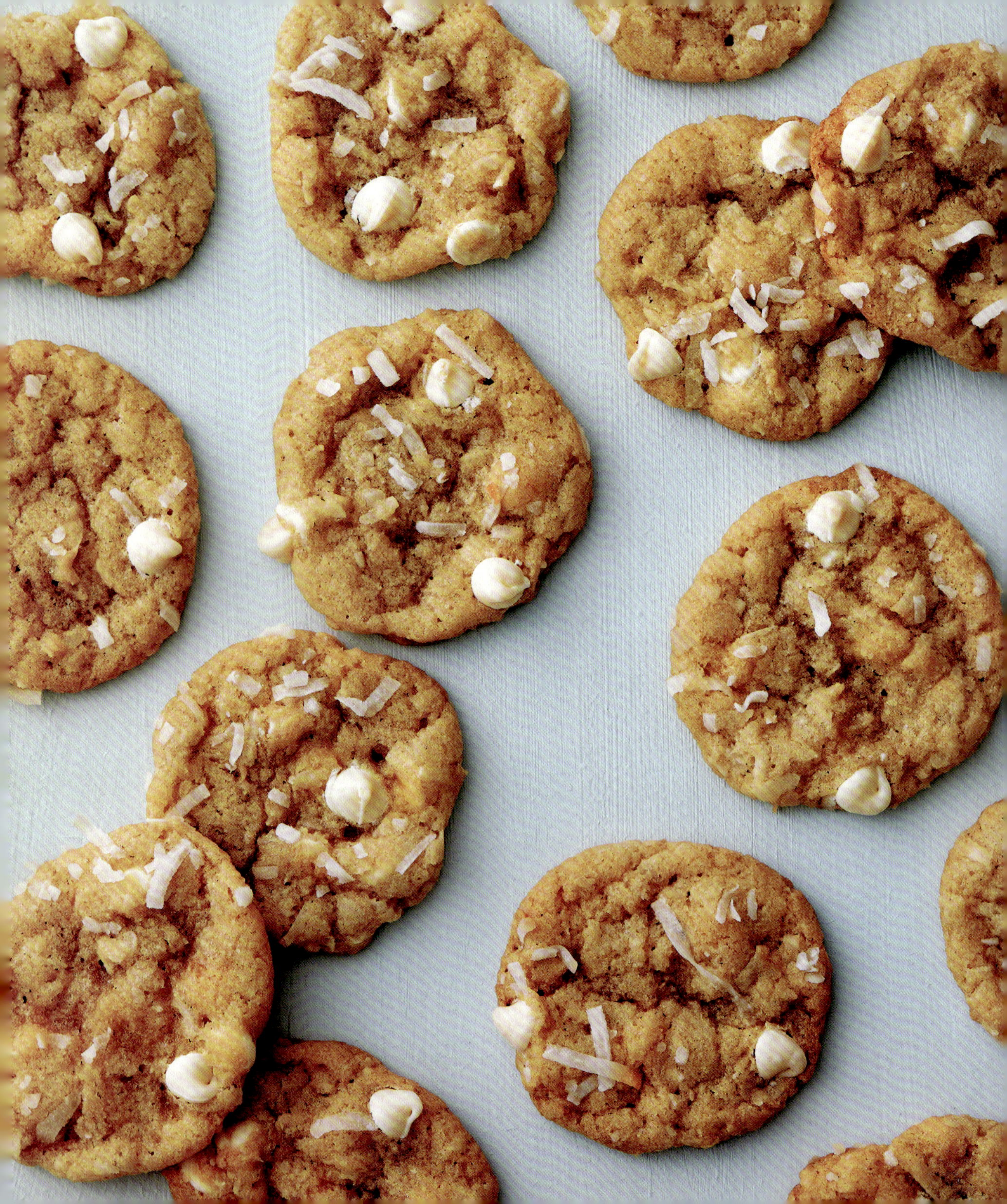

Chewy White Chocolate Coconut Cookies

Shredded coconut gives these yummy cookies an extra layer of chewiness. If you'd like to change up the flavor a little, use semisweet or milk chocolate chips in place of the white chocolate chips—or try butterscotch or peanut butter chips.

MAKES ABOUT 20 COOKIES

1⅓ cups all-purpose flour

½ teaspoon baking powder

½ teaspoon baking soda

½ teaspoon salt

½ cup (1 stick) unsalted butter, at room temperature

½ cup firmly packed light brown sugar

½ cup granulated sugar

1 large egg

½ teaspoon vanilla extract

1¼ cups sweetened shredded coconut

½ cup white chocolate chips

Preheat the oven to 325°F. Line 2 cookie sheets with parchment paper.

In a medium bowl, whisk together the flour, baking powder, baking soda, and salt. In a large bowl, using an electric mixer, beat the butter, brown sugar, and granulated sugar on medium speed until light and fluffy, about 3 minutes. Reduce the speed to low, add the egg and vanilla, and beat until combined, about 1 minute. Turn off the mixer and scrape down the bowl with a rubber spatula. Add the flour mixture and beat on low speed just until blended. Turn off the mixer, add the coconut and white chocolate chips, and stir with a wooden spoon until the coconut and chips are evenly mixed into the dough.

Drop rounded tablespoons of the dough onto the prepared cookie sheets, spacing the mounds about 2 inches apart. Bake 1 cookie sheet at a time until the cookies are golden brown, 14 to 16 minutes. Remove the sheet from the oven and set it on a wire rack. Let cool for 5 minutes, then use a metal spatula to move the cookies directly to the rack. Repeat to bake the rest of the cookies. Let cool completely and serve.

Chocolate-Covered Mint Wafers

If Girl Scouts Thin Mints are one of your favorite cookies, then you'll love these minty, chocolate-dipped wafers. For deep, dark chocolaty goodness, make sure to use Dutch-process cocoa powder, not natural cocoa powder, in the cookies.

MAKES ABOUT 40 COOKIES

COOKIES

- 1¼ cups all-purpose flour
- ¾ cup granulated sugar
- ¾ cup unsweetened Dutch-process cocoa powder
- 1 teaspoon baking soda
- ¼ teaspoon baking powder
- ½ teaspoon salt
- ¾ cup (1½ sticks) unsalted butter, at room temperature
- 1 large egg
- 1 teaspoon vanilla extract
- ½ teaspoon peppermint extract
- 1 tablespoon heavy cream

(See additional ingredients on page 56)

To make the cookies, in a medium bowl, whisk together the flour, granulated sugar, cocoa powder, baking soda, baking powder, and salt. In a large bowl, using an electric mixer, beat the butter on medium speed until light and fluffy, about 3 minutes. Add the egg and beat on low speed until well blended. Add the flour mixture and beat on low speed until combined, about 2 minutes. Turn off the mixer and scrape down the bowl with a rubber spatula. Add the vanilla and peppermint extracts and the cream. Raise the speed to medium and beat until the dough comes together, about 2 minutes.

Using the rubber spatula, scrape the dough out onto the work surface. Using your hands, form the dough into a disk, wrap it tightly in plastic wrap, and refrigerate until well chilled, about 30 minutes.

Preheat the oven to 375°F. Line 2 cookie sheets with parchment paper.

Dust your work surface lightly with flour, unwrap the dough, and set it on the surface. Dust your rolling pin with flour and roll out the dough to an even ¼-inch thickness. Using a 2½-inch round cookie cutter, cut out rounds from the dough. Using a metal spatula, carefully move the cutouts to the prepared cookie sheets, spacing them about 1 inch apart. Gather the dough scraps and press them together, then roll them out and cut out more rounds. If the dough is too soft and sticky to roll, wrap it in plastic wrap and refrigerate until slightly firm, about 15 minutes.

Continued on page 56

Chill out!
These double-chocolate treats are extra yummy when they're cold, so pop a few in the freezer to snack on anytime.

> **Chocolate shortcut**
> Look for chocolate discs, also called coating wafers, for the minty glaze. They're easy to melt and stir, so they're great for dipping.

GLAZE

1¼ pounds semisweet or bittersweet chocolate, finely chopped

½ teaspoon canola oil

½ teaspoon peppermint extract

~ *Continued from page 54* ~

Bake 1 cookie sheet at a time until the centers of the cookies are firm to the touch, 8 to 10 minutes. (Be careful when touching the cookies—they're very hot!) Remove the sheet from the oven and set it on a wire rack. Let cool for 5 minutes, then use a metal spatula to move the cookies directly to the rack. Repeat to bake the remaining cookies. Let cool completely. Reserve the parchment-lined cookie sheets.

To make the glaze, place the chocolate in a medium microwave-safe bowl. Microwave on high power, stirring every 30 seconds, just until the chocolate is melted and smooth. Don't let it get too hot! Stir in the oil and peppermint extract.

Dip each cookie into the glaze and use 2 forks to turn the cookie so that it's coated on both sides. Using the forks, lift out the cookie and gently shake it, allowing excess glaze to fall back into the bowl. Place the glazed cookie back on 1 of the parchment-lined cookie sheets. Repeat with the remaining cookies and glaze. (If the glaze starts to harden, microwave it on high power, stirring every 15 seconds, until it has remelted.) Refrigerate the cookies uncovered until the glaze is set, about 20 minutes. Serve the cookies chilled or at room temperature. (To store the cookies, layer them between pieces of parchment paper in an airtight container. They will keep for up to 3 days in the refrigerator.)

Chocolate-Filled Vanilla Sandwich Cookies

The dough for these cookies is piped with a pastry bag into rosettes, which is just a fancy word for small flower-like shapes. Make sure the ingredients are at room temperature, so the dough is soft enough to squeeze through the tip of the pastry bag.

MAKES ABOUT 15 COOKIES

2¼ cups all-purpose flour

½ teaspoon salt

¾ cup (1½ sticks) plus 2 tablespoons unsalted butter, at room temperature

1 cup powdered sugar

1 large egg

1 teaspoon vanilla extract

Chocolate Glaze (page 267), chilled

Preheat the oven to 325°F. Grease 2 cookie sheets with nonstick cooking spray and line them with parchment paper.

In a medium bowl, whisk together the flour and salt. In a large bowl, using an electric mixer, beat the ¾ cup butter and sugar on medium-high speed until light and fluffy, 2 to 3 minutes. Add the egg and vanilla and beat on low speed until combined. Add the flour mixture and mix on low speed just until blended. Scrape the dough to a pastry bag fitted with a ¾-inch open star tip (see page 9).

Using firm pressure and a circular motion, pipe 1¼-inch rosettes onto the prepared cookie sheets, spacing them about 1 inch apart. Refrigerate or freeze the cookie sheets until the dough is firm, about 15 minutes.

Bake 1 cookie sheet at a time until the cookies are firm to the touch but have not yet started to brown, 15 to 17 minutes. Remove the sheet from the oven and set it on a wire rack. Let cool for 5 minutes, then use a metal spatula to move the cookies directly to the rack. Let cool completely.

Turn half of the cookies bottom side up and spoon about 1 to 2 teaspoons of the chocolate glaze onto each, almost touching the edges. Top with the remaining cookies, bottom side down. Refrigerate until the filling is firm, about 1 hour. Serve chilled or at room temperature.

Sugar Cookie Cutouts

Buttery and crisp, these sugar cookies have a delicate vanilla flavor that makes them delicious on their own, but they are also perfect for decorating. Cut out shapes using your favorite cutters, then give the cookies pizzazz with colorful icings and cute sprinkles.

MAKES ABOUT 30 (3-INCH) COOKIES

3 cups all-purpose flour

1 teaspoon baking powder

½ teaspoon salt

1 cup (2 sticks) unsalted butter, at room temperature

1¼ cups sugar

1 large egg

2 teaspoons vanilla extract

1 tablespoon heavy cream

Royal Icing (page 256) or Vanilla Icing (page 60)

Rainbow sprinkles, sanding sugar, or other decorations of your choice

Step 1: In a medium bowl, whisk together the flour, baking powder, and salt. In a large bowl, using an electric mixer, beat the butter and sugar on medium-high speed until light and fluffy, 2 to 3 minutes. Add the egg and vanilla and beat on low speed until well combined. Turn off the mixer and scrape down the bowl with a rubber spatula. Add the flour mixture in three batches, mixing on low speed after each addition, until the flour is almost blended in. Turn off the mixer and scrape down the bowl again. Add the cream and beat on low speed just until combined.

Step 2: Lightly dust a clean work surface with flour. Using the rubber spatula, scrape the dough out onto the work surface, then use your hands to shape it into a flattened rectangle. Wrap the dough in plastic wrap and refrigerate until firm, at least 1 hour or up to overnight. (The dough can be wrapped in a second layer of plastic wrap and frozen for up to 1 month. Let it thaw overnight in the refrigerator before rolling and baking.)

Preheat the oven to 350°F. Line 2 cookie sheets with parchment paper.

Lightly dust your work surface with flour, unwrap the dough, and set it on the surface. If the dough is too hard to roll directly from the refrigerator, let it stand at room temperature for a few minutes. Dust your rolling pin with flour and roll out the dough to an even ¼-inch thickness.

Continued on page 60

Smart cookie
Dip cookie cutters in flour before pressing them into the dough, and place them close together to minimize scraps.

~ *Continued from page 59* ~

Use your hands to help mold the dough into a ball before rolling if it starts to crumble. Using your choice of cookie cutters, cut out shapes from the dough. With a metal spatula, carefully move the cutouts to the prepared cookie sheets, spacing them about 1 inch apart. Gather the dough scraps and press them together, then roll them out and cut out additional shapes.

Bake 1 cookie sheet at a time until just the edges, not the centers, of the cookies are light golden brown, 14 to 16 minutes. Remove the sheet from the oven and set it on a wire rack. Let cool for 5 minutes, then use the metal spatula to move the cookies directly to the rack. Repeat to bake the rest of the cookies. Let cool completely.

Using icing and sprinkles—and your creativity!—decorate the cookies. Let the icing dry at room temperature until firm, at least 6 hours or up to overnight.

Vanilla Icing
In a medium bowl, whisk together 2 cups powdered sugar, 2 tablespoons warm water, 1 tablespoon light corn syrup, and 1 teaspoon vanilla extract until smooth. Add 2–3 dabs of gel paste food coloring, if you like, and whisk to combine. Add more water if icing is too thick.

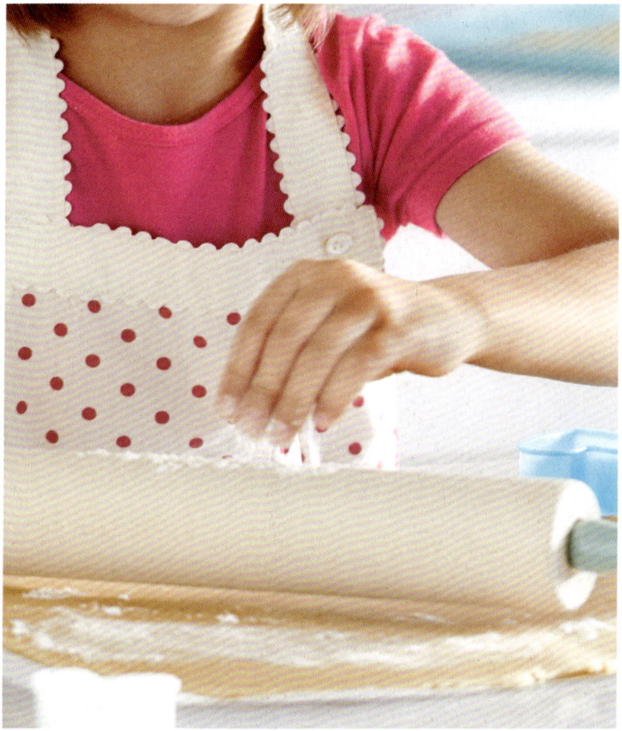
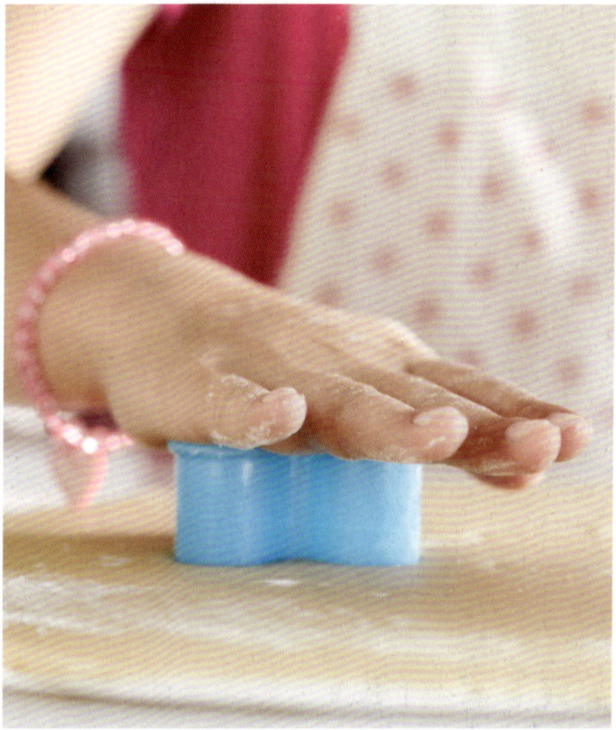
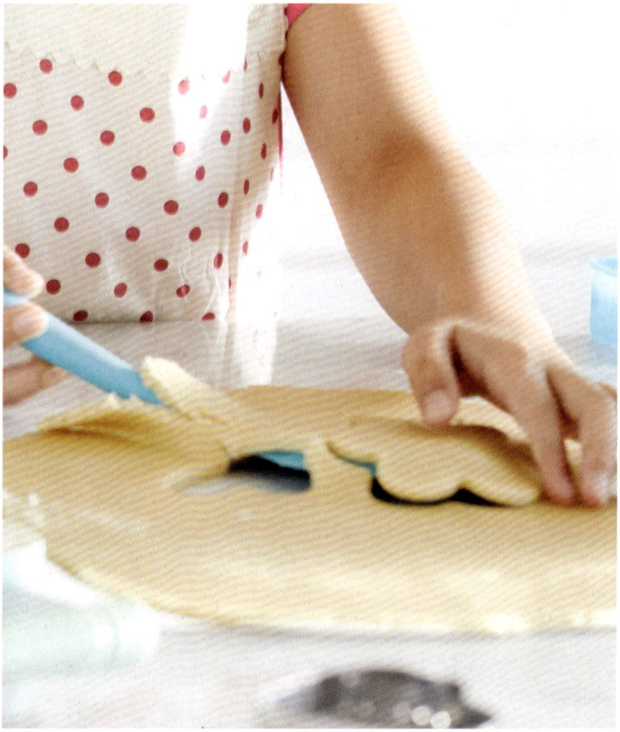
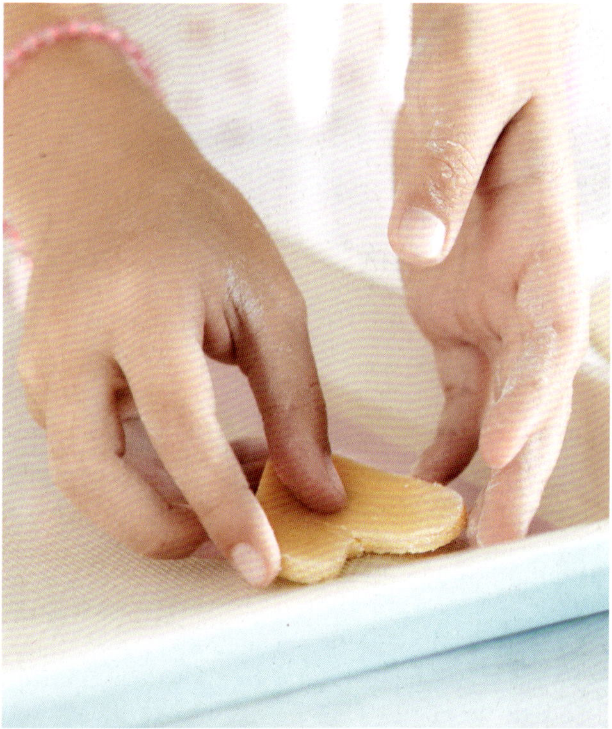

Classic Peanut Butter Cookies

You'll have lots of fun shaping this cookie dough with your hands. Peanut butter cookies are always best when they're soft and chewy, so take care not to overbake these treats. Definitely serve these cookies with tall glasses of ice-cold milk.

MAKES ABOUT 36 COOKIES

- 1⅓ cups all-purpose flour
- ½ teaspoon baking powder
- ½ teaspoon baking soda
- ½ teaspoon salt
- ½ cup (1 stick) unsalted butter, melted
- ½ cup firmly packed light brown sugar
- ½ cup granulated sugar
- 1 cup chunky peanut butter
- 1 large egg
- 1 teaspoon vanilla extract

In a medium bowl, whisk together the flour, baking powder, baking soda, and salt. In a large bowl, using an electric mixer, beat the butter, brown sugar, granulated sugar, peanut butter, egg, and vanilla on medium speed until well blended, about 3 minutes. Turn off the mixer and scrape down the bowl with a rubber spatula. Add the flour mixture and mix on low speed just until combined. Cover the bowl with plastic wrap and refrigerate until the dough is firm, about 2 hours.

Preheat the oven to 350°F. Line 2 cookie sheets with parchment paper.

Lightly moisten your hands with water, pinch off about 1 tablespoon of dough, and roll the dough into a ball between your palms. Place the ball on 1 of the prepared baking sheets. Repeat with the remaining dough, spacing the balls about 2 inches apart.

Dip the tines of a fork in flour, then lightly press the tines into each dough ball to flatten it slightly and create a set of parallel lines in one direction, and then repeat in the other direction to make a crosshatch pattern. Bake 1 cookie sheet at a time until the edges are golden brown, 12 to 15 minutes. Remove the sheet from the oven and set it on a wire rack. Let cool for 5 minutes, then use a metal spatula to move the cookies directly to the rack. Repeat to bake the rest of the cookies. Let cool completely and serve.

Chocolate-Drizzled Almond Florentines

The crisp, lacy cookies known as Florentines originated in Italy. They're the perfect mix of nutty caramel flavor and chocolate. What's not to love? Spoon the batter onto the cookie sheets soon after removing it from the heat because it will harden when cool.

MAKES ABOUT 24 COOKIES

COOKIES

¼ cup all-purpose flour

1 teaspoon finely grated orange zest

5 tablespoons unsalted butter, cut into pieces

½ cup sugar

¼ cup heavy cream

2 tablespoons honey

¾ cup sliced blanched almonds

CHOCOLATE GLAZE

6 ounces semisweet chocolate, finely chopped

½ cup (1 stick) unsalted butter

1 tablespoon light corn syrup

To make the cookies, preheat the oven to 325°F. Line 2 cookie sheets with parchment paper.

In a small bowl, stir together the flour and orange zest until the zest is coated. Set aside. In a saucepan, combine the butter, sugar, cream, and honey. Set the pan over low heat and cook, stirring, until the butter melts and the sugar dissolves. Raise the heat to medium-high and bring to a boil, stirring constantly, then boil for 2 minutes. Remove from the heat and carefully stir in the almonds, followed by the flour-zest mixture. The batter will be thick.

Drop the batter by 2-teaspoon scoops onto the prepared cookie sheets, spacing the cookies about 3 inches apart. Flatten each cookie with the back of the spoon. Bake 1 cookie sheet at a time until the cookies are bubbling vigorously and have light brown edges, 8 to 10 minutes. Remove the cookie sheet from the oven and set it on a wire rack. Let cool for 10 minutes, then use a wide metal spatula to move the cookies directly to the rack. Let cool completely.

To make the chocolate glaze, fill a saucepan one-third full with water and place over medium heat. Rest a bowl on the saucepan so it is over (but not touching) the water. Add the chocolate, butter, and corn syrup to the bowl and heat, stirring often with a rubber spatula, just until the chocolate is melted and smooth. Remove the bowl from the heat. Let cool to lukewarm before using.

Using a spoon, drizzle the chocolate glaze over the top of each cookie.

Donut Cookies

Super bright and cheery, donut cookies will make everyone's day. Don't be afraid to use bold icing colors and sprinkles—the crazier the better! Bake a bunch and invite friends over to help you decorate them.

MAKES ABOUT 40 COOKIES

Dough for Sugar Cookie Cutouts (page 59), prepared through Step 2

Royal Icing (page 256)

Pink and blue gel paste food coloring, or any 2 to 3 colors of your choice

Rainbow sprinkles, for decorating

Preheat the oven to 350°F. Line 2 cookie sheets with parchment paper.

Lightly dust your work surface with flour and set the dough on the surface. If the dough is too hard to roll directly from the refrigerator, let it stand at room temperature for a few minutes. Dust your rolling pin with flour and roll out the dough to ¼-inch thickness. Using a 4-inch donut cutter, cut out rounds from the dough, then remove the center "hole" from each round. With a metal spatula, carefully move the cutouts to the prepared cookie sheets, spacing them about 1 inch apart. Gather the dough scraps and press them together, then roll them out and cut out additional shapes.

Bake 1 cookie sheet at a time until the edges of the cookies are light golden brown, about 12 minutes. Remove the sheet from the oven and set it on a wire rack. Let cool for 5 minutes, then use the metal spatula to move the cookies directly to the rack. Repeat to bake the rest of the cookies. Let cool completely.

Divide the icing evenly among 3 small bowls. Add a very small amount of pink food coloring to one bowl, a larger amount of pink food coloring to the second bowl, and blue food coloring to the third bowl, then mix well; if needed, stir in more food coloring until the desired color is reached. Using a pastry bag or small icing spatula, spread icing over a cookie. Gently tap the cookie against the work surface to get the icing to settle into a smooth, even layer, then decorate with sprinkles. Repeat to ice and decorate the remaining cookies. Let the icing dry at room temperature until firm, at least 6 hours or up to overnight.

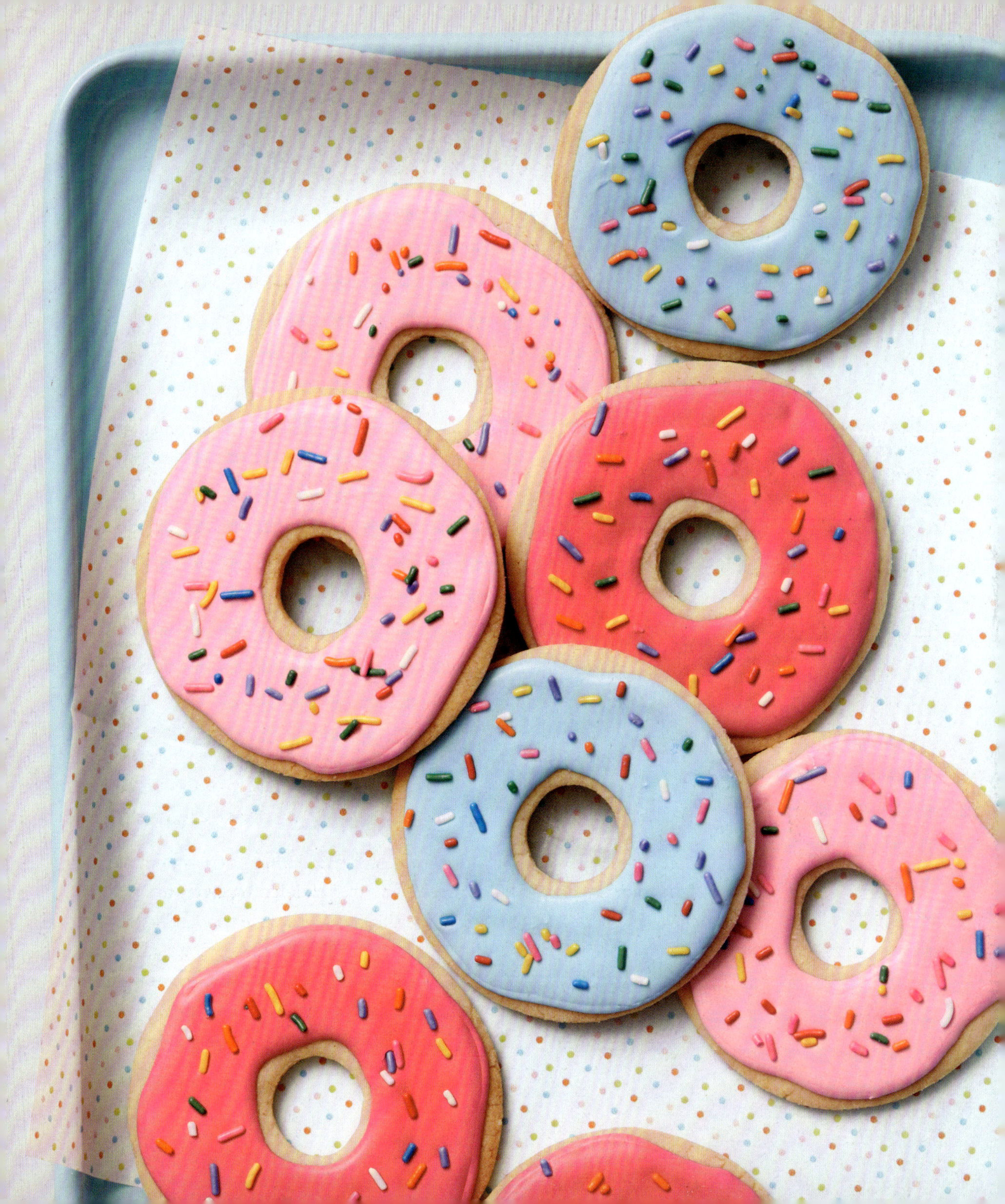

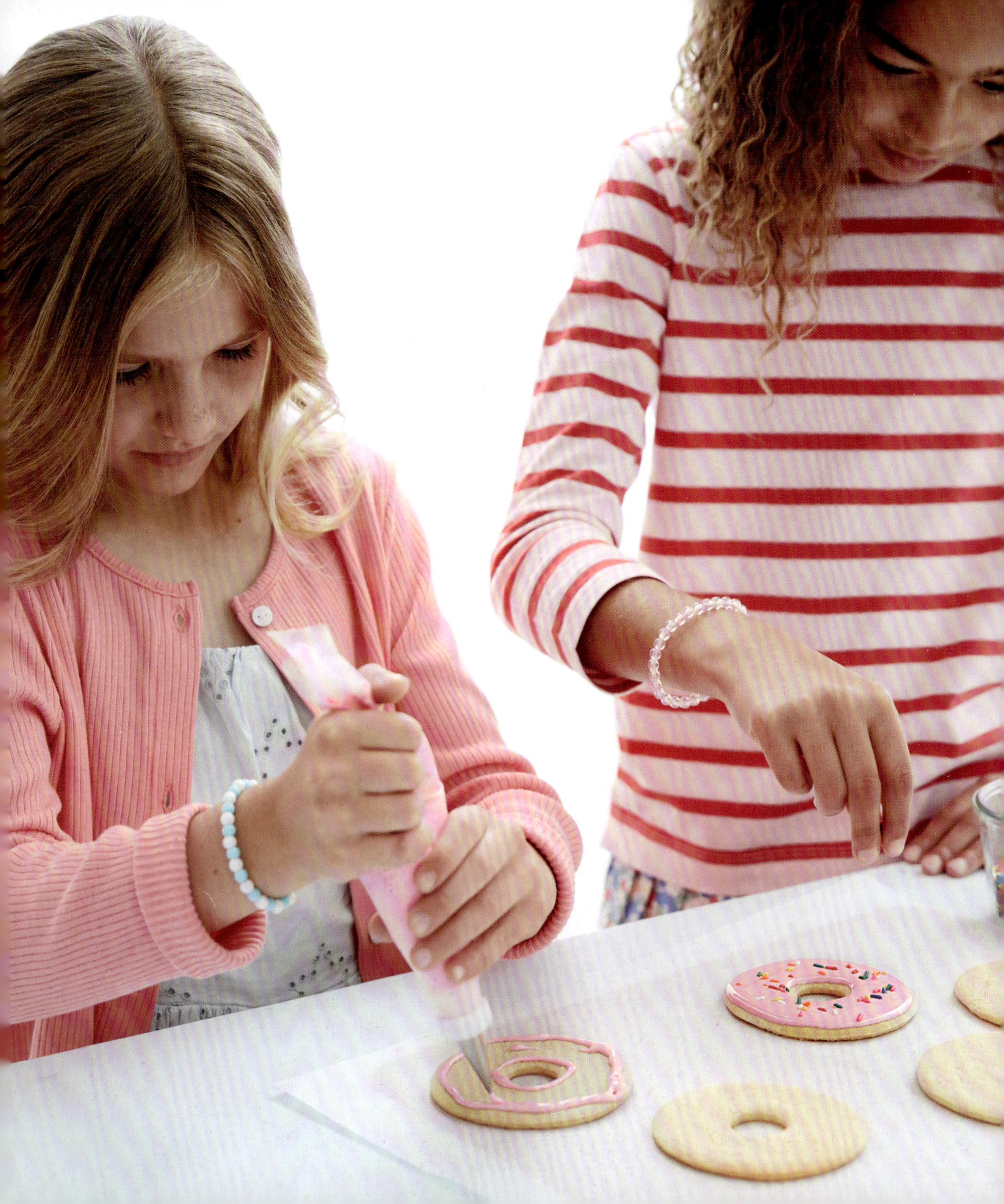

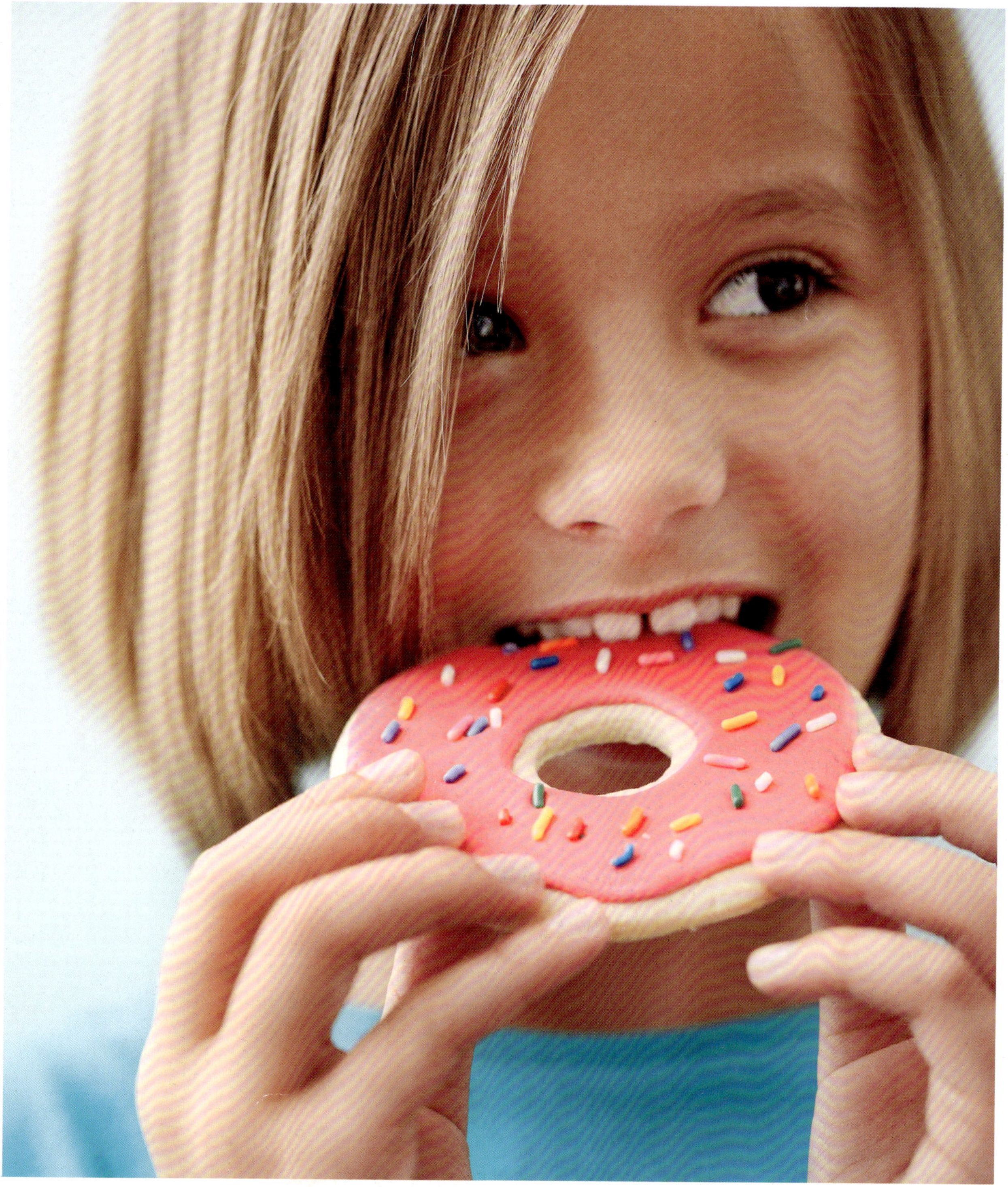

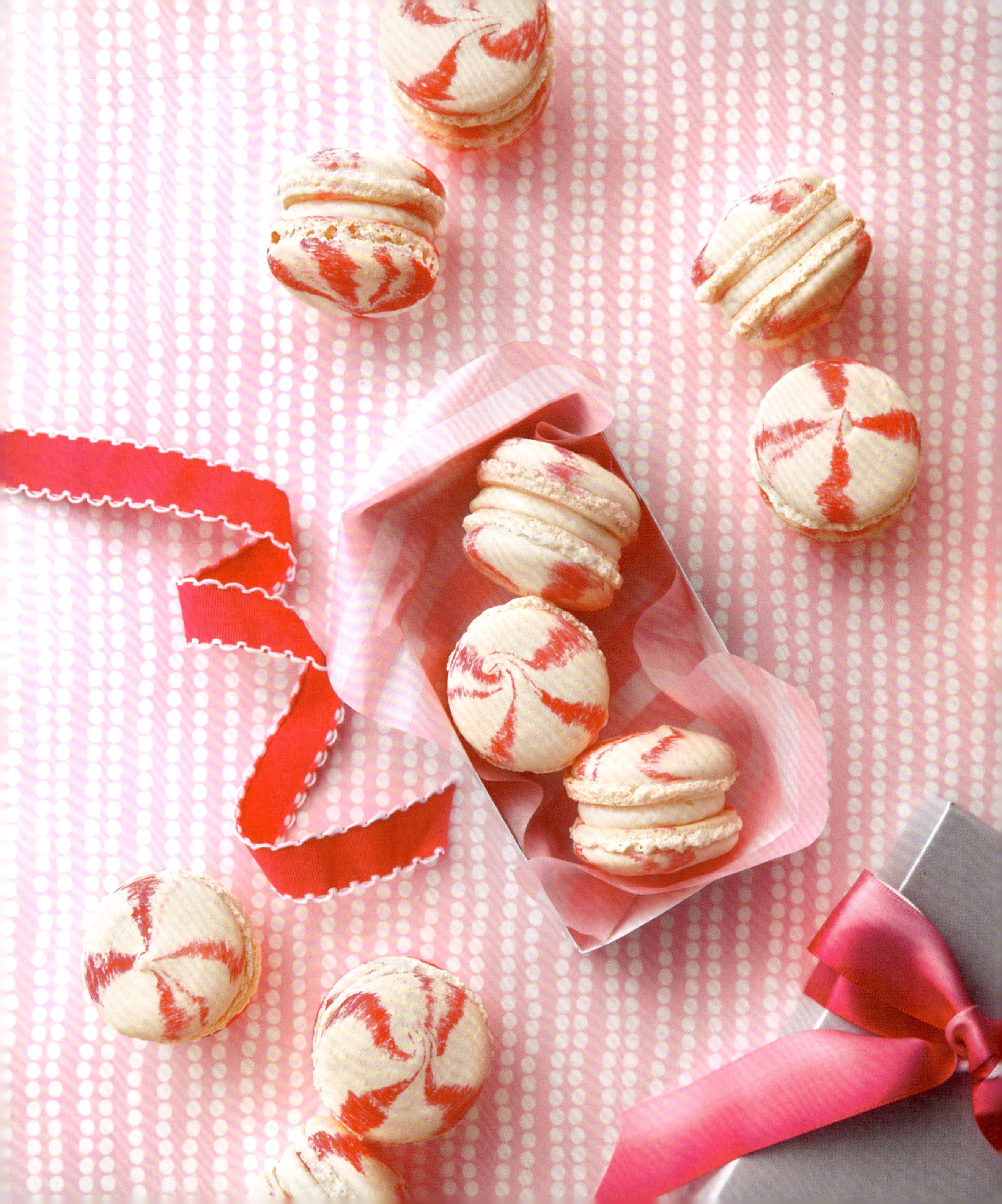

Peppermint Swirl Macarons

Light as a feather, these French macarons are the perfect balance of crisp and chewy. The red food coloring adds whimsy, but you can use any color you like, skip it altogether, or just stir a few drops of coloring into the batter toward the end of folding.

MAKES 24 COOKIES

2 cups powdered sugar

1⅓ cups superfine almond flour

3 large egg whites

1 teaspoon vanilla extract

½ teaspoon almond extract

¼ teaspoon cream of tartar

⅛ teaspoon salt

About 1 teaspoon red gel paste food coloring

1¼ cups (½ recipe) White Chocolate–Peppermint Frosting (page 259)

Line 2 cookie sheets with parchment paper. Using a 1½-inch circular guide (such as a biscuit cutter), draw 24 circles on each parchment sheet, spacing them about 1 inch apart. Turn the parchment paper over.

Combine 1 cup of the powdered sugar and the almond flour in a sifter or fine-mesh sieve. Set aside.

In a large bowl, using an electric mixer, beat the egg whites, vanilla and almond extracts, cream of tartar, and salt on medium speed until soft peaks form when the beaters are lifted (turn off the mixer first!), about 3 minutes. Raise the speed to high and gradually beat in the remaining 1 cup sugar, beating until stiff peaks form when the beaters are lifted (turn off the mixer first!), about 2 minutes longer.

Sift about one-third of the powdered sugar–almond flour mixture over the beaten whites. Using a rubber spatula, gently fold it in just until blended. Repeat to fold in the remaining powdered sugar mixture in 2 more additions until incorporated. Continue to fold the mixture just until the ingredients are completely combined and the batter flows in a slow, thick ribbon.

Fit a piping bag with a ⅜-inch round tip. Using a small, clean paintbrush, paint thin vertical stripes of the food coloring up the insides of the bag, spacing them evenly around the bag. (See step-by-step photos on page 71.)

Continued on page 70

> **Piping technique**
> Before piping, twist the full bag closed at the top, then squeeze it gently from the top to force the meringue through the opening.

Continued from page 69

Place the bag tip-end down in a glass and carefully spoon the batter into the piping bag using a rubber spatula, trying not to disturb the lines of food coloring; leave about 2 inches free at the top. Gently twist the bag closed.

Holding the piping bag with the tip about ½ inch above the prepared cookie sheet, pipe mounds of batter onto each sheet, using the circles as a guide. Pipe even mounds spaced about 1 inch apart, making the mounds as smooth as possible by moving the bag off to one side after piping each mound. Tap each sheet firmly against the work surface 2 or 3 times to release any air bubbles. Let the cookies stand at room temperature until they look less wet and are a little tacky, 45 to 60 minutes.

Preheat the oven to 300°F.

Bake 1 cookie sheet at a time until the cookies are risen and set but not browned, about 20 minutes. The bottoms of the cookies should be dry and firm to the touch (ask an adult for help) and not stick to the parchment paper (if they stick, bake them a few minutes longer). Remove the cookie sheet from the oven and set it on a wire rack. Let cool for 1 minute, then use a metal spatula to move the cookies directly to the rack. Repeat to bake the rest of the cookies. Let cool completely.

Prepare the white chocolate–peppermint frosting.

Spread about ½ teaspoon frosting over the flat side of half of the cookies. Top them with the remaining cookies, flat side down. Place the cookies in a single layer on a baking sheet, cover with plastic wrap, and refrigerate for at least 1 day or up to 3 days, or freeze for up to 6 months. (If frozen, thaw in the refrigerator before serving.) Serve chilled or at cool room temperature.

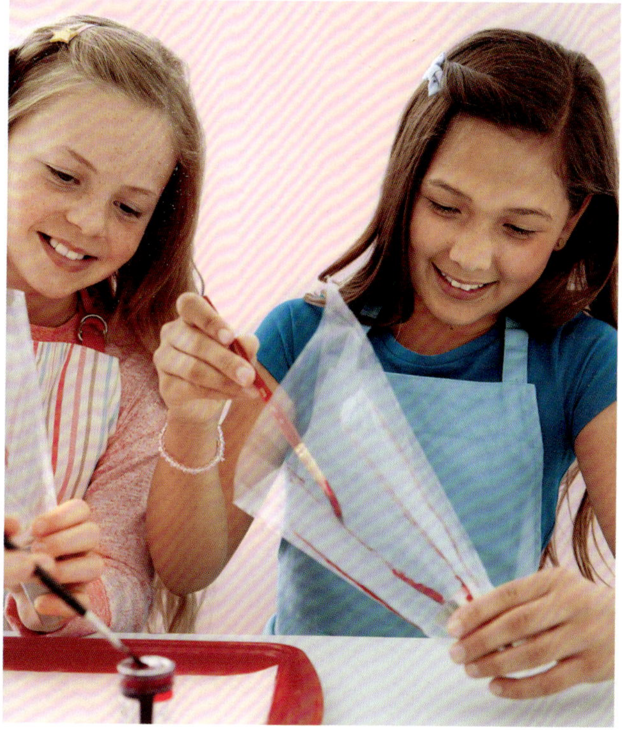
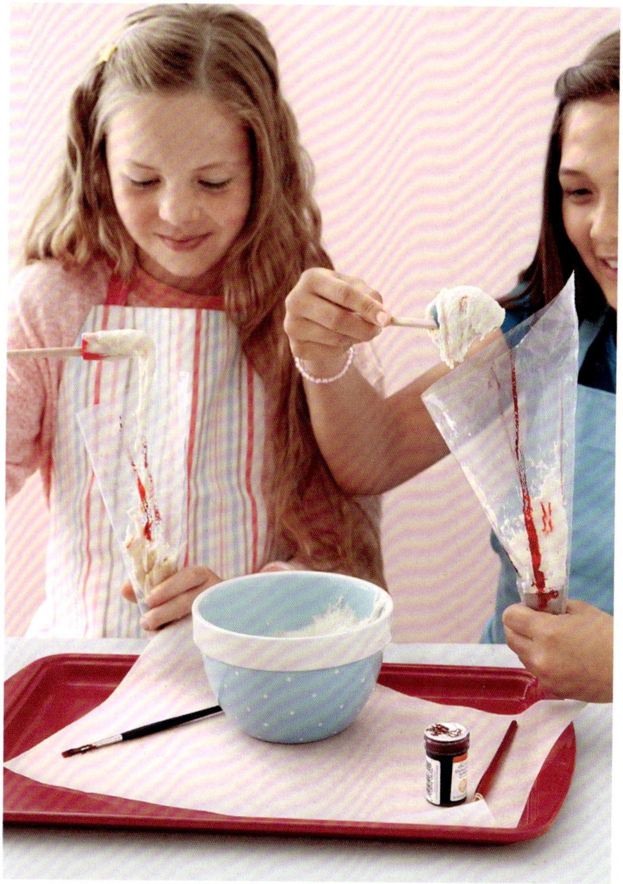
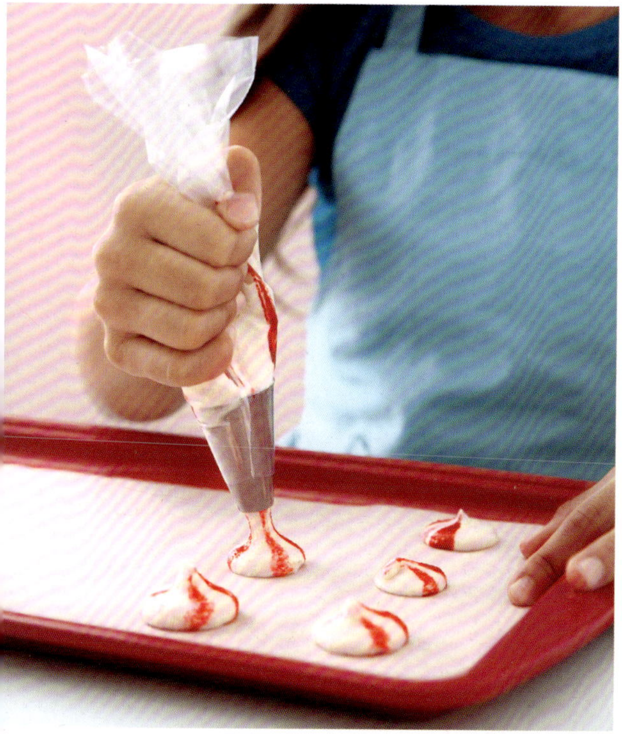
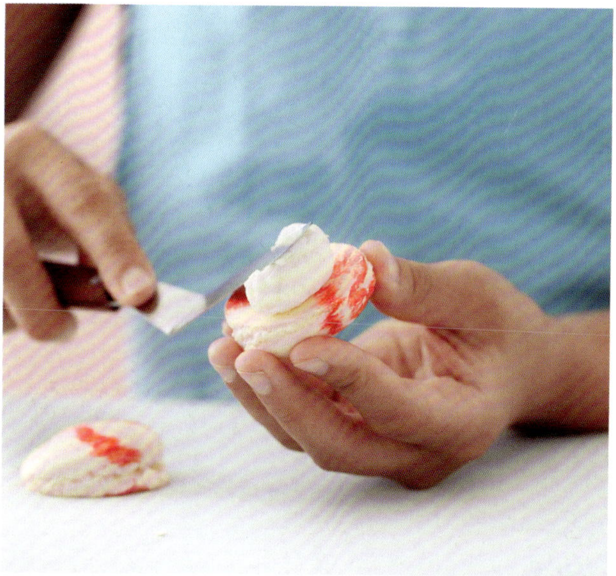

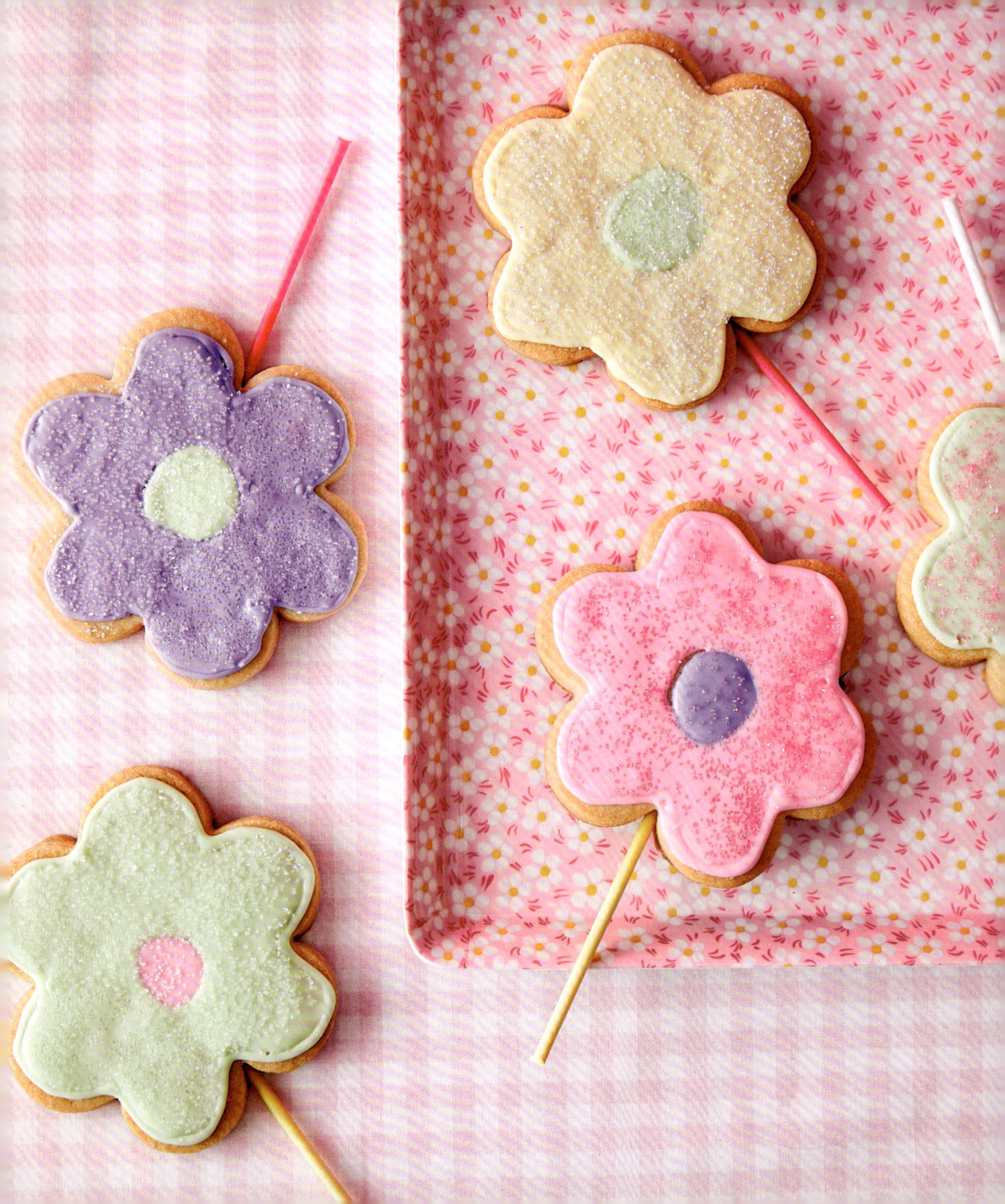

Flower Cookie Pops

Use icing in a variety of different hues to make a garden's worth of summery cookie pops. Arrange the pops on the cookie sheet with the sticks pointing towards the pan center to prevent the sticks from browning during baking.

MAKES ABOUT 20 COOKIE POPS

3 cups all-purpose flour

1 teaspoon baking powder

½ teaspoon salt

1 cup (2 sticks) unsalted butter, at room temperature

1¼ cups sugar

1 large egg

2 teaspoons vanilla extract

1 tablespoon heavy cream

(See additional ingredients on page 74)

In a medium bowl, whisk together the flour, baking powder, and salt. In a large bowl, using an electric mixer, beat the butter and sugar on medium-high speed until light and fluffy, 2 to 3 minutes. Add the egg and vanilla and beat on low speed until well combined. Add the flour mixture in three batches, mixing on low speed after each addition, until the flour is almost blended in. Turn off the mixer and scrape down the bowl with a rubber spatula. Add the cream and beat on low speed just until combined.

Scrape the dough onto a piece of plastic wrap, cover it with the wrap, and shape it into a disc. Refrigerate until firm, at least 1 hour or up to overnight.

Preheat the oven to 350°F. Line 2 cookie sheets with parchment paper. Lightly dust your work surface with flour, unwrap the dough, and set it on the surface. If the dough is too hard to roll directly from the refrigerator, let it stand at room temperature for a few minutes. Dust your rolling pin with flour and roll out the dough to an even ⅜-inch thickness.

Using a 3-inch flower-shaped cookie cutter, cut out shapes from the dough. With a metal spatula, carefully move the cutouts to the prepared cookie sheets, arranging them 3 across and 4 down around the perimeter of the pan and spacing them about 1 inch apart. Gather the dough scraps and press them together, then roll them out and cut out additional shapes. Gently insert an ice pop stick into the side of each cookie, pointing the sticks towards the center of the pan to prevent burning.

~ Continued on page 74 ~

~ *Continued from page 73* ~

ROYAL ICING

4 cups powdered sugar

3 tablespoons meringue powder

½ cup warm water, plus more as needed

½ teaspoon vanilla extract or ¼ teaspoon almond extract (optional)

Food coloring of your choice

Rainbow sprinkles, sanding sugar, or other decorations of your choice

20 wooden ice pop sticks

Bake 1 cookie sheet at a time until the edges of the cookies are light golden brown, 14 to 16 minutes. Remove the sheet from the oven and set it on a wire rack. Let cool for 5 minutes, then use the metal spatula to move the cookies directly to the rack. Repeat to bake the rest of the cookies. Let cool completely.

Meanwhile, make the royal icing: In a large bowl, using an electric mixer, beat the sugar, meringue powder, ½ cup warm water, and vanilla (if using) on medium speed until the mixture is very thick but drizzleable, 7 to 8 minutes.

Divide the icing among small bowls, using one bowl for each color. Stir 2 to 3 drops of food coloring into each bowl. Spoon each color of icing into a pastry bag with a plain tip or a lock-top plastic bag with a corner snipped.

Pipe icing around the edge of a cookie to form a border, then pipe icing—the same color or a different one—into the center of the cookie, letting it run to the border. Gently tap the cookie against the work surface a couple of times to get the icing to settle into a smooth, even layer, then sprinkle with sanding sugar or sprinkles. Repeat with the remaining cookies and icing.

Let the icing on the cookies dry at room temperature until firm, at least 6 hours or up to overnight. (To store the cookies, layer them between pieces of parchment paper in an airtight container. They will keep for up to 3 days at room temperature.)

Colorful Macarons

These delicate sandwich cookies take a little time and patience to prepare, but they're worth it. Choose your favorite color to tint the batter; you can also tint the filling with the same color or a different one, or keep it white. Cream of tartar is a powder that helps the egg whites whisk up nice and fluffy.

MAKES 12 MACARONS

2 cups powdered sugar

1⅓ cups almond flour

3 large egg whites

1 teaspoon vanilla extract

½ teaspoon almond extract

¼ teaspoon cream of tartar

⅛ teaspoon salt

½ teaspoon pink or orange gel food coloring

Fluffy White Chocolate Frosting (page 260)

Edible white glitter or pearl dust, for decorating (optional)

Line 2 cookie sheets with parchment paper. Use a 1½-inch round cookie cutter and a pen, trace 12 circles on each sheet of parchment. Turn the parchment over. The circle outlines will be visible through the paper.

Combine 1 cup of the powdered sugar and all the almond flour in a fine-mesh sieve. Set aside.

In a large bowl, using an electric mixer, beat together the egg whites, vanilla and almond extracts, cream of tartar, and salt on medium-high speed until foamy, about 30 seconds. Raise the speed to high and gradually beat in the remaining 1 cup powdered sugar, then continue beating until stiff, glossy peaks form, about 2 minutes longer.

Sift about one-third of the powdered sugar–almond flour mixture over the egg white mixture. Using a rubber spatula, fold it in gently just until blended. Repeat to fold in the remaining powdered sugar mixture in 2 batches. Add the food coloring and continue to fold the mixture just until the ingredients are fully combined and the batter flows in a thick, slow ribbon (about 40 strokes).

Spoon the batter into a piping bag fitted with a medium round tip (about ⅜ inch in diameter). Holding the piping bag so that the tip is about ½ inch above a circle outline on one of the parchment sheets, use the outline as a

~ Continued on page 76 ~

> **Test for doneness**
> *If the cookies seem done but still stick to the parchment, pop the macarons back into the oven for a few minutes longer.*

~ *Continued from page 75* ~

guide as you pipe the batter thickly onto each circle, piping the outline first and then filling in the middle. Tap each cookie sheet firmly against the work surface two or three times to release any air bubbles in the batter. Let the cookies stand at room temperature until they look less wet and are a little tacky, 45 to 60 minutes.

Preheat the oven to 300°F. Bake, one sheet at a time, until the cookies have risen and set but not browned, about 20 minutes. The bottoms of the cookies should be dry and firm to the touch. Let the cookies cool on the cookie sheet on a wire rack for 1 minute, then transfer to the rack and let cool completely. Repeat to bake the remaining cookies.

While the cookies bake and cool, make the frosting.

Turn half of the cookies bottom side up. Spread about 1½ teaspoons of the frosting onto each cookie. Top with the remaining cookies, bottom side down, pressing the bases together gently.

Place the cookies in a single layer on a rimmed cookie sheet, cover with plastic wrap, and refrigerate for at least 1 day or up to 3 days, or freeze in an airtight container for up to 6 months. If freezing, once the macarons are frozen, stack them in an airtight container, then thaw in the refrigerator before serving. Just before serving, dust the tops with edible glitter, if using. Serve chilled or at cool room temperature.

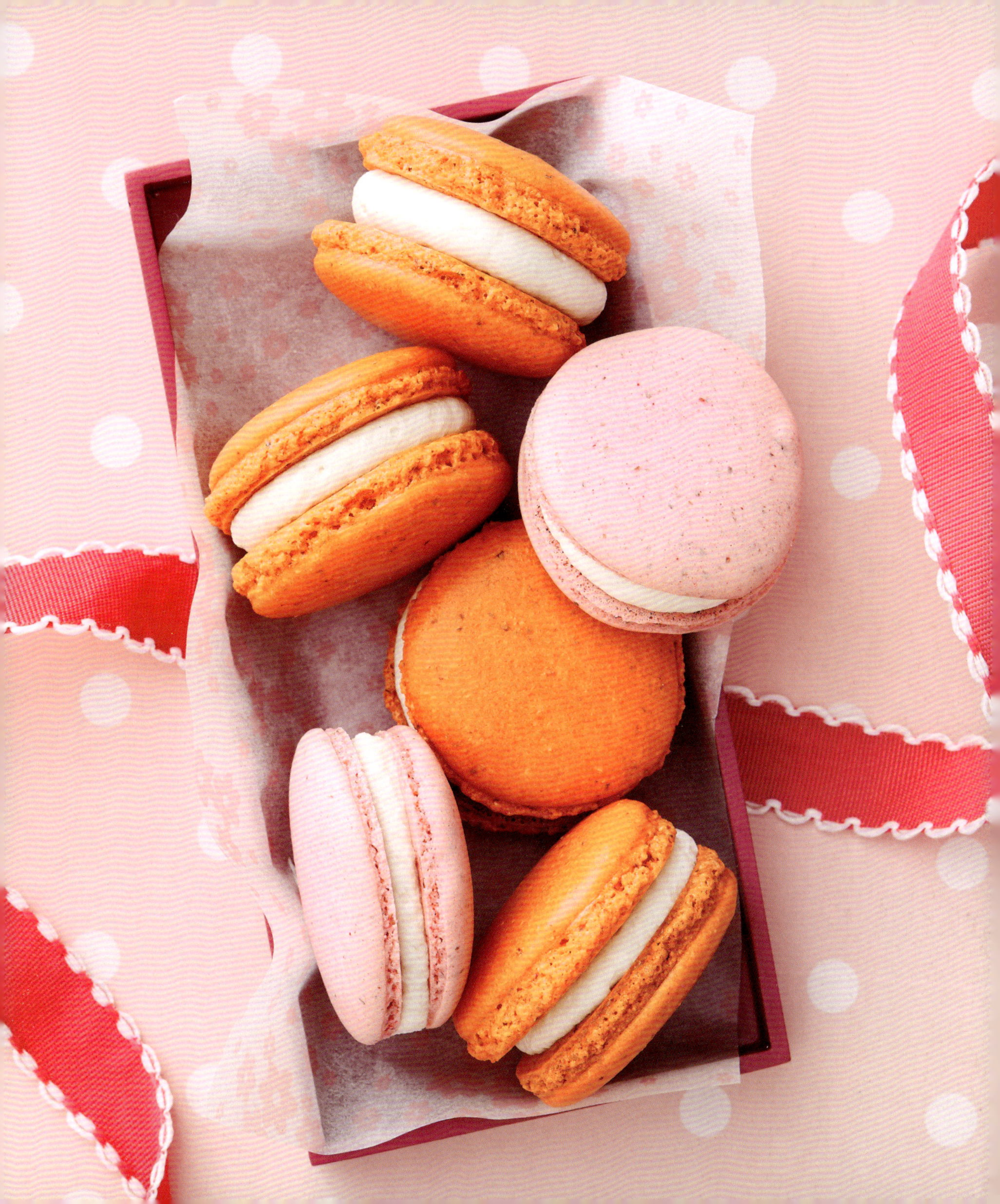

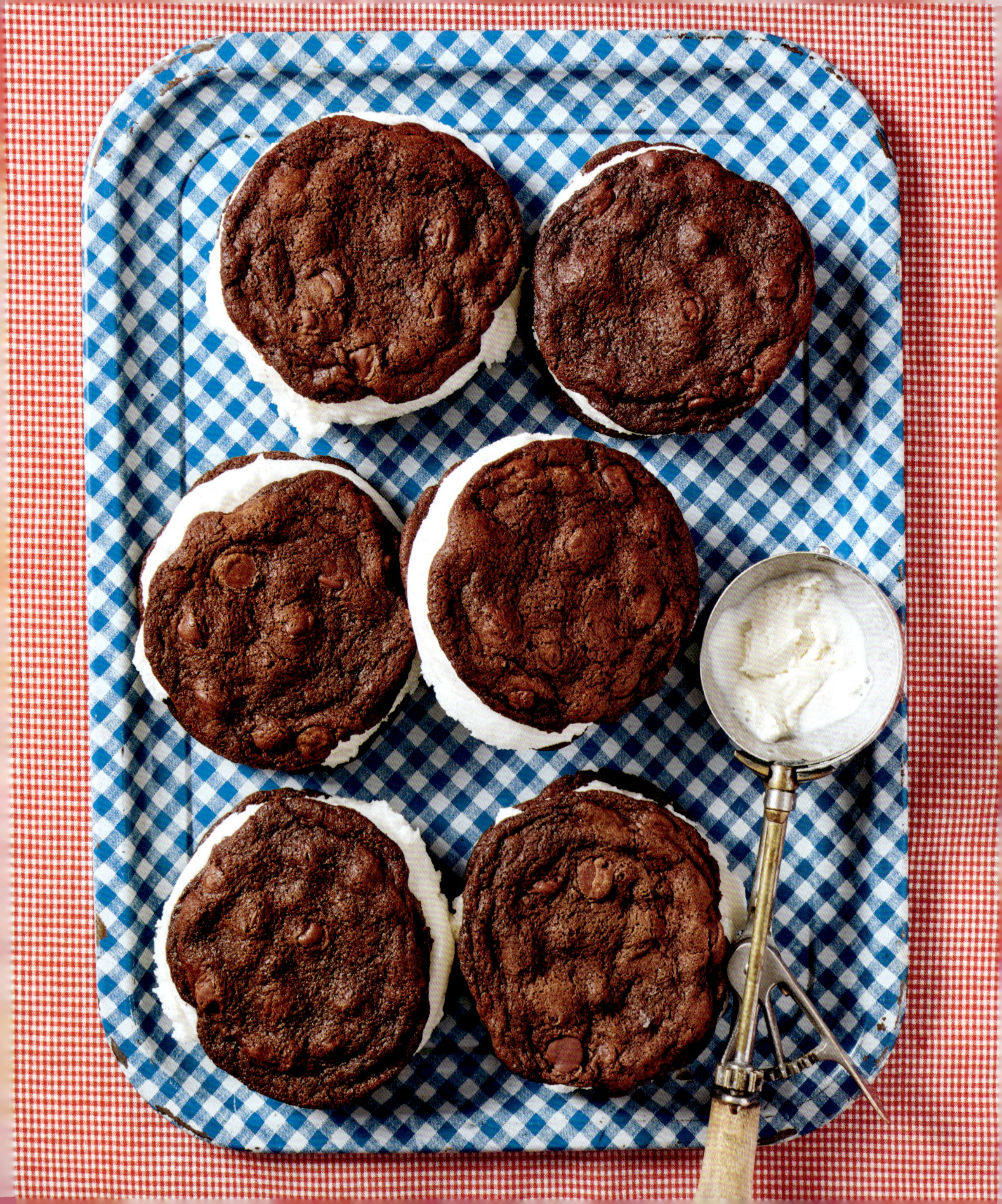

Ice Cream Sandwiches

These creamy, luscious ice cream sandwiches are a favorite anytime treat. Choose whatever flavor you'd like to smoosh between the dark chocolate cookies: vanilla, coffee, strawberry, or mint chip. If you like, roll the edges of the assembled sandwiches in chopped toasted peanuts or mini chocolate chips before freezing.

MAKES 6 ICE CREAM SANDWICHES

1¼ cups firmly packed dark brown sugar

½ cup (1 stick) unsalted butter, plus butter for greasing

3 ounces unsweetened chocolate, coarsely chopped

1 large egg

2 teaspoons vanilla extract

1¼ cups all-purpose flour

¾ teaspoon baking soda

¼ teaspoon salt

1½ cups semisweet chocolate chips

1½ pints ice cream, such as vanilla or chocolate, slightly softened

Preheat the oven to 350°F. Lightly butter 2 cookie sheets.

In a heavy saucepan over low heat, combine the brown sugar, butter, and chopped chocolate. Heat, stirring often, until the chocolate and butter melts. Transfer the mixture to a large bowl and let cool to lukewarm. Add the flour mixture to the chocolate mixture and whisk until smooth. In another bowl, whisk together the flour, baking soda, and salt. Add the dry ingredients to the chocolate mixture and stir until blended. Stir in the chocolate chips. Cover the bowl with plastic wrap and refrigerate until firm, about 30 minutes.

Drop the dough by generous tablespoonfuls onto the prepared cookie sheets, spacing the cookies at least 3 inches apart. You should have 12 cookies. With dampened fingers, smooth the cookies into slightly flattened rounds about 3 inches in diameter. Bake the cookies until the edges darken and the centers are still slightly soft, about 10 minutes. Remove the cookie sheet from the oven and set it on a wire rack. Let cool for 5 minutes, then use a metal spatula to move the cookies directly to the rack. Let cool completely.

Lay half of the cookies, flat side up, on a work surface. Spread about ½ cup of the ice cream on each cookie, then top the ice cream with 1 of the remaining cookies, flat side down. Smooth out the sides using a small icing spatula and wrap each sandwich in plastic wrap. Lay on a clean, dry cookie sheet and freeze until firm, at least 2 hours or up to 3 days.

Moon Pies

These full-moon-shaped pies make a stellar afternoon snack and baking adventure. Prepared with homemade graham cookies sandwiched with gooey marshmallow crème, the pies are dipped in dark-as-night chocolate. They take time to put together but are totally worth it.

MAKES ABOUT 15 MOON PIES

GRAHAM COOKIES

1 cup finely ground graham cracker crumbs (about 6 whole crackers)

1 cup all-purpose flour, plus flour for dusting

½ teaspoon baking powder

½ teaspoon ground cinnamon

½ teaspoon salt

½ cup (1 stick) unsalted butter, at room temperature

½ cup firmly packed dark brown sugar

1 large egg

1 teaspoon vanilla extract

2 tablespoons whole milk

About 1¾ cups marshmallow crème

(See additional ingredients on page 82)

To make the cookies, in a medium bowl, stir together the graham cracker crumbs, flour, baking powder, cinnamon, and salt. In a large bowl, using an electric mixer, beat the butter and sugar on medium-high speed until light and fluffy, about 1 minute. Add the egg and vanilla and beat until blended. Turn off the mixer and scrape down the bowl with a rubber spatula. Add the graham cracker mixture and beat on low speed until combined. Add the milk and beat just until the dough comes together. Transfer the dough to a clean work surface and press into a thick disk. Wrap the disk in plastic wrap and refrigerate for at least 1 hour or up to overnight.

Preheat the oven to 350°F. Line 2 cookie sheets with parchment paper.

On a lightly floured surface, roll out the dough into a round about ⅛ inch thick. Using a fluted 2¾-inch round cookie cutter, cut out as many cookies as possible. Transfer the cookies to the prepared cookie sheets, spacing them at least 1 inch apart. Gather up the dough scraps, press them together, roll them out again, and cut out more cookies. You should have about 30 cookies.

Bake 1 cookie sheet at a time until the cookies are lightly golden around the edges, about 13 minutes. Remove the cookie sheet from the oven and set it on a wire rack. Let cool for 5 minutes, then use a metal spatula to move the cookies directly to the rack and let cool completely. Repeat to bake the rest of the

~ Continued on page 82 ~

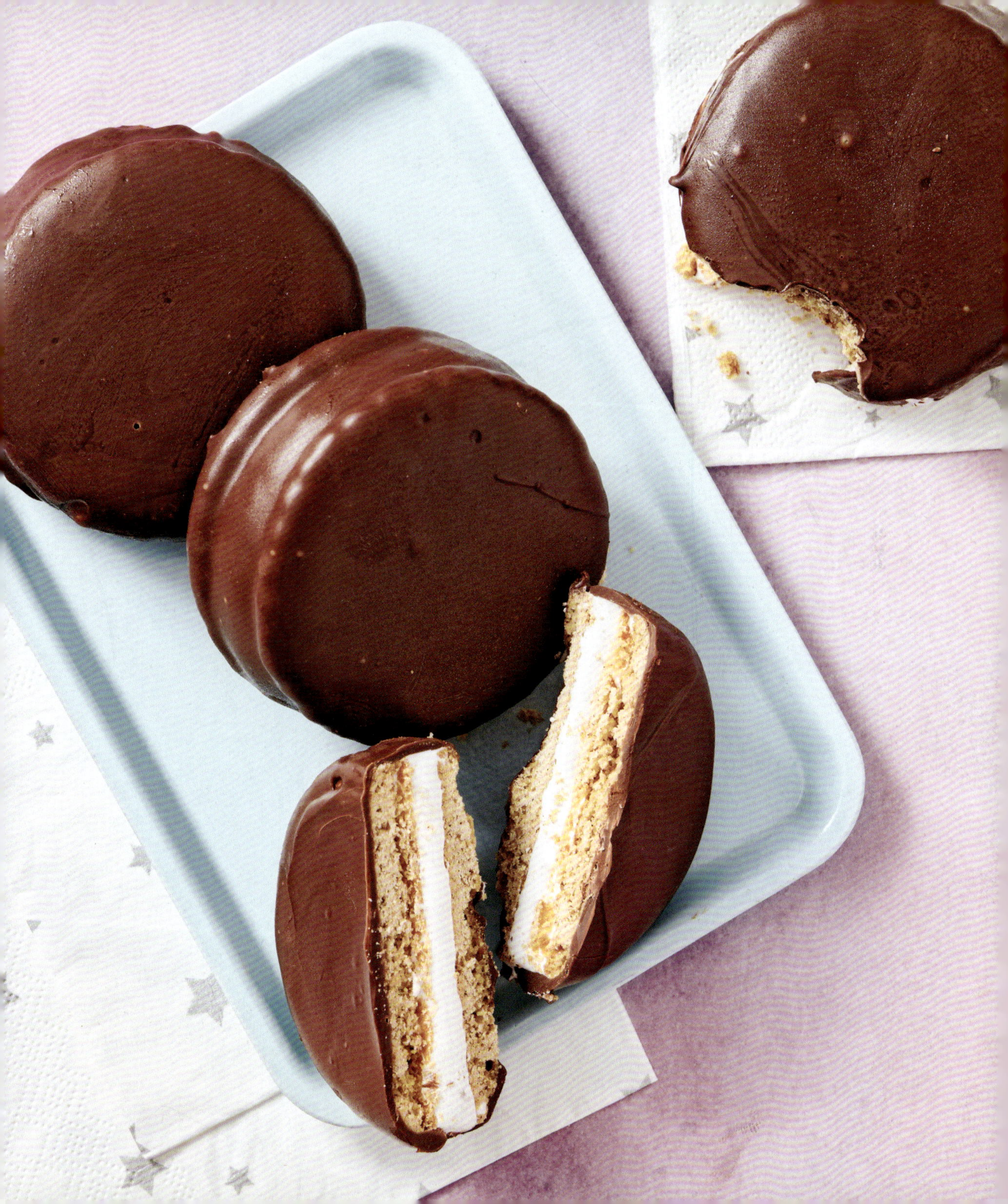

~ *Continued from page 80* ~

CHOCOLATE COATING

2⅔ cups semisweet chocolate chips

2 tablespoons vegetable oil

cookies. Turn half of the cookies bottom side up. Dollop about 2 tablespoons marshmallow crème onto the center of each overturned cookie. Top with a second cookie, bottom side down, and press the top cookie gently so the crème fills the sandwich. Place the filled cookies on a cookie sheet, cover with plastic wrap, and place in the freezer to firm up, at least 20 minutes or up to overnight.

To make the coating, in a small saucepan, pour water to a depth of about 1 inch. Set the pan over medium-low heat and bring to a gentle simmer. Rest a bowl on the saucepan so that it is over (but not touching) the water. Add the chocolate chips to the bowl and heat, stirring occasionally with a rubber spatula, until the chocolate is melted and is smooth. Remove the bowl from the heat and let cool slightly, then stir in the oil. Let cool for about 5 minutes.

To coat the moon pies, place a wire rack on a cookie sheet. Immerse a chilled moon pie into the melted chocolate and use 2 forks to maneuver it so it is evenly coated. Transfer to the wire rack. Repeat with the remaining moon pies. Refrigerate the moon pies until the chocolate hardens, at least 30 minutes. Serve chilled or at room temperature.

Gingerbread Cookies

Baking these chewy gingerbread cookies will fill your home with the most delectable spicy aroma. Double the recipe if you like, and keep extra logs of the dough in the freezer for up to 1 month; to bake, thaw a log partially, then slice and bake as directed.

MAKES ABOUT 4 DOZEN COOKIES

2½ cups all-purpose flour

2½ teaspoons baking soda

1½ tablespoons ground ginger

½ teaspoon ground cinnamon

½ teaspoon salt

¼ teaspoon ground white pepper

¾ cup (1½ sticks), plus 2 tablespoons unsalted butter, at room temperature

1¼ cups sugar, plus more for sprinkling

1 large egg

½ cup unsulphured dark molasses

¼ cup minced crystallized ginger

In a medium bowl, sift together the flour, baking soda, ground ginger, cinnamon, salt, and white pepper. Set aside. In a large bowl, using an electric mixer, beat the butter and sugar on medium-high speed until creamy, about 5 minutes. Add the egg and beat until the mixture is fluffy, about 5 minutes. Add the molasses and beat until incorporated. Reduce the speed to low, slowly add the flour mixture, and beat until fully incorporated, 2 to 3 minutes. Stir in the crystallized ginger until evenly distributed.

Lay a sheet of waxed paper on a work surface. Divide the dough in half. Place half of the dough in the center of the waxed paper and form it into a rough log. Fold 1 side of the paper over the dough and press to shape it into an even log about 1½ inches in diameter. Wrap tightly in the waxed paper. Repeat with the remaining dough. Refrigerate the logs until firm, at least 4 hours or up to 2 days.

Preheat the oven to 325°F. Line 2 cookie sheets with parchment paper.

Unwrap the chilled dough and slice into rounds ⅛ inch thick. Arrange the rounds on the prepared cookie sheets, spacing them about 1 inch apart.

Bake until the cookies are golden, 8 to 10 minutes. Remove the cookie sheets from the oven and set them on wire racks. Let cool for 5 minutes, then use a metal spatula to move the cookies directly to the racks. Sprinkle with sugar and let cool completely.

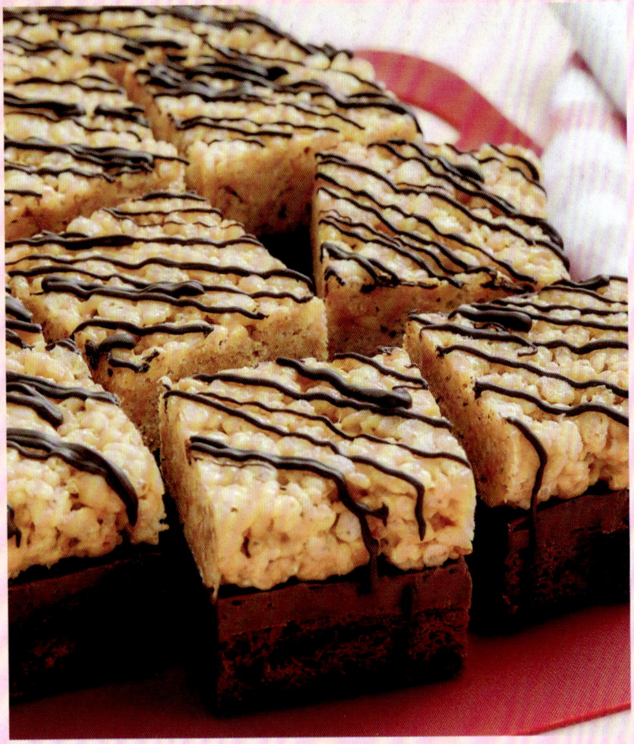
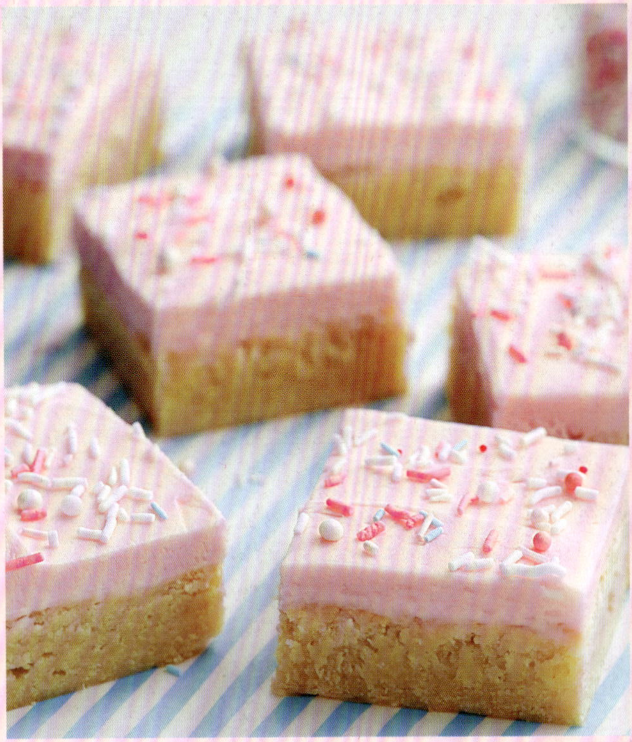
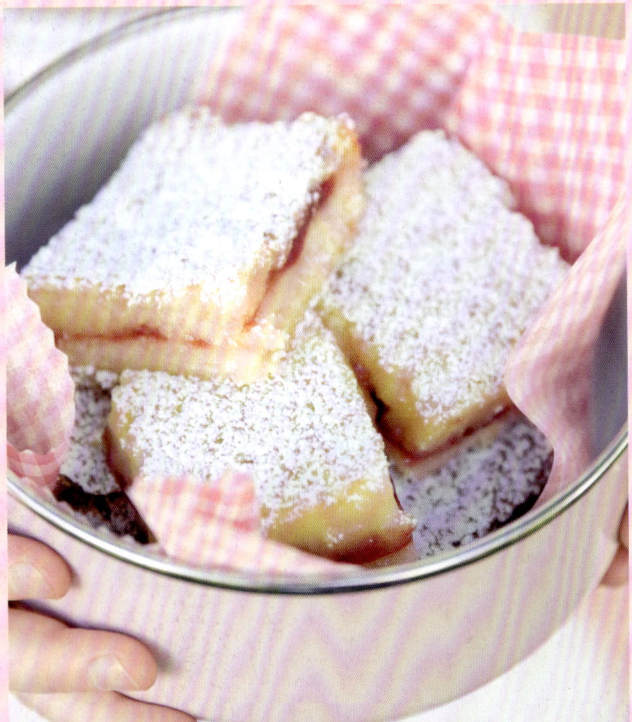
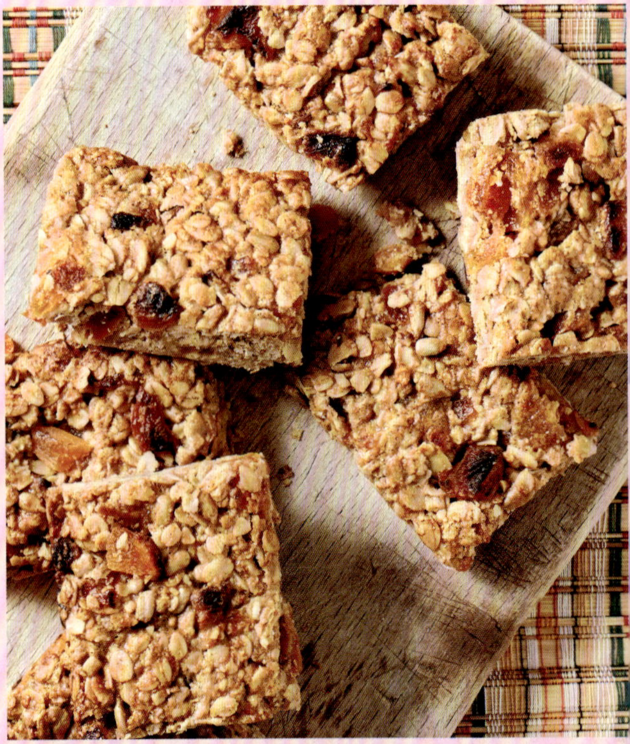

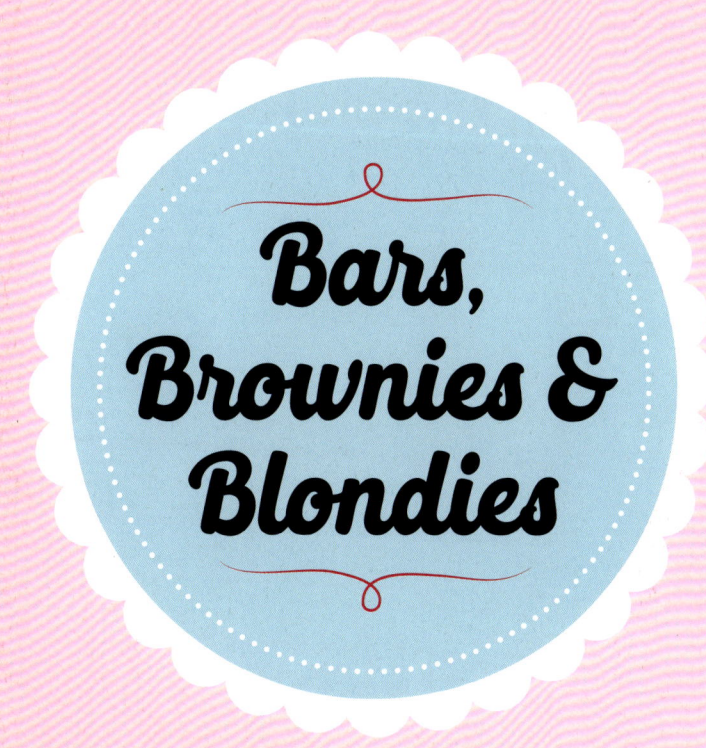

Bars, Brownies & Blondies

Caramel-Glazed Blondies

Blondies are like brownies, but they have a yummy brown-sugar flavor instead of chocolate and are lighter in color. These are covered in a sweet, creamy glaze to make them even more delicious! Bake them for your next sleepover.

MAKES 16 BLONDIES

BLONDIES

½ cup (1 stick) unsalted butter

1 cup firmly packed dark brown sugar

1½ cups all-purpose flour

1 teaspoon baking powder

¼ teaspoon salt

2 large eggs

1 teaspoon vanilla extract

CARAMEL GLAZE

¼ cup (½ stick) unsalted butter

¾ cup firmly packed dark brown sugar

½ cup heavy cream

1 teaspoon vanilla extract

½ cup powdered sugar, sifted

Preheat the oven to 325°F. Line a 9-inch square baking pan with parchment paper, extending it up and over the sides on two sides.

To make the blondies, in a small saucepan, combine the butter and brown sugar. Ask an adult to help you set the pan over medium heat and warm the mixture, stirring often, until melted and smooth. Using a rubber spatula, scrape the mixture into a large bowl and let cool slightly.

In a small bowl, whisk together the flour, baking powder, and salt. Add the eggs and vanilla to the butter mixture and mix with a large spoon until smooth. Add the flour mixture and stir just until combined. Pour the batter into the prepared pan. Put the pan in the oven and bake until a toothpick inserted into the center comes out with moist crumbs attached (ask an adult for help!), 20 to 25 minutes. Ask an adult to help you remove the pan from the oven and set it on a wire rack. Let cool completely.

To make the glaze, in a saucepan, combine the butter, brown sugar, and cream. Ask an adult to help you set the pan over medium heat and warm the mixture, stirring, until melted. Raise the heat to medium-high and let the mixture boil for 2 minutes. Remove from the heat, stir in the vanilla, and let cool. Stir in the powdered sugar. Spread the glaze evenly over the blondies. Let stand until set.

Holding the ends of the parchment, lift the blondies onto a cutting board. Use a warm knife to cut into 16 squares and serve.

Blondie sundae
For a special treat, omit the glaze and top blondie squares with vanilla ice cream, hot fudge, and sliced almonds.

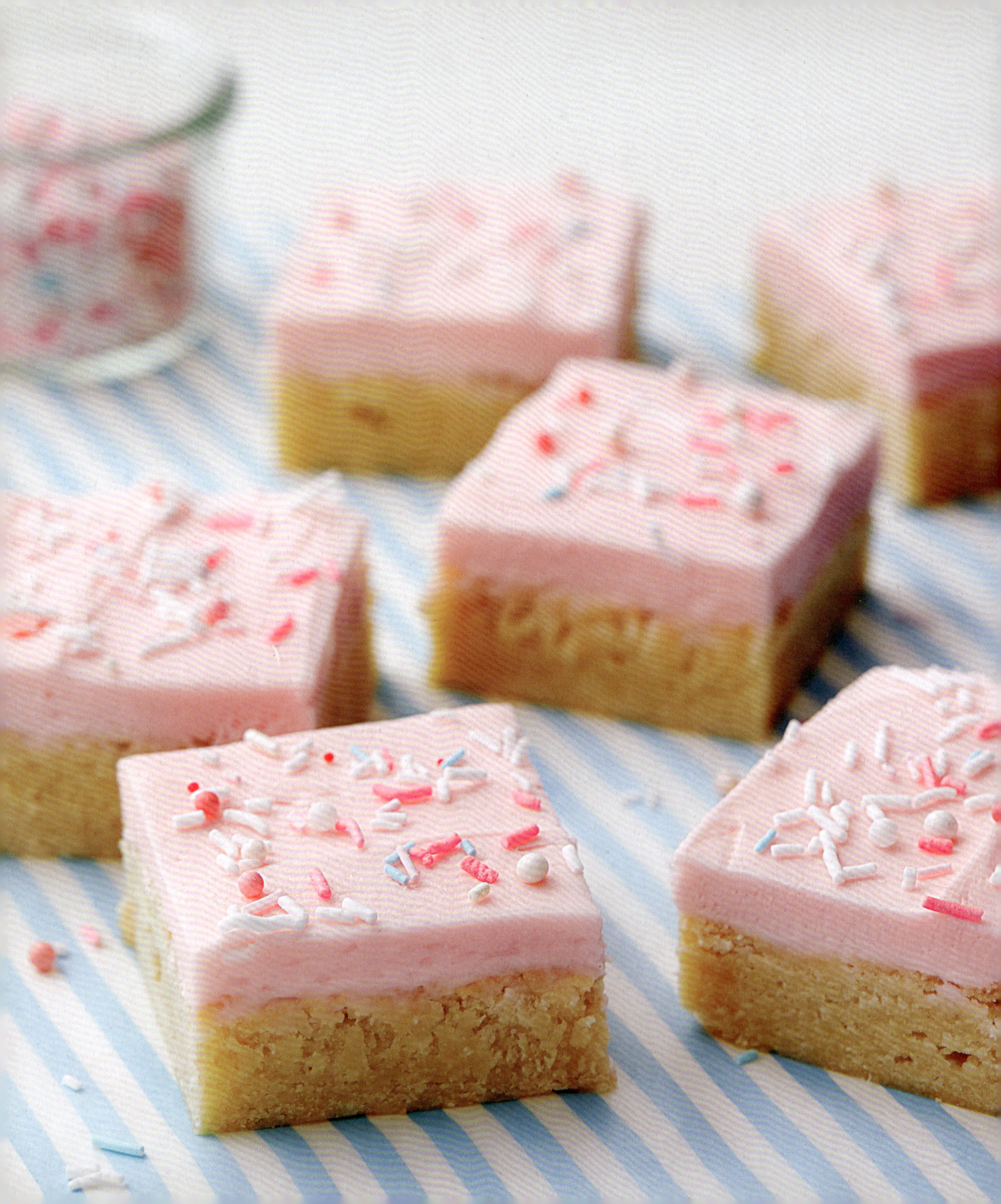

Sugar Cookie Bars

This bar-shaped sugar cookie is super chewy, thanks to the cream cheese in the dough. And, topped with fluffy pink frosting and colorful sprinkles, it's also super pretty! Instead of rainbow sprinkles, you can use confetti, heart-shaped, or star-shaped sprinkles.

MAKES 20 BARS

SUGAR COOKIE

2¾ cups all-purpose flour

½ teaspoon salt

1 cup (2 sticks) unsalted butter, at room temperature

1 (8-ounce) package cream cheese, at room temperature

1½ cups granulated sugar

1 large egg

2 teaspoons vanilla extract

FROSTING

¾ cup (1½ sticks) unsalted butter, at room temperature

4 cups powdered sugar

2 teaspoons vanilla extract

¼ cup fresh blood orange juice or ¼ cup whole milk, plus a few dabs of red gel paste food coloring

Salt

Rainbow sprinkles, for decorating

Preheat the oven to 350°F. Lightly butter a 9-by-13-inch baking pan. Line the pan with parchment paper, running it up the two long sides of the pan and letting it extend past the rim by about 2 inches. Butter the parchment.

To make the sugar cookie, in a medium bowl, whisk together the flour and salt. In a large bowl, using an electric mixer, beat the butter and cream cheese on medium speed until well blended, about 1 minute. Add the granulated sugar and beat until smooth. Add the egg and vanilla and beat on low speed until well combined. Turn off the mixer and scrape down the bowl with a rubber spatula. Add the flour mixture and mix on low speed just until blended.

Scrape the dough into the prepared baking pan and press it into an even layer with the spatula. Bake until the edges are light brown, about 30 minutes. Remove the pan from the oven and set it on a wire rack. Let cool completely.

To make the frosting, place the butter in a large bowl. Using an electric mixer, beat the butter on medium speed until creamy, about 1 minute. Add the powdered sugar 1 cup at a time, beating on low speed until combined after each addition. Add the vanilla, blood orange juice, and a pinch of salt and beat on medium speed until the frosting is light and fluffy.

Holding the ends of the parchment paper like handles, lift the cookie out of the pan and set it on a cutting board. Using a spatula, spread the frosting on top, then decorate with rainbow sprinkles. Cut it into 20 bars and serve.

Ooey-Gooey Layer Bars

You don't even need a mixing bowl to make these buttery, nutty, chocolaty bars! Just layer the ingredients in the baking pan and pop the whole thing in the oven. If you like, you can swap the butterscotch chips for peanut butter chips.

MAKES 20 BARS

10 graham crackers, broken into pieces

½ cup (1 stick) unsalted butter, melted

1½ cups semisweet chocolate chips

1 cup butterscotch chips

1 cup old-fashioned rolled oats

1 cup pecans, toasted and chopped (optional)

1 cup walnuts, toasted and chopped (optional)

1 (14-ounce) can sweetened condensed milk

1½ cups shredded dried unsweetened coconut

Preheat the oven to 350°F. Put the graham cracker pieces in a zipper-lock plastic bag. Press out the air and seal the bag. Use a rolling pin to crush the crackers into fine crumbs, pounding them lightly or using a gentle back-and-forth rolling motion. You should have about 1½ cups of crumbs.

Pour the butter into a 9-by-13-inch baking pan and carefully tilt the pan to coat the sides. Sprinkle the graham cracker crumbs in an even layer in the pan. Layer in the chocolate chips, butterscotch chips, oats, and, if using, the pecans and walnuts. Pour the condensed milk evenly over the top, then sprinkle with the coconut. Bake until the coconut is golden brown, 20 to 25 minutes. Remove the pan from the oven and set it on a wire rack. Let cool completely.

Cut the bar into 20 rectangles and serve.

Share the love
Wrap individual bars in a piece of colored paper and tie with twine for a super cute homemade gift.

Lemon-Blackberry Crumb Bars

The double dose of lemon juice and zest in the cake batter really brings out the flavor of the berries. You could swap in blueberries or raspberries for the blackberries, or use any combo of the three. Be sure to zest the lemon before you juice it.

MAKES ABOUT 18 BARS

TOPPING

¾ cup all-purpose flour

⅓ cup firmly packed light brown sugar

¼ cup granulated sugar

1 teaspoon ground cinnamon

½ cup (1 stick) cold unsalted butter

CAKE

1½ cups all-purpose flour

¾ cup granulated sugar

1½ teaspoons baking powder

½ teaspoon salt

4 tablespoons (½ stick) unsalted butter

1 large egg

½ cup whole milk

1 teaspoon vanilla extract

Zest and juice of 1 lemon

5 cups blackberries

¼ cup granulated sugar

Preheat the oven to 350°F. Butter a 9-by-13-inch metal or glass baking pan.

To make the topping, in a medium bowl, mix the flour, both sugars, and cinnamon. Cut the butter into ½-inch pieces and, using a fork or your hands, rub the butter into the flour mixture until coarse crumbs form. Set aside.

To make the cake, in a medium bowl, whisk together the flour, granulated sugar, baking powder, and salt. Cut the butter into chunks, place it in a microwave-safe bowl, and microwave on high until melted, about 20 seconds. In a large bowl, using an electric mixer, beat the egg, melted butter, milk, vanilla, and lemon zest and juice on medium speed until creamy, about 1 minute. Turn off the mixer and scrape down the bowl with a rubber spatula. Add the flour mixture and beat on low speed just until combined. Turn off the mixer and scrape down the bowl. Pour the batter into the prepared pan.

In a medium bowl, toss together the blackberries and granulated sugar. Scatter the berries on top of the cake batter. Sprinkle the topping evenly over the berries.

Bake until the cake is golden brown and a wooden skewer inserted into the center comes out clean, 35 to 40 minutes. Using oven mitts, remove the pan from the oven and set it on a wire rack. Let cool for at least 20 minutes. Cut the cake into bars and serve.

Frosted Chocolate Brownies

Just in case you can't get enough chocolate, these gooey brownies are topped with a fluffy chocolate frosting. If you're packing these treats to go, skip the frosting because it will get smooshed—or bring it with you in a separate container.

MAKES 16 BROWNIES

BROWNIES

¾ cup (1½ sticks) unsalted butter, at room temperature

5 ounces unsweetened chocolate, chopped

1 cup all-purpose flour

¼ teaspoon salt

4 large eggs

2 cups granulated sugar

1 teaspoon vanilla extract

FROSTING

2 ounces bittersweet chocolate, chopped

½ cup (1 stick) unsalted butter, at room temperature

1 cup powdered sugar

1 teaspoon vanilla extract

1 tablespoon heavy cream

Preheat the oven to 325°F. Lightly butter a 9-by-13-inch baking pan. Line the pan with parchment paper, running it up the two long sides of the pan and letting it extend past the rim by about 2 inches. Butter the parchment.

To make the brownies, in a large microwave-safe bowl, combine the butter and chocolate. Microwave on high power, stirring every 30 seconds, just until the mixture is melted and smooth. Don't let it get too hot! Set aside to cool slightly.

In a small bowl, whisk together the flour and salt; set aside. Add the eggs to the warm chocolate mixture and whisk until well blended. Add the sugar and vanilla and whisk until well combined. Add the flour mixture and whisk just until there are no white streaks in the batter. Pour into the prepared pan and bake until a toothpick inserted in the center comes out with moist crumbs, 30 to 35 minutes. Remove from the oven and let cool completely on a wire rack.

Meanwhile, make the frosting. Melt the chocolate as you did for the brownies. Let cool for about 5 minutes. In a large bowl, using an electric mixer, beat the butter and powdered sugar on medium speed until well blended, about 1 minute. Add the vanilla, cream, and melted chocolate and beat on medium speed until the mixture is evenly colored and the frosting is fluffy, about 2 minutes.

Holding the ends of the parchment paper like handles, lift the brownie out of the pan and set it on a cutting board. Using an offset spatula, spread the frosting evenly on the brownie. Carefully cut it into 16 squares and serve.

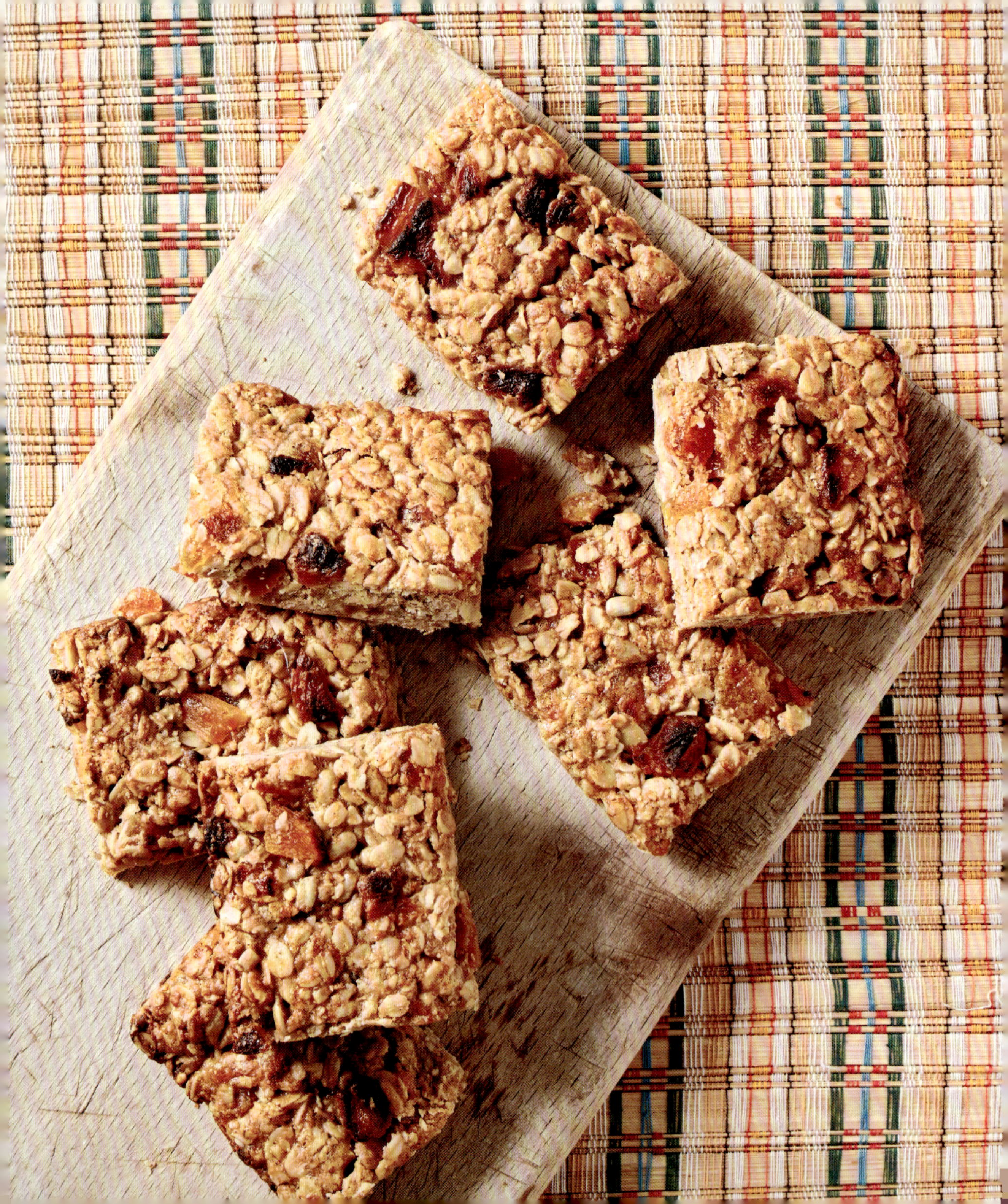

Nut, Seed & Fruit Granola Bars

These chewy bars are a healthy on-the-go snack, perfect for traveling, and packed with seeds, nut butter, and dried fruits. You can swap out the dried apricots with dried cranberries or raisins.

MAKES 12 TO 16 BARS

Nonstick cooking spray

2½ cups old-fashioned rolled oats

1½ cups finely chopped dried apricots

½ cup toasted sunflower seeds

½ cup wheat germ

1 teaspoon ground cinnamon

½ teaspoon salt

½ cup (1 stick) unsalted butter, cut into pieces

½ cup firmly packed light brown sugar

½ cup creamy almond or peanut butter

⅓ cup maple syrup

2 large egg whites

Preheat the oven to 350°F. Spray a 9-by-13-inch baking pan with nonstick cooking spray.

In a large bowl, combine the oats, apricots, sunflower seeds, wheat germ, cinnamon, and salt and stir with a rubber spatula. Set aside. In a small saucepan, combine the butter, brown sugar, almond butter, and maple syrup. Set the pan over medium heat, bring to a simmer, and cook for 1 minute, stirring constantly with the spatula. Remove from the heat and pour over the oat mixture. Stir with the spatula to mix well. Let cool for 5 minutes.

In a small bowl, whisk the egg whites until frothy, about 30 seconds. Add the egg whites to the oat mixture and stir to combine.

Pour the mixture into the prepared pan. Using the spatula, press the mixture firmly to create an even layer.

Bake until the edges are golden brown and the top is no longer sticky to the touch, 20 to 25 minutes. Remove the pan from the oven and set it on a wire rack. Let cool slightly. Cut into 12 rectangular or 16 square bars, then let cool completely in the pan for 1 hour.

Lemony Berry Bars

The easy press-in crust for these sweet-tart jam-filled bars is partly baked before you add the filling, to make sure that everything bakes up perfectly in the end.

MAKES ABOUT 16 BARS

CRUST

½ cup (1 stick) unsalted butter, at room temperature

1 cup all-purpose flour

¼ cup powdered sugar, sifted

1 tablespoon ice water

1 teaspoon vanilla extract

½ teaspoon salt

FILLING

¾ cup raspberry jam or other berry jam

6 large eggs

2 cups granulated sugar

¾ cup lemon juice

¼ cup all-purpose flour

¾ teaspoon baking powder

¼ teaspoon salt

½ cup powdered sugar, sifted

Preheat the oven to 350°F. Grease a 9-inch square baking pan.

To make the crust, in a medium bowl, using an electric mixer, beat the butter on medium speed until creamy. Turn off the mixer. Add the flour, powdered sugar, ice water, vanilla, and salt and beat on low speed just until the mixture is well blended and forms small clumps that hold together when pressed between two fingers. Using clean hands, scoop the dough into the prepared pan and press to form an even layer in the bottom of the pan. Refrigerate for 10 minutes.

Put the pan in the oven and bake the crust until golden, about 15 minutes. Ask an adult to help you remove the pan from the oven and set it on a wire rack. Reduce the oven temperature to 325°F.

To make the filling, using a rubber spatula, ask an adult to help you carefully spread the jam evenly over the warm crust. In a medium bowl, whisk the eggs, granulated sugar, lemon juice, flour, baking powder, and salt until well combined. Pour the egg mixture over the jam-topped crust, carefully spreading it with the spatula to form an even layer.

Return the pan to the oven and bake until the filling doesn't jiggle when you gently shake the pan (ask an adult for help!), 40 to 45 minutes. Ask an adult to help you remove the pan from the oven and set it on a wire rack. Let cool, then transfer to the refrigerator to cool completely. Ask an adult to help you cut around the edges of the pan to loosen the sides; then cut the bars into small rectangles or squares. Just before serving, put the powdered sugar in a fine-mesh sieve and dust the bars with sugar.

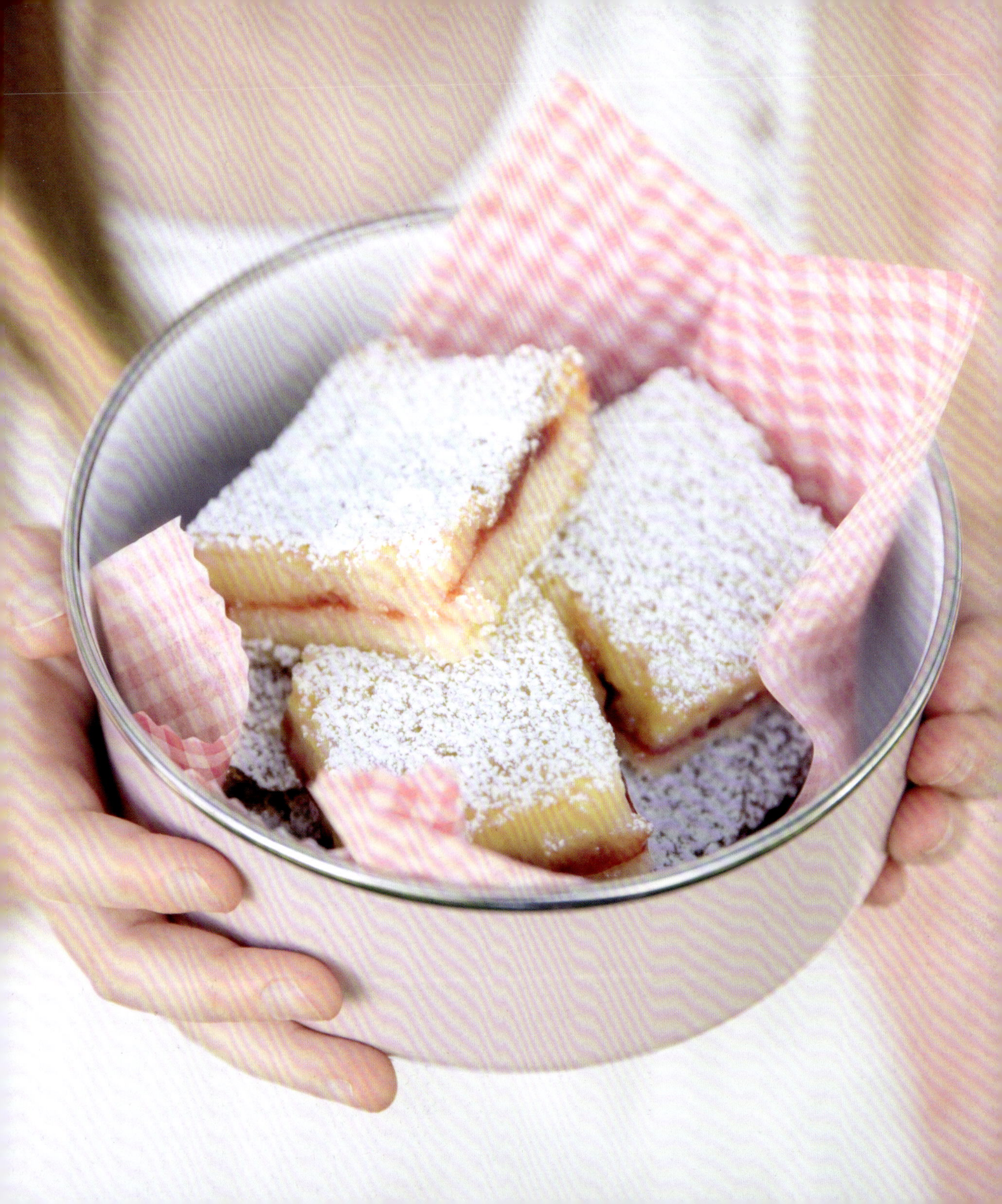

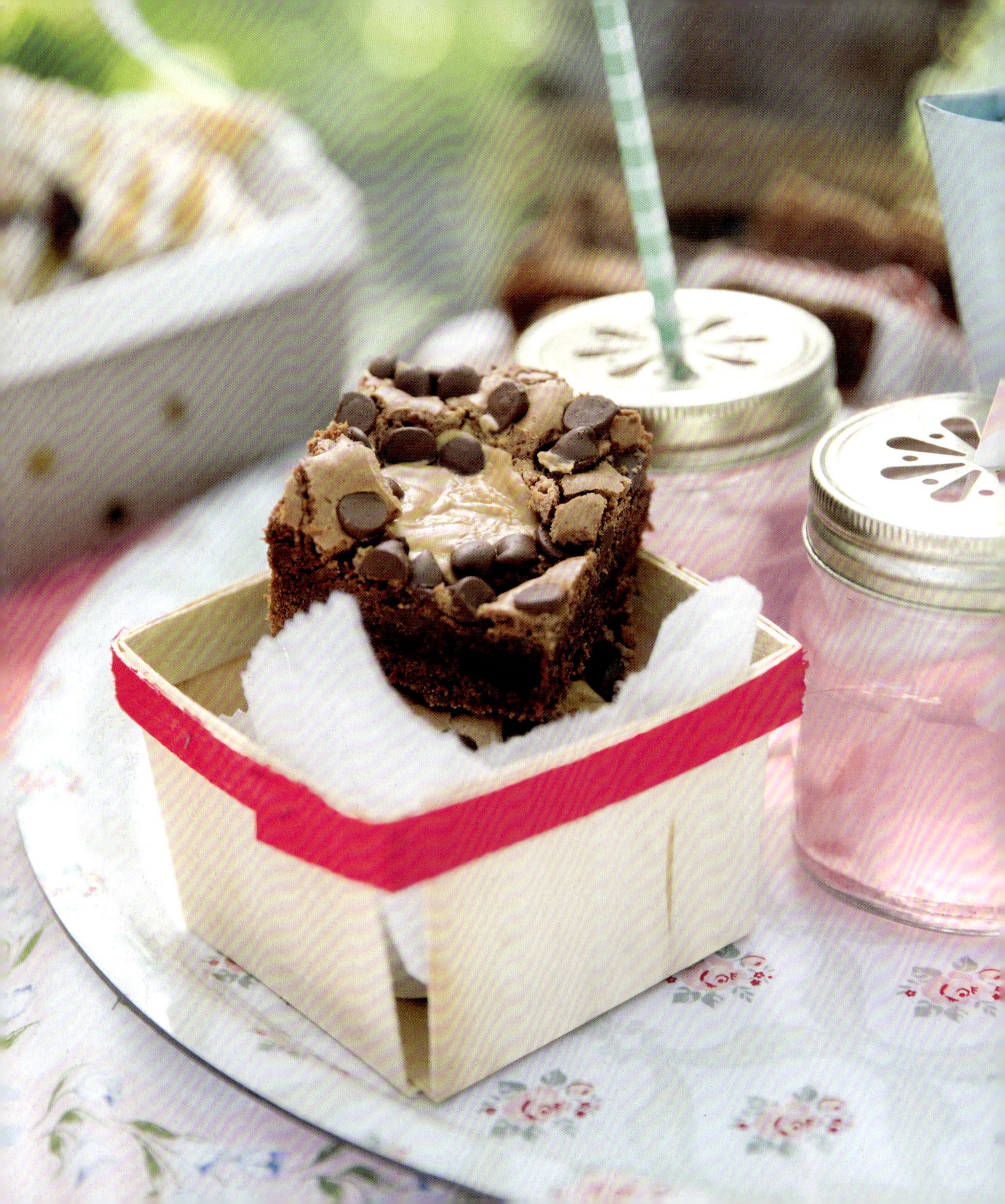

Chocolate-Peanut Butter Brownies

A big pan of fudgy brownies is one of the best things to share with your friends. Creamy pools of peanut butter make these an even more delicious treats!

MAKES 16 BROWNIES

¾ cup (1½ sticks) unsalted butter

8 ounces semisweet chocolate, chopped into small pieces

4 large eggs

1 cup sugar

1 teaspoon vanilla extract

¼ teaspoon salt

1 cup all-purpose flour

8 tablespoons smooth peanut butter

¾ cup semisweet chocolate chips

Preheat the oven to 350°F. Line a 9-inch square baking pan with parchment paper, extending it up and over the sides on 2 sides.

Select a saucepan and a heatproof bowl that fits snugly on top of the pan. Fill the pan one-third full of water, making sure the water doesn't touch the bottom of the bowl. Ask an adult to help you place the saucepan over medium heat. When the water is steaming, place the bowl on top of the saucepan and add the butter and chocolate to the bowl. Heat, stirring with a rubber spatula, until the mixture is melted and smooth, about 5 minutes. Don't let the chocolate get too hot! Ask an adult to help you remove the bowl from the saucepan (the bowl will be hot!) and set aside to cool slightly.

In a bowl, using an electric mixer, beat the eggs on medium speed until pale, about 4 minutes. Add the sugar, vanilla, and salt and beat until well combined. Turn off the mixer. Add the chocolate mixture and beat until blended. Turn off the mixer and scrape down the bowl with a rubber spatula. Stir in the flour with the rubber spatula just until blended.

Scrape the batter into the pan and smooth the top. Using a tablespoon measure, drop 8 dollops of peanut butter over the top, spacing them evenly. Sprinkle with the chocolate chips. Bake until a toothpick inserted into the center comes out clean (ask an adult for help!), 25 to 30 minutes. Ask an adult to help you remove the pan from the oven and put it on a wire rack. Let cool completely, then use the edges of the parchment paper to lift the brownie "cake" from the pan. Place on a cutting board and cut into 16 squares and serve.

Crispy Rice and Chocolate Layer Brownies

Crispy, chewy, peanut buttery, and oh-so chocolaty, these eye-catching bar cookies are sure to be crowd-pleasers. The trick to easy assembly is making sure that each layer is completely cooled before adding the next one.

MAKES 16 BROWNIES

BROWNIES

½ cup (1 stick) unsalted butter, cut into 4 pieces

3 ounces unsweetened chocolate, finely chopped

1 cup sugar

Pinch of salt

2 large eggs

1 teaspoon vanilla extract

¾ cup all-purpose flour

¾ cup bittersweet chocolate chips

CHOCOLATE LAYER

1⅓ cups semisweet or bittersweet chocolate chips

1 cup heavy cream

Pinch of salt

(See additional ingredients on page 103)

Preheat the oven to 325°F. Butter an 8-inch square baking pan. Line the pan with parchment paper, letting it extend past the rim on two sides by about 2 inches. Butter the parchment.

To make the brownies, in a large microwave-safe bowl, combine the butter and chocolate. Microwave on high power, stirring every 30 seconds, just until the mixture is melted and smooth. Don't let it get too hot! Add the sugar and salt and whisk until blended. Add the eggs and vanilla and whisk until well combined. Add the flour and bittersweet chocolate chips and stir with a wooden spoon just until there are no white streaks in the batter and the chips are evenly mixed in.

Pour the batter into the prepared pan and use a rubber spatula to spread evenly. Bake until a toothpick inserted into the center of the brownies comes out with a few moist crumbs attached, about 30 minutes. Remove the pan from the oven and set it on a wire rack. Let cool to room temperature.

To make the chocolate layer, put the semisweet chocolate chips in a heatproof medium bowl. Pour the cream into a small saucepan and bring it to a boil over medium-high heat. Immediately pour the cream over the chocolate chips and add the salt. Let stand for 10 minutes, then whisk until smooth and shiny. Refrigerate until the mixture is chilled but not hardened, about 20 minutes.

~ Continued on page 103 ~

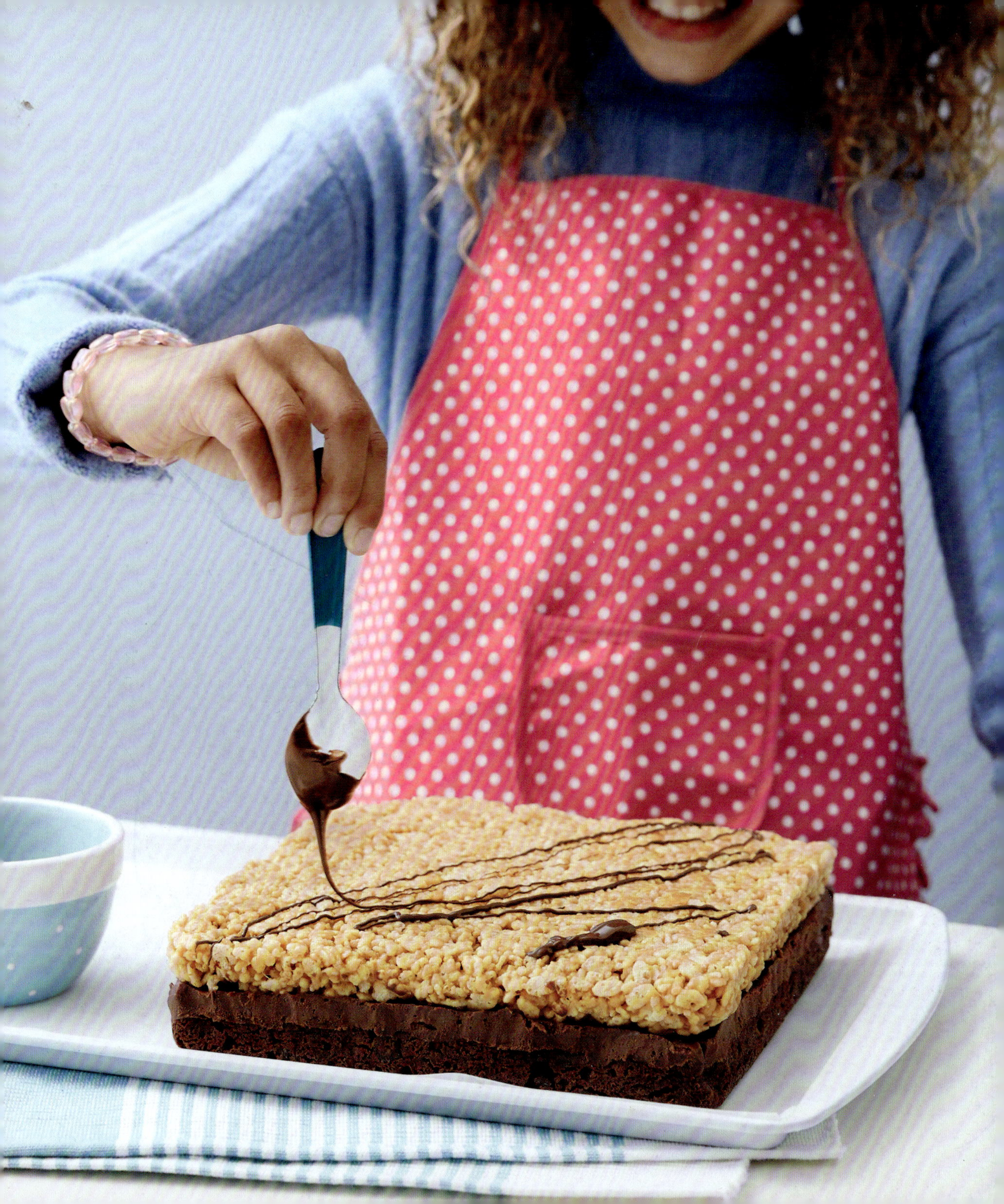

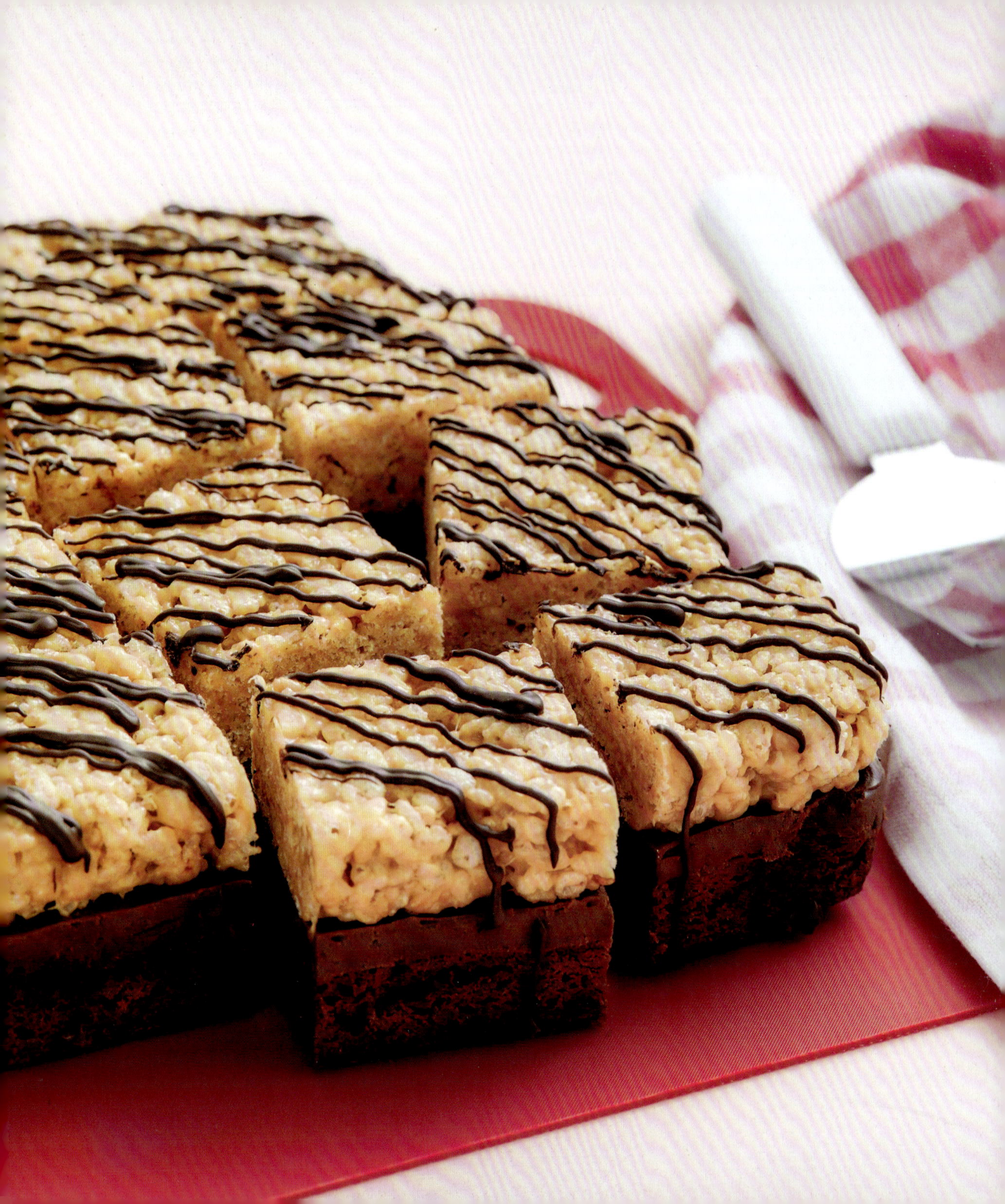

> **Try this!**
> To cut gooey bars and treats with less mess, dip your knife into a glass of hot water before you use it.

~ *Continued from page 100* ~

Measure out ¼ cup of the chocolate mixture and set aside. Pour the remaining chocolate mixture onto the brownies and spread it evenly with a spatula. Place the pan in the refrigerator.

To make the peanut butter crispy rice, in a large saucepan, melt the butter over low heat. Add the marshmallows and stir with a wooden spoon until melted. Remove the pan from the heat, add the peanut butter, and stir until fully blended. Add the rice cereal and stir until evenly coated. Let cool completely.

Scoop the peanut butter–rice cereal mixture on top of the chocolate layer. Using a rubber spatula, gently press it into an even layer. Using a spoon, drizzle the reserved chocolate mixture on top. Let cool.

Holding the ends of the parchment paper like handles, lift the bar out of the pan and set it on a cutting board. Cut it into 16 squares and serve.

PEANUT BUTTER CRISPY RICE

5 tablespoons unsalted butter

5 cups mini marshmallows

½ cup creamy peanut butter

5 cups crispy rice cereal

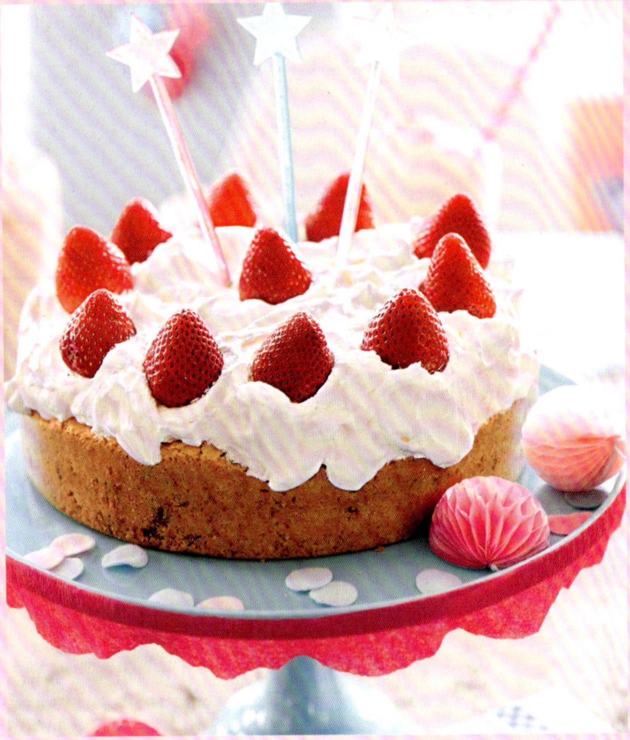
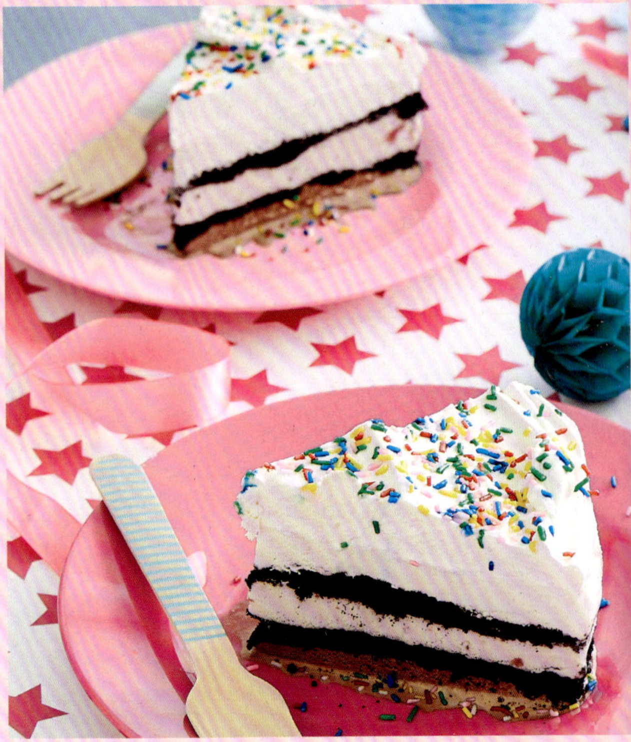
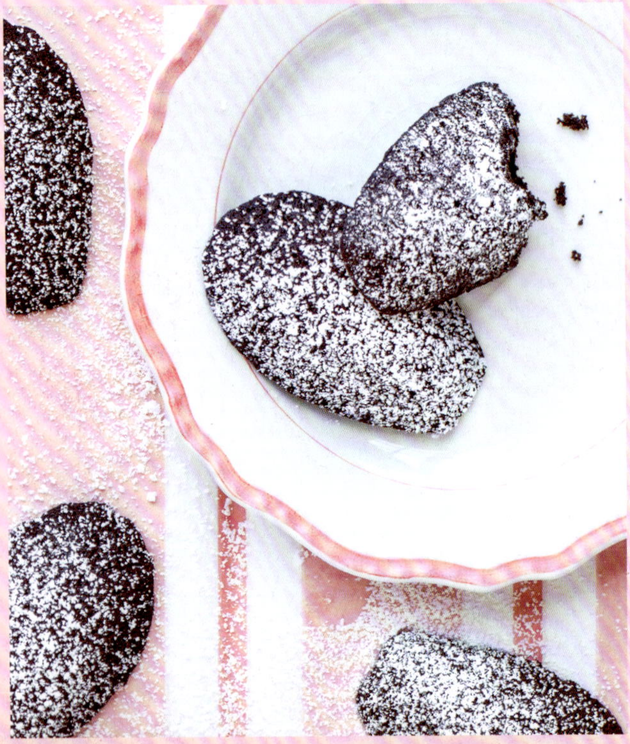
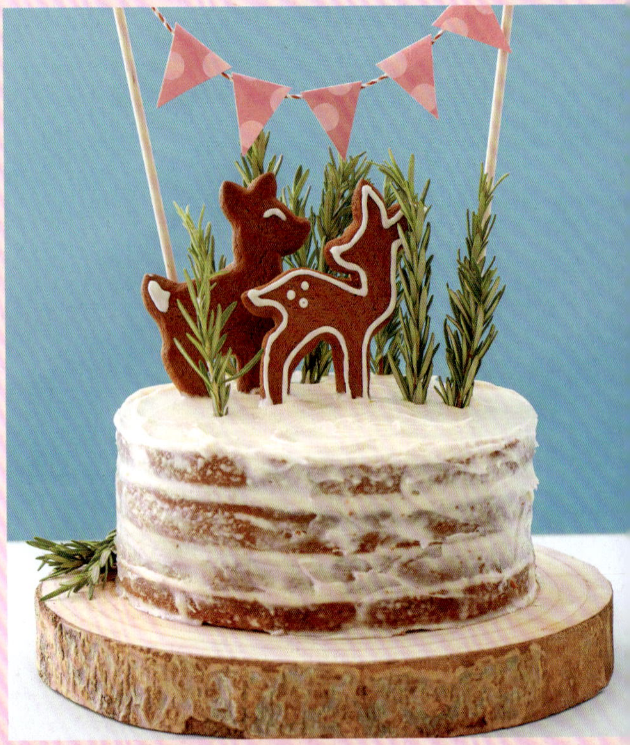

Cakes

Golden Layer Cake with Chocolate Frosting

This towering chocolate-frosted vanilla butter cake will make your friends and family say, "Wow!" Decorate it with your favorite colored sprinkles for a birthday, write a fun message on top with icing, or mound fresh raspberries onto the center.

MAKES 8–10 SERVINGS

CAKE

3 cups all-purpose flour

2 teaspoons baking powder

½ teaspoon salt

1 cup (2 sticks) unsalted butter, at room temperature

2 cups granulated sugar

4 large eggs

1 cup buttermilk

FROSTING

2 cups semisweet chocolate chips

½ cup (1 stick) unsalted butter, at room temperature

1 cup sour cream

2 teaspoons vanilla extract

5 cups powdered sugar, sifted

Sprinkles and/or candies, for decorating

Preheat the oven to 350°F. Trace the bottom of two 8-inch round cake pans onto sheets of parchment paper and cut out the circles with scissors. Rub the insides of the cake pans with a little butter. Put the paper circles in the bottom of the pans and butter the paper.

To make the cake, in a medium bowl, whisk together the flour, baking powder, and salt. In a large bowl, using an electric mixer, beat the butter and granulated sugar on medium-high speed until fluffy and pale, 3 to 4 minutes. Turn off the mixer and scrape down the bowl with a rubber spatula. Add 2 of the eggs to the butter mixture and beat on medium speed until well combined. Turn off the mixer. Add the remaining 2 eggs and beat on medium speed until well combined. Turn off the mixer and scrape down the bowl. Add half of the flour mixture and mix on low speed just until blended. Turn off the mixer. Pour in the buttermilk and mix on low speed just until blended. Turn off the mixer. Add the remaining flour mixture and mix just until blended. Turn off the mixer one last time and scrape down the bowl.

Divide the batter evenly between the cake pans and gently smooth the tops with the rubber spatula. Put the cake pans in the oven and bake until the cakes are golden brown and a wooden skewer inserted into the centers of the cakes comes out clean (ask an adult for help!), 45 to 50 minutes.

~ Continued on page 109 ~

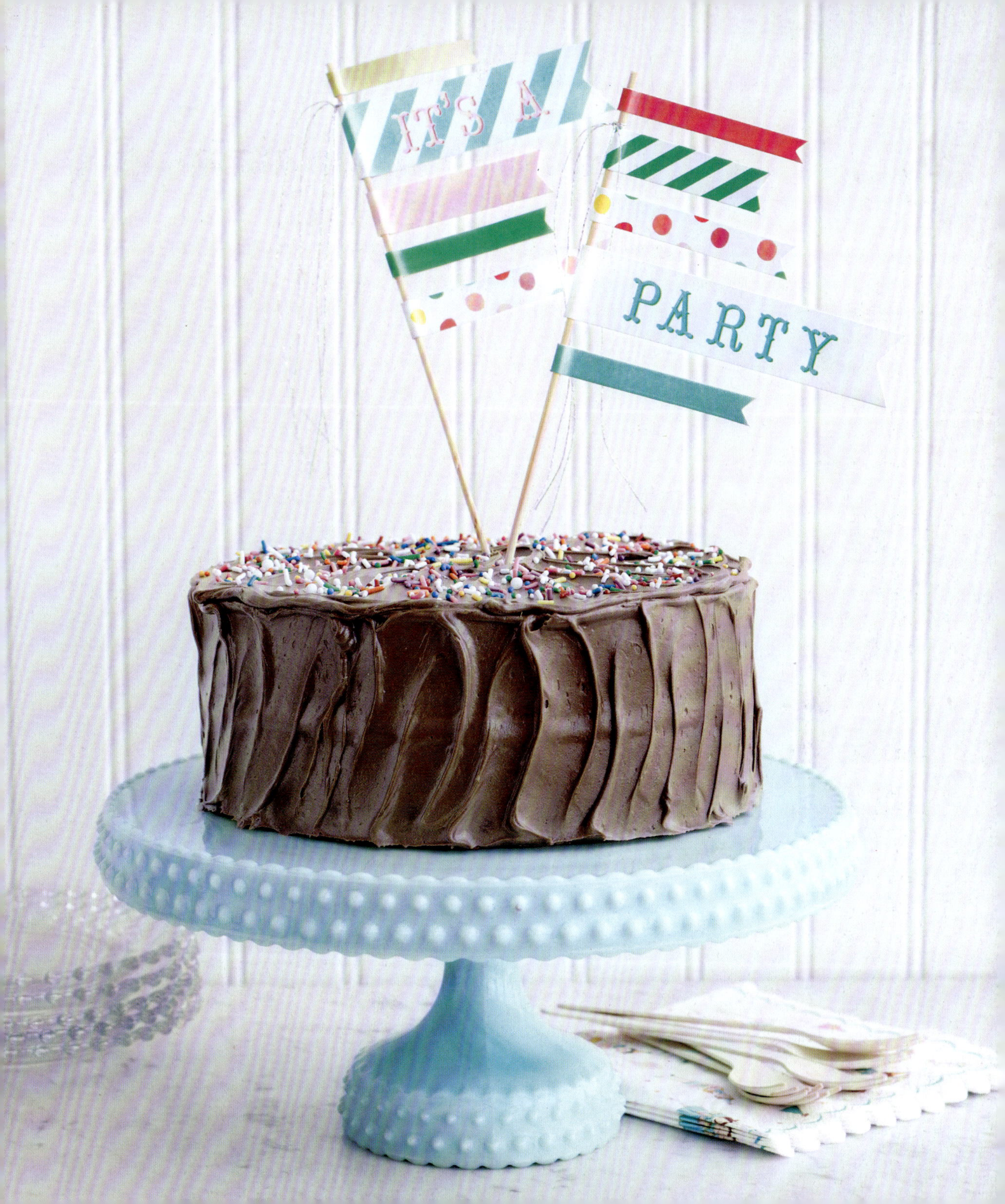
IT'S A
PARTY

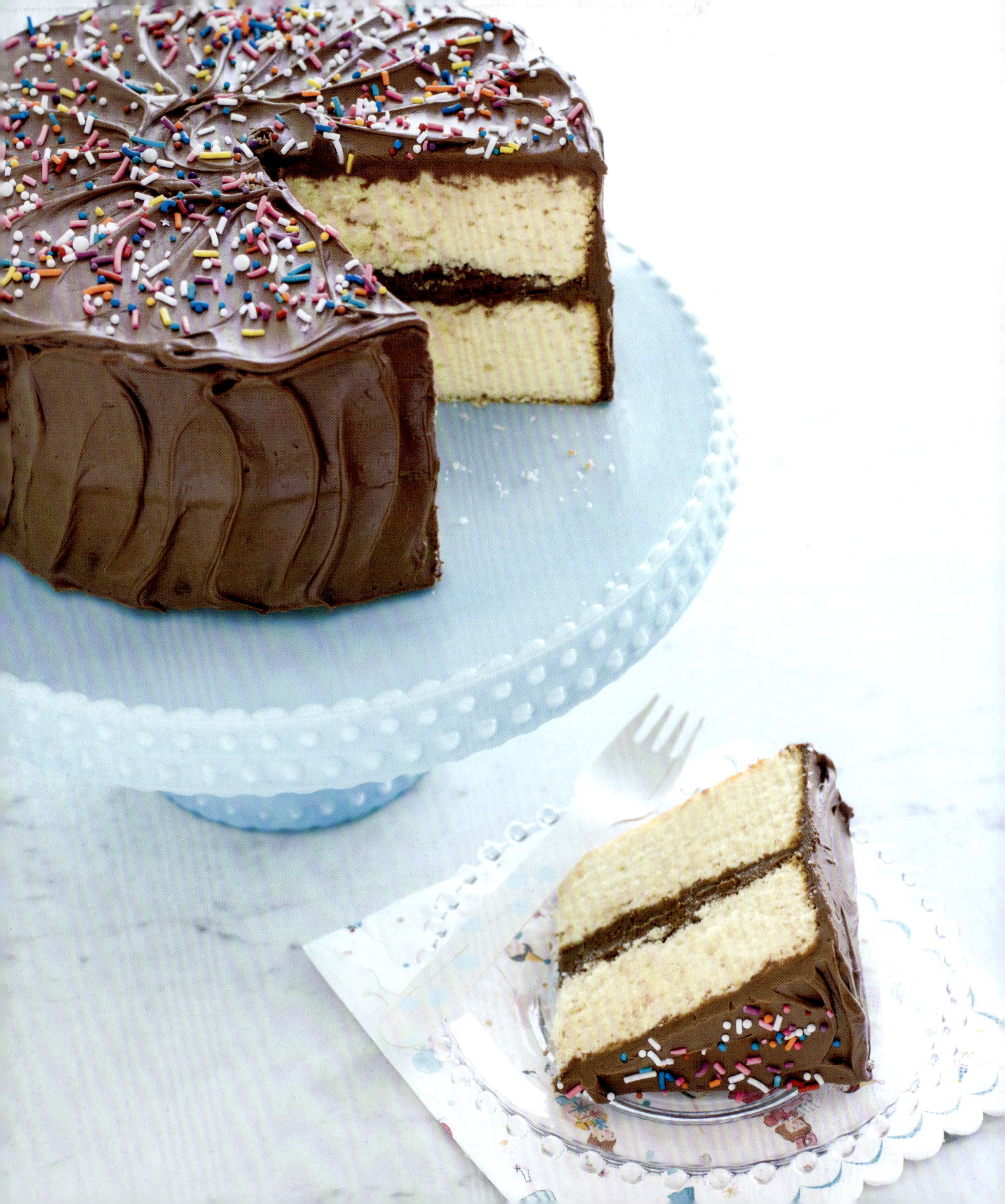

~ *Continued from page 106* ~

Ask an adult to help you remove the cake pans from the oven and set them on wire racks. Let cool for 20 minutes, then run a table knife around the inside edge of each cake pan. Turn the pans over onto the racks. Lift away the pans and the parchment paper and let the cakes cool completely, upside down, about 2 hours.

To make the frosting, put the chocolate chips in a microwave-safe bowl. Ask an adult to help you microwave the chips on high heat, stirring every 20 seconds until they are melted and smooth. Don't let the chocolate get too hot!

In a large bowl, using the electric mixer, beat the butter, sour cream, and vanilla until smooth. Add the melted chocolate and beat until smooth. With the electric mixer on low speed, beat in the powdered sugar ½ cup at a time. When all of the sugar has been added, raise the speed to high and beat until the frosting is nice and smooth. Scrape down the bowl with the spatula and beat for 1 minute more.

When the cakes have cooled, place one layer on a cake stand or plate. Using an offset spatula, spread some of the frosting over the top, nearly to the edge, making a thick layer as even as possible. Place the second cake layer on top of the frosting, trying to line up the sides of the cakes. Spread more frosting over the top of the cake and down the sides, creating a thick layer. Decorate the cake with sprinkles and/or candies.

Serve the cake right away or cover it loosely with plastic wrap and refrigerate for up to 3 days. Ask an adult to help you cut the cake into wedges for serving.

Cake 'n' ice cream
Serve slices of the cake with big scoops of your favorite ice cream for an extra-special treat!

Black Forest Cake

In this majestic German dessert, chocolate cake layers are filled with cherry-studded whipped cream and topped with more whipped cream. You can make the cake layers a day ahead, wrap them well in plastic wrap, and store them at room temperature.

MAKES 8 TO 10 SERVINGS

CAKE

½ cup cake flour

½ cup unsweetened Dutch-process cocoa powder

½ cup (1 stick) unsalted butter, melted and cooled

6 large eggs

¾ cup granulated sugar

1½ teaspoons vanilla extract

½ teaspoon salt

1 (24-ounce) jar pitted red sour cherries in light syrup

2 cups heavy cream

2 tablespoons powdered sugar

1½ teaspoons vanilla extract

1 cup chocolate sprinkles

To make the cake, preheat the oven to 350°F. Line the bottoms of two 9-inch round cake pans with parchment paper rounds. (Place each cake pan on a piece of parchment paper, trace around the bottom with a pencil, and then use scissors to cut out the circle, cutting just inside of the pencil line.)

Sift the flour and cocoa powder into a bowl. Put the melted butter in a medium bowl. In a large bowl, using an electric mixer, beat the eggs, granulated sugar, vanilla, and salt on high speed until light and fluffy, about 5 minutes. Sprinkle the flour mixture over the egg mixture and, using a large rubber spatula, gently fold just until combined. Stir a big spoonful of the batter into the melted butter until well blended, and then add this mixture back into the batter and gently fold with the spatula until well combined. Divide the batter evenly between the prepared pans.

Bake the cakes until a wooden skewer inserted into the center comes out clean, about 20 minutes. Remove from the oven and let cool in the pans on a wire rack for about 20 minutes.

One cake at a time, slide a paring knife between the edge of the cake and the sides of the pan to loosen and carefully invert the cake onto the rack. Lift off the cake pan, peel off the parchment round, and let cool completely.

Set a fine-mesh sieve over a bowl and drain the cherries, reserving the juice.

Cherry-licious!

Save leftover cherries from this recipe for oatmeal and boil down their juice to make a syrup for sparkling water.

Set aside 13 of the prettiest cherries in a small bowl. Measure out 1 cup of drained cherries and put them in a medium bowl.

In a large bowl, using an electric mixer, beat the cream, powdered sugar, and vanilla on low speed until slightly thickened, 1 to 2 minutes. Gradually increase the speed to medium-high and continue to beat until the cream holds medium-stiff peaks when the beaters are lifted, 3 to 4 minutes longer. Take care not to overwhip the cream.

To assemble the cake, very carefully place one cake layer on a cake platter or cake stand. Add 1 cup of the whipped cream to the cherries in the bowl and gently fold together to combine. Spread this mixture on top of the first cake layer. Carefully place the second cake layer on top, lining up the layers. If you like, fit a pastry bag with a star tip and put about ½ cup of the whipped cream in the bag; set the bag aside. Using an icing spatula, spread the remaining whipped cream all over the top and sides of the cake, smoothing the surfaces as best you can.

Cover the top and sides of the cake with the chocolate sprinkles. If you saved whipped cream in a pastry bag, twist the wide end of the bag to push the cream to the tip and pipe 12 rosettes (rose-shaped decorations that are made with the star tip of a piping bag) on top of the cake, evenly spaced around the edge, and 1 in the center. Place 1 cherry in each rosette. (If you are not piping rosettes, place 12 of the reserved cherries on top of the cake, evenly spaced around the edge, and 1 in the center.) Serve right away or refrigerate for up to 2 hours.

Tres Leches Cakes

Tres leches means "three milks" in Spanish. This favorite Latin American treat gets its name because a trio of sweetened condensed, evaporated, and whole milk is used to soak the cake after baking so that it's incredibly moist and delicious.

MAKES 12 SERVINGS

Unsalted butter, for greasing the pan

1 (12-ounce) can sweetened condensed milk

1 (12-ounce) can evaporated milk

1 cup heavy cream

1 cup all-purpose flour

¾ cup granulated sugar

1 teaspoon baking powder

¼ teaspoon salt

3 large eggs, at room temperature

½ cup whole milk

1 teaspoon vanilla extract

Whipped cream (see page 128), for serving

Preheat the oven to 350°F. Butter a standard 12-cup muffin pan.

To make the cakes, in a 9-by-13-inch glass baking dish, stir together the sweetened condensed milk, evaporated milk, and heavy cream until well combined and set aside. In a large bowl, whisk together the flour, granulated sugar, baking powder, and salt. In a medium bowl, whisk the eggs, milk, and vanilla until well combined. Pour the egg mixture into the flour mixture and whisk gently just until the batter is evenly moistened.

Divide the batter evenly among the prepared muffin cups. Bake until the cakes are light golden brown and a wooden skewer inserted in the center of a cake comes out clean, 18 to 20 minutes. Remove from the oven and poke each cake several times with the skewer. While the cakes are still hot, carefully invert them onto a wire rack to remove them from the pan, and place them in a single layer in the baking dish with the milk and cream mixture. Generously spoon the milk and cream mixture over each cake. Let the soaked cakes cool completely in the baking dish, about 1 hour.

Transfer the cakes to an airtight container, arranging them in a single layer, and cover. Pour the soaking mixture into a separate container and cover. Refrigerate both the cakes and the soaking mixture for at least 4 hours or up to 2 days, spooning more soaking mixture over the cakes a few times to keep them moist.

Before serving, let the cakes stand at room temperature for about 10 minutes. Put the cakes in individual bowls and the soaking liquid on top so that it pools in the bowl. Dollop each with whipped cream and serve right away.

Baking game plan
Start preparing these cakes in the morning since they need time to soak up the sweet milky sauce.

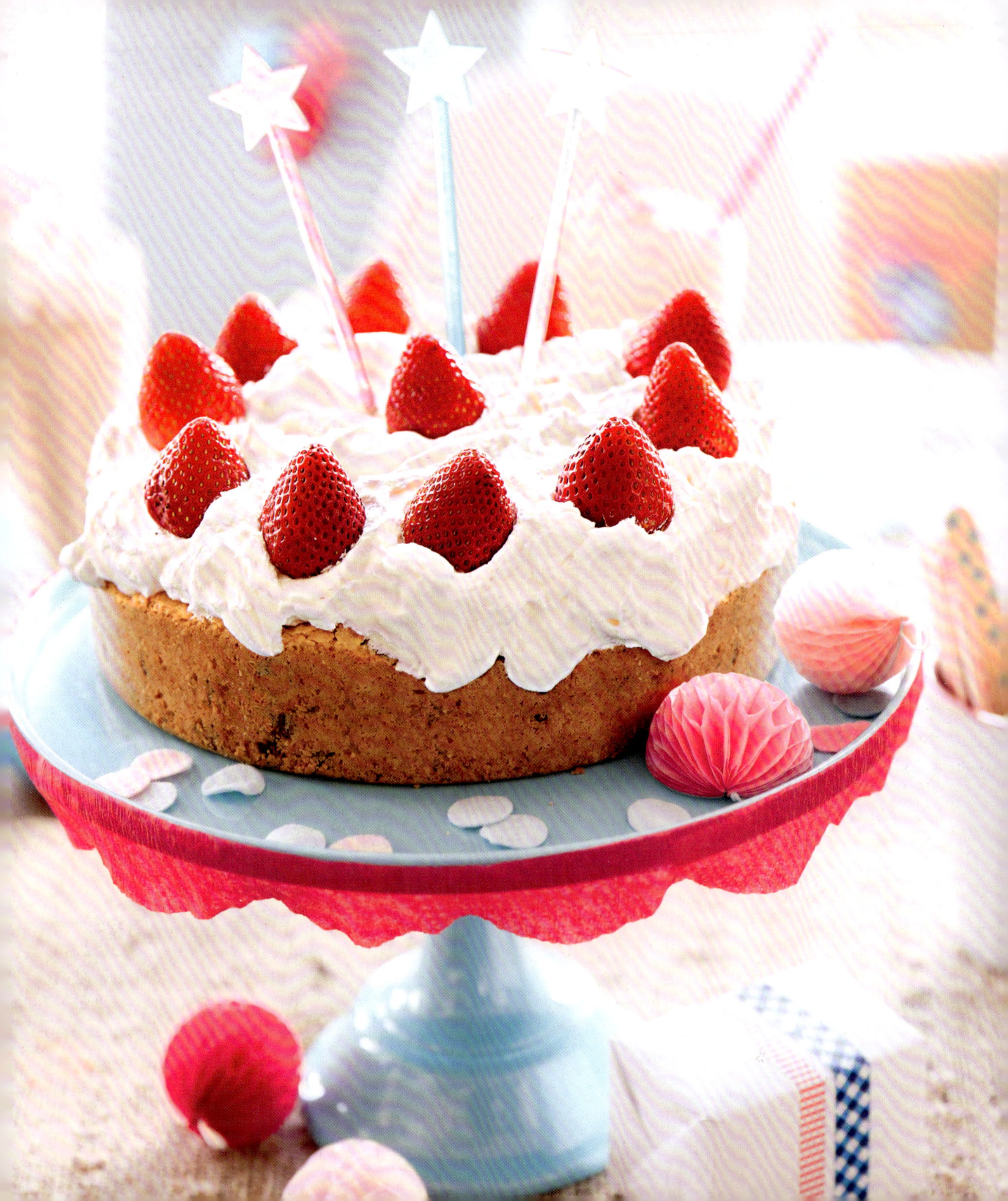

Chocolate Chip Cookie Birthday Cake

A birthday party just isn't a birthday party without a festive cake. This cake is like a giant chocolate chip cookie, so what's not to love? Decorate the cake as suggested, or double the recipe to make two cakes and layer with your favorite chocolate frosting.

MAKES 25 TARTLETS

2 cups all-purpose flour

2 teaspoons baking powder

½ teaspoon salt

¾ cup (1½ sticks) unsalted butter, at room temperature, plus more for greasing the pan

1⅓ cups firmly packed light brown sugar

2 large eggs

1½ teaspoons vanilla extract

1½ cups semisweet chocolate chips

Whipped Cream (page 128)

11 strawberries, hulled

Preheat the oven to 350°F. Grease a 9-inch round cake pan with butter. Sprinkle some flour in the pan and shake and tilt the pan to evenly coat the bottom and sides. Turn the pan upside down and tap out the excess flour.

In a small bowl, whisk together the flour, baking powder, and salt. In a large bowl, using an electric mixer, beat the butter and sugar on medium speed until creamy, about 3 minutes. Turn off the mixer and scrape down the bowl with a rubber spatula. Add the eggs, one at a time, beating on medium speed until blended. Add the vanilla and beat until blended. Turn off the mixer. Add the flour mixture and mix on low speed just until blended. Stir in the chocolate chips. The dough will be very thick. Scrape the dough into the prepared pan and spread it into an even layer.

Bake until a toothpick inserted into the center of the cake comes out with a few crumbs clinging to it, 40–45 minutes. Remove the pan from the oven and set it on a wire rack. Let cool for 30 minutes. Run a paring knife around the inside edge of the pan to loosen the cake. Ask an adult to help you place the rack upside down on top of the pan and, holding the two together, turn them over. Lift off the pan. Place a serving plate upside down on top of the cake and invert the cake right side up onto the plate. Let the cake cool completely.

Mound the whipped cream on top of the cake and spread it evenly over the top. Place 10 strawberries, pointed sides up, around the edge and 1 in the center. Serve right away.

Pink Orange Cake

This pretty cake has a naturally pink frosting from the juice of blood oranges. Blood oranges have a relatively short winter season, so if you don't have any, you can just stick to regular oranges, although the glaze won't have the same pink hue.

MAKES ABOUT 8 SERVINGS

CAKE

1½ cups all-purpose flour

½ teaspoon baking powder

3 large eggs

¼ cup fresh orange juice

1 teaspoon vanilla extract

1 cup granulated sugar

¾ cup (1½ sticks) unsalted butter, at room temperature

Grated zest of 2 oranges

½ teaspoon salt

GLAZE

1 cup powdered sugar

1 tablespoon plus ½ teaspoon fresh blood orange juice or orange juice, plus more as needed

About 4 very thin slices blood orange, seeded, or a handful of edible flowers (optional)

Preheat the oven to 350°F. Generously butter a 9-by-5-inch loaf pan, then line it with a piece of parchment paper, extending it up and over the sides.

To make the cake, in a small bowl, whisk together the flour and baking powder. In a glass measuring pitcher, whisk together the eggs, orange juice, and vanilla.

In a large bowl, using an electric mixer, beat the granulated sugar, butter, orange zest, and salt on medium-high speed until fluffy and pale, about 3 minutes. Turn off the mixer and scrape down the bowl with a rubber spatula. Add the egg mixture, a third of it at a time, and beat until well blended (the mixture will look a little curdled but this is okay). Turn off the mixer. Add the flour mixture, half of it at a time, and beat until just combined. Do not overmix. Give the batter a final stir with a rubber spatula to make sure it is fully combined.

~ Continued on page 118 ~

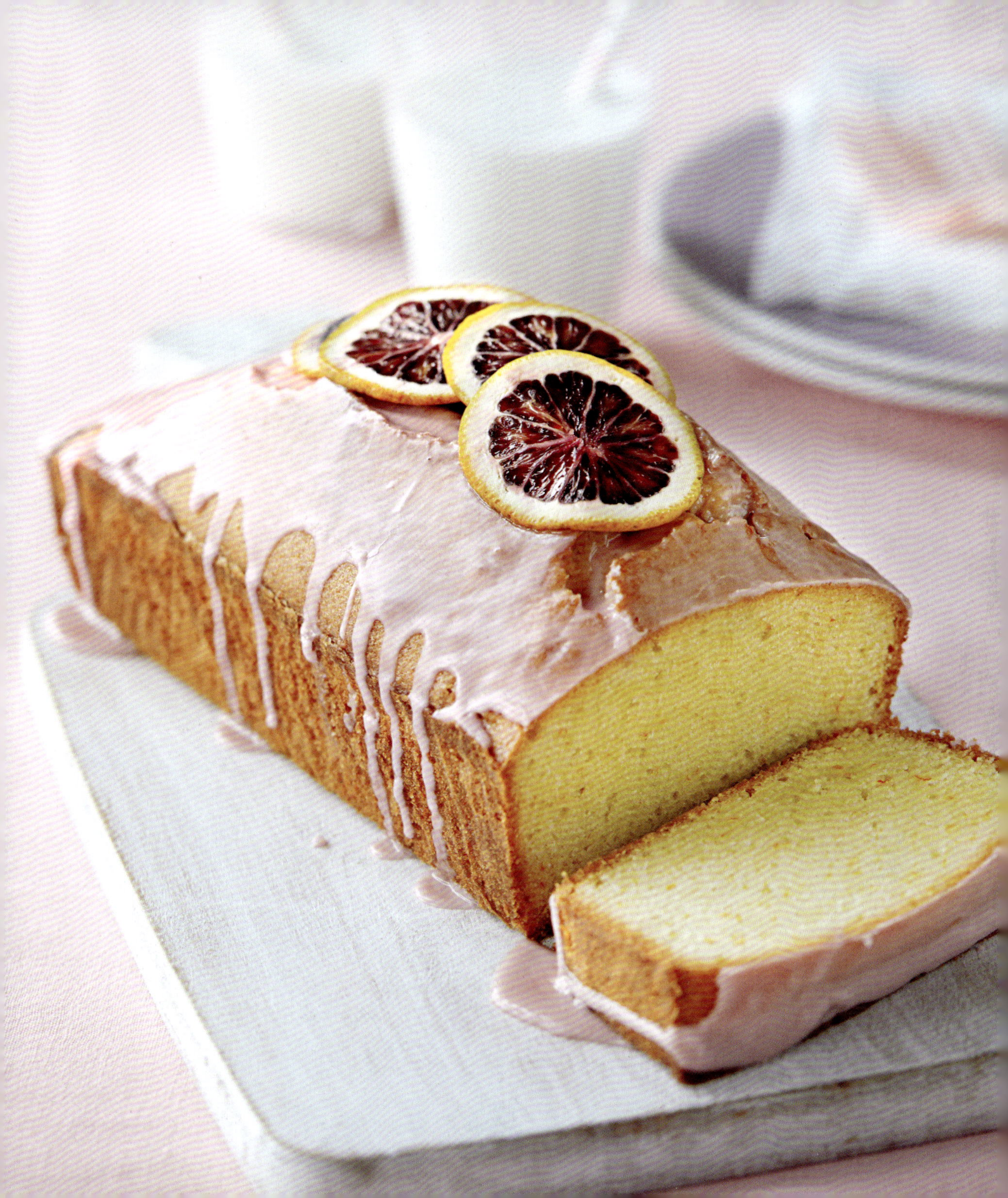

> **Juicy how-to**
> *Be sure to zest your oranges before juicing them. It's really hard to zest squishy orange peels!*

~ *Continued from page 116* ~

Pour the batter into the prepared pan and spread the top evenly.

Bake until the top of the cake is golden brown and a wooden skewer inserted into the center comes out clean, about 65 minutes. If the cake browns too quickly, cover the top with aluminum foil after about 45 minutes. Remove the loaf pan from the oven and set atop a wire rack. Let cool in the pan for about 10 minutes, then, using the parchment, carefully lift the cake out of the pan. Remove the parchment and place the cake on the rack. Let cool completely.

To make the glaze, sift the powdered sugar into a bowl. Add the blood orange juice and whisk until smooth. It should be thick but fall in ribbons from the spoon; if it's too thick, add a few drops more juice, but be careful a not to add too much at once. Using a large spoon, drizzle the glaze over the top of the cake, allowing it to drip down the sides. Let stand for 2 minutes to set, then lay the blood orange slices or edible flowers (if using) decoratively over the top. Cut the cake into thick slices and serve right away.

Frosted Apple Cake

This cake is great for an after-school snack or big get-togethers. You can use a variety of apples, such as McIntosh, Fuji, pippin, or Granny Smith. We used a combo of thinly sliced rings of green Granny Smith and red Gravenstein apples for the garnish.

MAKES 12 SERVINGS

CAKE

2 cups all-purpose flour

1 teaspoon baking powder

1 teaspoon baking soda

1 teaspoon ground cinnamon

½ teaspoon ground nutmeg

½ teaspoon ground cloves

½ teaspoon salt

¾ cup (1½ sticks) unsalted butter, at room temperature

1½ cups granulated sugar

3 large eggs, at room temperature

½ cup buttermilk, at room temperature

2 cups peeled diced apples (from about 3 apples)

½ cup walnuts, toasted and chopped (optional)

(See additional ingredients on page 121)

Preheat the oven to 350°F. Line a 9-by-13-inch baking pan with a piece of parchment paper, extending it up and over the short sides.

To make the cake, sift together the flour, baking powder, baking soda, cinnamon, nutmeg, cloves, and salt onto a sheet of parchment paper. In a large bowl, using an electric mixer, beat the butter and granulated sugar on medium-high speed until fluffy and pale, 3 to 5 minutes. Add the eggs, 1 at a time, beating well after each addition. Turn off the mixer and scrape down the bowl with a rubber spatula.

Using the spatula, gently fold in about a third of the flour mixture. Stir in half of the buttermilk. Add another third of the flour mixture and fold just until combined. Stir in the rest of the buttermilk, then add the rest of the flour mixture and fold just until combined. Fold in the apples and the walnuts (if using). Do not fold too vigorously or the cake will be tough. Pour the batter into the prepared pan and spread the top evenly.

Bake until the top is brown and a wooden skewer inserted into the center of the cake comes out clean, 35 to 40 minutes. Ask an adult to help you remove the baking pan from the oven and set it atop a wire rack. Let cool completely.

~ Continued on page 121 ~

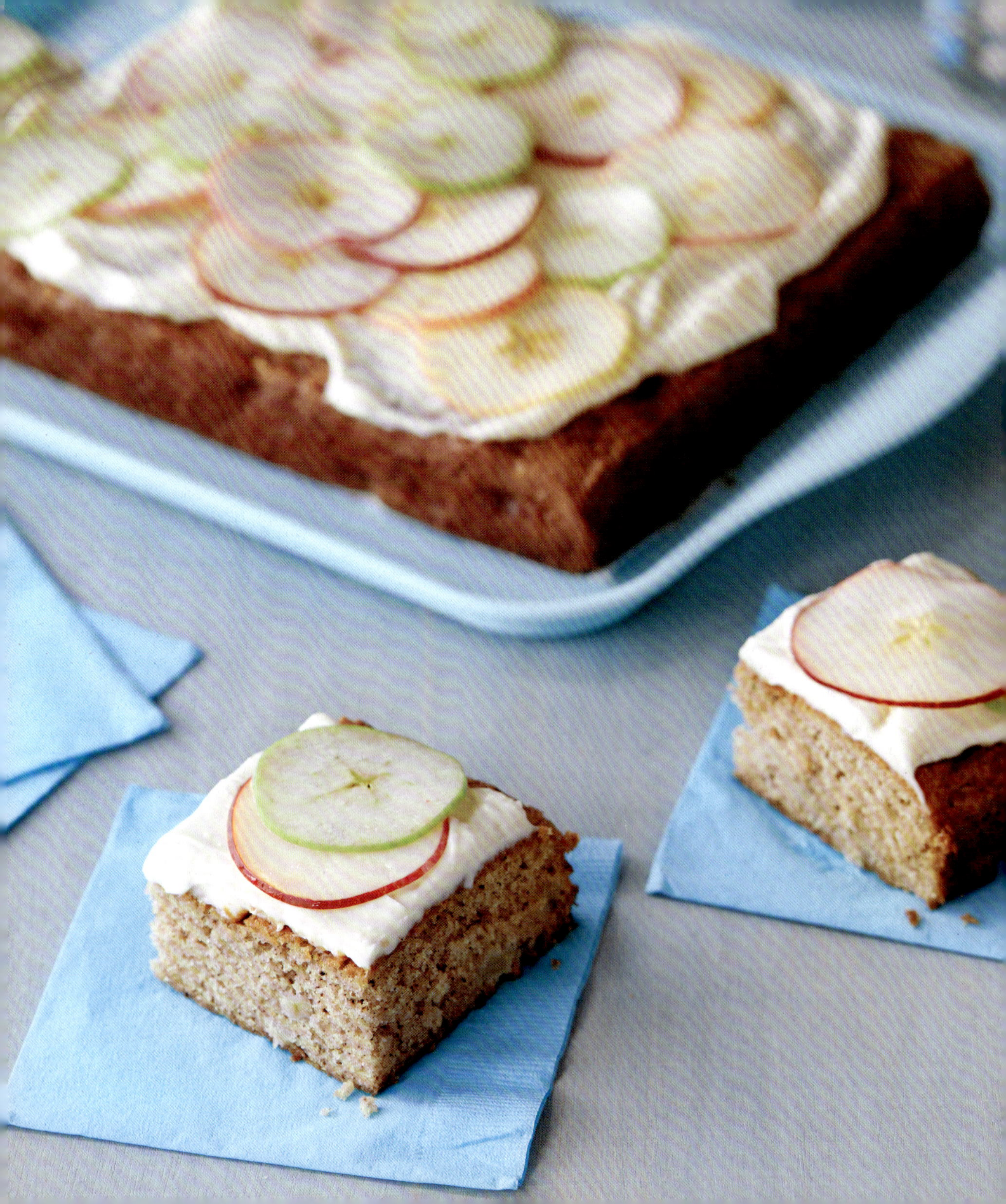

Packable snack
Skip the frosting (it can get messy) and wrap up pieces of this cake to enjoy after lunch or after school.

~ **Continued from page 119** ~

While the cake cools, make the cream cheese frosting. In a large bowl, using an electric mixer, beat the cream cheese and butter on medium-high speed until smooth, 3 to 5 minutes. Reduce the speed to low, add the powdered sugar, and beat until smooth, about 2 minutes. Beat in the vanilla. Turn off the mixer and scrape down the bowl with a rubber spatula.

When the cake is cool, using the parchment, carefully lift the cake out. Remove the parchment and place the cake on a tray or platter. Using a long offset spatula, spread the frosting over the top of the cake. Arrange the apple slices in overlapping rows across the top. Cut the cake into squares and serve right away.

FROSTING

2 (8-ounce) packages cream cheese, at room temperature

6 tablespoons unsalted butter, at room temperature

1¼ cups powdered sugar

1½ teaspoons vanilla extract

Thin apple slices, for garnish

Spiced Apple & Honey Cake

Surprise your family with a memorable cake that's layered with fluffy honey frosting. You can transform it into a forest wonderland by decorating it with rosemary "trees" and Gingerbread Cookies (page 83) cut into the shape of deer.

MAKES 10–12 SERVINGS

2 cups cake flour, plus flour for dusting

1 ½ teaspoons baking soda

1 teaspoon baking powder

¾ teaspoon ground cinnamon

¾ teaspoon ground cardamom

¼ teaspoon salt

¾ cup (1½ sticks) unsalted butter, plus butter for greasing

1¼ cups firmly packed light brown sugar

3 large eggs

1 teaspoon vanilla extract

1 cup unsweetened apple sauce, pear sauce, or a blend, at room temperature

⅔ cup whole milk, at room temperature

Whipped Honey Frosting (page 272)

Rosemary sprigs for decorating (optional)

Preheat the oven to 350°F. Trace the bottom of two 8-inch round cake pans onto sheets of parchment paper and cut out the circles with scissors. Rub the insides of the cake pans with a little butter. Put the paper circles in the bottoms of the pans and butter the paper. Dust the insides of the cake pans with flour, shaking out the excess.

In a medium bowl, mix the flour, baking soda, baking powder, cinnamon, cardamom, and salt. In a large bowl, using an electric mixer, beat the butter and brown sugar on medium-high speed until light and fluffy, 2 to 3 minutes. Add the eggs one at a time, beating well after each addition. Beat in the vanilla. Turn off the mixer and scrape down the bowl with a rubber spatula.

In a liquid measuring cup, combine the applesauce and milk. Add about one-third of the flour mixture to the mixing bowl. Mix on low speed just until blended. Pour in about half of the applesauce mixture and mix just until combined. Add about half of the remaining flour mixture and mix just until blended. Pour in the remaining applesauce mixture and mix just until combined. Add the remaining flour mixture and mix just until blended. Turn off the mixer, scrape down the bowl, and give the batter a final stir with the spatula.

Continued on page 124

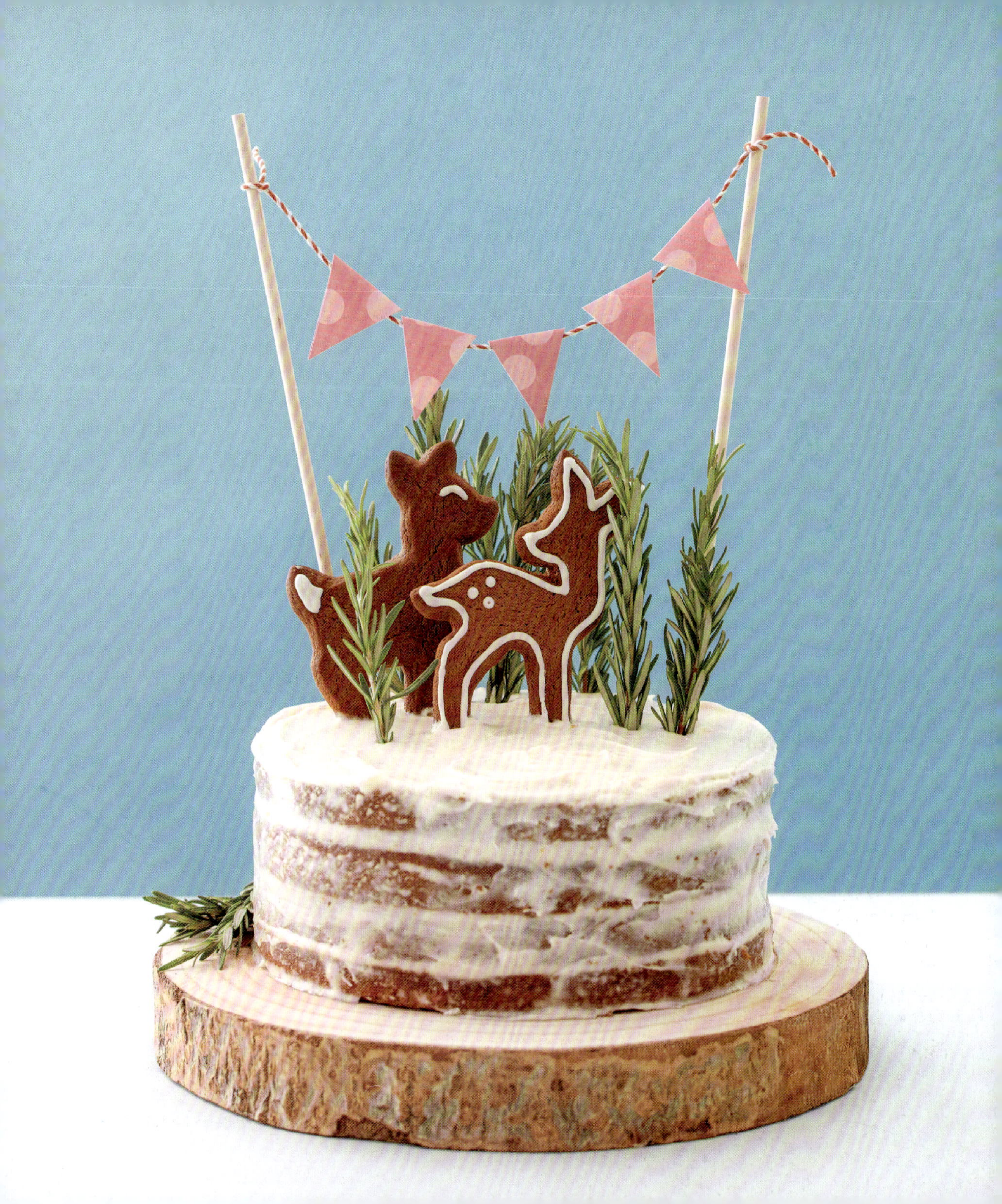

> **Frosting tips**
> *For a modern frosting technique, use an offset spatula (shown on page 273) to spread a sheer coat of frosting over the cake side.*

~ *Continued from page 122* ~

Divide the batter evenly between the prepared cake pans and spread in an even layer. Bake until the cakes are golden and a wooden skewer inserted into the centers comes out clean, 40 to 45 minutes. Remove the pans from the oven and set them on wire racks. Let cool for 15 minutes. Turn the pans over onto the racks. Lift off the pans, peel off the parchment paper, and let the cakes cool completely.

Make the whipped honey frosting.

Using a serrated knife, cut each cake layer in half horizontally. Place the bottom of 1 cake layer on a cake stand or plate. Using an offset spatula, spread some of the frosting over the top, making a thin, even layer about ¼ inch thick. Place a second cake layer, cut side down, on top of the frosting, lining up the sides of the cakes. Spread more frosting over the top. Repeat with the remaining 2 layers. Spread a thick layer of the remaining frosting over the cake top. Smooth the frosting around the sides with the spatula so that the sides of cake are peeking through. Decorate the cake as desired. Cut the cake into wedges and serve.

Southern Tea Cakes

Buttermilk gives these sweet treats a cakelike texture, and plenty of lemon zest and juice add a zingy flavor. Many traditional recipes for tea cakes use molasses to flavor the cookies; this version swaps in sugar.

MAKES ABOUT 48 COOKIES

2 cups all-purpose flour, plus flour for dusting

¾ teaspoon baking soda

½ teaspoon kosher salt

¾ cup (1½ sticks) unsalted butter, at room temperature

1 cup sugar

1 large egg

2 tablespoons finely grated lemon zest

3 tablespoons buttermilk

1 teaspoon fresh lemon juice

In a medium bowl, whisk together the flour, baking soda, and salt. Set aside. In a large bowl, using an electric mixer, beat the butter and sugar on medium-high speed until light and fluffy, 2 to 3 minutes. Add the egg and lemon zest and beat on low speed until the egg is incorporated. On low speed, mix in the dry ingredients. Add the buttermilk and lemon juice and beat until just incorporated.

Sprinkle a work surface with flour. Transfer the dough to the floured surface. Form the dough into an even log about 12 inches long. Wrap tightly in parchment paper and refrigerate until firm, at least 3 hours or up to overnight.

Position 2 racks in the oven so that they are evenly space apart and preheat the oven to 350°F. Line 2 cookie sheets with parchment paper.

Unwrap the chilled dough and slice into rounds ½ inch thick. Arrange the rounds on the prepared cookie sheets, spacing them about 1 inch apart.

Bake until the edges are lightly golden, about 12 minutes, rotating the cookie sheets from front to back and between the racks. Let the cookies cool on the sheets for 5 minutes, then use a metal spatula to move the cookies directly to a wire rack. Let cool completely.

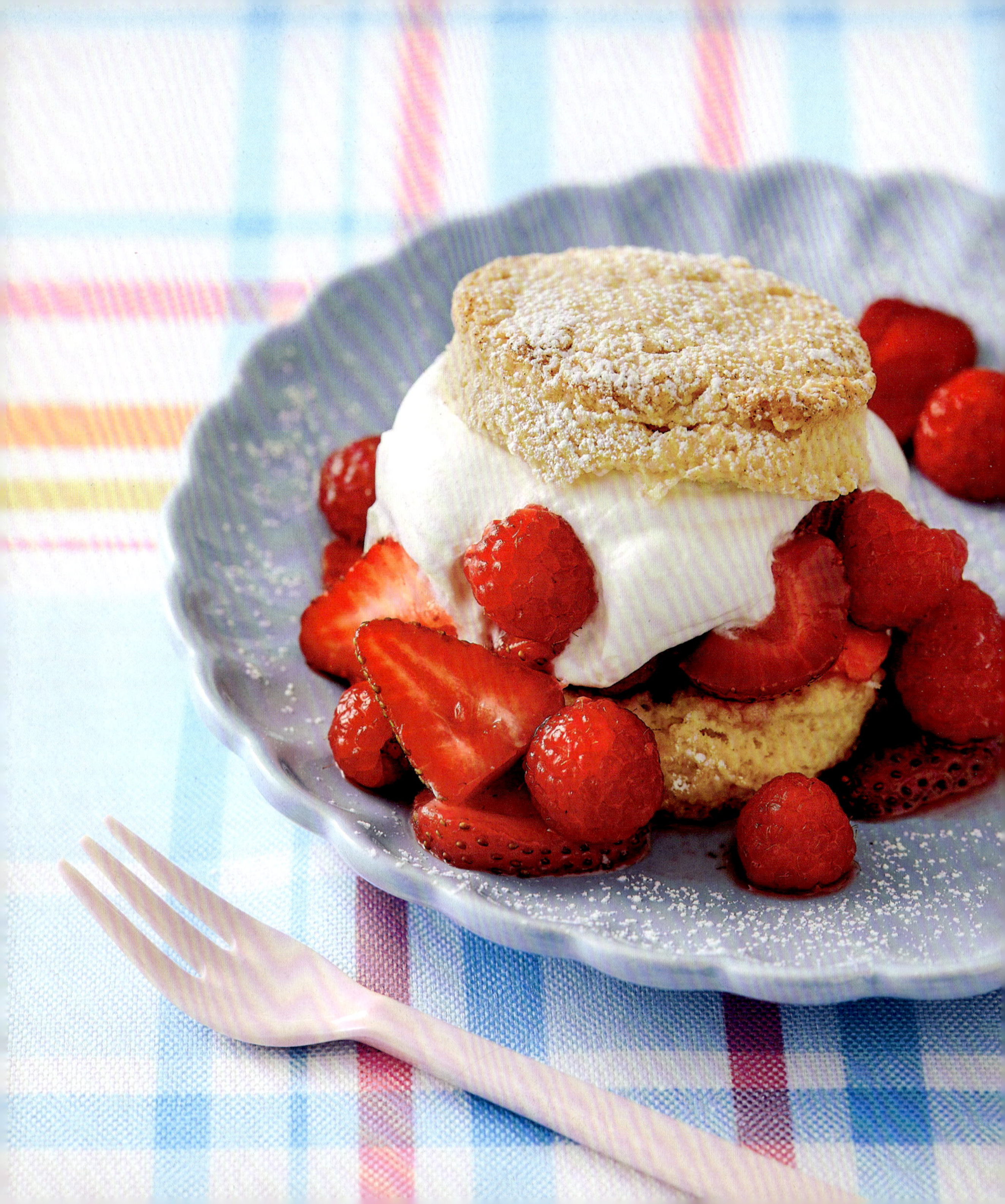

Mixed Berry Shortcake

If you have any leftover shortcakes and berries, make a delicious sundae the next day. Crumble the shortcakes into an ice cream glass, top with a scoop of vanilla or strawberry ice cream and the extra berries, and finish with a dollop of whipped cream. Then dig in!

MAKES 6 SERVINGS

2 cups all-purpose flour, plus flour for dusting

¼ cup plus 1 to 2 tablespoons granulated sugar

2 teaspoons baking powder

¼ teaspoon salt

6 tablespoons (¾ stick) cold unsalted butter, cut into small cubes

¾ cup heavy cream

2 cups mixed berries, such as raspberries and strawberries

WHIPPED CREAM

1 cup heavy cream

1 tablespoon granulated sugar

1 teaspoon vanilla extract

Powdered sugar for dusting

Preheat the oven to 375°F. Line a cookie sheet with parchment paper.

In a large bowl, whisk together the flour, the ¼ cup granulated sugar, the baking powder, and salt. Add the butter and, using a pastry blender or 2 knives, make quick, firm chopping motions to cut the butter into the flour mixture until it looks like coarse crumbs, with some chunks the size of peas. Add the cream and stir until the dough starts to come together.

Sprinkle a work surface with flour. Dump the dough onto the floured surface and pat it into a disk. Using a rolling pin, roll out the dough, giving the disk a quarter turn now and then, into a round slab that's 1 inch thick. Pat the sides to make them neat.

Using a 3-inch biscuit cutter, cut out 4 rounds. Gather the dough scraps, roll them out again, and cut out 2 more rounds.

Transfer the dough rounds to the prepared cookie sheet, spacing them evenly apart. Bake until the shortcakes are golden brown on top, 18 to 20 minutes. Using oven mitts, remove the cookie sheet from the oven and set it on a wire rack. Let the shortcakes cool for 10 to 15 minutes.

Continued on page 128

> **Fruity twist**
> Sub in any of your favorite summer fruits for the berries. Try sliced peaches, nectarines, plums, pluots, or cherries, selecting the best seasonal fruit.

~ *Continued from page 127* ~

Meanwhile, put the strawberries on a cutting board. Pull or cut out the stem and white core from the center of each strawberry, then cut them into thin slices. Put all of the berries in a medium bowl and sprinkle with the remaining 1 to 2 tablespoons granulated sugar (the amount depends on how sweet the berries are—taste one!). Let the berries stand for about 10 minutes.

In a large bowl, using an electric mixer, beat the cream, granulated sugar, and vanilla on low speed until the cream begins to thicken and no longer splatters, about 2 minutes. Raise the speed to medium-high and beat until the cream forms soft peaks that fall to one side when the beaters are lifted (turn off the mixer first!), about 3 minutes.

Cut each cooled shortcake in half horizontally. Place the shortcake bottoms, cut side up, on serving plates and spoon the berries on top, dividing them equally. Add a big spoonful of whipped cream and top with the shortcake tops. Put the powdered sugar in a fine-mesh sieve, hold it over the shortcakes, and tap the side to dust the shortcakes with an even layer of the sugar. Serve right away.

Chocolate Ice Box Cake

The longer this cake sits in the refrigerator, the tastier it gets. Allow at least a few hours for it to set, or make it a few days ahead of when you want to serve it. Leftover cookies can be crumbled and used to decorate the top of the cake.

MAKES 10 TO 12 SERVINGS

CHOCOLATE COOKIES

1¼ cups all-purpose flour, plus flour for dusting

¾ cup granulated sugar

¾ cup unsweetened cocoa powder

1 teaspoon baking soda

½ teaspoon salt

¼ teaspoon baking powder

12 tablespoons (1½ sticks) unsalted butter, at room temperature

1 large egg, plus 1 large egg yolk

WHIPPED CREAM

3 cups heavy cream

2 teaspoons vanilla extract

½ cup powdered sugar

Preheat the oven to 375°F. Line 2 cookie sheets with parchment paper.

To make the cookies, in a large bowl, whisk together the flour, granulated sugar, cocoa powder, baking soda, salt, and baking powder. Add the butter and, using an electric mixer, beat on low speed for 2 minutes. Add the egg and egg yolk and beat on low speed until a dough forms, about 1 minute. Turn off the mixer and scrape down the bowl with a rubber spatula.

Dump the dough onto a lightly floured work surface. Using a floured rolling pin, roll out the dough until it is about ¼ inch thick. Using a 2½-inch round cookie cutter, cut out as many cookies as possible. Transfer the cookies to the prepared cookie sheets, spacing them about 1 inch apart. Press the dough scraps together, roll out, and cut out more cookies. If the dough is too sticky to roll, wrap it in plastic wrap and refrigerate until slightly firm, about 15 minutes.

When both cookie sheets are full, bake 1 cookie sheet at a time until the centers of the cookies are firm to the touch, 8 to 10 minutes. Using oven mitts, remove the cookie sheet from the oven and set it on a wire rack. Let cool for 5 minutes, then use a metal spatula to move the cookies directly to the rack. Repeat to bake the rest of the cookies. Let cool completely.

Continued on page 130

> **Time-saving tip**
> Need dessert in a hurry? Skip the homemade cookies here and sub in two dozen purchased chocolate wafer cookies instead.

~ Continued from page 129 ~

To make the whipped cream, in a large bowl, using an electric mixer, beat the cream, vanilla, and powdered sugar on medium speed until soft peaks form when the beaters are lifted (turn off the mixer first!), 2 to 3 minutes.

To assemble, place the cookies in a single layer, as close together as possible, in a 9-by-3-inch round cake pan or ceramic dish. If needed, break some cookies in half to fill in the center of the circle. Spread a thick layer of the whipped cream on top of the cookies. Top with another layer of cookies, followed by another layer of whipped cream. Repeat until you reach the top of the pan, ending with a layer of whipped cream. Crumble any remaining cookies and sprinkle them on top of the cake, if desired. Cover the pan with plastic wrap and refrigerate until set, at least 4 hours or up to 3 days. Cut the cake into slices and serve cold.

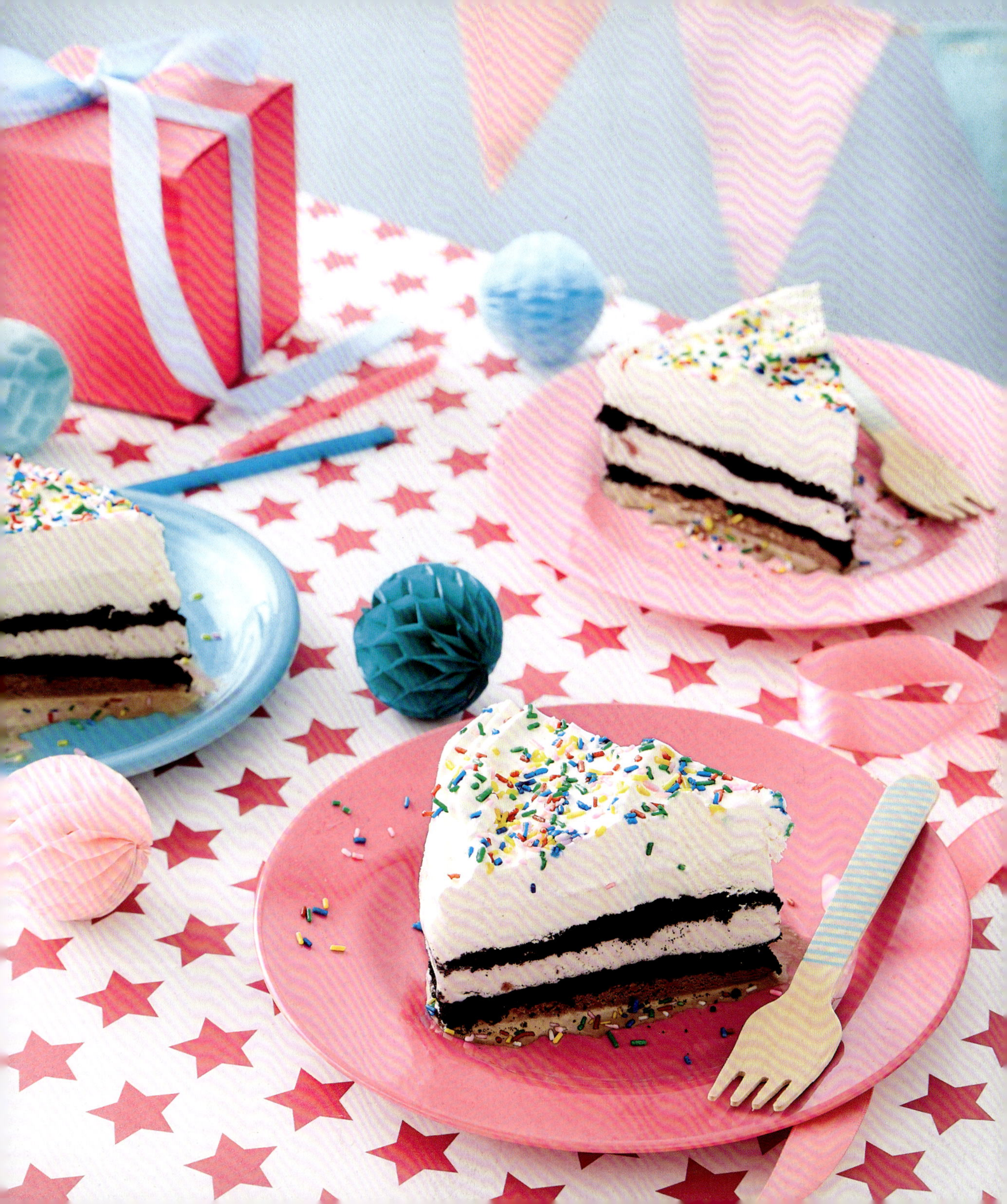

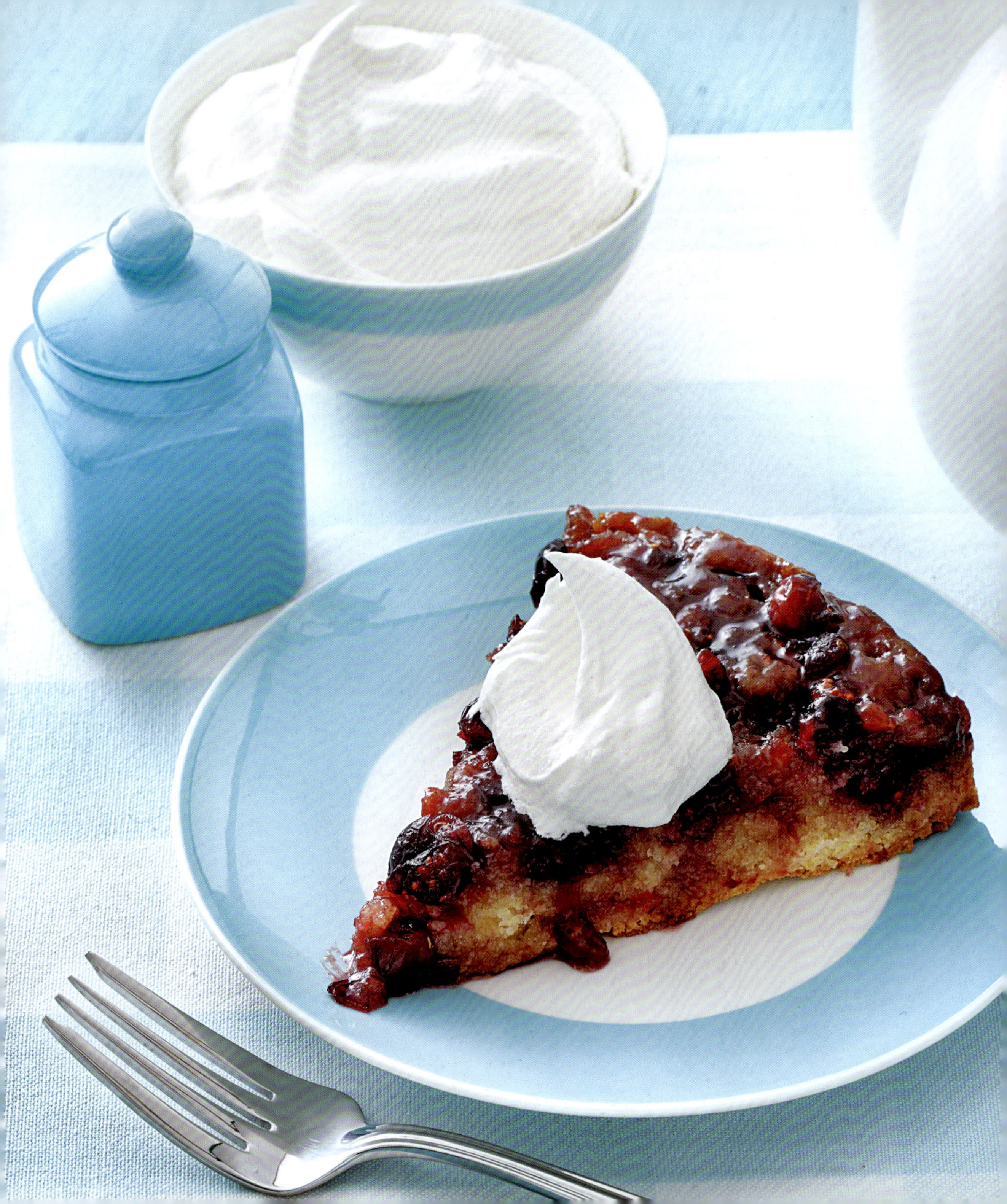

Cranberry Upside-Down Cake

Show off your baking skills with this colorful cake that's topped with juicy cranberries. Be sure to line the pan with parchment paper—this prevents the berries and glaze from sticking when you flip the pan over.

MAKES 8 SERVINGS

4 tablespoons (½ stick) unsalted butter, plus butter for greasing

¾ cup firmly packed light brown sugar

2 cups fresh or thawed frozen cranberries

1¼ cups all-purpose flour

½ teaspoon baking powder

¼ teaspoon baking soda

¼ teaspoon salt

1 large egg

1 cup granulated sugar

½ cup canola oil

1 teaspoon vanilla extract

½ cup sour cream

Whipped cream (page 128) for serving (optional)

Preheat the oven to 350°F. Trace the bottom of a 9-inch round cake pan onto a sheet of parchment paper and cut out the circle with scissors. Rub the insides of the cake pan with a little butter. Put the paper circle in the bottom of the pan and butter the paper.

In a small saucepan, combine the butter and brown sugar. Set the pan over medium-low heat and cook, stirring, until the butter is melted and the mixture is smooth. Carefully scrape the glaze into the prepared pan, tilting the pan to spread it evenly. Arrange the cranberries evenly over the glaze.

Sift together the flour, baking powder, baking soda, and salt into a medium bowl. In a large bowl, using an electric mixer, beat the egg and granulated sugar on medium speed until light and fluffy, about 2 minutes. Turn off the mixer and scrape down the bowl with a rubber spatula. Slowly add the oil and vanilla and beat on low speed until blended. Mix in the sour cream just until no white streaks remain. Turn off the mixer and add the flour mixture. Mix on low speed until incorporated. Scrape down the bowl. Carefully pour the batter over the cranberries, spreading it evenly.

Bake until a wooden skewer inserted into the center of the cake comes out clean, about 45 minutes. Remove the pan from the oven and let cool on a wire rack for about 10 minutes. Run a table knife around the inside edge of the pan. Place a plate upside down on top of the pan and turn the pan and plate over together to unmold the cake. Lift off the pan and peel off the parchment paper. Cut the cake into wedges. Serve with whipped cream, if desired.

Baked Nectarines with Cinnamon Streusel

Streusel is a crumbly mixture of flour, sugar, butter, nuts, and spices that is used as a topping for cakes and muffins—and fruit! You can use peaches, plums, or pluots instead of the nectarines for this recipe, and a scoop of vanilla ice cream on top is always a hit.

MAKES 4 SERVINGS

4 firm, ripe nectarines, halved and pitted

¼ cup plus 2 tablespoons whole wheat flour

¼ cup plus 2 tablespoons firmly packed light brown sugar

½ teaspoon ground cinnamon

⅛ teaspoon salt

2 tablespoons cold unsalted butter, cut into small pieces

⅓ cup roasted almonds, chopped

Preheat the oven to 400°F. Line a rimmed cookie sheet with parchment paper.

Arrange the nectarines, cut side up, on the prepared cookie sheet. Cut a thin slice off the round side of each half to help them sit flat, if you like. Set aside.

In a food processor, combine the flour, brown sugar, cinnamon, and salt and pulse a few times to mix. Scatter the butter pieces over the flour mixture and pulse just until the mixture resembles coarse crumbs. Do not overmix. Transfer to a bowl and stir in the almonds. Squeeze the flour-sugar-butter mixture into small handfuls and scatter it evenly over the nectarine halves, pressing it lightly so that it sticks to the nectarines.

Bake until the nectarines are tender when pierced with a small knife and the topping is nicely browned, about 20 minutes. Arrange 2 nectarine halves on each of 4 dessert plates and serve right away.

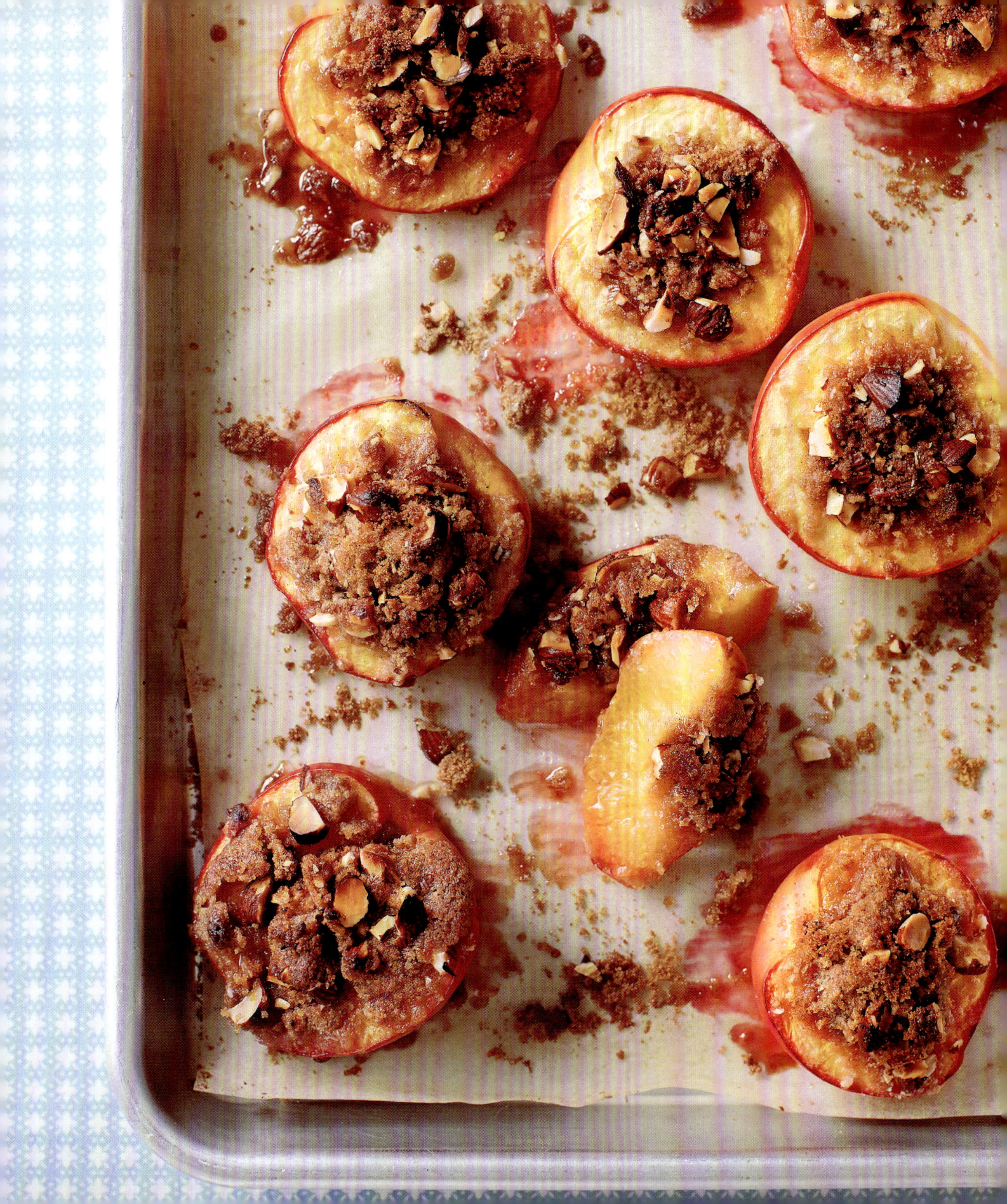

Honey Madeleines

These buttery, honey-licious cakes are surprisingly easy to make. You need only a few ingredients, an electric mixer, and a shell-shaped mold. And with a little imagination, you'll feel like you're in a bakery in Paris!

MAKES 12 MADELEINES

5 tablespoons unsalted butter, melted and cooled

½ cup cake flour, plus more for dusting the pan

½ teaspoon baking powder

1 large egg

3 tablespoons sugar

2 tablespoons honey

2 teaspoons orange flower water

Position a rack in the lower third of the oven and preheat the oven to 400°F. Using a pastry brush and 1 tablespoon of the butter, coat the 12 molds of a madeleine pan with a thick layer of butter, making sure you coat each and every ridge. Dust the molds with flour, tilting the pan to coat all of the surfaces. Turn the pan upside down over the kitchen sink and tap it gently to knock out the excess flour.

Sift together the flour and baking powder into a bowl. In another bowl, using an electric mixer, beat together the egg and sugar on medium speed for 30 seconds. Increase the speed to high and beat until very thick and quadrupled in bulk, about 10 minutes. Add the honey and orange flower water and beat until combined. Turn off the mixer. Sprinkle the flour mixture over the egg mixture. Using a rubber spatula, gently fold in the flour mixture, then fold in the remaining 4 tablespoons butter.

Scoop a heaping tablespoonful of batter into each mold. The molds should be three-fourths full. Bake until the cookies are golden brown at the edges and the tops spring back when lightly touched (ask an adult for help!), 10 to 12 minutes. Ask an adult to help you remove the pan from the oven, invert it onto a wire rack right away, and tap the pan on the rack to release the madeleines. If any of the cookies stick, use a butter knife to loosen the edges, being careful not to touch the hot pan, and invert and tap again. Serve slightly warm. These are best eaten the same day they are baked.

Tea perfect!
These sweet little cakes are ideal for an afternoon tea party. Serve them with fresh berries and fruity herbal tea.

Orange Madeleines

A little freshly grated orange zest gives these adorable shell-shaped mini cakes an amazing aroma and lots of flair. The zest adds pretty orange flecks to the cakes, too.

MAKES 12 MADELEINES

2 large eggs

⅓ cup granulated sugar

¼ teaspoon salt

½ teaspoon vanilla extract

¼ teaspoon almond extract

1 teaspoon grated orange zest

½ cup all-purpose flour, plus more for dusting the pan

¼ cup unsalted butter, melted and cooled, plus room-temperature butter for the pan

Confectioners' (powdered) sugar for dusting

Preheat the oven to 375°F. Using a pastry brush, coat the 12 molds of a madeleine pan with room-temperature butter, making sure you coat each and every ridge. Dust the molds with flour, tilting the pan to coat all of the surfaces. Turn the pan upside down over the kitchen sink and tap it gently to knock out the excess flour.

In a bowl, using an electric mixer, beat together the eggs, sugar, and salt on medium-high speed until light and fluffy, about 5 minutes. Beat in the vanilla and almond extracts, and the orange zest. Turn off the mixer. Sift the flour over the egg mixture and mix on low speed to incorporate. Using a rubber spatula, gently fold in one-half of the melted butter just until blended. Fold in the remaining melted butter.

Scoop a heaping tablespoonful of the batter into each mold. Bake until the tops spring back when lightly touched (ask an adult for help!), 10 to 12 minutes. Ask an adult to help you remove the pan from the oven, invert it onto a wire rack right away, and tap the pan on the rack to release the madeleines. If any of the cookies stick, use a butter knife to loosen the edges, being careful not to touch the hot pan, and invert and tap again. Use a fine-mesh sieve or a sifter, dust them with confectioners' sugar. Serve slightly warm.

Chocolate Madeleines

These scrumptious little cakes are perfect for baking with your friends. To make them super-duper choco-rific, dip the madeleines in melted chocolate chips (see page 140).

MAKES 12 MADELEINES

⅓ cup all-purpose flour, plus more for dusting the pan

¼ cup unsweetened cocoa powder

2 large eggs

½ cup granulated sugar

¼ teaspoon salt

1 teaspoon vanilla extract

6 tablespoon unsalted butter, melted and cooled, plus room-temperature butter for the pan

Confectioners' (powdered) sugar for dusting

Preheat the oven to 375°F. Using a pastry brush, coat the 12 molds of a madeleine pan with room temperature butter, making sure you coat each and every ridge. Dust the molds with flour, tilting the pan to coat all of the surfaces. Turn the pan upside down over the kitchen sink and tap it gently to knock out the excess flour.

Sift together the flour and cocoa powder into a bowl. In another bowl, using an electric mixer, beat together the eggs, sugar, and salt on medium-high speed until light and fluffy, about 3 minutes. Beat in the vanilla. Turn off the mixer. Sprinkle the flour mixture over the egg mixture and mix on low speed to incorporate. Using a rubber spatula, gently fold in one-half of the melted butter just until blended. Fold in the remaining melted butter.

Scoop a heaping tablespoonful of the batter into each mold. Bake until the tops spring back when lightly touched (ask an adult for help!), about 12 minutes. Ask an adult to help you remove the pan from the oven, invert it onto a wire rack right away, and tap the pan on the rack to release the madeleines. If any of the cookies stick, use a butter knife to loosen the edges, being careful not to touch the hot pan, and invert and tap again. Use a fine-mesh sieve or a sifter, dust them with confectioners' sugar. Serve slightly warm.

Chocolate-Dipped Vanilla Madeleines

Sweet and fancy French madeleines are très cute when dipped into rich melted chocolate. Serve these at your next tea party. Bon appétit!

MAKES 12 MADELEINES

2 large eggs

⅓ cup granulated sugar

¼ teaspoon salt

1 teaspoon vanilla extract

½ cup all-purpose flour, plus more for dusting the pan

¼ cup unsalted butter, melted and cooled, plus room-temperature butter for the pan

⅓ cup semisweet chocolate chips

Preheat the oven to 375°F. Using a pastry brush, coat the 12 molds of a madeleine pan with room-temperature butter, making sure you coat each and every ridge. Dust the molds with flour, tilting the pan to coat all of the surfaces. Turn the pan upside down over the kitchen sink and tap it gently to knock out the excess flour.

In a bowl, using an electric mixer, beat together the eggs, sugar, and salt on medium-high speed until light and fluffy, about 5 minutes. Beat in the vanilla extract. Turn off the mixer. Sift the flour over the egg mixture and mix on low speed to incorporate. Using a rubber spatula, gently fold in one-half of the melted butter just until blended. Fold in the remaining melted butter.

Scoop a heaping tablespoonful of the batter into each mold. Bake until the tops spring back when lightly touched (ask an adult for help!), 10 to 12 minutes. Ask an adult to help you remove the pan from the oven, invert it onto a wire rack right away, and tap the pan on the rack to release the madeleines. If any of the cookies stick, use a butter knife to loosen the edges, being careful not to touch the hot pan, and invert and tap again. Let cool while you melt the chocolate for dipping.

To dip the madeleines in chocolate, line a cookie sheet with parchment paper. Place the chocolate chips in a small microwave-safe bowl. Ask an adult to help you microwave the chocolate on high heat, stirring every 20 seconds, until it's melted and smooth. Don't let the chocolate get too hot! One at a time, carefully dip the wide, rounded end of each madeleine into the chocolate, then set it, shell-side up, on the prepared cookie sheet.

Refrigerate the cookies until the chocolate is set, 10 to 15 minutes, and serve.

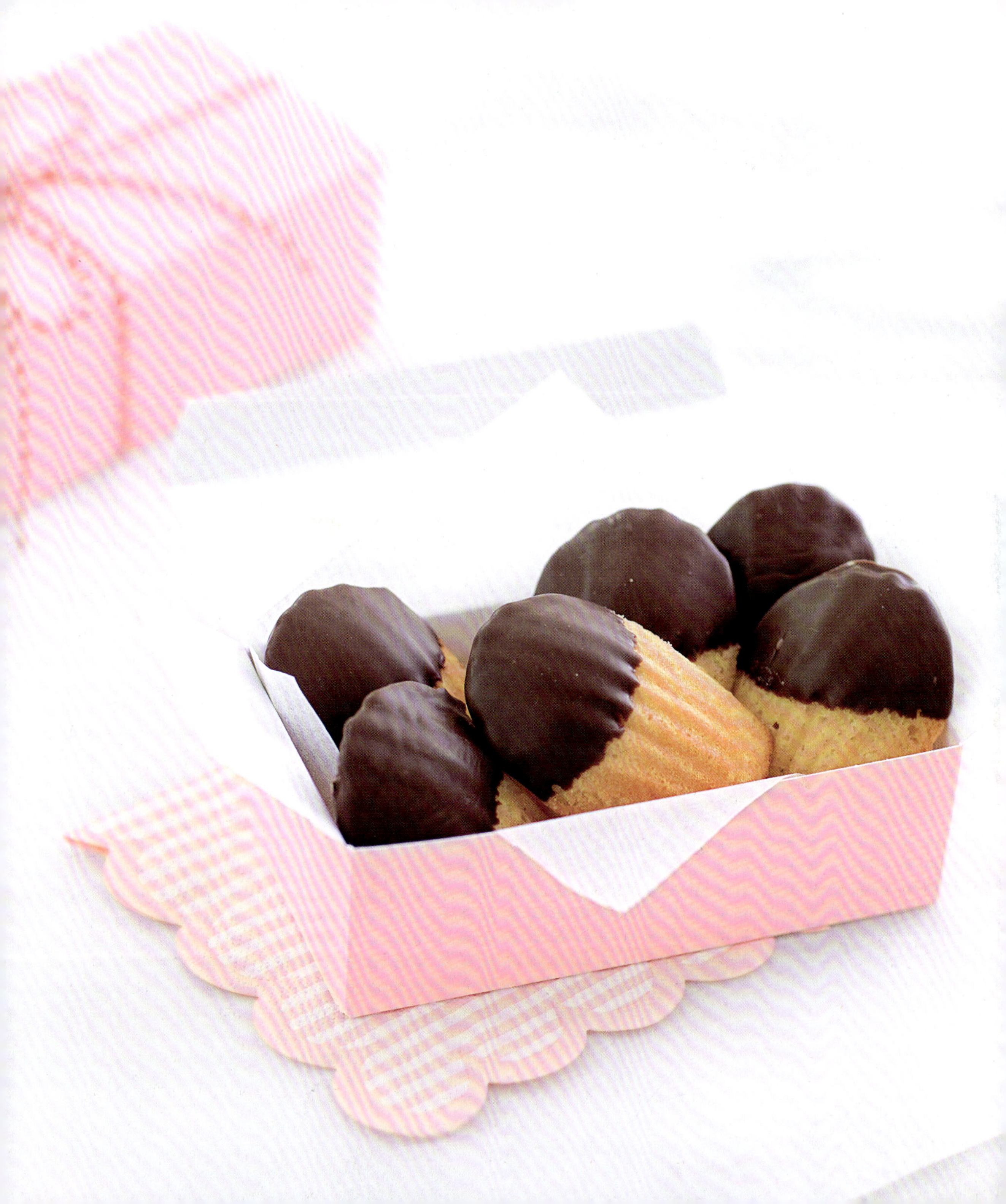

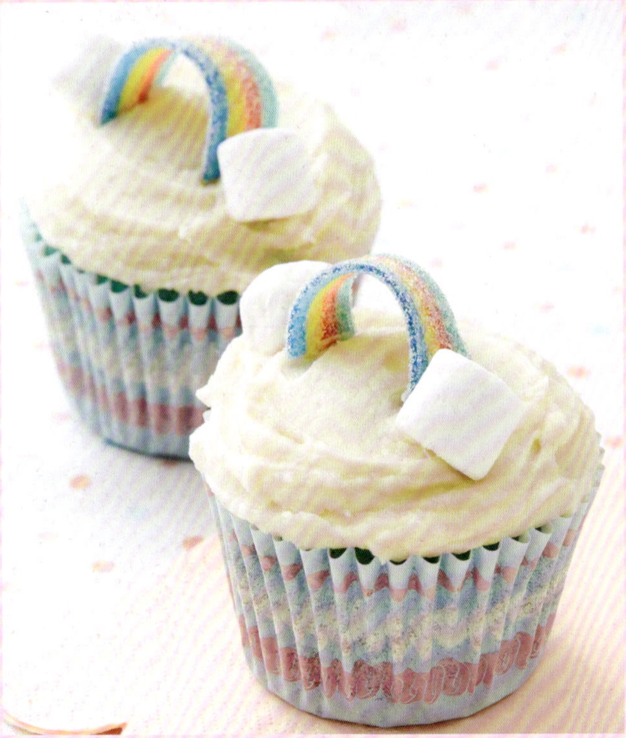
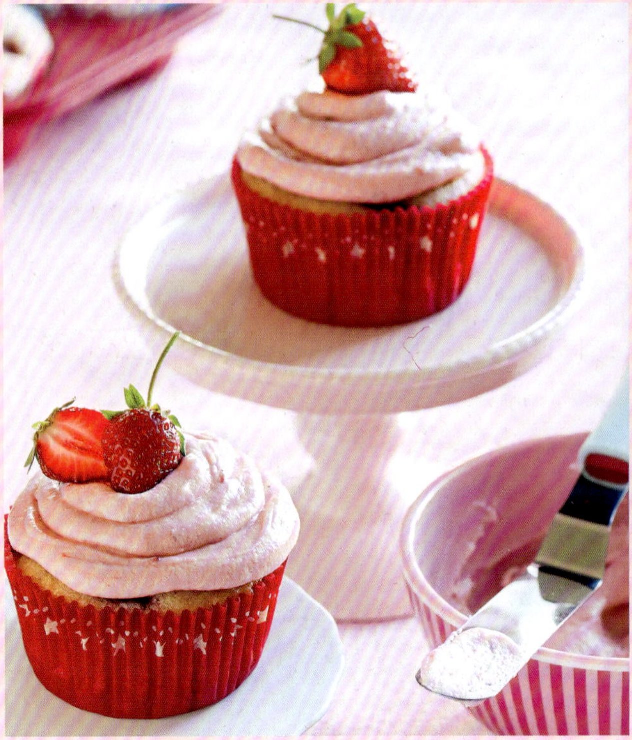
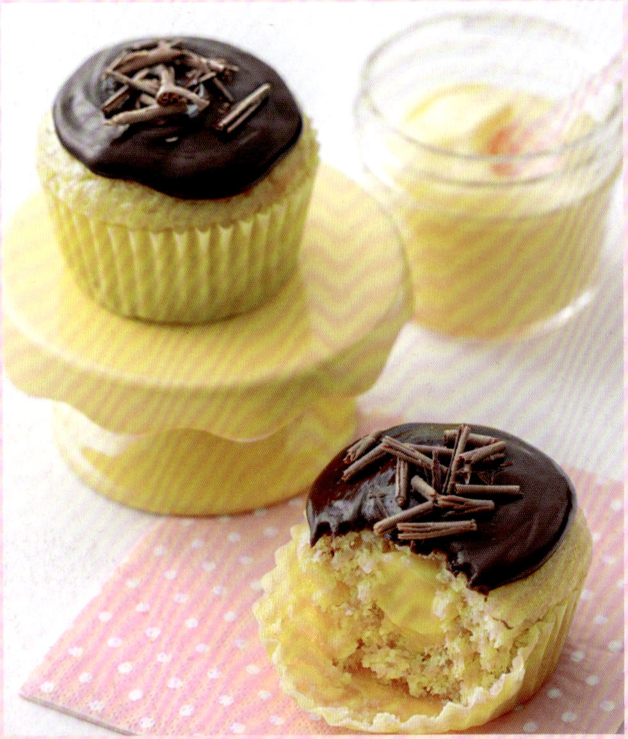
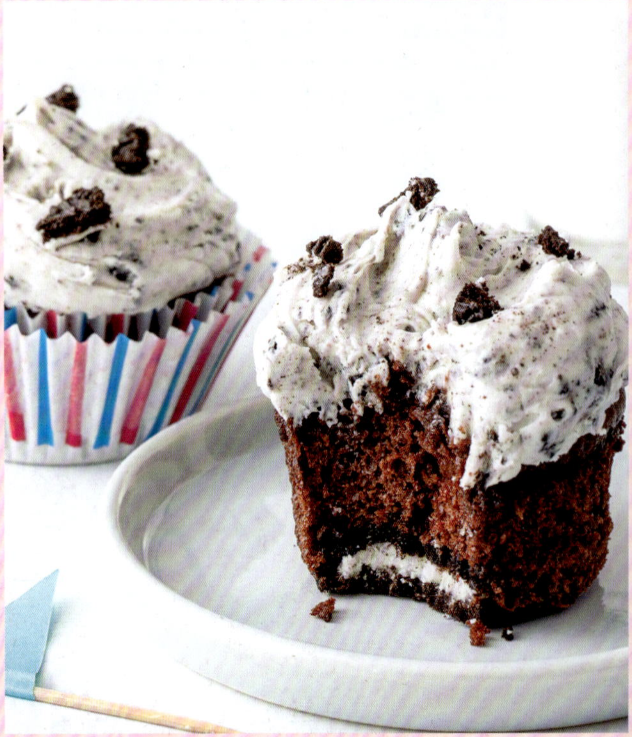

Cupcakes

Devil's Food Cupcakes

Despite their name, these cupcakes are anything but devilish. Moist chocolate cake and rich chocolate frosting—decorated with plenty of rainbow sprinkles or other candies—are just heavenly good!

MAKES 12 CUPCAKES

CUPCAKES

1 cup all-purpose flour

¼ cup unsweetened cocoa powder

1 teaspoon baking soda

¼ teaspoon salt

⅓ cup granulated sugar

⅓ cup firmly packed light brown sugar

4 tablespoons (½ stick) unsalted butter, at room temperature

1 large egg

1 teaspoon vanilla extract

¾ cup buttermilk

CHOCOLATE FROSTING

3½ cups powdered sugar

1 cup cocoa powder

½ cup (1 stick) unsalted butter, at room temperature

1 teaspoon vanilla extract

1 cup heavy cream

Preheat the oven to 350°F. Line a standard 12-cup muffin pan.

To make the cupcakes, in a bowl, whisk together the flour, cocoa, baking soda, and salt. In a large bowl, using an electric mixer, beat the granulated sugar, brown sugar, and butter on medium-high speed until fluffy, about 3 minutes. Add the egg and vanilla and beat until combined. Turn off the mixer and scrape down the bowl with a rubber spatula. Add half of the flour mixture and mix on low speed just until blended. Turn off the mixer. Pour in the buttermilk and mix on low speed just until combined. Turn off the mixer. Add the rest of the flour mixture and mix just until blended. Scrape down the bowl.

Divide the batter evenly among the prepared muffin cups, filling each about three-fourths full. Bake until a wooden skewer inserted into the center of a cupcake comes out clean (ask an adult for help!), 18 to 20 minutes. Ask an adult to help you remove the pan from the oven and set it on a wire rack. Let the cupcakes cool for 10 minutes, then transfer them to the rack. Let cool.

To make the frosting, sift together the powdered sugar and cocoa into a bowl. Add the butter. Using an electric mixer, beat the mixture on low speed until crumbly. Add the vanilla and beat until combined. Turn off the mixer. Add the cream and beat until the frosting is smooth, about 1 minute. If the frosting is too thick, add more of the cream until it becomes smooth and spreadable.

Frost the cupcakes. Decorate with sprinkles or candies, if you like, and serve.

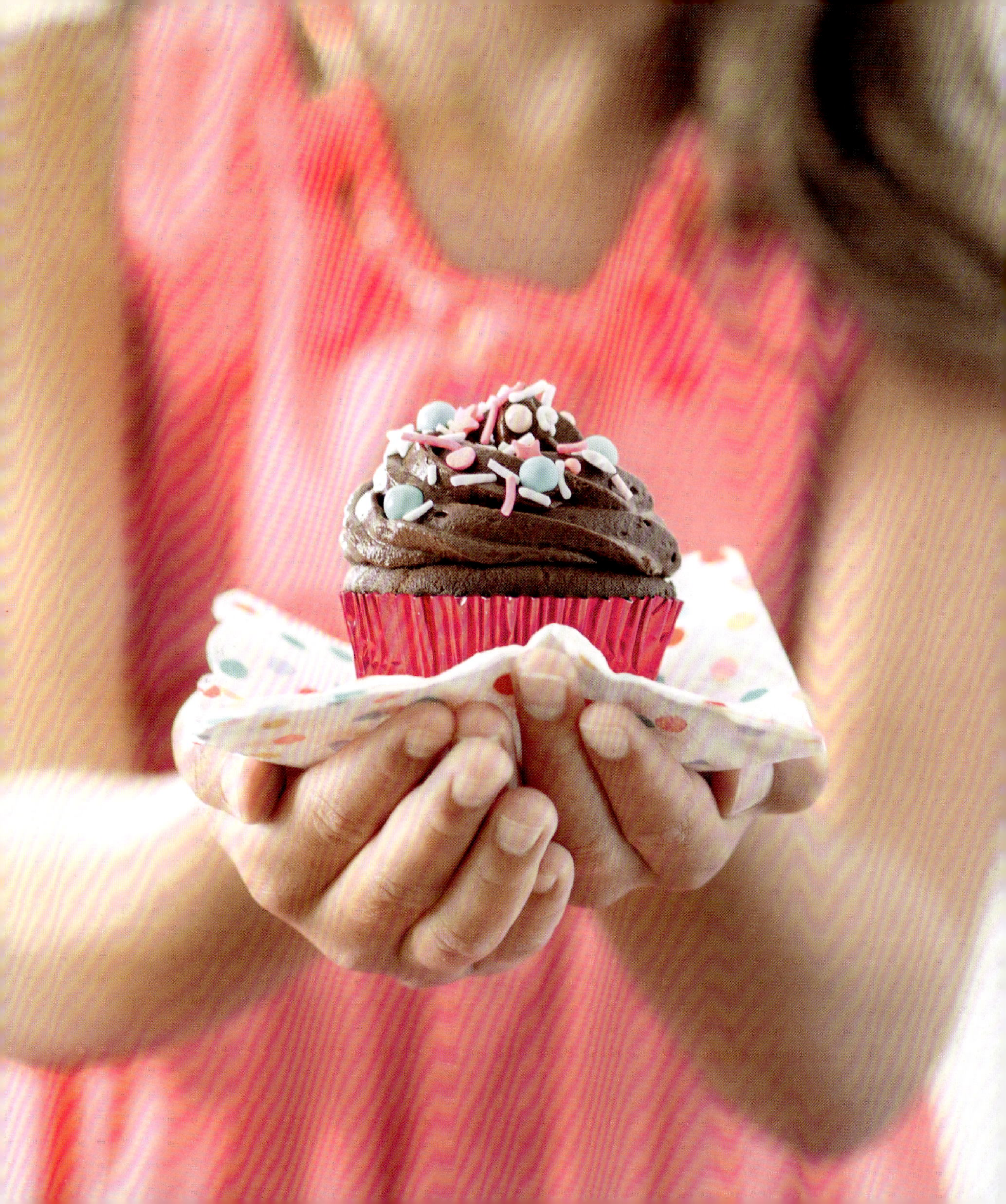

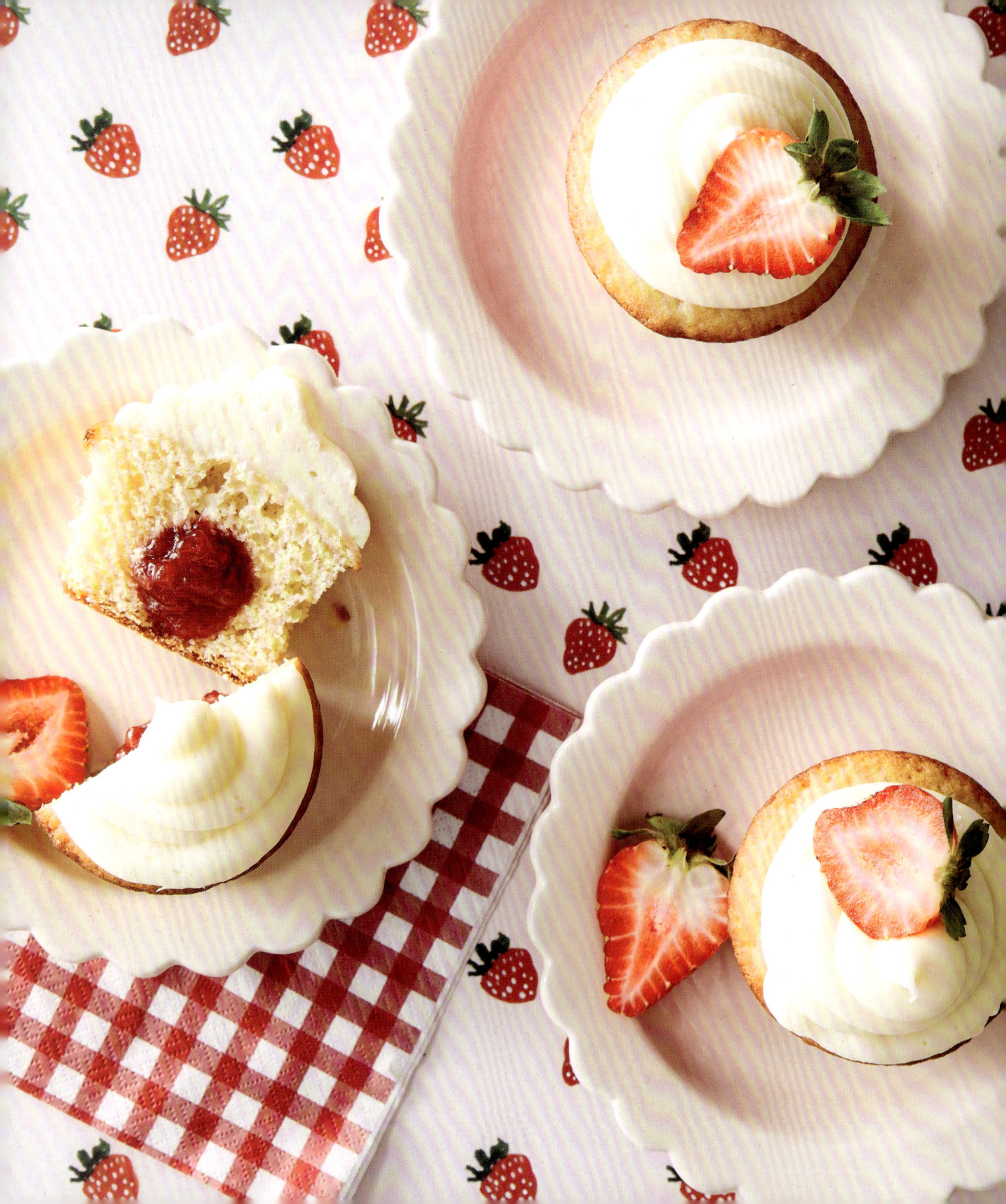

Strawberries & Cream Cupcakes

Give classic vanilla cupcakes a fruity, creamy makeover by adding some strawberry jam inside, then topping them with a swirl of irresistible cream cheese frosting and a fresh strawberry. These taste best during summer, when berries are in season.

MAKES 12 CUPCAKES

FOR THE CUPCAKES

1¼ cups all-purpose flour

1¼ teaspoons baking powder

¼ teaspoon salt

¾ cup sugar

6 tablespoons (¾ stick) unsalted butter, at room temperature

2 large eggs

1 teaspoon vanilla extract

⅓ cup whole milk

¼ cup strawberry jam or preserves

Cream Cheese Frosting (page 263)

12 strawberries

Preheat the oven to 350°F. Line a standard 12-cup muffin pan with paper or foil liners.

In a medium bowl, whisk together the flour, baking powder, and salt. In a large bowl, using an electric mixer, beat the sugar and butter on medium-high speed until light and fluffy, 2 to 3 minutes. Add the eggs, one at a time, beating well after each addition. Turn off the mixer and scrape down the bowl with a rubber spatula. Add the vanilla and beat until combined. Add about half of the flour mixture and mix on low speed just until blended. Add the milk and mix on low speed until combined. Add the remaining flour mixture and mix just until blended. Turn off the mixer, scrape down the bowl, and give the batter a final stir with the spatula.

Divide the batter evenly among the prepared muffin cups. Drop 1 teaspoon jam onto the center of each (the jam will sink into the batter during baking). Bake until the tops are light golden brown and a wooden skewer inserted into the center of a cupcake comes out with only a few crumbs and some jam attached, 18 to 20 minutes. Let the cupcakes cool in the pan on a wire rack for 10 minutes, then carefully transfer the cupcakes directly to the rack. Let cool completely, about 1 hour. While the cupcakes cool, make the frosting.

Using a small icing spatula or a butter knife, or a piping bag fitted with a large round tip, top the cupcakes with frosting and place a strawberry in the center.

Snowball Cupcakes

These tender vanilla treats are covered in shredded coconut, so they look like fluffy snowballs—but they taste way yummier! You can color the frosting and the coconut by mixing a few drops of food coloring into each before decorating the cupcakes.

MAKES 24 CUPCAKES

2¾ cups all-purpose flour

2 tablespoons cornstarch

1 tablespoon baking powder

⅛ teaspoon salt

1½ cups sugar

¾ cup (1½ sticks) unsalted butter, at room temperature

3 large eggs

¾ cup whole milk

½ cup water

1 tablespoon vanilla extract

Cream Cheese Frosting (page 263)

2 cups shredded sweetened coconut

Preheat the oven to 350°F. Line two standard 12-cup muffin pans with paper or foil liners.

In a medium bowl, whisk together the flour, cornstarch, baking powder, and salt. In a large bowl, using an electric mixer, beat the sugar and the butter on medium-high speed until fluffy and pale, about 3 minutes. Add the eggs, one at a time, beating well after adding each one. Turn off the mixer and scrape down the bowl with a rubber spatula. Add the milk, water, and vanilla and beat until combined. Turn off the mixer and scrape down the bowl. Add half of the flour mixture and mix on low speed just until blended. Turn off the mixer. Add the rest of the flour mixture and mix just until blended. Scrape down the bowl.

Divide the batter evenly among the prepared muffin cups, filling them about two-thirds full. Put the pans in the oven and bake until a toothpick inserted into the center of a cupcake comes out clean (ask an adult for help!), 18 to 20 minutes. Ask an adult to help you remove the pans from the oven and set them on wire racks. Let the cupcakes cool in the pans for 10 minutes, then lift them out and set them directly on the racks. Let cool completely.

Using a small icing spatula or a butter knife, frost the cupcakes. Sprinkle them with the shredded coconut and serve.

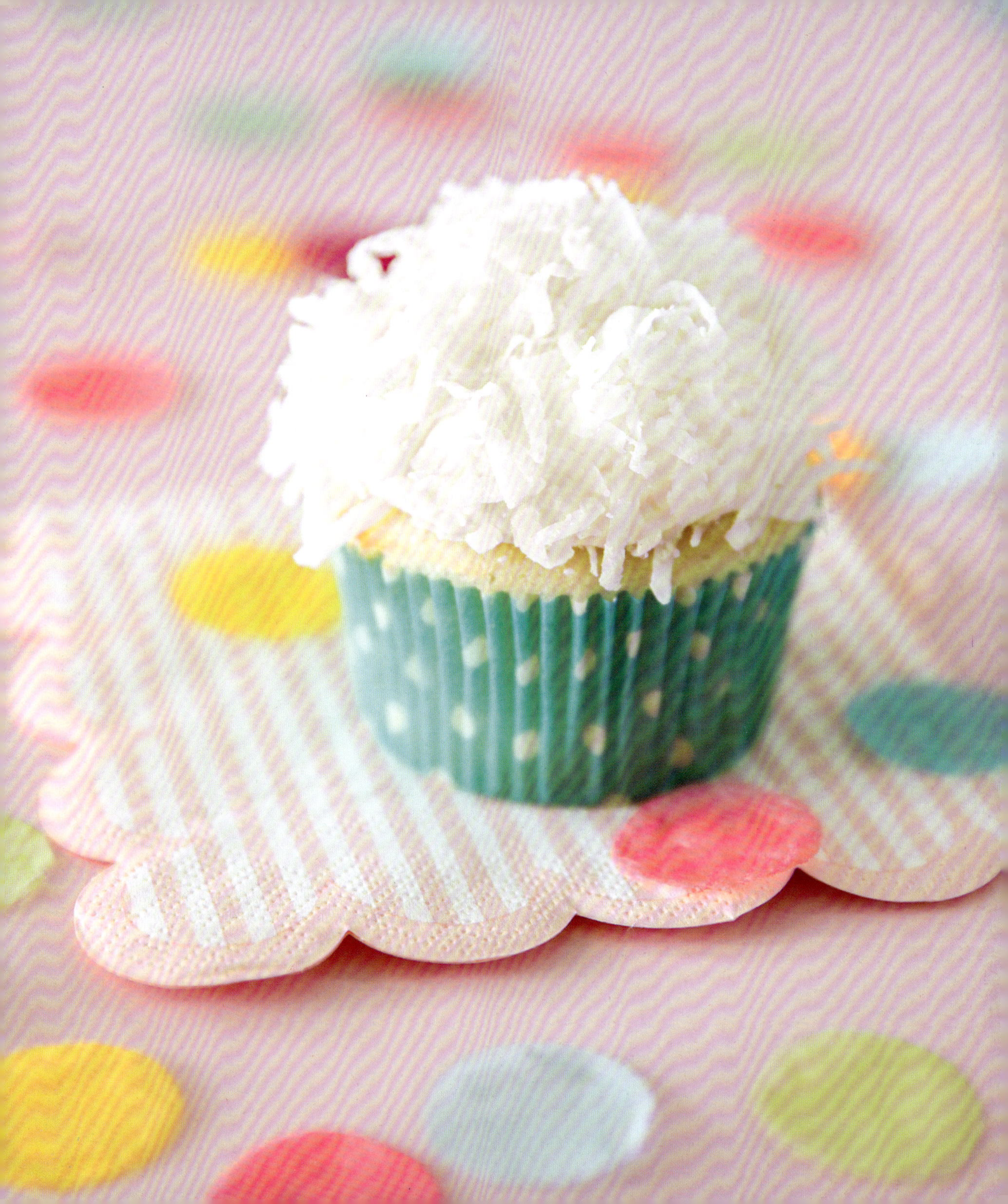

Frilly fun
Decorate your cupcakes with fun, colorful toothpick flags, pinwheels, and other cute toppers.

Sweet Lemony Cupcakes

These cupcakes are sweet, tart, and perfect for enjoying in the summer sunshine. Bake up a batch or two to sell at your lemonade stand and you'll have customers coming back for more!

MAKES 24 CUPCAKES

CUPCAKES

2¼ cups all-purpose flour

1½ teaspoons baking powder

¾ teaspoon salt

5 teaspoons poppy seeds

¾ cup (1½ sticks) unsalted butter, at room temperature

1½ cups granulated sugar

2 teaspoons finely grated lemon zest

2 large eggs

¾ cup whole milk

GLAZE

2 cups powdered sugar, sifted

3 tablespoons lemon juice

Yellow decorating sugar or white and yellow sprinkles, for decorating

Preheat the oven to 325°F. Line 2 standard 12-cup muffin pans.

To make the cupcakes, in a bowl, whisk together the flour, baking powder, salt, and poppy seeds. In a large bowl, using an electric mixer, beat the butter, granulated sugar, and lemon zest on medium-high speed until fluffy and pale, about 3 minutes. Add the eggs one at a time, beating well after adding each one. Turn off the mixer and scrape down the bowl with a rubber spatula. Add half of the flour mixture and mix on low speed just until blended. Turn off the mixer. Pour in the milk and mix on low speed until combined. Turn off the mixer. Add the rest of the flour mixture and mix just until blended. Turn off the mixer and scrape down the bowl.

Divide the batter evenly among the muffin cups, filling each three-fourths full. Bake until golden brown and a wooden skewer inserted into the center of a cupcake comes out clean (ask an adult for help!), 18 to 20 minutes. Ask an adult to help you remove the pans from the oven and set them on wire racks. Let the cupcakes cool for 10 minutes, then transfer them to the racks. Let cool.

To make the icing, in a bowl, whisk together the powdered sugar and lemon juice. Spoon some icing on top of each cooled cupcake and use the back of the spoon to spread it to the edge. Let the icing stand for a minute, until it smooths out. While the icing is soft, sprinkle the cupcakes with the sugar or sprinkles. Don't wait too long or the icing will harden and the decorations won't stick! Let the icing dry for about 20 minutes and serve.

White Chocolate & Raspberry Cupcakes

These sweet, berry-licious cupcakes are decorated with powdered sugar, not frosting, so they're perfect for taking on a picnic or packing in a lunchbox. If you like, you can stir in chopped strawberries or blackberries instead of raspberries.

MAKES 12 CUPCAKES

1¼ cups all-purpose flour

1½ teaspoon baking powder

⅛ teaspoon salt

⅔ cup granulated sugar

4 tablespoons (½ stick) unsalted butter, at room temperature

1 large egg

1 teaspoon vanilla extract

½ cup whole milk

½ cup white chocolate chips

1 cup raspberries, halved if large

Powdered sugar, for dusting

Preheat the oven to 350°F. Line a standard 12-cup muffin pan.

In a medium bowl, whisk together the flour, baking powder, and salt. In a large bowl, using an electric mixer, beat the granulated sugar and butter on medium-high speed until fluffy and pale, about 3 minutes. Add the egg and vanilla and beat until combined. Turn off the mixer and scrape down the bowl with a rubber spatula. Add half of the flour mixture and mix on low speed just until blended. Turn off the mixer. Pour in the milk and mix on low speed just until combined. Turn off the mixer. Add the rest of the flour mixture and mix just until blended. Turn off the mixer. Add the white chocolate chips and stir gently with the rubber spatula, then add the raspberries and stir gently just until combined.

Divide the batter evenly among the prepared muffin cups, filling each about three-fourths full. Bake until lightly golden and a wooden skewer inserted into the center of a cupcake comes out clean (ask an adult for help!), 18 to 20 minutes. Ask an adult to help you remove the pan from the oven and set it on a wire rack. Let the cupcakes cool in the pan for 10 minutes, then lift them out and set them directly on the rack. Let cool completely.

Put the powdered sugar in a fine-mesh sieve and dust the cupcakes with sugar. Serve right away.

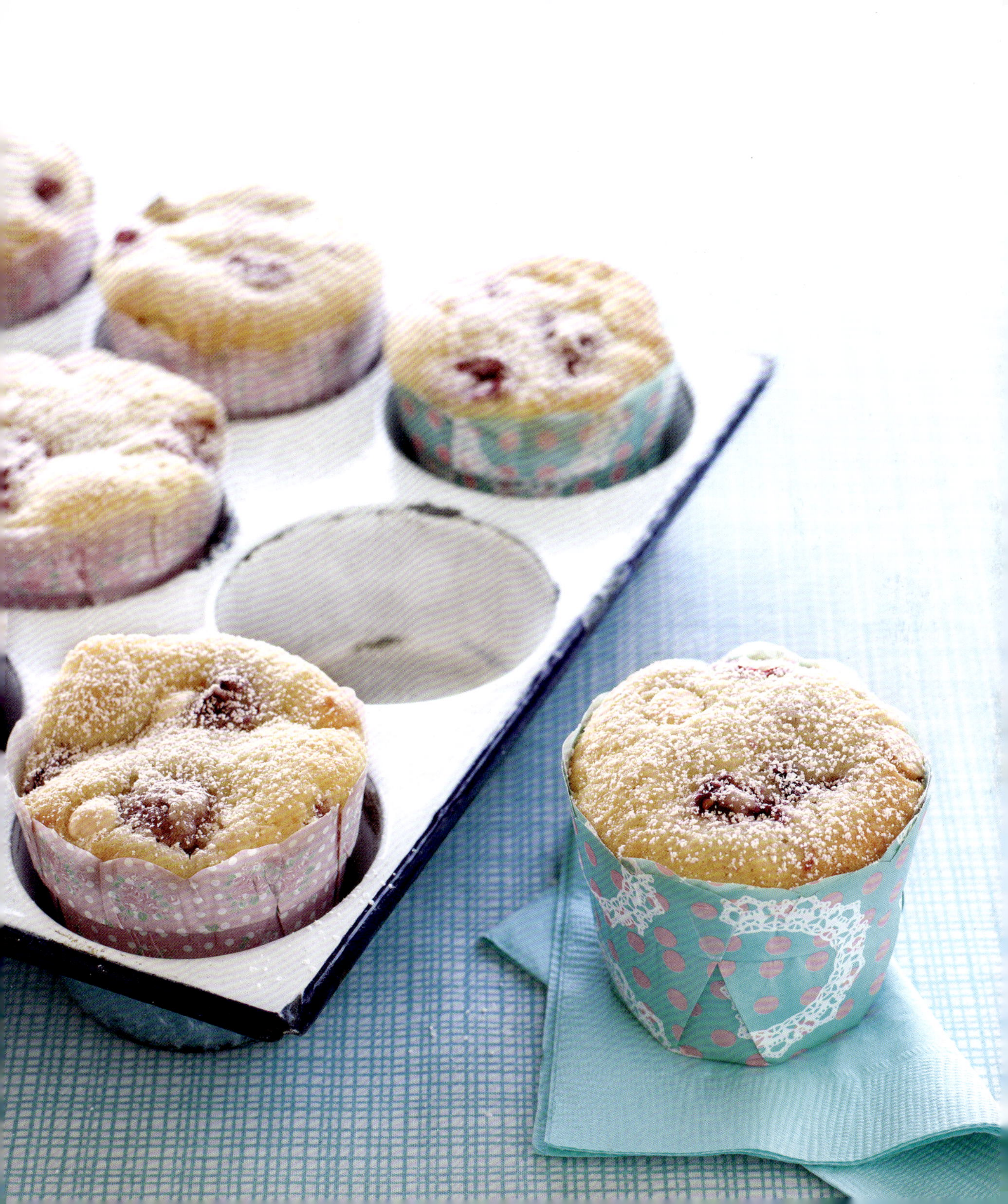

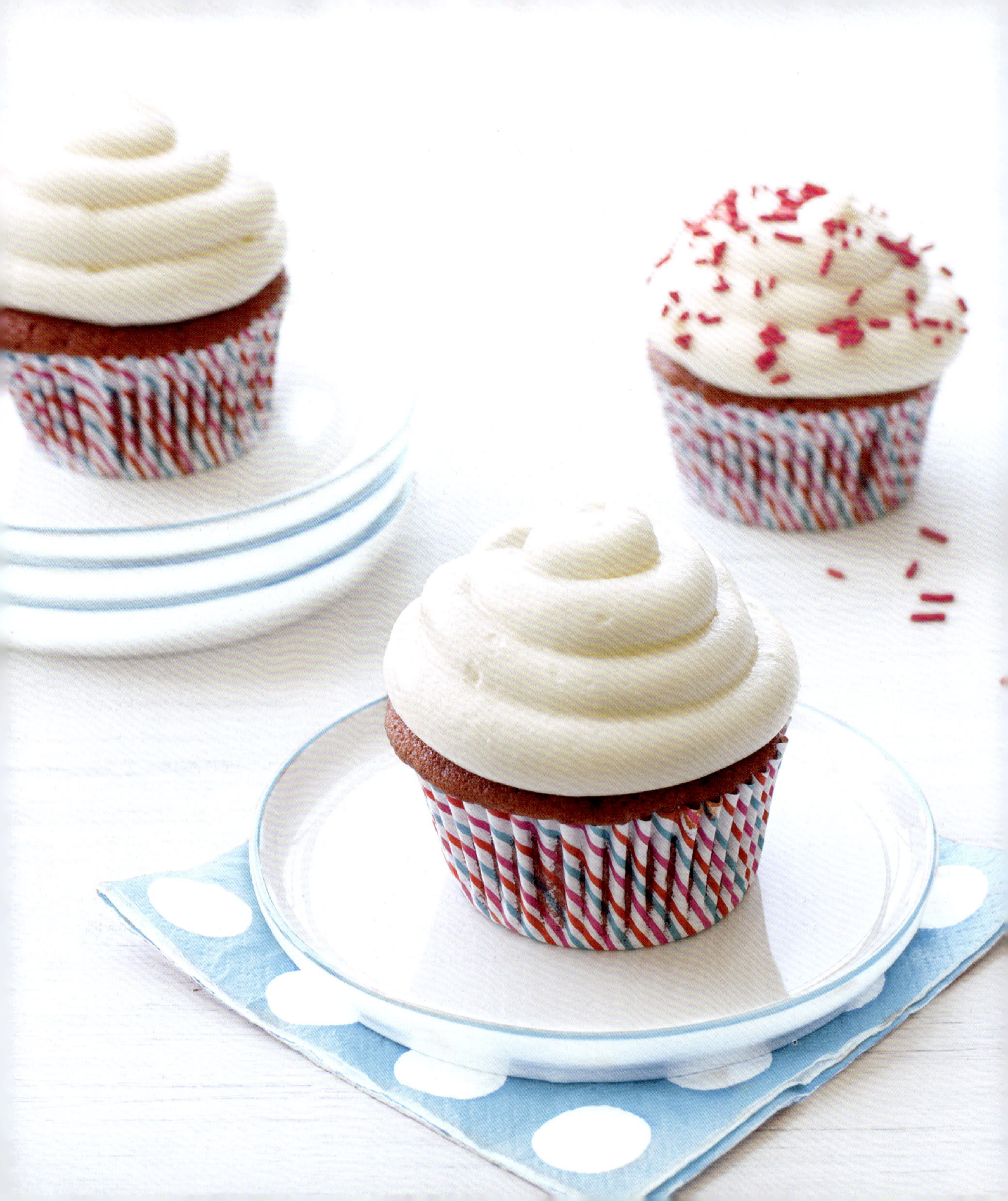

Red Velvet Cupcakes

These red velvet cupcakes have just a hint of cocoa and get their jewel-like red color from a little food coloring. Piled high with cream cheese frosting, these festive treats are ready for a party!

MAKES 18 CUPCAKES

2 tablespoons unsweetened cocoa powder, sifted

⅓ cup boiling water

1 cup buttermilk

12 tablespoons (1½ sticks) unsalted butter, at room temperature

1½ cups sugar

3 large eggs

2 to 3 teaspoons red food coloring

2 teaspoons vanilla extract

¼ teaspoon salt

2½ cups all-purpose flour

1½ teaspoons baking soda

1 teaspoon white vinegar

Cream Cheese Frosting (page 263)

Preheat the oven to 350°F. Line 18 cups (of two 12-cup muffin pans).

In a heatproof bowl, whisk together the cocoa and the boiling water, then whisk in the buttermilk. In a large bowl, using an electric mixer, beat the butter and sugar on medium-high speed until fluffy and pale, about 3 minutes. Add the eggs one at a time, beating well after adding each one. Add the food coloring, vanilla, and salt and beat until combined. Turn off the mixer and scrape down the bowl with a rubber spatula. Add half of the flour and beat on low speed just until blended. Turn off the mixer. Pour in the buttermilk mixture and mix on low speed just until blended. Turn off the mixer. Add the remaining flour and mix just until blended. Turn off the mixer one last time and scrape down the bowl. In a small bowl, stir together the baking soda and vinegar, then quickly stir the mixture into the batter with the rubber spatula.

Divide the batter among the prepared muffin cups, filling them about three-fourths full. Put the pans in the oven and bake until a wooden skewer inserted into the center of a cupcake comes out clean (ask an adult for help!), about 18 minutes. Ask an adult to help you remove the pans from the oven and set them on wire racks. Let the cupcakes cool in the pans for 10 minutes, then transfer them to the racks. Let cool completely.

Using a small icing spatula or a butter knife (or a piping bag), frost the cupcakes and serve.

PB & J Cupcakes

Inspired by peanut butter and jelly sandwiches, these jam-filled vanilla cupcakes are topped with peanut butter frosting. Add one to your lunchbox for a sweet treat!

MAKES 12 CUPCAKES

CUPCAKES

1¼ cups all-purpose flour

1¼ teaspoons baking powder

¼ teaspoon salt

¾ cup granulated sugar

6 tablespoons (¾ stick) unsalted butter, at room temperature

2 large eggs

1 teaspoon vanilla extract

⅓ cup whole milk

PB FROSTING

6 tablespoons (¾ stick) unsalted butter, at room temperature

¾ cup smooth peanut butter

¾ cup powdered sugar, sifted

¼ cup heavy cream

¾ cup fruit jam or preserves

Preheat the oven to 350°F. Line a standard 12-cup muffin pan.

To make the cupcakes, in a bowl, whisk together the flour, baking powder, and salt. In another bowl, using an electric mixer, beat the granulated sugar and butter on medium-high speed until fluffy and pale, about 3 minutes. Add the eggs and vanilla and beat until combined. Turn off the mixer and scrape down the bowl with a rubber spatula. Add half of the flour mixture and mix on low speed just until blended. Turn off the mixer. Pour in the milk and mix on low speed just until combined. Turn off the mixer. Add the rest of the flour mixture and mix just until blended. Scrape down the bowl.

Divide the batter evenly among the prepared muffin cups, filling each about three-fourths full. Bake until lightly golden and a wooden skewer inserted into the center of a cupcake comes out clean (ask an adult for help!), 18 to 20 minutes. Ask an adult to help you remove the pan from the oven and set it on a wire rack. Let the cupcakes cool in the pan for 10 minutes, then transfer them to the rack. Let cool completely.

To make the frosting, in a bowl, using an electric mixer, beat the butter, peanut butter, powdered sugar, and cream on medium-low speed until smooth and combined, about 2 minutes. Ask an adult to help you use a serrated knife and halve each cupcake horizontally. Spread about 1 tablespoon of jam on each cupcake bottom, then replace the tops. Using a small icing spatula or a butter knife, frost the cupcakes and serve.

Yellow Cupcakes

These cupcakes are the classic choice for birthday parties, but they're perfect for any occasion. Choose between a gooey chocolate frosting and a smooth chocolate glaze, then decorate them with oodles of sprinkles.

MAKES 24 CUPCAKES

2¾ cups cake flour

1 tablespoon baking powder

½ teaspoon salt

1 cup (2 sticks) unsalted butter, at room temperature

1¾ cups sugar

4 large eggs, plus 2 large egg yolks

2 teaspoons vanilla extract

1 cup sour cream

Chocolate Frosting (page 264) or Rich Chocolate Glaze (page 267)

Sprinkles, for decorating (optional)

Preheat the oven to 350°F. Line 24 cups of two standard muffin pans with paper or foil liners.

In a medium bowl, whisk together the flour, baking powder, and salt. In a large bowl, using an electric mixer, beat the butter and sugar on medium-high speed until light and fluffy, 2 to 3 minutes. Add the eggs and yolks one at a time, beating well after each addition. Turn off the mixer and scrape down the bowl with a rubber spatula. Add the vanilla and beat until combined. Add about half of the flour mixture and mix on low speed just until blended. Add the sour cream and mix on low speed just until combined. Add the remaining flour mixture and mix just until blended.

Divide the batter evenly among the prepared muffin cups. Bake until the tops are light golden brown and a toothpick inserted into the center of a cupcake comes out clean, 22 to 24 minutes. Remove the pans from the oven and set them on a wire rack. Let cool for 10 minutes, then carefully transfer the cupcakes directly to the rack. Let cool completely, about 1 hour.

If decorating the cupcakes with chocolate frosting, use a small icing spatula or a butter knife, or a pastry bag fitted with a plain or star tip, top the cupcakes with the frosting, then decorate them with sprinkles (if using). If glazing the cupcakes, spoon the chocolate glaze over the cupcakes, then decorate them with sprinkles (if using).

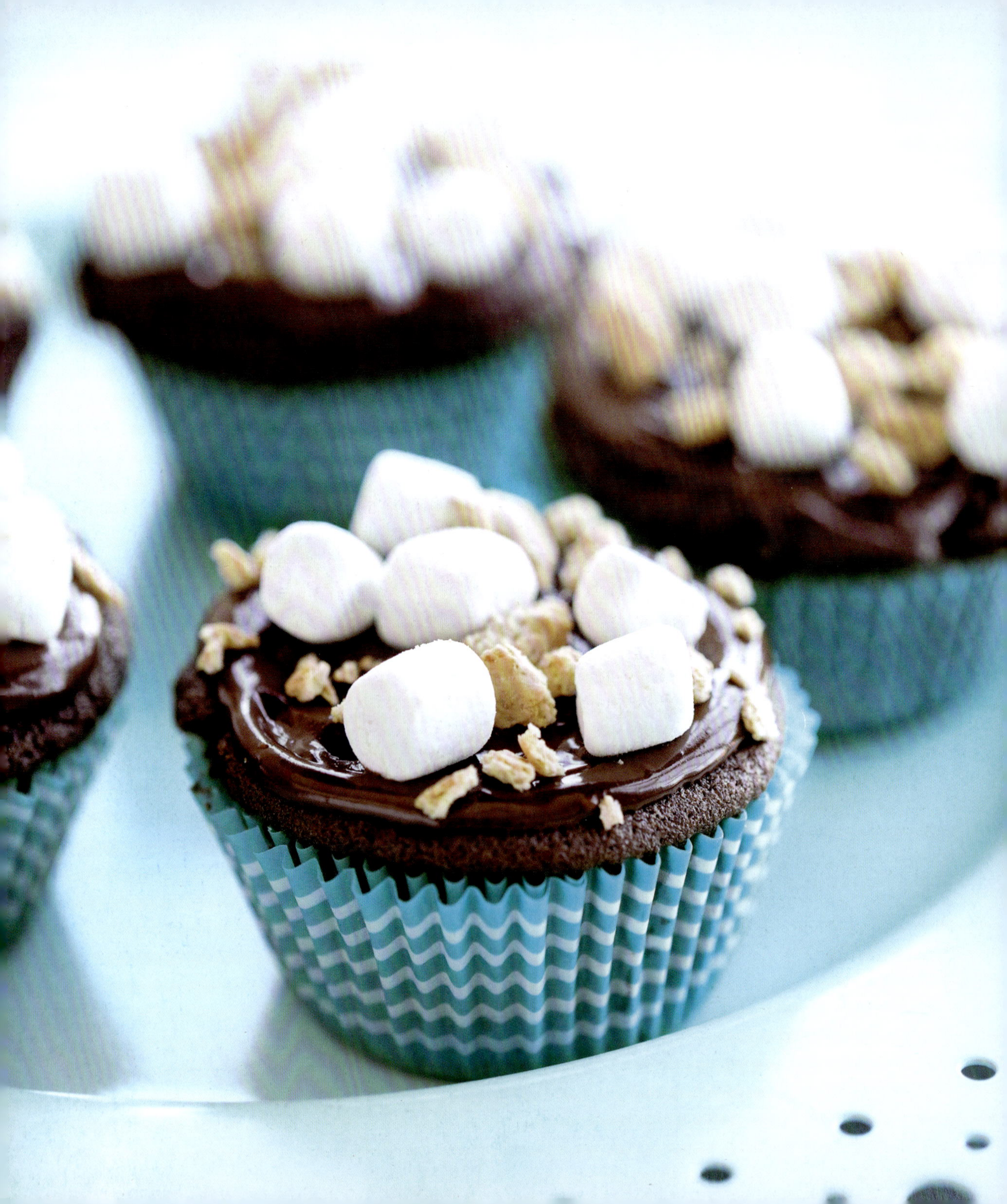

S'mores Cupcakes

No campfire? No problem! Here's a way to turn everyone's favorite camping treat into delicious oven-baked goodies. These rich chocolate cupcakes are loaded with mini marshmallows and crumbled graham crackers. Yum!

MAKES 18 CUPCAKES

1 cup all-purpose flour

¼ cup unsweetened cocoa powder, sifted

¾ teaspoon baking soda

¼ teaspoon salt

6 tablespoons (¾ stick) unsalted butter, at room temperature

½ cup granulated sugar

⅓ cup firmly packed light brown sugar

1 large egg

1 teaspoon vanilla extract

¾ cup buttermilk

⅔ cup roughly crumbled graham crackers (about 3 crackers), plus more for decorating

⅓ cup mini marshmallows, plus more for decorating

⅔ cup semisweet chocolate chips

Preheat the oven to 350°F. Line 18 cups (of two 12-cup muffin pans).

In a medium bowl, whisk together the flour, cocoa, baking soda, and salt. In another bowl, using an electric mixer, beat the butter and sugars on medium-high speed until fluffy and pale, about 3 minutes. Add the egg and vanilla and beat until combined. Turn off the mixer and scrape down the bowl with a rubber spatula. Add half of the flour mixture and mix on low speed just until blended. Turn off the mixer. Pour in the buttermilk and mix on low speed just until combined. Turn off the mixer. Add the rest of the flour mixture and mix just until blended. Turn off the mixer. Using a rubber spatula, stir in the graham crackers and marshmallows.

Divide the batter evenly among the prepared muffin cups, filling each about two-thirds full. Bake until a wooden skewer inserted into the center of a cupcake comes out clean (ask an adult for help!), 18 to 20 minutes. Ask an adult to help you remove the pans from the oven and set them on wire racks. Let the cupcakes cool for 10 minutes, then transfer them to the racks. Let cool.

Place the chocolate chips in a small microwave-safe bowl. Ask an adult to help you microwave the chocolate on high heat, stirring every 20 seconds, until it's melted and smooth. Don't let the chocolate get too hot!

Spread a thin layer of melted chocolate on each cupcake, then top with graham crackers and marshmallows. Let the chocolate set, then serve.

Pumpkin Cupcakes

Thick, tangy cream cheese frosting is the perfect topping for these delicious spiced cupcakes. Surprise your family and serve them for a winter holiday or bake them for a special autumn birthday party.

MAKES 12 CUPCAKES

1½ cups all-purpose flour

2 teaspoons baking powder

½ teaspoon baking soda

2 teaspoons ground cinnamon

1 teaspoon ground ginger

¼ teaspoon ground nutmeg

¼ teaspoon salt

½ cup (1 stick) unsalted butter, at room temperature

⅔ cup firmly packed light brown sugar

2 large eggs

½ cup canned pumpkin puree

½ cup sour cream

Cream Cheese Frosting (page 263)

Preheat the oven to 350°F. Line a standard 12-cup muffin pan with paper or foil liners.

In a medium bowl, whisk together the flour, baking powder, baking soda, cinnamon, ginger, nutmeg, and salt. In a large bowl, using an electric mixer, beat the butter and brown sugar on medium-high speed until fluffy, about 3 minutes. Add the eggs one at a time, beating well after adding each one. Turn off the mixer and scrape down the bowl with a rubber spatula. Add the pumpkin puree and sour cream and mix with the rubber spatula until blended. Add the flour mixture and stir with the rubber spatula just until blended. The batter will be thick.

Divide the batter evenly among the muffin cups, filling them nearly full. Bake until a wooden skewer inserted into the center of a cupcake comes out clean (ask an adult for help!), about 18 minutes. Ask an adult to help you remove the pan from the oven and set it on a wire rack. Let the cupcakes cool in the pan for 10 minutes, then lift them out and set them directly on the rack. Let cool completely.

Using a small icing spatula or a butter knife (or a piping bag), frost the cupcakes and serve.

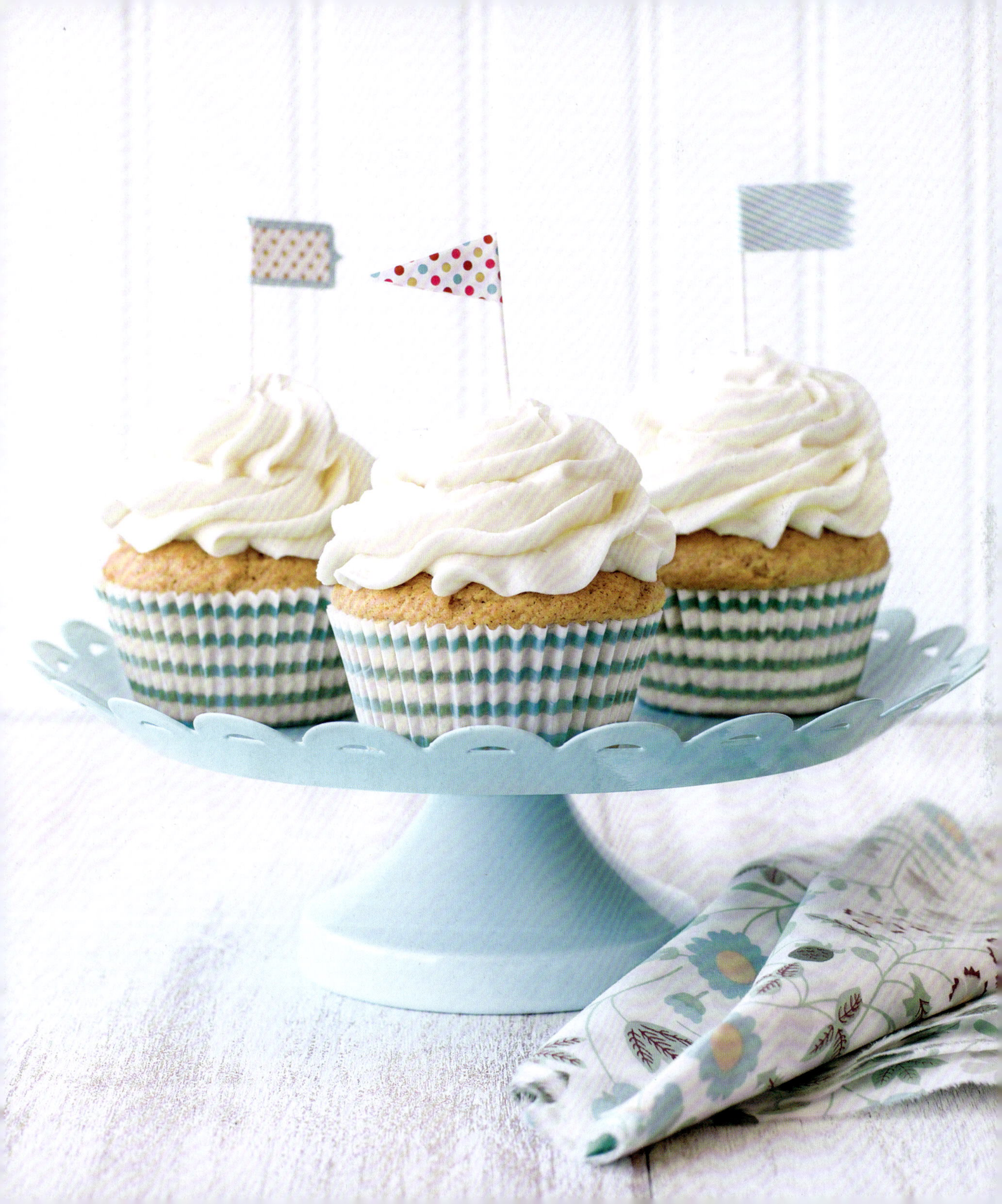

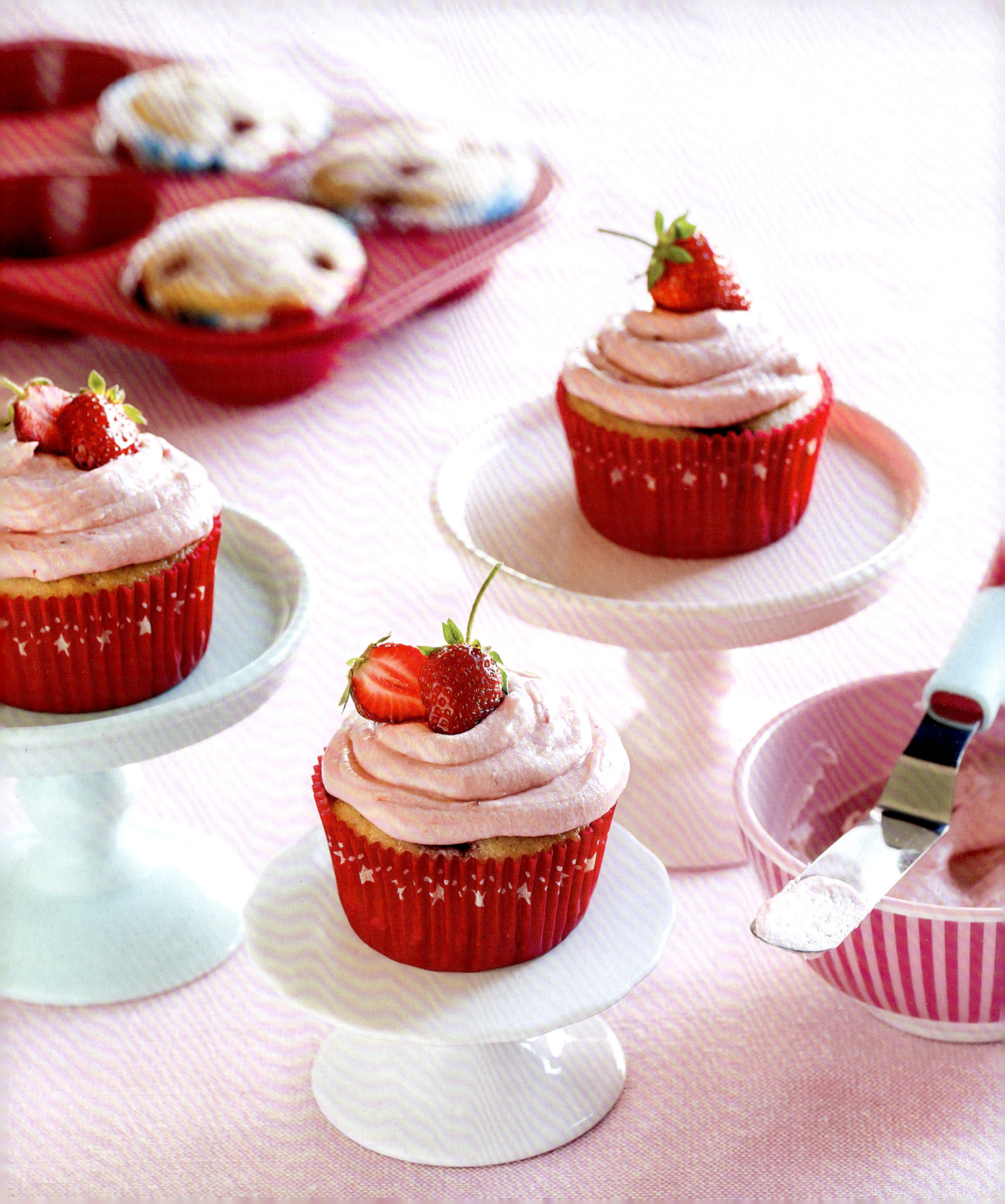

Strawberry Cupcakes

A triple dose of strawberries—in the cupcakes, frosting, and decorations—will make strawberry lovers really happy. If you want to punch up the pink color, add a few drops of red food coloring to the batter or buttercream.

MAKES 12 CUPCAKES

CUPCAKES

2 tablespoons strawberry jam

¼ cup finely chopped strawberries, plus 12 whole strawberries for garnish

1¼ cups all-purpose flour

1¼ teaspoons baking powder

¼ teaspoon salt

¾ cup granulated sugar

½ cup (1 stick) unsalted butter, at room temperature

3 large egg whites, at room temperature

½ teaspoon vanilla extract

4 drops red food coloring (optional)

⅓ cup whole milk

(See additional ingredients on page 164)

Preheat the oven to 350°F. Line a standard 12-cup muffin pan with paper or foil liners.

To make the cupcakes, in a small bowl, stir together the jam and chopped strawberries.

In a medium bowl, whisk together the flour, baking powder, and salt. In a large bowl, using an electric mixer, beat the granulated sugar and butter on medium-high speed until fluffy and pale, 2 to 3 minutes. Add the egg whites, vanilla, and red food coloring (if using), and beat until combined. Turn off the mixer and scrape down the bowl with a rubber spatula. Add about a third of the flour mixture and beat on low speed until just combined. Beat in half of the milk. Turn off the mixer. Add another third of the flour mixture and beat until just combined. Beat in the rest of the milk. Turn off the mixer. Add the rest of the flour mixture and beat until just combined. Fold in the strawberry jam mixture until just combined.

Divide the batter evenly among the prepared muffin cups, filling each about three-fourths full. Bake until lightly golden and a wooden skewer inserted in the center of a cupcake comes out clean, about 25 minutes. Remove the muffin pan from the oven and set it atop a wire rack. Let cool for 5 minutes, then carefully transfer the cupcakes directly to the rack. Let cool completely.

~ Continued on page 164 ~

> **Cupcakes for days!**
> *Refrigerate frosted cupcakes in an airtight container for up to 3 days. Bring to room temperature before serving.*

FROSTING

1 cup (2 sticks) unsalted butter, at room temperature

6 cups powdered sugar

1 tablespoon vanilla extract

¼ cup heavy cream

⅓ to ⅔ cup strawberry jam

6 drops red food coloring (optional)

~ *Continued from page 163* ~

While the cupcakes cool, make the frosting. In the bowl of a stand mixer fitted with the paddle attachment, or in a large bowl using an electric mixer, beat the butter on medium-high speed until fluffy and pale, about 2 minutes. Add half of the powdered sugar and beat until just combined. Add the vanilla and beat until smooth, about 1 minute. Turn off the mixer and scrape down the bowl with a rubber spatula. Add the cream and beat until thick and creamy, about 3 minutes. Turn off the mixer. Add the jam and red food coloring (if using), and beat until combined.

Using a small icing spatula or a butter knife, frost the cupcakes. Top each with a fresh strawberry and serve right away.

Chocolate-Banana Cream Pie Cupcakes

Banana cupcakes filled with vanilla cream and topped with chocolate glaze? Yes, please! For the best taste and texture, make sure your bananas are nice and ripe—they should be spotty brown and a little soft to the touch.

MAKES 18 CUPCAKES

BANANA CUPCAKES

2 cups all-purpose flour

2 teaspoons baking powder

½ teaspoon baking soda

½ teaspoon salt

½ cup (1 stick) unsalted butter, at room temperature

1¼ cups sugar

2 large eggs

1 teaspoon vanilla extract

2 ripe bananas, peeled and mashed (about 1 cup)

½ cup buttermilk

Vanilla Custard (page 269)

Rich Chocolate Glaze (page 267)

Chunk of dark chocolate, for decorating (optional)

To make the cupcakes, preheat the oven to 350°F. Line 18 cups of two standard muffin pans with paper or foil liners.

In a medium bowl, whisk together the flour, baking powder, baking soda, and salt. In a large bowl, using an electric mixer, beat the butter and sugar on medium-high speed until light and fluffy, 2 to 3 minutes. Add the eggs one at a time, beating well after each addition. Turn off the mixer and scrape down the bowl with a rubber spatula. Add the vanilla and bananas and beat until combined.

Turn off the mixer. Add half of the flour mixture and mix on low speed just until blended. Pour in the buttermilk and mix on low speed just until combined. Add the remaining flour mixture and mix on low speed just until blended. Turn off the mixer, scrape down the bowl, and give the batter a final stir with the spatula.

Divide the batter evenly among the prepared muffin cups. Bake until light golden brown and a toothpick inserted into the center of a cupcake comes out clean, 18 to 20 minutes. Remove the pan from the oven and set it on a wire rack. Let cool for 10 minutes, then carefully transfer the cupcakes directly to the rack. Let cool completely, about 1 hour.

~ Continued on page 166 ~

Cool cupcakes

These cream-filled treats taste yummy straight from the refrigerator—no need to let them warm up before munching.

~ **Continued from page 165** ~

Using a paring knife, cut a 1½-inch-diameter round about 1 inch deep in the center of each cupcake, then remove the rounds and set them aside. Fill each hollow with about 1 teaspoon of vanilla custard. Cut the rounds that you removed from the cupcakes in half horizontally; reserve the tops and discard—or eat!—the rest. Return the tops to the cupcakes, covering the filling, then gently press down on each to fit it into the hole.

Spoon the chocolate glaze over the cupcakes. If decorating with chocolate, use a vegetable peeler to shave the chunk of chocolate over the cupcakes, letting the shavings fall onto the glaze. Place the cupcakes on a rimmed baking sheet and refrigerate until the glaze is set, about 10 minutes.

Chocolate Éclair Cupcakes

Follow the recipe for Chocolate-Banana Cream Pie Cupcakes, swapping in vanilla-flavored cupcakes (page 173) for the banana-flavored cupcakes.

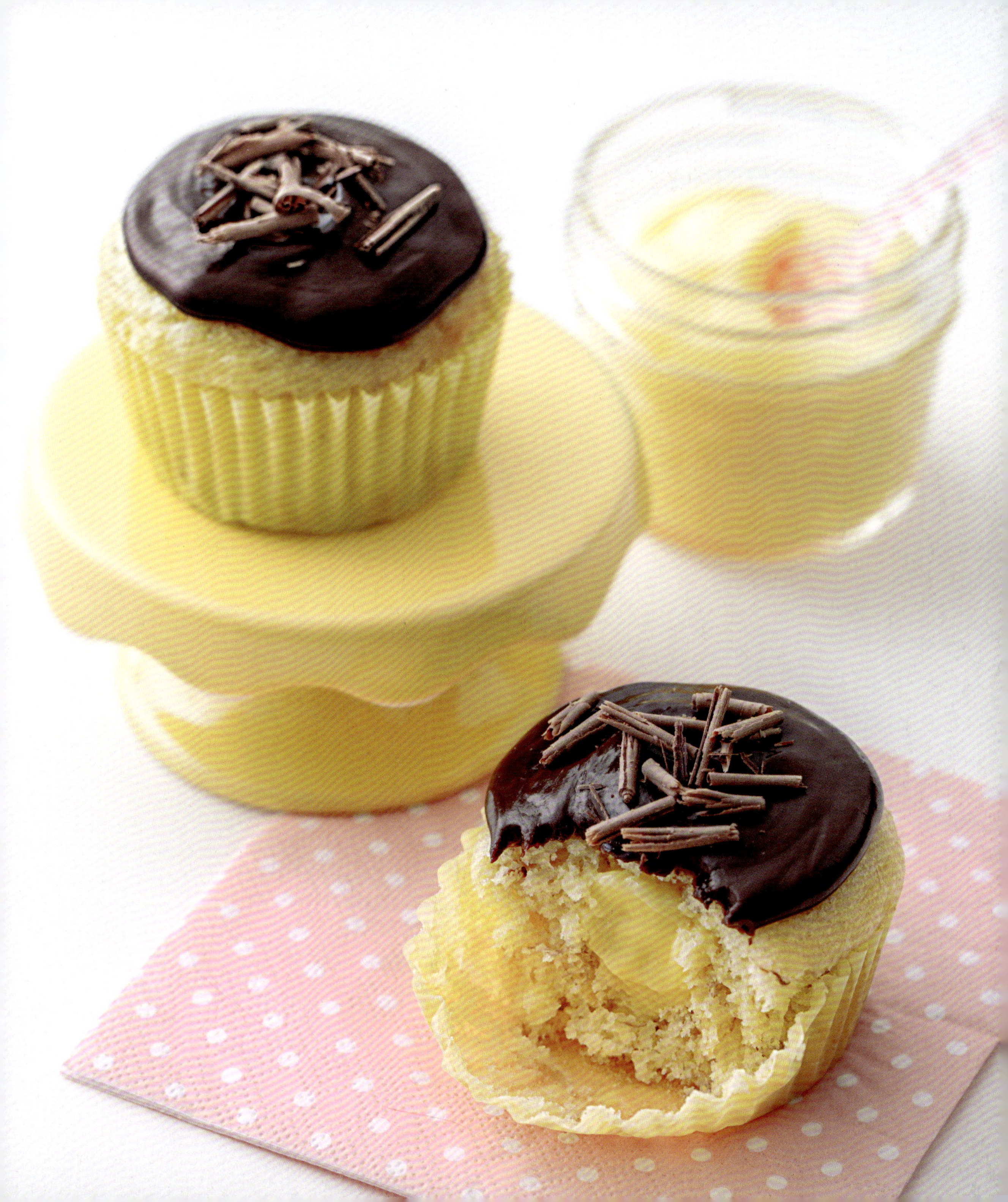

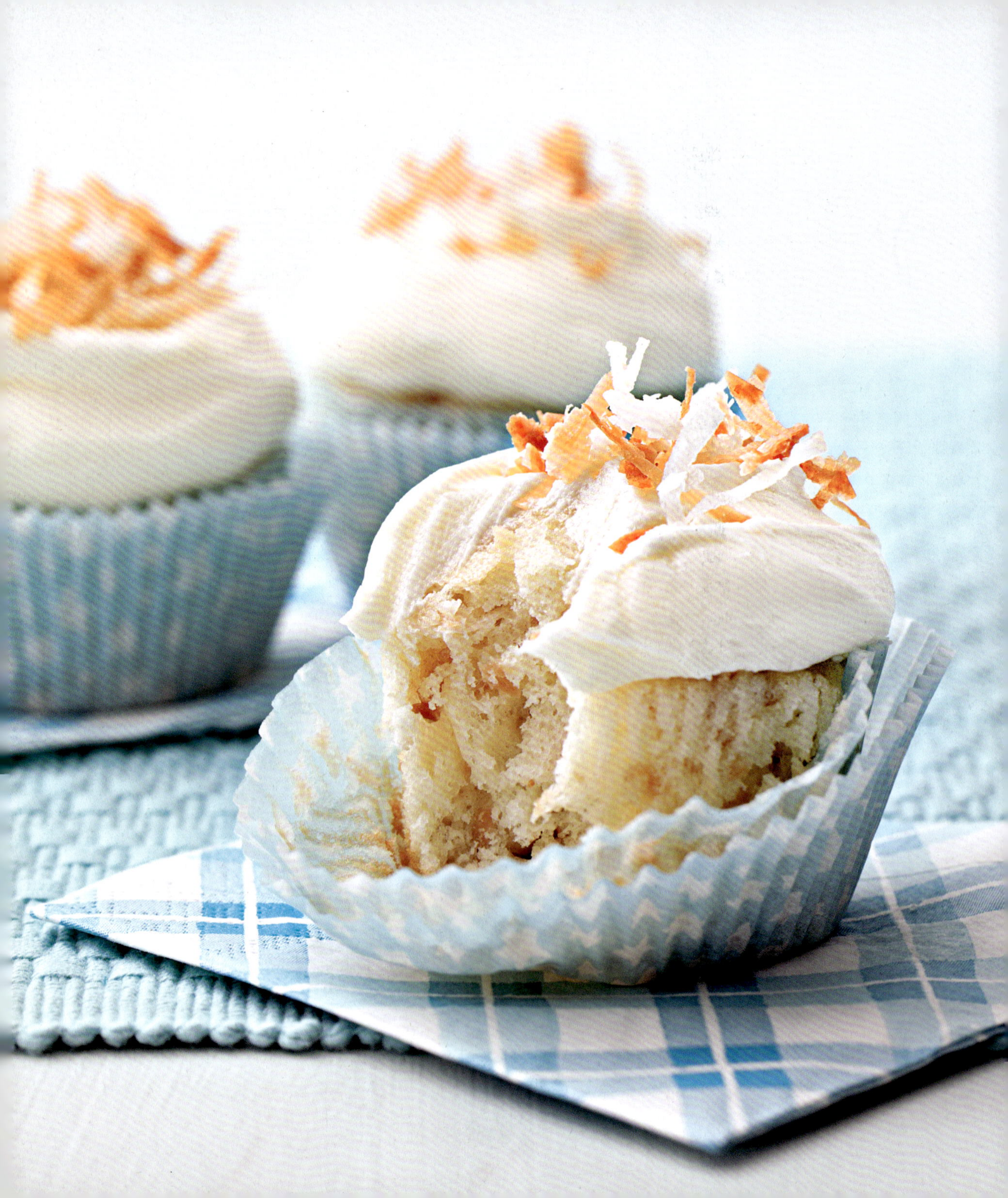

Toasted Coconut Cupcakes

If you love coconut, these cupcakes are for you. Toasting brings out coconut's sweet flavor and adds a pretty golden-brown tint to these scrumptious little cakes. Sprinkle toasted coconut on top of the frosting for a fun, easy, and delicious decoration.

MAKES 12 CUPCAKES

2 cups sweetened shredded coconut

1½ cups all-purpose flour

1¼ teaspoons baking powder

¼ teaspoon salt

¾ cup, plus 2 tablespoons sugar

½ cup (1 stick) unsalted butter, at room temperature

1 large egg, plus 1 large egg white

1 teaspoon vanilla extract

½ cup canned coconut milk

Fluffy Vanilla Frosting or Fluffy Coconut Frosting (page 260)

Preheat the oven to 350°F. Line a rimmed cookie sheet with parchment paper. Line a standard 12-cup muffin pan with paper or foil liners.

Spread the coconut in an even layer on the prepared cookie sheet. Bake until the coconut is golden brown at the edges, 5 to 7 minutes. Remove from the oven, set on a wire rack, and let cool completely.

In a medium bowl, whisk together the flour, baking powder, salt, and 1 cup of the toasted coconut. In a large bowl, using an electric mixer, beat the sugar and butter on medium-high speed until light and fluffy, 2 to 3 minutes. Add the egg, egg white, and vanilla and beat until combined. Turn off the mixer and scrape down the bowl with a rubber spatula. Add half of the flour mixture and mix on low speed just until blended. Pour in the coconut milk and mix on low speed just until combined. Add the remaining flour mixture and mix on low speed just until blended. Turn off the mixer and scrape down the bowl. Divide the batter evenly among the prepared muffin cups. Bake until the tops are light golden brown and a toothpick inserted into the center of a cupcake comes out clean, 18 to 20 minutes. Remove the pan from the oven and set it on a wire rack. Let cool for 10 minutes, then carefully transfer the cupcakes directly to the rack. Let cool completely, about 1 hour.

Using a small icing spatula or a butter knife, or a pastry bag fitted with a large plain tip, top the cupcakes with the frosting. Sprinkle with the remaining toasted coconut, dividing it evenly.

Pink Velvet Cupcakes

This playful and pretty take on red velvet cake is flavored with strawberries inside and on top. Freeze-dried strawberries are sold in the same aisle as the dried fruits and nuts in most grocery stores, but if you can't find any, increase the flour in the batter to 2½ cups.

MAKES 20 CUPCAKES

2 tablespoons unsweetened cocoa powder, sifted

⅓ cup boiling water

1 cup buttermilk

1 cup freeze-dried strawberries

2 cups all-purpose flour

¼ teaspoon salt

¾ cup (1½ sticks) unsalted butter, at room temperature

1½ cups sugar

3 large eggs

2 teaspoons vanilla extract

Pink gel paste food coloring

1½ teaspoons baking soda

1 teaspoon white vinegar

Double recipe Strawberry–Cream Cheese Frosting (page 263)

Heart-shaped sprinkles, for decorating (optional)

Preheat the oven to 350°F. Line 20 cups of two standard 12-cup muffin pans with paper or foil liners.

In a medium heatproof bowl, whisk the cocoa and boiling water until well combined, then whisk in the buttermilk. Set aside.

Place the strawberries in a quart-size zipper-lock bag and seal the bag. Using a rolling pin or wooden spoon, crush the strawberries to a fine powder. In a small bowl, whisk together the flour, salt, and strawberry powder.

In a large bowl, using an electric mixer, beat the butter and sugar on medium speed until light and fluffy, 2 to 3 minutes. Add the eggs one at a time, beating well after each addition. Add the vanilla and 3 dabs of food coloring and beat until combined. Add half of the flour mixture and mix on low speed just until blended. Pour in the cocoa-buttermilk mixture and mix on low speed until combined. Add the remaining flour mixture and beat just until blended. In a small bowl, stir together the baking soda and vinegar, then quickly add the mixture to the batter and stir with a rubber spatula until combined.

Divide the batter evenly among the prepared muffin cups. Bake until a toothpick inserted into the center of a cupcake comes out clean, about 18 minutes. Remove the pans from the oven and let cool on a wire rack for 10 minutes, then transfer the cupcakes to the rack to cool completely, about 1 hour.

Using a pastry bag fitted with a star tip, frost the cupcakes, then decorate them with sprinkles (if using).

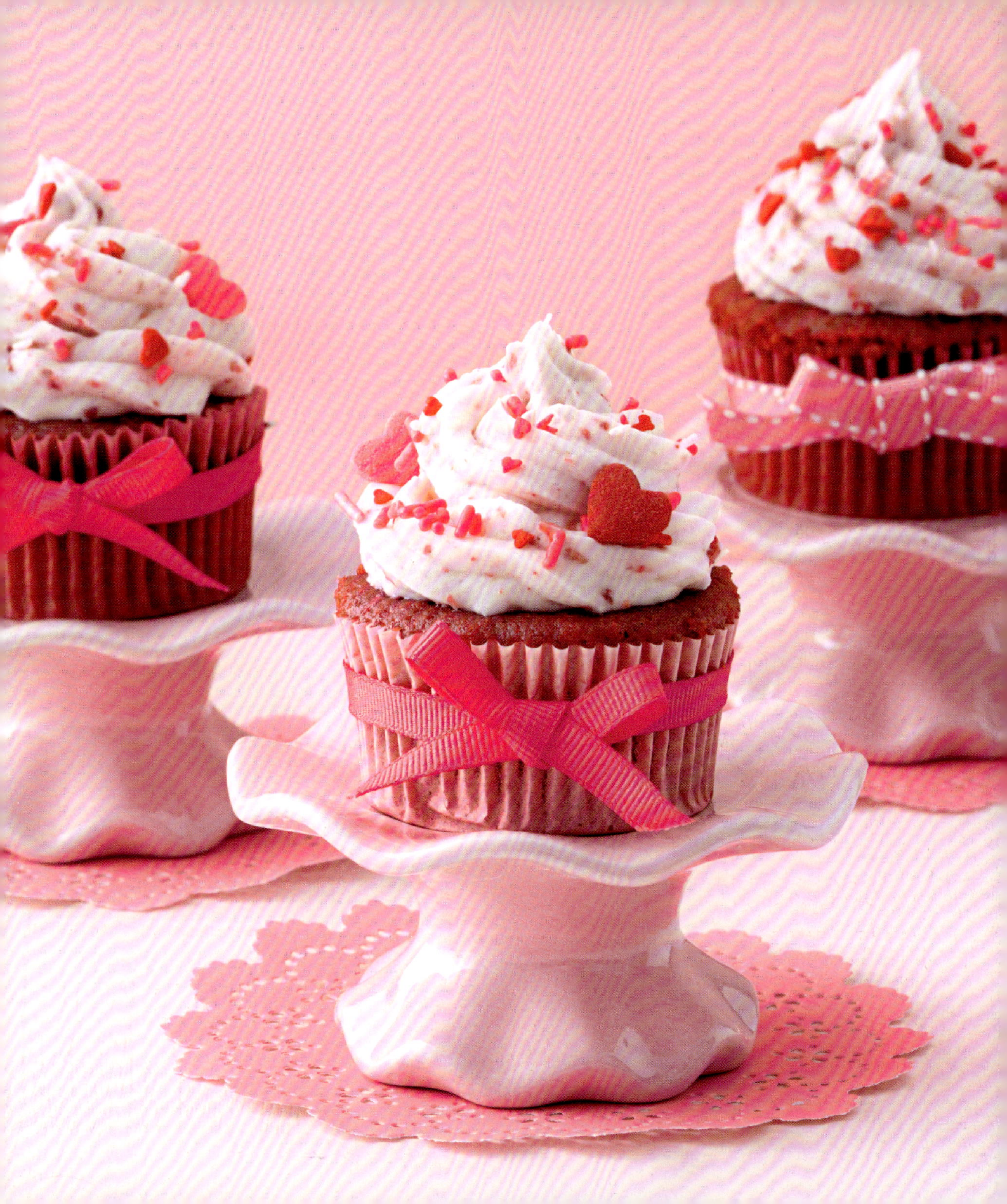

Sweet swoops
Use a small icing spatula to create the soft, natural-looking swirls of frosting on these cupcakes.

Snow White Cupcakes

All-white decorations on snowy mounds of frosting give these vanilla cupcakes an angelic look, but if you like, use bold, colorful sprinkles instead. Buttermilk in the batter makes them super moist and tender.

MAKES 18 CUPCAKES

2 cups all-purpose flour

2 teaspoons baking powder

½ teaspoon baking soda

½ teaspoon salt

½ cup, plus 2 tablespoons (1¼ sticks) unsalted butter, at room temperature

1 cup sugar

2 large eggs

2 teaspoons vanilla extract

1⅓ cups buttermilk

Fluffy Vanilla Frosting (page 260)

Edible white pearl beads and/or white sanding sugar, for decorating

Preheat the oven to 375°F. Line 18 cups of two standard muffin pans with paper or foil liners.

In a medium bowl, whisk together the flour, baking powder, baking soda, and salt. In a large bowl, using an electric mixer, beat the butter and sugar on medium-high speed until light and fluffy, 2 to 3 minutes. Add the eggs one at a time, beating well after each addition. Turn off the mixer and scrape down the bowl with a rubber spatula. Add the vanilla and beat until combined. Turn off the mixer. Add about half of the flour mixture and mix on low speed just until blended. Pour in the buttermilk and mix on low speed until combined. Add the remaining flour mixture and mix just until blended. Turn off the mixer, scrape down the bowl, and give the batter a final stir with the spatula. The batter will be thick.

Divide the batter evenly among the prepared muffin cups. Bake until the tops are light golden brown and a toothpick inserted into the center of a cupcake comes out clean, about 17 minutes. Remove the pans from the oven and set them on a wire rack. Let cool for 10 minutes, then carefully transfer the cupcakes directly to the rack. Let cool completely, about 1 hour.

Using a small icing spatula or a butter knife, or a pastry bag fitted with a large plain tip, top the cupcakes with the frosting, then decorate them with edible beads and/or sparkling sugar.

Cookies 'n' Cream Cupcakes

Have you ever had a cookie in your cupcake? A chocolate sandwich cookie hides at the bottom of each of these sweet treats, and crushed cookies add crunchy bites to the vanilla frosting for the ultimate cookies 'n' cream dream.

MAKES 16 CUPCAKES

24 chocolate-creme sandwich cookies

Devil's Food Cupcakes (page 144), prepared through step 2; omit the chocolate glaze and sugared flowers

Fluffy Vanilla Frosting (page 260)

Preheat the oven to 350°F. Line 16 cups of two standard muffin pans with paper or foil liners. Place 1 cookie in the bottom of each cup.

Divide the cupcake batter evenly among the muffin cups. Bake until a toothpick inserted into the center of a cupcake comes out clean, 18 to 20 minutes. Remove the pans from the oven and set them on a wire rack. Let cool for 10 minutes, then carefully transfer the cupcakes directly to the rack. Let cool completely, about 1 hour.

Place the remaining 8 cookies in a zipper-lock bag, seal the bag, and use a rolling pin or wooden spoon to crush the cookies to small pieces.

Place the frosting in a medium bowl, then add the cookie pieces. Beat on medium speed until well combined and the cookies are broken into coarse crumbs. If you will be piping the frosting onto the cupcakes, the cookie crumbs need to be fine enough to pass through the pastry tip.

Using a small icing spatula or a butter knife, or a pastry bag fitted with a plain tip (see page 9), top the cupcakes with the frosting.

Cookie-tastic
For an extra-crunchy cupcake, sprinkle big chunks of crushed cookies on top of the cookie frosting.

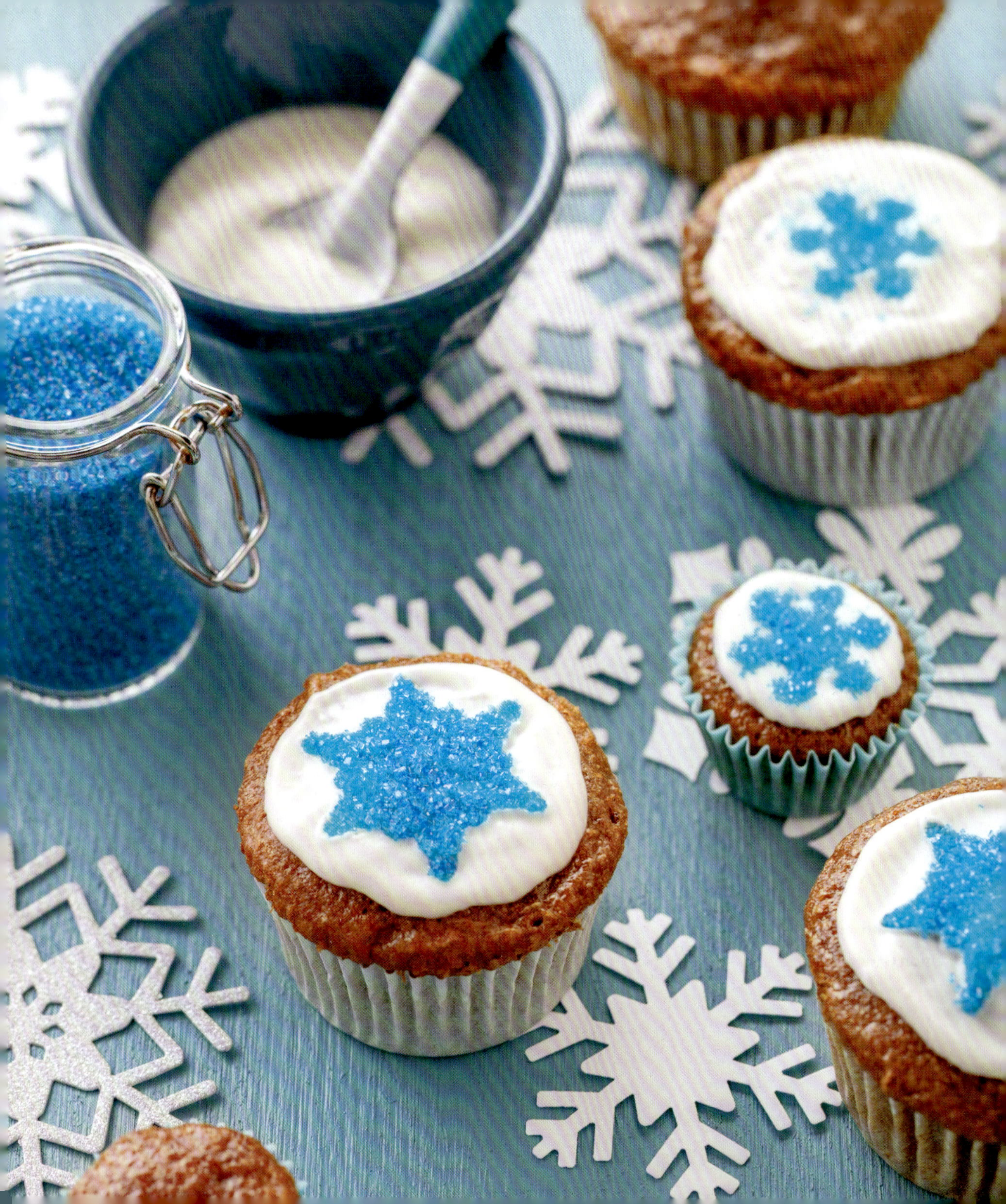

Gingerbread Cupcakes

As these cupcakes bake, they'll fill your kitchen with the amazing aroma of sweet, warm spices. You'll need a small snowflake cookie cutter to make a wintry design on these tasty treats, but if you don't have one, decorate the glazed cupcakes with sprinkles as you like.

MAKES 12 CUPCAKES

1¼ cups all-purpose flour

1¼ teaspoons baking powder

¼ teaspoon salt

1 teaspoon ground ginger

1 teaspoon ground cinnamon

¼ teaspoon ground allspice

Pinch of ground nutmeg

½ cup firmly packed light brown sugar

⅓ cup light molasses

4 tablespoons (½ stick) unsalted butter, at room temperature

1 large egg

2 teaspoons grated fresh ginger

⅓ cup whole milk

Lemon Glaze (page 267)

Blue sprinkles or sanding sugar, for decorating

Preheat the oven to 350°F. Line a standard 12-cup muffin pan with paper or foil liners.

In a medium bowl, whisk together the flour, baking powder, salt, ground ginger, cinnamon, allspice, and nutmeg. In a large bowl, using an electric mixer, beat the brown sugar, molasses, and butter on medium-high speed until light and fluffy, 2 to 3 minutes. Add the egg and fresh ginger and beat until combined. Turn off the mixer and scrape down the bowl with a rubber spatula. Add about half of the flour mixture and mix on low speed just until blended. Pour in the milk and mix on low speed until combined. Add the remaining flour mixture and mix just until blended. Turn off the mixer, scrape down the bowl, and give the batter a final stir with the spatula.

Divide the batter evenly among the prepared muffin cups. Bake until a toothpick inserted into the center of a cupcake comes out clean, 20 to 22 minutes. Remove the pan from the oven and set it on a wire rack. Let cool for 10 minutes, then carefully transfer the cupcakes directly to the rack. Let cool completely, about 1 hour.

Spoon the glaze onto the cupcakes and let dry for about 5 minutes. Place a small snowflake cookie cutter on top of a cupcake and carefully pour sprinkles or sanding sugar inside the cookie cutter until the glaze is covered. Carefully lift off the cookie cutter. Decorate the remaining cupcakes in the same way, then let them dry until the glaze is set, about 30 minutes.

Rainbow Cupcakes

Sky blue and topped with mini marshmallow clouds and rainbow sour belts, these almost too-cute-to-eat cupcakes will get all the attention at your tea party. Bake them in patterned or metallic blue foil liners for an extra dose of color.

MAKES 24 CUPCAKES

- 2¾ cups cake flour
- 1 tablespoon baking powder
- ½ teaspoon salt
- 1 cup (2 sticks) unsalted butter, at room temperature
- 1¾ cups sugar
- 4 large whole eggs
- 2 large egg yolks
- 2 teaspoons vanilla extract
- 1 cup sour cream
- 8 drops of blue food coloring
- Fluffy Frosting (page 260)
- Rainbow sour belts, for decorating
- Mini marshmallows, for decorating

Preheat the oven to 350°F. Line 2 standard 12-cup muffin pans with paper or foil liners.

In a medium bowl, whisk together the flour, baking powder, and salt. In a large bowl, using an electric mixer, beat together the butter and sugar on medium-high speed until light and fluffy, 2 to 3 minutes. Add the whole eggs and egg yolks one at a time, beating well after each addition. Turn off the mixer and scrape down the bowl. Add the vanilla and beat on medium-high speed until combined. Reduce the speed to low, add about half of the flour mixture, and mix just until blended. Add the sour cream and food coloring and beat just until combined. Add the remaining flour mixture and beat just until blended.

Divide the batter evenly among the prepared muffin cups. Bake the cupcakes until the tops are light golden brown and a wooden skewer inserted into the center of a cupcake comes out clean, 22 to 24 minutes. Let the cupcakes cool in the pans on wire racks for 10 minutes, then carefully transfer the cupcakes directly to the racks. Let cool completely, about 1 hour. While the cupcakes are cooling, make the frosting.

Using an icing spatula, spread the tops of the cupcakes with frosting. Cut the sour belts into twenty-four 2-inch lengths crosswise. Arc half of a sour belt like a rainbow and insert the ends into the frosting on each cupcake. Arrange marshmallows at the base of each arc to simulate clouds. Arrange the cupcakes on a large platter or tray and serve.

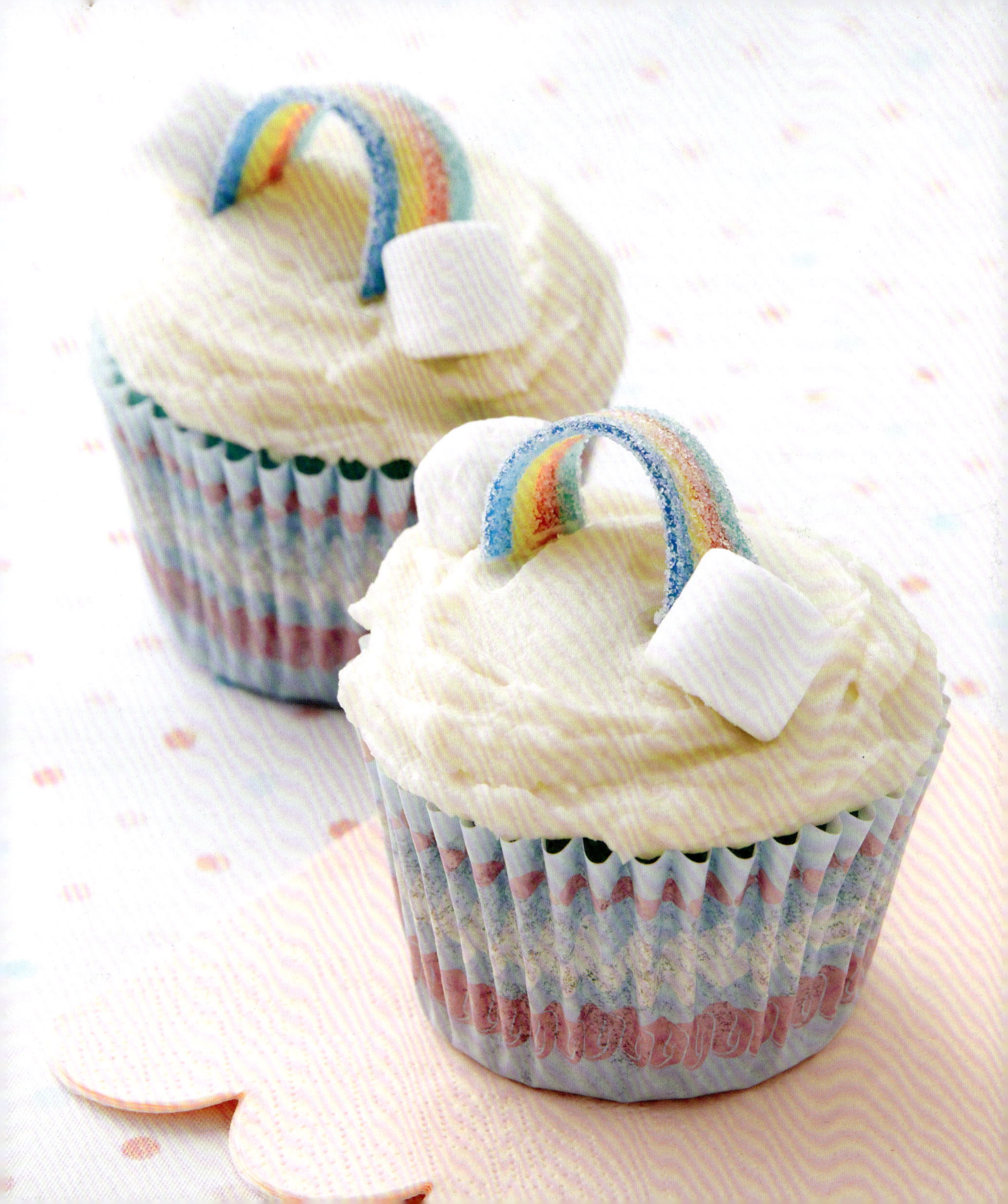

Triple Chocolate Cupcakes

Milk chocolate cupcakes filled with gooey dark chocolate and topped with white chocolate frosting are a chocolate lover's dream. To warm the glaze filling, heat it in a bowl set over, but not touching, a saucepan of simmering water until it is spoonable.

MAKES 12 CUPCAKES

½ cup (1 stick) plus 3 tablespoons unsalted butter, cut into chunks

3 ounces milk chocolate, chopped

⅔ cup all-purpose flour

2½ tablespoons unsweetened cocoa powder

¾ teaspoon baking powder

¼ teaspoon salt

¾ cup sugar

3 large eggs

1 teaspoon vanilla extract

¾ cup Rich Chocolate Glaze (page 267), warm

Fluffy White Chocolate Frosting (page 260)

Preheat the oven to 350°F. Line a standard 12-cup muffin pan with paper or foil liners.

In a large microwave-safe bowl, combine the butter and chocolate. Microwave on high power, stirring every 20 seconds, just until the mixture is melted and smooth. Don't let it get too hot! Let cool completely.

In a medium bowl, whisk together the flour, cocoa powder, baking powder, and salt. Add the sugar to the chocolate mixture and whisk until blended. Whisk in the eggs one at a time, mixing until well combined after each addition. Whisk in the vanilla. Add the flour mixture and fold gently with a rubber spatula.

Divide the batter evenly among the prepared muffin cups. Bake until a toothpick inserted into the center of a cupcake comes out with only a few crumbs attached, 22 to 24 minutes. Remove the pan from the oven and set it on a wire rack. Let cool for 10 minutes, then carefully transfer the cupcakes directly to the rack. Let cool completely, about 1 hour.

Using a paring knife, cut a 1½-inch-diameter round about 1 inch deep in the center of each cupcake, then remove the rounds (and enjoy them as a baker's treat). Fill each hollow with about 1 tablespoon of the chocolate glaze. Place the filled cupcakes on a rimmed cookie sheet and refrigerate until the filling is set, about 10 minutes.

Using a small icing spatula or a butter knife, frost the cupcakes.

Butterfly Cupcakes

For these fancy-looking treats, the cupcake tops are sliced off, cut in half, and perched in the frosting topping to resemble butterfly wings. They're the perfect addition to a nature-inspired outdoor garden party. Use colorful paper liners to make them even more festive.

MAKES 12 CUPCAKES

1⅔ cups all-purpose flour

1¼ teaspoons baking powder

½ teaspoon salt

½ cup (1 stick) unsalted butter, at room temperature

¾ cup granulated sugar

2 large eggs, at room temperature

½ teaspoon vanilla extract

½ cup whole milk

Fluffy Frosting (page 260)

Strawberry or raspberry jam

Preheat the oven to 350°F. Line a standard 12-cup muffin pan with paper or foil liners.

In a small bowl, whisk together the flour, baking powder, and salt. In a large bowl, using an electric mixer, beat the butter on medium speed until smooth, about 1 minute. Add the sugar, raise the speed to medium-high, and beat until fluffy and lighter in color, 2 to 3 minutes. Add 1 egg, beat well, and add the vanilla with the second egg. On low speed, add about half of the flour mixture and mix just until blended, then add the milk and mix until blended. Add the remaining flour mixture and mix just until blended.

Divide the batter evenly among the prepared muffin cups and smooth it with an icing spatula. Bake until the tops are light golden brown and a wooden skewer inserted into the center of a cupcake comes out clean, 17 to 19 minutes. Let the cupcakes cool in the pan on a wire rack for 15 minutes. Lift the cupcakes from the pan and arrange, top side up, on the rack. Let cool completely. While the cupcakes are cooling, make the frosting.

Using a serrated knife, cut off the domed top from each cupcake and cut it in half to form the butterfly "wings". Using an icing spatula, spread the tops of the cupcakes with frosting. Put a small dollop (about ¼ teaspoon) of the jam in the center of the frosting. Gently push 2 wings, cut side down and at a slight angle, into the frosting, positioning them on either side of the jam. Serve right away.

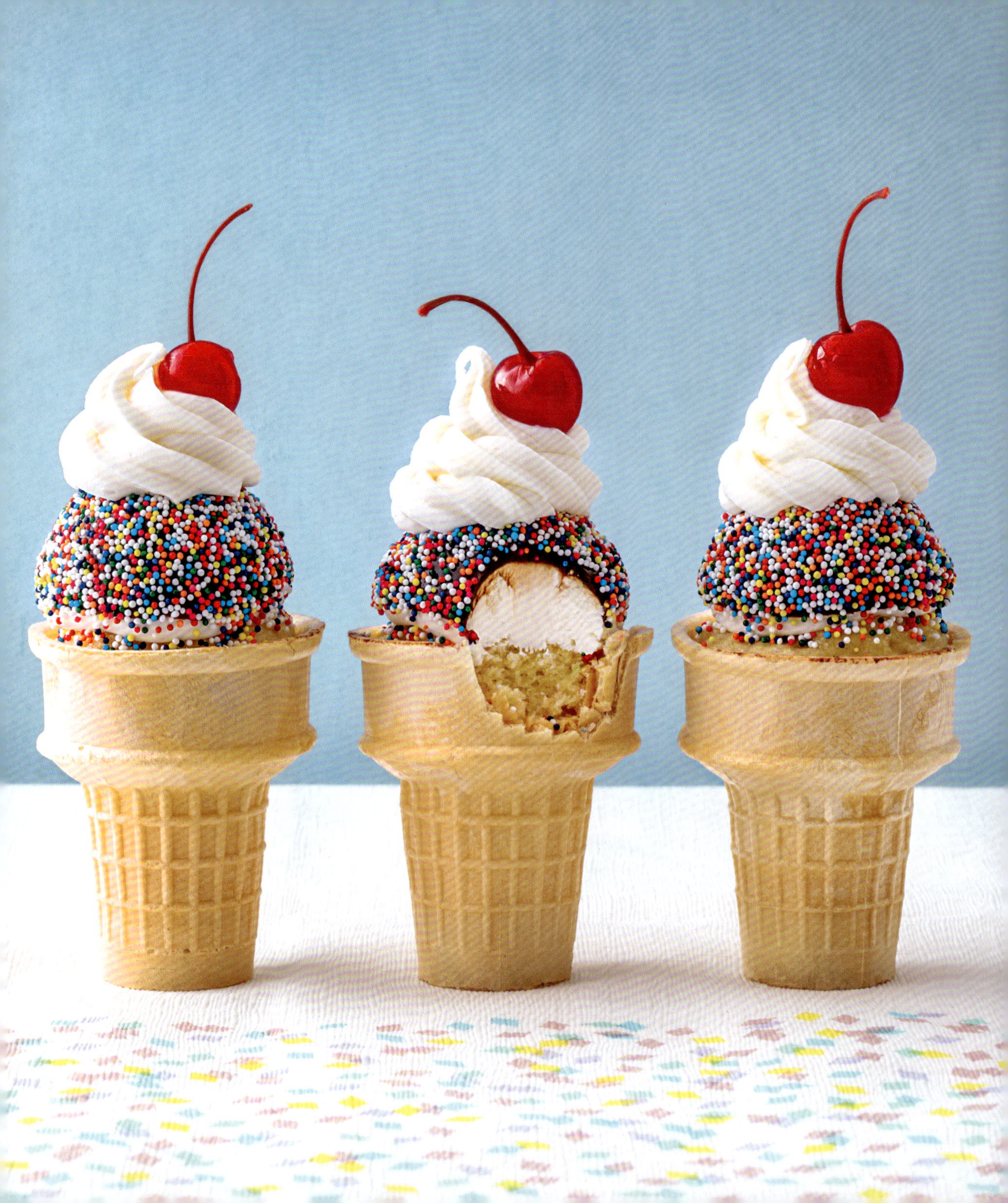

Cupcake Cones

It's surprisingly simple to create these faux ice cream cones! Just fill wafer cones with cupcake batter, then bake them in a standard muffin pan. You can vary the batter, frosting, and sprinkles to create different looks and flavor combos.

MAKES 12 CUPCAKE CONES

12 jumbo flat-bottomed wafer ice cream cones

Vanilla Cupcakes (page 173) prepared through step 3

Double recipe Fluffy Vanilla Frosting (page 260)

Rich Chocolate Glaze (page 267), warm

Rainbow nonpareil sprinkles (about 1/2 cup)

12 maraschino cherries

Place an ice cream cone in each cup of a standard 12-cup muffin pan. Divide the batter evenly among the cones, filling each about two-thirds full. Bake until the tops are light golden brown and a toothpick inserted into the center of a cupcake comes out clean, 18 to 20 minutes. Remove the pan from the oven and set it on a wire rack. Let cool for 10 minutes, then carefully transfer the cones directly to the rack. Let cool completely, about 1 hour.

Fit a pastry bag with a large round tip (we used Ateco 809) and fill it with one batch of the frosting. Pipe frosting on a cupcake in a thick, even layer, starting from the outer edge and spiraling toward the center. Repeat with the remaining cupcakes, then place them on a rimmed cookie sheet and freeze them for 20 minutes to firm up the frosting.

Place the warm chocolate glaze in a medium bowl and pour the sprinkles onto a small plate. One at a time, dip just the frosted part of each chilled cupcake into the glaze, then into the sprinkles. Return the cupcake cones to the cookie sheet and freeze for 5 minutes to firm up the glaze.

Fit another pastry bag with a large star tip (we used Ateco 826) and fill it with the second batch of frosting. Pipe the frosting on top of the cupcake cones, dividing it evenly, and top each with a maraschino cherry.

Iced Lemon Drizzle Cupcakes

Bake these double-lemon cupcakes (there's lemon in both the cake and the glaze) in colorful cupcake liners that match your party's theme, and adorn them with colorful sprinkles Adding sour cream to the batter keeps it moist. Be sure to zest the lemon before you juice it.

MAKES 12 CUPCAKES

FOR THE CUPCAKES

1¼ cups all-purpose flour

½ teaspoon baking powder

½ teaspoon baking soda

¼ teaspoon salt

4 tablespoons (½ stick) unsalted butter, at room temperature

¾ cup granulated sugar

2 teaspoons grated lemon zest

1 large egg

¾ cup sour cream

FOR THE GLAZE

1 cup powdered sugar

2 tablespoons fresh lemon juice, plus more if needed

Metallic sprinkles, for decorating (optional)

Preheat the oven to 325°F. Line a standard 12-cup muffin pan with paper or foil liners.

To make the cupcakes, in a medium bowl, whisk together the flour, baking powder, baking soda, and salt. In a large bowl, using an electric mixer, beat together the butter, granulated sugar, and lemon zest on medium speed until fluffy and pale, about 3 minutes. Add the egg and beat until combined. Turn off the mixer and scrape down the bowl with a rubber spatula. Add half of the flour mixture and beat on low speed just until combined. Then add the sour cream and beat just until combined. Add the remaining flour mixture and beat just until combined. Turn off the mixer, scrape down the bowl, and give the batter a final stir.

Divide the batter evenly among the prepared muffin cups, filling them about three-fourths full. Bake the cupcakes until golden brown and a wooden skewer inserted into the center of a cupcake comes out clean, 18 to 20 minutes. Let the cupcakes cool in the muffin pan on a wire rack for 10 minutes, then carefully transfer the cupcakes directly to the rack. Let cool completely.

To make the glaze, in a small bowl, whisk together the powdered sugar and lemon juice until smooth and spreadable, adding more lemon juice, if needed, until the glaze is thick but pourable. Spoon some of the glaze on top of each cooled cupcake and, using the back of the spoon, spread it to the edge. Decorate with sprinkles, if you like. Let the glaze stand for 1 to 2 minutes until it sets, then serve.

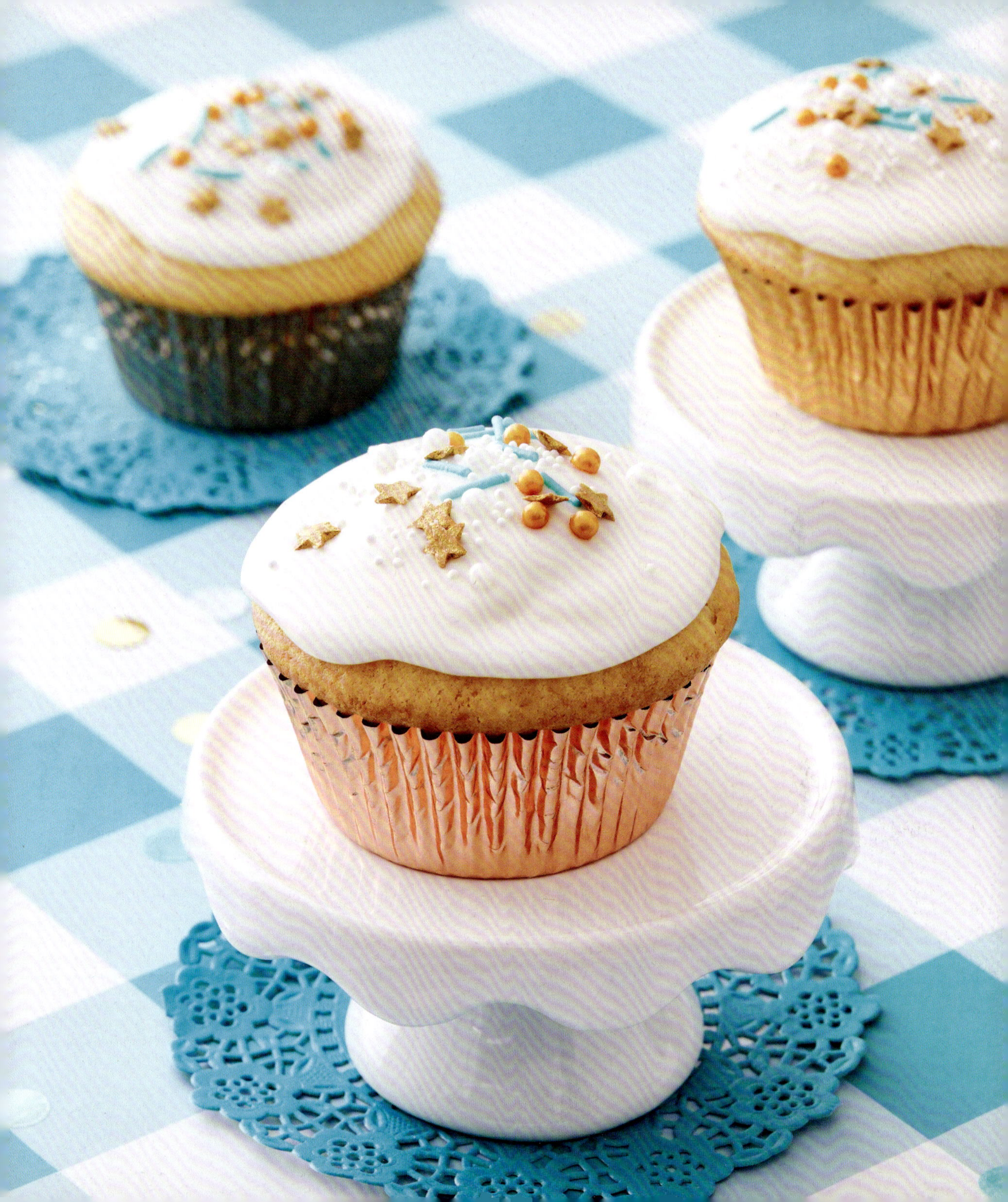

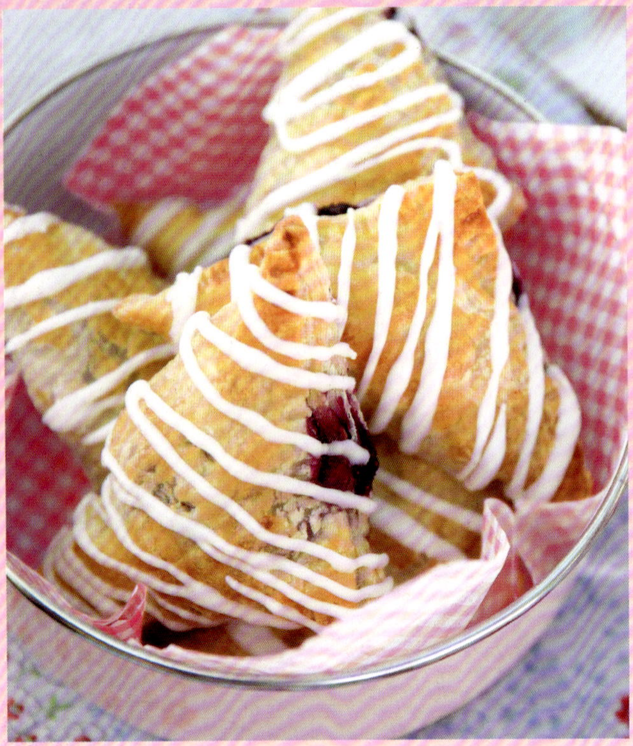
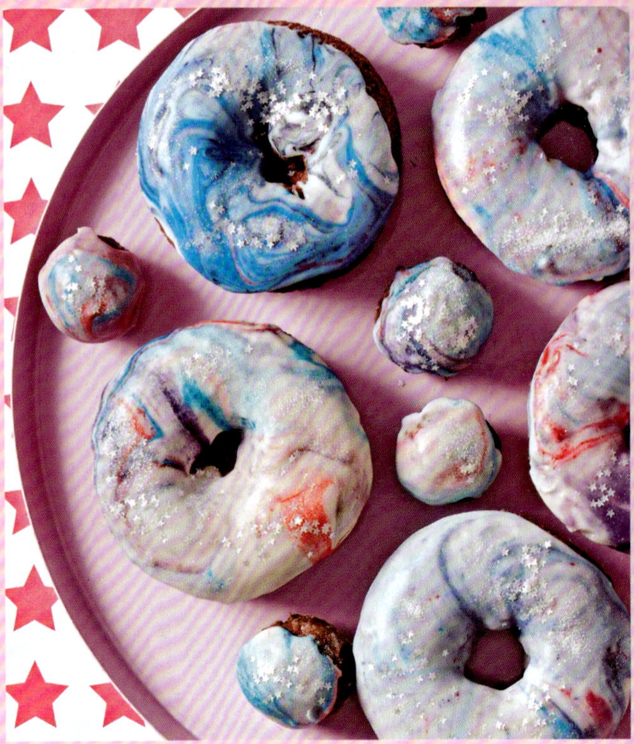
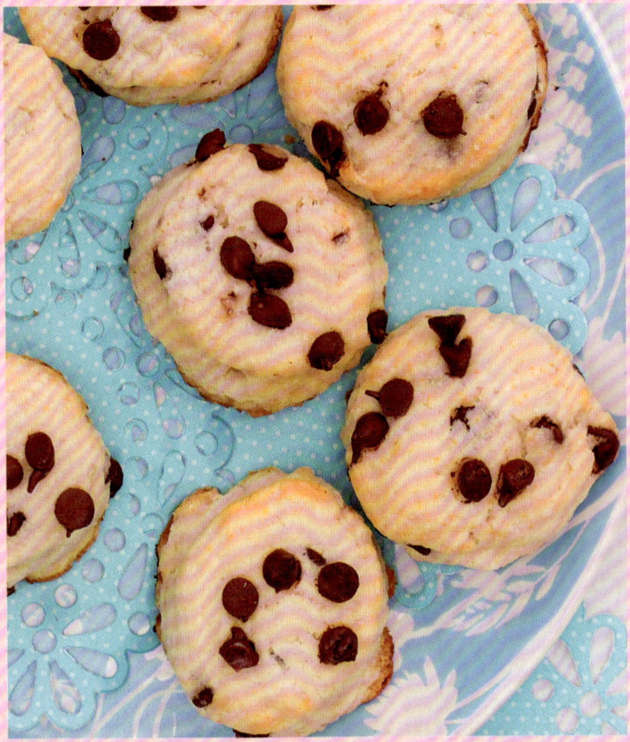
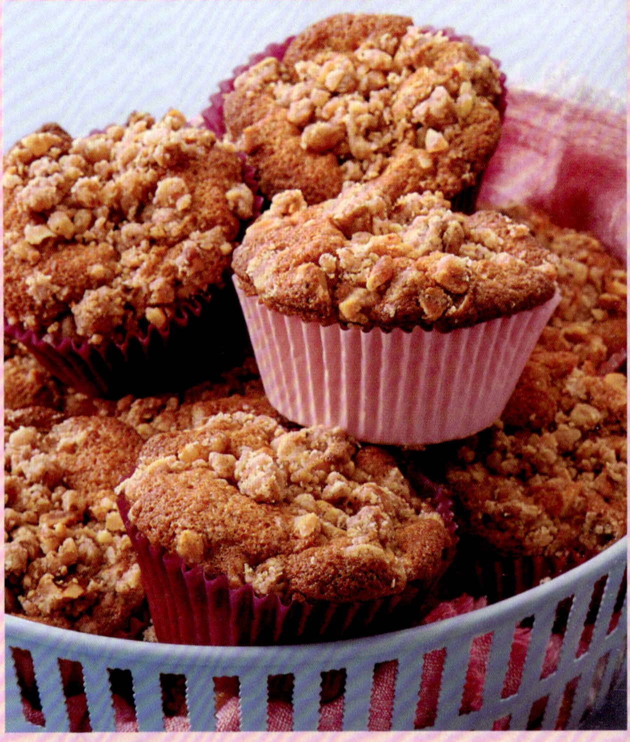

Muffins & Pastries

Sugar-and-Spice Popovers

There's a lot to love about these popovers. They rise dramatically as they bake and emerge from the oven with a crisp golden crust and a moist, hollow interior. Brushed with butter and coated with cinnamon-sugar, they're perfect for special occasions.

MAKES 12 POPOVERS

1 cup all-purpose flour

½ teaspoon salt

1 cup whole milk

2 large eggs, beaten

½ cup (1 stick) unsalted butter, melted and cooled

½ cup sugar

1 teaspoon ground cinnamon

Preheat the oven to 450°F.

In a bowl, stir together the flour and salt. Make a well in the center of the flour mixture, add the milk and eggs, and whisk just until combined. Pour the batter into a glass measuring cup or a pitcher.

Place a 12-cup popover pan or a standard 12-cup muffin pan in the oven and heat until hot, about 2 minutes. Spoon 1 teaspoon of the melted butter into each cup. Divide the batter evenly among the cups, filling them half-full.

Bake for 10 minutes. Reduce the oven temperature to 375°F and continue to bake, without opening the oven door, until the popovers are puffed, crisp, and golden brown, 20 to 25 minutes longer. Remove the pan from the oven. Using a small butter knife, gently remove the popovers from the pan.

In a shallow bowl, stir together the sugar and cinnamon until evenly blended. Using a pastry brush, brush the popovers all over with the remaining melted butter, then toss gently in the cinnamon-sugar mixture until evenly coated. Return the popovers to the pan to keep warm until serving, or arrange them in a napkin-lined serving basket or bowl. Serve right away.

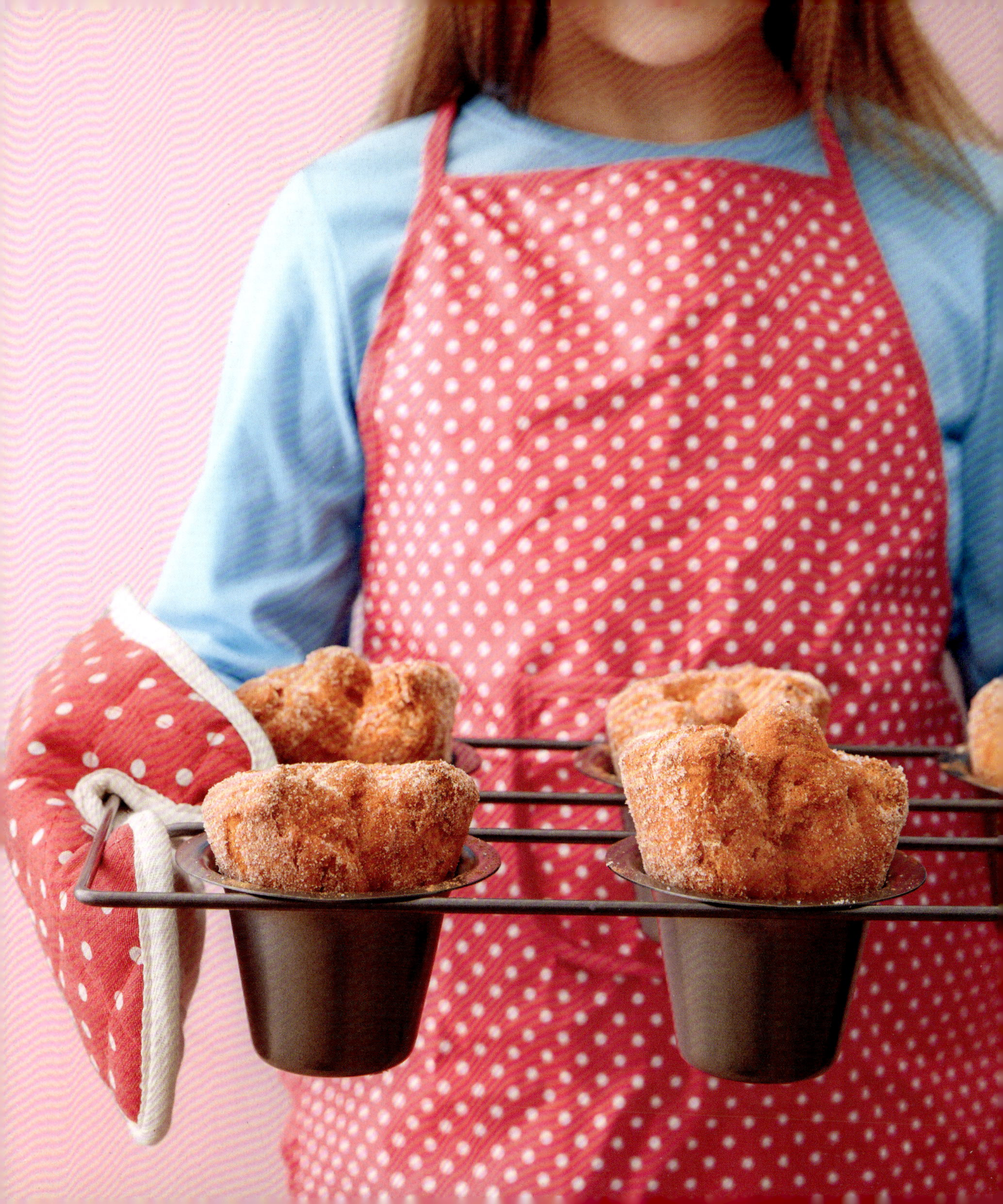

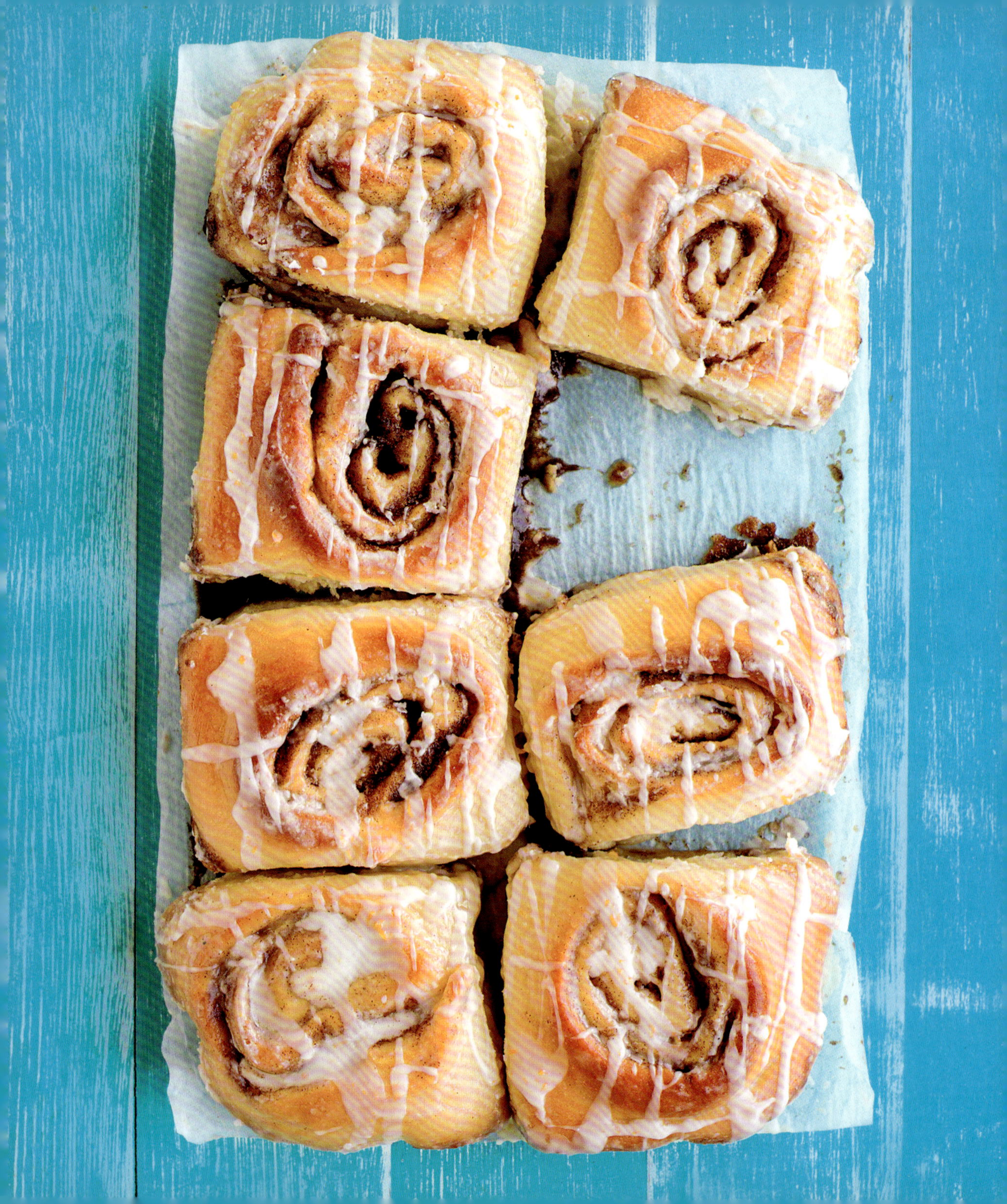

Cinnamon Rolls with Cream Cheese Icing

Cinnamon rolls baking in the oven is one of the best smells ever! These are downright irresistible. You can make the dough and shape the rolls the night before so that all you have to do in the morning is take them out of the refrigerator and bake them.

MAKES 8 ROLLS

DOUGH

1 cup whole milk

½ cup granulated sugar

5 tablespoons unsalted butter, melted, plus more for greasing the bowl and baking pan

3 large eggs

1 package (2½ teaspoons) quick-rise yeast

4½ cups all-purpose flour, plus more as needed

1¼ teaspoons salt

FILLING

½ cup firmly packed light brown sugar

2 teaspoons ground cinnamon

6 tablespoons (¾ stick) unsalted butter, at room temperature

(See additional ingredients on page 192)

To make the dough, in the bowl of a stand mixer, combine the milk, sugar, melted butter, eggs, and yeast and whisk until blended. Add 4½ cups of the flour and the salt. Attach the flat beater to the stand mixer and mix on medium-low speed, adding up to ½ cup flour to make a soft dough that does not stick to the bowl. Remove the flat beater and fit the stand mixer with the dough hook attachment. Knead the dough on medium-low speed, adding more flour if needed, until the dough is smooth but still soft, 6 to 7 minutes. Remove the dough from the bowl and shape it into a ball. Brush a large bowl with melted butter. Add the dough to the bowl and turn to coat its entire surface with butter. Cover with plastic wrap and let rise in a warm place until the dough has doubled in bulk, 1½ to 2 hours.

While the dough is rising, make the filling: In the stand-mixer bowl, combine the brown sugar, cinnamon, and butter. Attach the flat beater and beat on medium speed until combined, about 30 seconds. Set aside.

When the dough has doubled in bulk, use your hand to gently punch down and deflate the dough. Lightly flour a clean work surface. Turn the dough out onto the floured surface and dust the top with flour. Using a rolling pin, roll out the dough to a 16-by-14-inch rectangle, with a long side facing you. Spread the filling evenly over the dough, leaving a 1-inch uncovered border at the top and bottom. Starting at the long side of the rectangle farthest from you, roll up the rectangle into a log. Pinch the seam to seal. Using a sharp knife, cut

~ Continued on page 192 ~

> **Try this!**
> Sprinkle ½ cup raisins, dried cherries, or chopped pecans over the filling before rolling up the dough.

~ Continued from page 191 ~

the log crosswise into 8 equal slices. Brush a 9-by-13-inch baking pan with melted butter. Arrange the slices, cut side up, in the pan, spacing them evenly. Cover loosely with plastic wrap and let rise in a warm place until doubled in bulk, 1¼ to 1½ hours. (If making the night before, refrigerate for 8 to 12 hours; remove from the refrigerator 1 hour before baking.)

ICING

1½ cups powdered sugar

2 ounces cream cheese, at room temperature

2 tablespoons unsalted butter, at room temperature

½ teaspoon vanilla extract

Finely grated zest of 1 orange

¼ cup whole milk, plus more as needed

Preheat the oven to 350°F.

Bake until the rolls are golden brown, about 30 minutes. Remove from the oven and let cool in the pan on a wire rack for 15 minutes.

Meanwhile, make the icing: Sift the powdered sugar into a medium bowl and add the cream cheese, butter, vanilla, and orange zest. Using an electric mixer, beat the mixture on low speed until crumbly. Gradually beat in the milk. The icing should be very thick but pourable; if needed, beat in more milk, 1 teaspoon at a time, until the icing has the correct consistency. Drizzle the icing over the warm rolls, or pour it over the rolls and use a butter knife to spread it out evenly. Let cool for at least 15 minutes. Serve the rolls warm or at room temperature.

Vanilla-Glazed "Toaster" Pastries

These pastries might look like the kind you can buy in a box, but the fresh-fruit filling makes them even more delish—and better for you, too. You can eat them at room temperature, or reheat them on a cookie sheet for a few minutes in a 300°F oven.

MAKES 4 PASTRIES

PASTRIES

1 large egg

2 cups fresh pitted cherries or blueberries

3 tablespoons sugar

½ teaspoon grated lemon zest

2 teaspoons lemon juice

⅛ teaspoon ground cinnamon (optional)

1 sheet frozen puff pastry, thawed

All-purpose flour, for dusting

GLAZE

¾ cup, plus 2 tablespoons powdered sugar

2½ tablespoons water

½ teaspoon vanilla extract

Preheat the oven to 350°F. Line a cookie sheet with parchment paper. In a small bowl, beat the egg with a fork.

In a medium bowl, combine the fruit, sugar, lemon zest, lemon juice, and ground cinnamon (if using). Set aside.

Place the puff pastry on a clean, lightly floured work surface. Using a rolling pin, roll out the pastry until it is a square that is ⅛ inch thick. Cut the pastry into 4 equal squares, then cut each square in half to make a total of 8 rectangles.

Place 2 dough rectangles on the prepared cookie sheet. Brush the edges of 1 rectangle with beaten egg, then spoon one-fourth of the fruit mixture onto the dough, leaving a ½-inch border uncovered. Using a knife, cut vents into the top of a second rectangle and carefully place it over the first one, sealing the fruit inside. Using the tines of a fork, crimp the edges. Repeat to form 3 more pastries on the cookie sheet.

Bake until the pastries are golden brown, about 25 minutes. Remove from the oven and let cool completely on the cookie sheet on a wire rack.

To make the glaze, in a small bowl, whisk the powdered sugar, water, and vanilla until smooth. Drizzle the glaze evenly over the pastries and serve.

Blueberry Turnovers

You can fill these charming handheld pies with any kind of berry you like: sliced strawberries, raspberries, and blackberries all work well. They're perfect for taking on adventures because they're small and travel well.

MAKES 9 TURNOVERS

TURNOVERS

1 sheet frozen puff pastry, thawed

2 cups blueberries

3 tablespoons granulated sugar

2 tablespoons all-purpose flour

½ teaspoon grated lemon zest

2 teaspoons lemon juice

1 large egg, lightly beaten

GLAZE

½ cup powdered sugar, sifted

1 tablespoon lemon juice

1 tablespoon orange juice

Preheat the oven to 400°F. Line a cookie sheet with parchment paper.

To make the turnovers, unfold the puff pastry and place it on a clean work surface. Using a rolling pin, roll out the pastry to a square that's ⅛ inch thick. Cut the pastry into 3 equal strips, then cut the strips crosswise to make a total of 9 squares. Place the squares on the prepared baking sheet, spacing them apart evenly.

In a medium bowl, combine the berries, granulated sugar, flour, lemon zest, and lemon juice. Divide the berry mixture evenly among the pastry squares, placing it in the center of each square. Brush the edges of each square with the beaten egg. Fold each square on the diagonal to enclose the filling and form a triangle. Gently press along the edge with the back of the tines of a fork to seal in the filling. Put the cookie sheet in the oven and bake until the turnovers are golden brown, about 15 minutes. Ask an adult to help you remove the cookie sheet from the oven and set it on a wire rack. Let the turnovers cool completely.

To make the glaze, in a small bowl, whisk together the powdered sugar, lemon juice, and orange juice. Drizzle the glaze over the cooled turnovers. Let the glaze dry for about 15 minutes and serve.

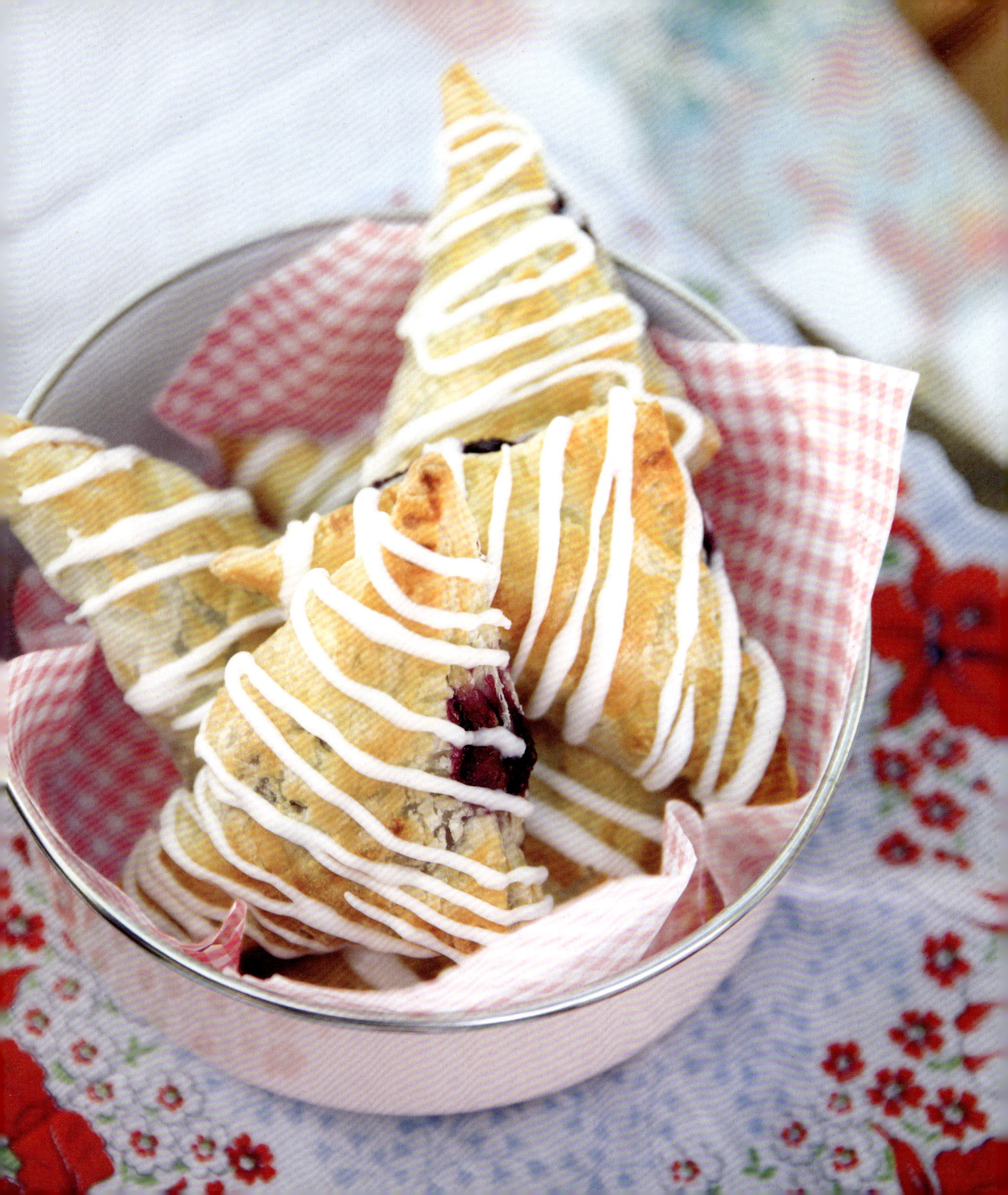

Apple Galettes

These rustic pastries are like flat, open-faced fruit pies. For a sweet and crusty finish, brush the pastry edges with egg white and sprinkle with sugar before baking. Serve each galette with a small scoop of your favorite ice cream on top.

MAKES 6 SMALL GALETTES

Pie Dough (page 232)

4 apples, preferably Granny Smith or Pippin, peeled, cored, and sliced ¼ inch thick

Finely grated zest of 1 lemon

1 tablespoon lemon juice

¼ cup sugar

½ teaspoon ground cinnamon

Pinch of salt

All-purpose flour for dusting

Vanilla or dulce de leche ice cream for serving

Prepare the pie dough, shape into a large, flat disk, and chill as directed. Line 2 baking sheets with parchment paper.

In a large bowl, toss together the apples, lemon zest, lemon juice, sugar, the cinnamon, and salt. Set aside.

Remove the dough disk from the refrigerator and let stand at room temperature for 5 minutes. Sprinkle a work surface with flour. Remove the dough disk from the plastic wrap and place it on the floured surface. Cut the dough into 6 equal pieces. Using a rolling pin, roll each piece into a round about ⅛ inch thick. Transfer the dough rounds to the prepared baking sheets, spacing them evenly. Divide the apple mixture evenly among the rounds, spreading it in an even layer and leaving a 1-inch border of dough uncovered along the edge. Fold the edge of the dough up and over the apples, loosely pleating the dough and leaving the galettes uncovered in the center. Refrigerate the galettes for about 30 minutes.

Meanwhile, preheat the oven to 400°F.

Bake the galettes until the crust is golden brown and the apples are tender, about 40 minutes. Using oven mitts, remove the baking sheets from the oven and set them on a wire rack. Let cool briefly. Serve each galette warm or at room temperature with a small scoop of ice cream on top.

Crumpets

These are just like pancakes but made with yeast (instead of baking soda or baking powder) to help them rise. Ring molds are open metal circles that bakers use to create fancy pastries. You can buy them at cooking-supply stores or online.

MAKES 12 CRUMPETS

3¼ cups all-purpose flour

4 teaspoons salt

½ teaspoon baking soda

2 cups whole milk, 1 cup heated to 115°F and 1 cup at room temperature

2 tablespoons sugar

1 teaspoon active dry yeast

Unsalted butter, for the molds, pan, and serving

Jam, for serving

In a medium bowl, whisk together the flour, salt, and baking soda. In a large bowl, combine the 1 cup heated milk, sugar, and yeast and let stand until foamy, about 10 minutes. With an electric mixer on low speed, slowly add the flour mixture and then the 1 cup room-temperature milk, beating until a smooth, thick batter forms. Cover the bowl loosely with plastic wrap and set in a warm place until the batter expands and becomes bubbly, about 1 hour.

Heat a large cast-iron frying pan or heavy-bottomed skillet over medium heat. While the pan is heating, butter as many 4-inch ring molds as will fit comfortably in the pan. When the pan is hot, lightly grease it with butter, then place the prepared molds in the pan. Fill each ring with about ⅓ cup batter and cook until bubbles appear on the surface, about 6 minutes. Carefully remove the rings and use a spatula to flip the crumpets over. Cook until the crumpets are golden on the second side and cooked through, about 5 minutes. Transfer to a plate and keep warm.

Repeat with the remaining batter, buttering the ring molds each time. Serve hot with butter and jam.

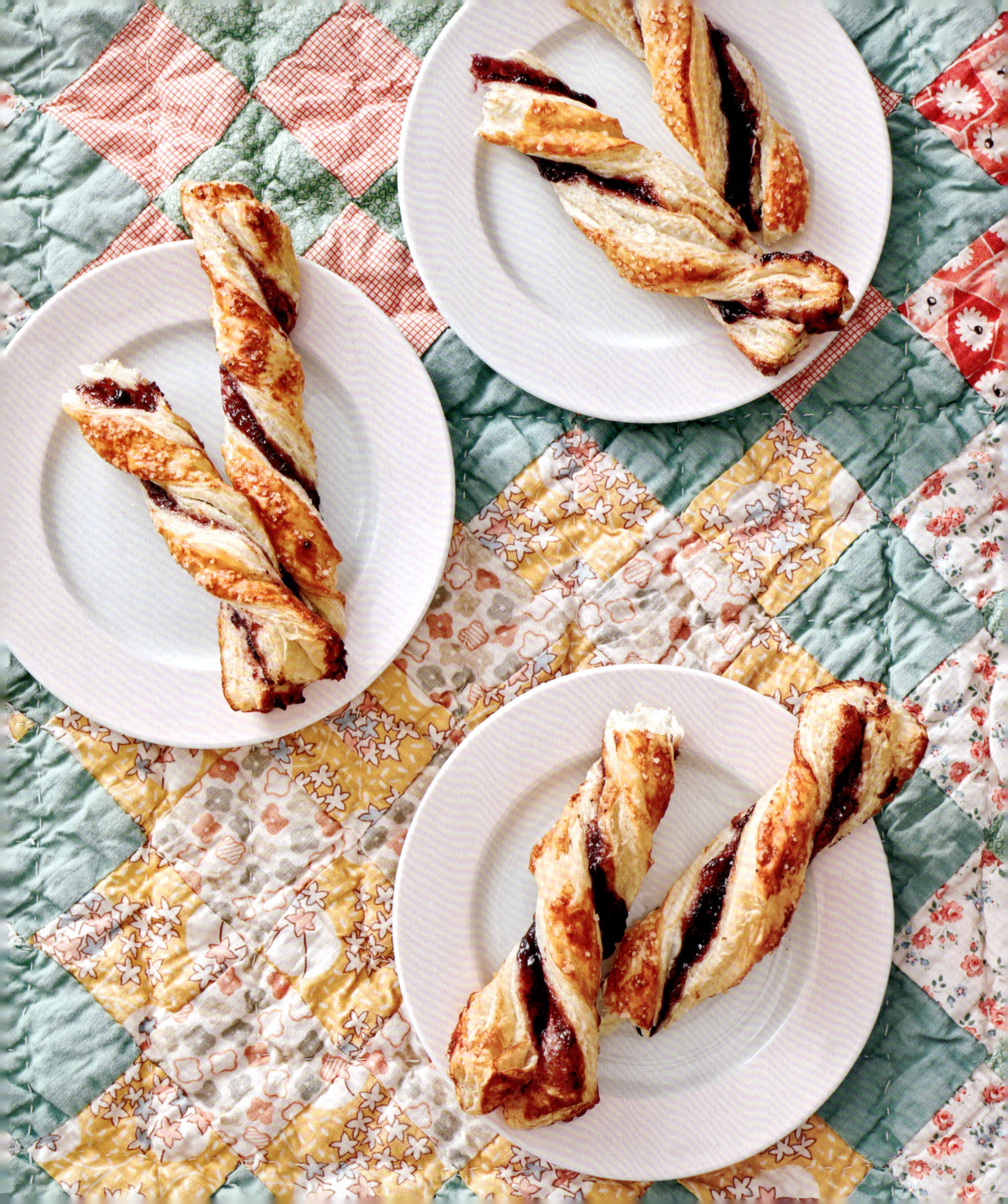

Jam Twists

You'd never guess that this spectacular-looking pastry is made from only four ingredients. You can use any jam you like, or a mix of sweet-tart flavors. For a special presentation, dust the cooled pastry with powdered sugar.

MAKES 6 TWISTS

All-purpose flour, for dusting

1 sheet (½ pound) frozen puff pastry, thawed

¼ cup berry jam, such as blueberry, cherry, or plum

1 large egg white

1 tablespoon turbinado sugar

Preheat the oven to 400°F. Line a cookie sheet with parchment paper.

Place the puff pastry on a lightly floured work surface, unfold, and press flat. Using a pizza cutter or a sharp knife, cut the sheet in half to make 2 rectangles. Spread the jam over 1 rectangle in an even layer. Place the other rectangle on top of the jam.

In a small bowl, using a fork, lightly beat the egg white. Using a pastry brush, lightly brush the top of the pastry with some of the egg white. Sprinkle half of the sugar evenly over the top, gently pressing the sugar into the dough so it adheres. Carefully turn the pastry over and brush the top side with the egg white. Sprinkle with the remaining sugar and gently press to adhere.

Using the pizza cutter or knife, cut the pastry rectangle lengthwise into 6 equal strips. Twist the ends of each strip in opposite directions to give the strip a spiraled look, then transfer the twists to the prepared cookie sheet, spacing them about 1½ inches apart. Refrigerate for 20 minutes.

Bake the pastry twists until they are puffed and golden and the jam is bubbling, about 15 minutes. Turn off the oven and leave the twists in the oven for 5 minutes longer to crisp. Remove the cookie sheet from the oven. Carefully transfer the twists to a wire rack and let cool briefly, then serve warm.

Bite-Sized Chocolate Chip Scones

No tea party is complete without scones, and these dainty ones are the best because they're studded with chocolate chips. To make regular-sized scones, use a 3-inch cutter and bake them a few minutes longer. Serve the scones with butter and strawberry jam.

MAKES ABOUT 16 MINI SCONES

2 cups all-purpose flour

3 tablespoons sugar

2½ teaspoons baking powder

¼ teaspoon salt

½ cup (1 stick) cold unsalted butter, cut into 8 chunks

½ cup mini semisweet chocolate chips

1 cup cold heavy cream

Preheat the oven to 400°F. Line a cookie sheet with parchment paper.

In a large bowl, whisk together the flour, sugar, baking powder, and salt. Scatter the butter chunks over the flour mixture and, using a pastry blender or 2 dinner knives, cut the butter into the dry ingredients until the mixture forms coarse crumbs about the size of peas. Stir in the chocolate chips. Pour in the cream and stir with a fork or rubber spatula just until combined.

Sprinkle a clean work surface with flour and turn the dough out onto the floured surface. Using floured hands, pat the dough into a round about ½ inch thick. Using a 1½-inch biscuit cutter, cut out as many rounds of the dough as possible. Gather up the scraps, knead briefly, and pat and cut out more rounds. Place the rounds on the prepared cookie sheet, spacing them apart evenly.

Bake until the scones are golden brown, about 10 minutes. Remove the cookie sheet from the oven and set it on a wire rack. Serve the scones warm or at room temperature.

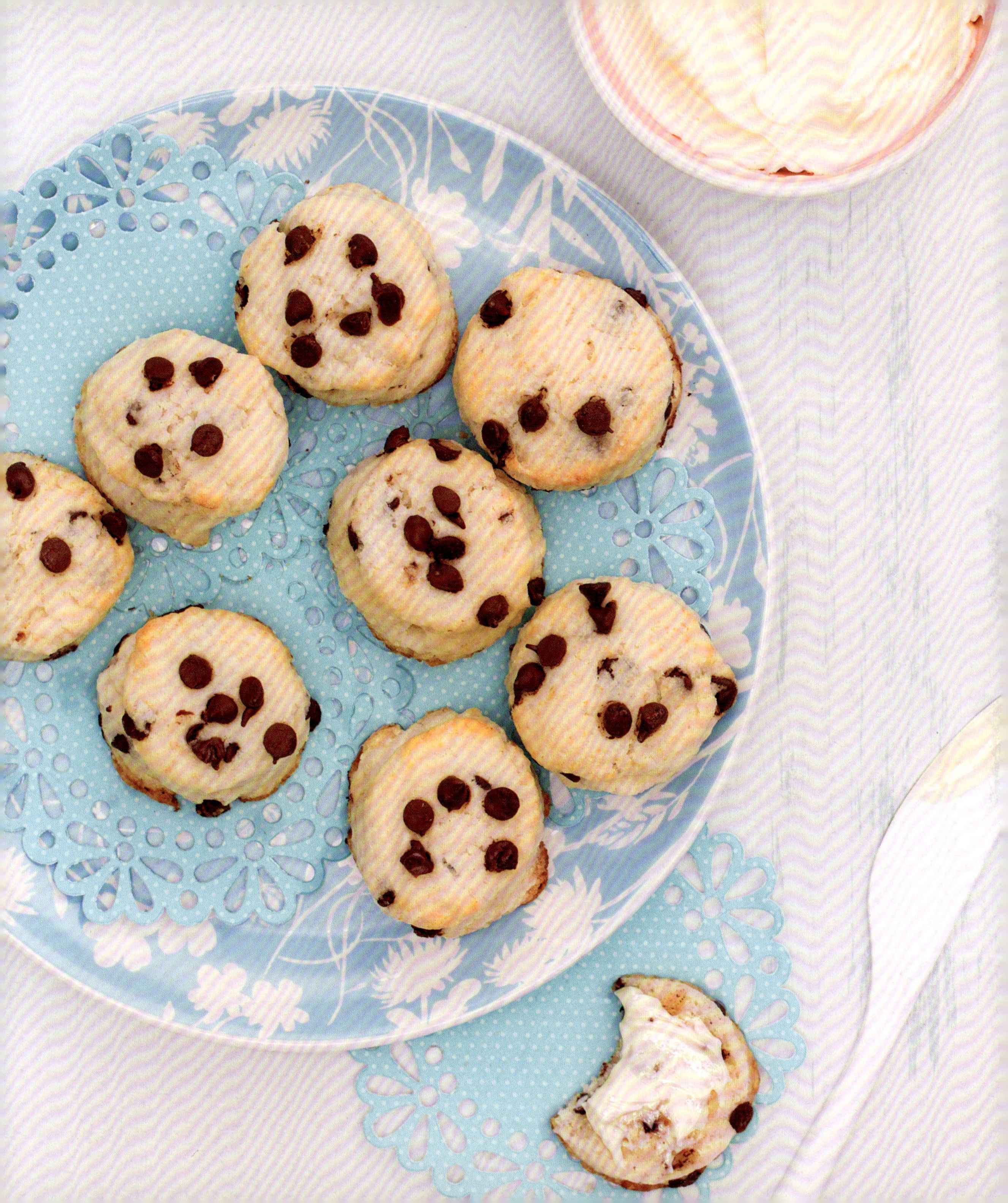

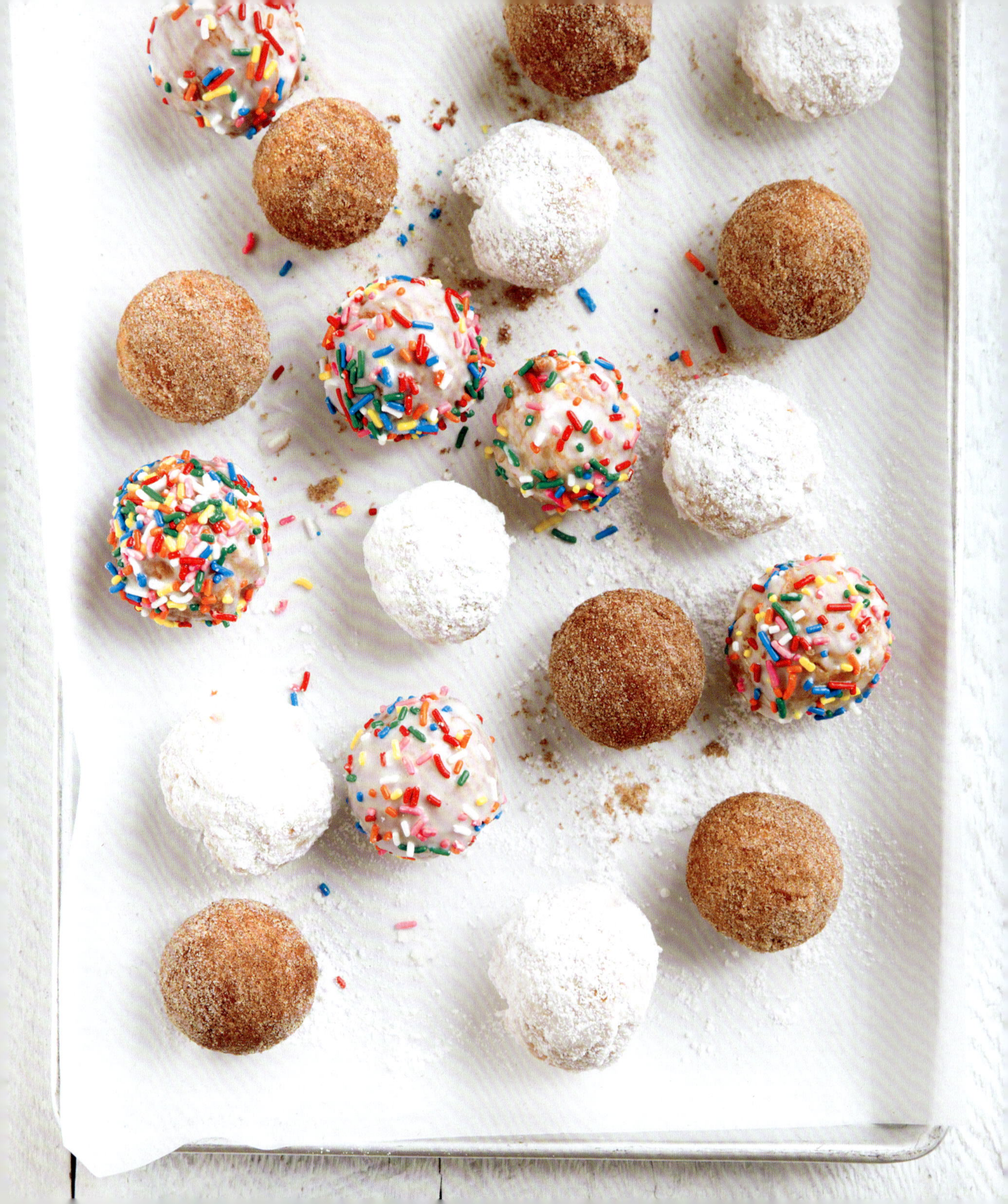

Cinnamon-Sugar Donut Holes

Surprise! You don't have to go to the trouble of making classic ring-shaped donuts to get donut holes! Invite friends over so you have lots of hands to help shape the dough. You can use the same recipe to make powdered-sugar and confetti versions.

MAKES ABOUT 40 DONUT HOLES

2¼ cups all-purpose flour

2 teaspoons ground cinnamon

1½ teaspoons baking powder

½ teaspoon salt

2 large eggs

1½ cups granulated sugar

½ cup whole milk

2 tablespoons unsalted butter, melted

1 teaspoon vanilla extract

Canola or peanut oil, for brushing and deep-frying

In a bowl, whisk together the flour, 1 teaspoon of the cinnamon, the baking powder, and the salt. In a large bowl, using an electric mixer, beat the eggs and ½ cup of the granulated sugar on low speed until creamy and pale, about 3 minutes. Turn off the mixer. Add half of the flour mixture and beat on low speed just until incorporated. Turn off the mixer and scrape down the bowl with a rubber spatula. Add the milk, melted butter, and vanilla and beat on low speed until well blended. Turn off the mixer. Add the remaining flour mixture and beat, still on low speed, just until the mixture comes together into a soft dough. Cover the bowl with plastic wrap and refrigerate until the dough is firm, at least 30 minutes or up to 1 hour.

Line a cookie sheet with waxed paper and brush the paper with oil. Line a second cookie sheet with paper towels. Pour oil to a depth of 2 inches into a deep-fryer or a large, heavy-bottomed saucepan and warm over medium-high heat until the oil registers 360°F on a deep-frying thermometer.

Meanwhile, lightly oil the palms of your hands. Pull off about 1 tablespoon of the dough and roll it between your palms into a smooth ball about 1 inch in diameter. Place it on the oiled paper. Shape the remaining dough in the same way, spacing the dough balls about 1 inch apart on the cookie sheet. You should have about 40 dough balls.

Continued on page 204

> **Try this!**
> *Donut holes are also tasty the next day. Just warm them on a cookie sheet for 5 to 7 minutes in a 300°F oven.*

~ *Continued from page 203* ~

Using tongs and handling only 1 at a time, carefully transfer 6 to 8 donut holes from the cookie sheet to the hot oil, gently placing them in. Don't overcrowd the pan. The donut holes should float to the top and puff to about double their size. Deep-fry until deep golden brown on the first side, about 1½ minutes. Using a slotted spoon, tongs, or a wire skimmer, turn each donut hole and fry until deep golden brown on the second side, about 1 minute longer. Transfer to the paper towel–lined cookie sheet to drain. Fry the remaining donut holes in the same way, allowing the oil to return to 360°F between batches.

In a wide, shallow bowl, stir together the remaining 1 teaspoon cinnamon and 1 cup granulated sugar. When the donut holes are cool enough to handle but still slightly warm, roll them in the cinnamon sugar until evenly coated and serve.

Powdered-Sugar Donut Holes Follow the recipe for Cinnamon-Sugar Donut Holes, replacing the cinnamon sugar with 1 cup sifted powdered sugar and coating the warm donut holes as directed.

Confetti Donut Holes In a medium bowl, whisk 2 cups powdered sugar, ½ teaspoon salt, ½ cup whole milk, and 2 teaspoons vanilla extract until smooth and well blended. Follow the recipe for Cinnamon-Sugar Donut Holes to make and fry the donut holes. When cool enough to handle, dip a few at a time into the glaze to coat evenly on all sides. Decorate with sprinkles and serve.

Apricot Puff-Pastry Twists

Super-flaky puff pastry is made up of lots of alternating layers of paper-thin dough and butter. For these adorable treats, cut store-bought pastry into strips and twist them. A pastry brush is a helpful tool.

MAKES 6 TWISTS

1 sheet store-bought frozen puff pastry (about ½ pound), thawed overnight in the refrigerator

All-purpose flour, for dusting

¼ cup apricot jam

1 large egg white

1 tablespoon turbinado or granulated sugar

Line a cookie sheet with parchment paper.

Place the puff pastry on a lightly floured work surface. Carefully unfold it and press it flat. Using a pizza cutter or sharp knife, cut the sheet in half to make 2 rectangles. Using a pastry brush, evenly brush 1 rectangle with the jam. Place the other rectangle on top of the jam-covered rectangle, lining up the edges and gently pressing them together. Put the egg white in a small bowl and beat it lightly with a fork. Using the pastry brush, lightly brush the top of the pastry with some of the egg white. Sprinkle half of the sugar evenly over the top, pressing it in gently so it adheres. Carefully turn the pastry over, brush the top side with the egg white, sprinkle with the remaining sugar, and again press so that the sugar adheres.

Using the pizza cutter or knife, cut the pastry rectangle lengthwise into 6 equal strips. Twist the ends of each strip in opposite directions to give the strip a spiraled look, then transfer the twists to the prepared cookie sheet, spacing them about 1½ inches apart. Refrigerate for 20 minutes.

While the twists are chilling, preheat the oven to 400°F.

Bake the pastry twists until they are golden brown and the jam is bubbling, about 15 minutes. Turn off the oven and leave the twists in the oven for 5 minutes longer to crisp. Transfer the twists to a wire rack to cool briefly, then serve warm.

Cosmos Doughnuts

Creative and artistic Luciana has a swirl of purple in her hair, much like the swirls of colorful icing atop these whimsical chocolate cake doughnuts. When frying doughnuts, make sure there's an adult nearby, and never overcrowd the pan. Decorate these with star-shaped, multicolored sprinkles, or dust with edible glitter for a truly out-of-this-world effect.

MAKES 10 DOUGHNUTS

CAKE DOUGHNUTS

1 cup all-purpose flour, plus flour for dusting

1 cup cake flour

¼ cup unsweetened natural cocoa powder

1 teaspoon baking powder

½ teaspoon baking soda

½ teaspoon salt

1 large egg

½ cup sugar

½ cup buttermilk

1 tablespoon unsalted butter, melted

1 teaspoon vanilla extract

Canola or peanut oil for deep-frying

To make the doughnuts, in a medium bowl, sift together the all-purpose flour, cake flour, cocoa powder, baking powder, baking soda, and salt. In a large bowl, using an electric mixer, beat the egg and sugar on low speed until creamy and pale, about 2 minutes. Add the buttermilk, melted butter, and vanilla and beat until blended. Add the flour mixture and beat just until the mixture comes together into a soft dough. Cover the bowl with plastic wrap and refrigerate the dough until firm, at least 30 minutes or up to 1 hour.

Line a cookie sheet with paper towels. Pour oil into a deep-fryer or a deep, heavy-bottomed sauté pan to a depth of 2 inches and warm over medium-high heat until it registers 360°F on a deep-frying thermometer.

On a generously floured work surface, roll out the dough into a round 10 inches in diameter and ½ inch thick. Using a 3-inch round doughnut cutter, cut out as many doughnuts and holes as possible. Gather up the dough scraps, press them together, roll them out again, and cut out more doughnuts.

Using a slotted or skimmer spoon, carefully lower 2 to 5 doughnuts and holes into the hot oil and deep-fry until dark brown and crusty on the first side, about 1½ minutes. Turn the doughnuts and holes over and fry until dark brown and crusty on the second side, about 1 minute longer. Transfer to the prepared cookie sheet. Repeat to fry the remaining doughnuts and holes, allowing the oil to return to 360°F between batches.

Continued on page 208

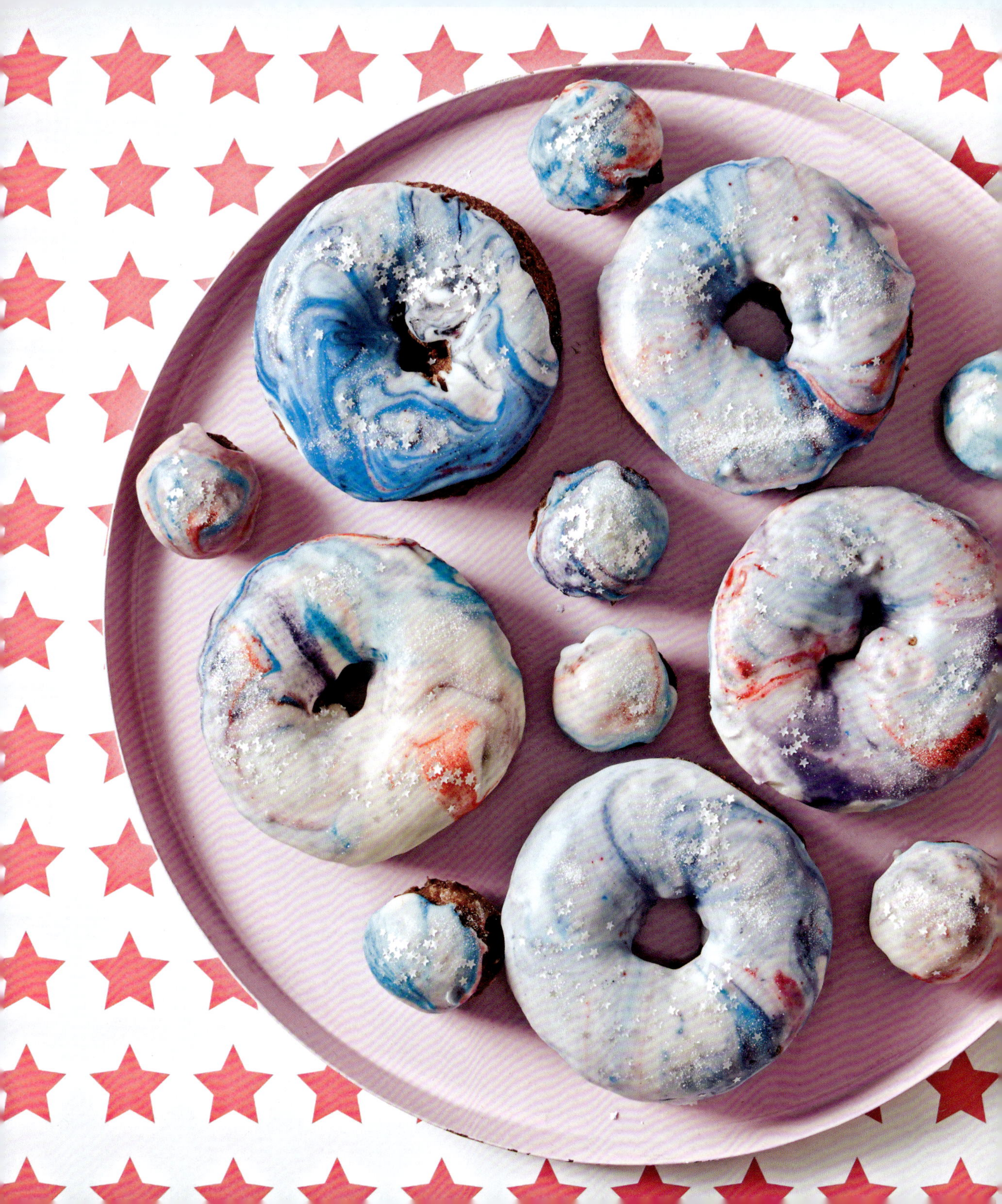

~ *Continued from page 206* ~

VANILLA GLAZE

6 tablespoons (¾ stick) unsalted butter, melted

2½ cups powdered sugar

5 tablespoons hot water, plus more if needed

1 teaspoon vanilla extract

Pink, blue, and purple gel food coloring

Edible glitter and/or edible silver star sprinkles for decorating (optional)

To make the glaze, in a bowl, whisk together the melted butter, sugar, hot water, and vanilla until smooth. Whisk in 1 to 2 teaspoons more hot water if needed to give the glaze a smooth consistency.

Divide the glaze evenly between 2 bowls. Dip a toothpick into the pink food coloring, then dip the coloring into a bowl of glaze. Dip a clean toothpick into the blue food coloring, then dip the coloring into the same bowl. Do the same with another clean toothpick and the purple food coloring. Then use the toothpick to gently swirl the food colorings into the glaze and create color streaks. Don't swirl the toothpick too much or the colors will blend together. Repeat this process with the second bowl of glaze.

Dip the top of a doughnut into the glaze and, as you lift the doughnut out of the glaze, gently twist it to let any excess glaze drip off. Place the doughnut, glaze side up, on a platter and sprinkle with edible glitter and/or stars (if using). Repeat with the remaining doughnuts and the holes. When the first bowl of glaze no longer has colored swirls, or if the colors have started to blend together too much, use the other bowl of glaze. Let the glaze set for 10 minutes, then serve.

Spiced Applesauce Muffins

Plenty of spices amp up the flavor of these tender applesauce muffins, which are perfect for breakfast or a midday snack. If you would prefer mini muffins, use a 24-cup mini muffin pan and decrease the cooking time by a few minutes.

MAKES 12 MUFFINS

2 cups all-purpose flour

⅔ cup firmly packed light brown sugar

2 teaspoons baking powder

1 teaspoon ground cinnamon

1 teaspoon ground allspice

½ teaspoon salt

1 heaping cup applesauce

⅓ cup avocado or canola oil

1 large egg

Preheat the oven to 350°F. Spray a standard 12-cup muffin pan with nonstick cooking spray.

In a bowl, stir together the flour, sugar, baking powder, cinnamon, allspice, and salt. In another bowl, whisk together the applesauce, oil, and egg until smooth. Make a well in the center of the flour mixture and stir in the applesauce mixture just until evenly moistened. Divide the batter evenly among the prepared muffin cups, filling them about three-fourths full.

Bake until the muffins are golden and springy to the touch and a wooden skewer inserted into the center of a muffin comes out clean, 25 to 30 minutes. Remove the pan from the oven and set it on a wire rack. Let the muffins cool in the pan for 5 minutes, then transfer them to the rack and let cool slightly before serving. Serve warm or at room temperature.

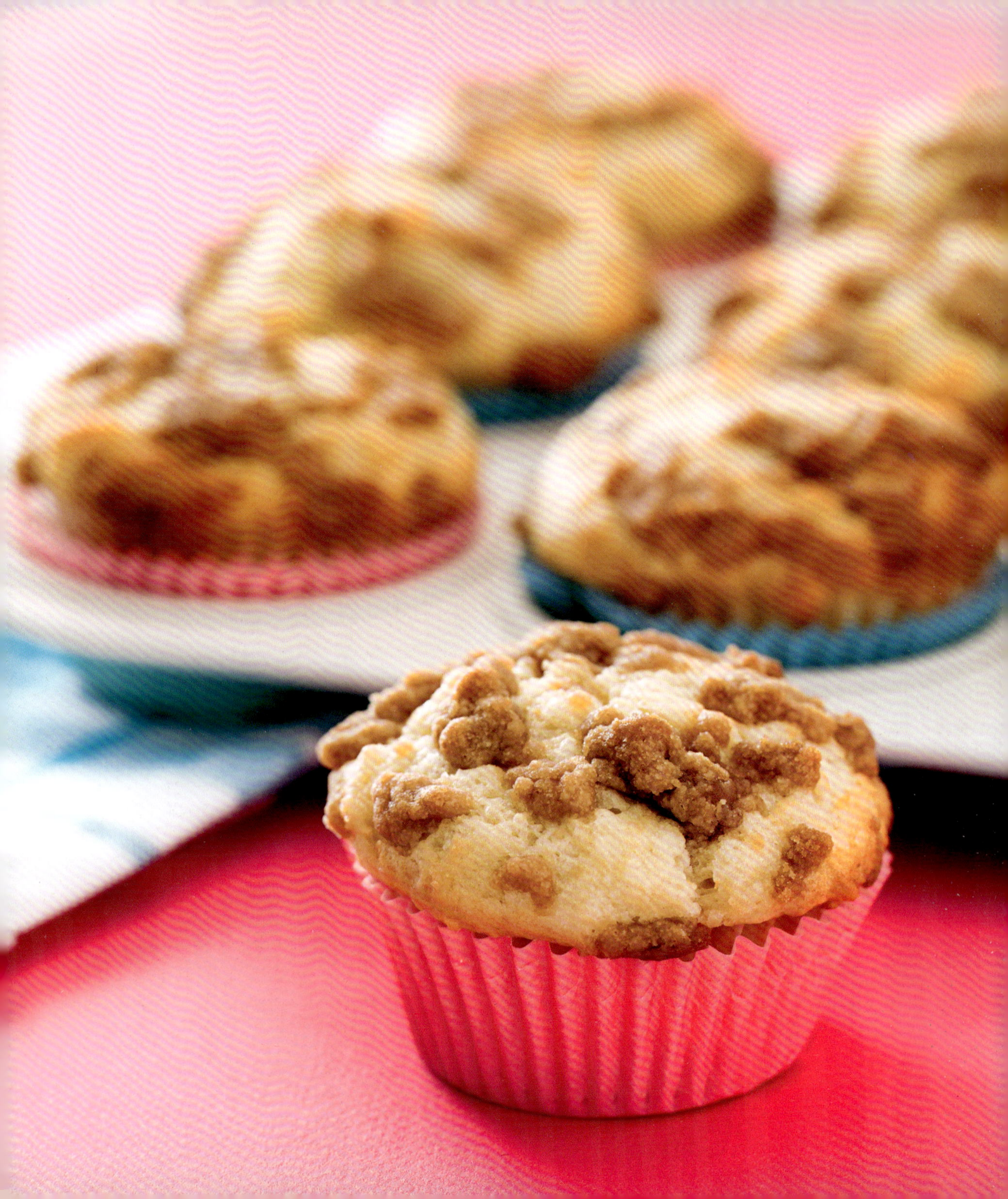

Coffee Cake Muffins

With a buttery crumb topping and pockets of sweet, sticky jam hiding inside, these muffins make mornings fun for everyone. Any type of jam is tasty here, so use your favorite. Hot chocolate is the perfect drink to serve with these muffins.

MAKES 12 MUFFINS

TOPPING
- ¼ cup all-purpose flour
- ¼ cup firmly packed light brown sugar
- 3 tablespoons cold unsalted butter, cut into small chunks

MUFFINS
- 2 cups all-purpose flour
- 2 teaspoons baking powder
- ½ teaspoon baking soda
- ¼ teaspoon salt
- ½ cup (1 stick) unsalted butter, at room temperature
- ½ cup granulated sugar
- 2 large eggs
- 2 teaspoons vanilla extract
- 1 cup sour cream
- ¼ cup fruit jam (use your favorite type)

Preheat the oven to 400°F. Line a standard 12-cup muffin pan with paper or foil liners.

To make the topping, in a small bowl, stir together the flour and brown sugar. Scatter the butter over the top and work it in with your fingertips until the mixture is evenly moistened and holds together when pinched. Put the topping in the freezer until needed.

To make the muffins, in a medium bowl, whisk together the flour, baking powder, baking soda, and salt. In a large bowl, using an electric mixer, beat the butter and granulated sugar on medium-high speed until fluffy, about 1 minute. Beat in the eggs, one at a time, and then add the vanilla and beat until well combined. Scrape down the bowl with a rubber spatula. Add the sour cream and beat on low speed to combine. Add the flour mixture and, using the rubber spatula, stir just until evenly moistened. The batter will be quite thick.

Fill each prepared muffin cup halfway full with batter. Drop 1 teaspoon jam onto the center of the batter in each cup. Divide the remaining batter evenly among the muffin cups, filling them almost to the rim. Sprinkle the muffins with the topping, dividing it evenly. Bake until golden brown and a wooden skewer inserted into the center of a muffin comes out clean, about 15 minutes. Remove from the oven and let cool in the pan on a wire rack for about 5 minutes, then carefully transfer them directly to the rack. Serve warm.

Strawberry Jam Muffins

Who doesn't love spreading jam on fresh-out-of-the-oven baked goods? Now you can have your jam and eat it too—but the jam is tucked inside these breakfast treats! The sour cream in the batter makes these muffins extra moist and delicious.

MAKES 12 MUFFINS

2 cups all-purpose flour

¾ cup sugar

1 tablespoon baking powder

½ teaspoon baking soda

½ teaspoon salt

2 large eggs

1¼ cups sour cream

6 tablespoons (¾ stick) unsalted butter, melted

1 teaspoon vanilla extract

½ cup strawberry jam

Preheat the oven to 375°F. Line a standard 12-cup muffin pan with paper or foil liners.

In a large bowl, whisk together the flour, sugar, baking powder, baking soda, and salt. In a medium bowl, whisk together the eggs, sour cream, melted butter, and vanilla until smooth. Add the egg mixture to the flour mixture and stir just until evenly moistened. The batter will be slightly lumpy.

Spoon batter into the prepared muffin cups, filling each about one-third full. Drop 2 teaspoons jam onto the center of the batter in each cup. Divide the remaining batter evenly among the muffin cups, filling them almost to the rim. Bake until golden brown and a wooden skewer inserted into the center of a muffin comes out clean, 20 to 25 minutes. Remove from the oven and let the muffins cool in the pan on a wire rack for about 5 minutes, then carefully transfer them directly to the rack. Let cool for few minutes longer and serve warm or at room temperature.

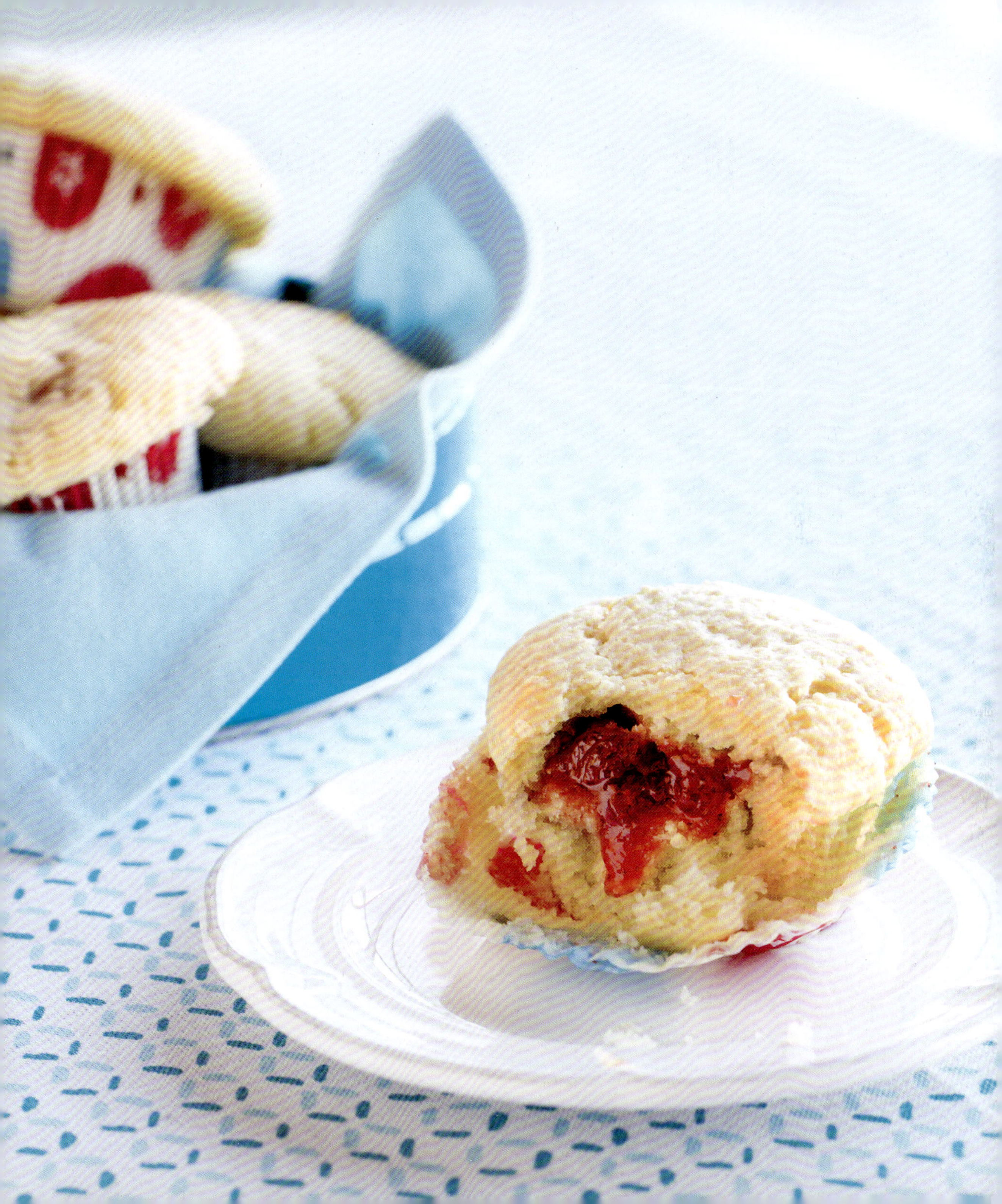

Packable snack
Muffins travel well and don't require a fork to eat, so they're a perfect choice for taking breakfast to go.

Mini Blueberry-Oat Muffins

Toasting the oats brings out their flavor and adds a subtle nutty taste. You can use fresh or frozen blueberries (thaw them first), so this is a great recipe to make at any time of year. Don't break the berries when you stir them or you'll end up with blue-gray muffins.

MAKES 24 MINI MUFFINS

1¼ cups quick-cooking rolled oats

1 cup all-purpose flour

¾ cup sugar

½ teaspoon ground cinnamon

1 teaspoon baking powder

½ teaspoon baking soda

½ teaspoon salt

1 large egg

1 cup buttermilk

4 tablespoons (½ stick) unsalted butter, melted

1 cup fresh or thawed frozen blueberries

Preheat the oven to 400°F. Line a 24-cup mini muffin pan with paper or foil liners.

Put the oats in a medium frying pan and set the pan over medium heat. Toast the oats, stirring constantly with a wooden spoon, until fragrant and just beginning to brown, 4 to 5 minutes. Remove from the heat and let cool slightly.

Pour the cooled oats into a large bowl. Add the flour, sugar, cinnamon, baking powder, baking soda, and salt and whisk to combine. In a medium bowl, whisk together the egg, buttermilk, and melted butter. Pour the buttermilk mixture into the dry ingredients and mix with a wooden spoon just until evenly moistened. Gently stir in the blueberries.

Divide the batter evenly among the prepared muffin cups, filling them nearly to the rim. Bake until lightly browned and a wooden skewer inserted into the center of a muffin comes out clean, 12 to 14 minutes. Let the muffins cool in the pan on a wire rack for about 5 minutes, then carefully transfer them directly to the rack. Let cool for a few minutes longer and serve warm or at room temperature.

Cranberry-Oat Muffins

Cranberries bring color and a juicy tart flavor to these oat-based muffins. Enjoy them warm from the oven and slathered with butter. For a fruit-and-nut variation, stir in ¼ cup each golden raisins and chopped nuts with the berries.

MAKES 16 MUFFINS

1⅓ cups all-purpose flour

2 teaspoons baking powder

½ teaspoon baking soda

½ teaspoon salt

2¼ cups rolled oats

¾ cup crème fraîche

½ cup whole milk, at room temperature

½ cup (1 stick) unsalted butter, melted and cooled

2 large eggs, lightly beaten

1 cup firmly packed brown sugar

1 cup chopped fresh or thawed frozen cranberries

Preheat the oven to 350°F. Line 16 cups of two standard 12-cup muffin pans with paper or foil liners.

In a medium bowl, mix the flour, baking powder, baking soda, and salt. In a large bowl, stir together 2 cups of the oats, the crème fraîche, milk, and melted butter until combined. Add the eggs, then the brown sugar, and stir until blended. Gently stir the flour mixture into the oat mixture, then stir in the cranberries.

Divide the batter evenly among the prepared muffin cups, filling them to the rims. Sprinkle the remaining ¼ cup oats evenly over the muffins. Bake until the muffins are golden brown and a wooden skewer inserted into the center of a muffin comes out clean, about 25 minutes. Remove the pan from the oven and set it on a wire rack. Let the muffins cool in the pan for 5 minutes, then transfer them directly to the rack. Serve warm or at room temperature.

Pumpkin Spice Muffins

These muffins are perfect for a fall or winter breakfast or brunch, but we love to make them all year round. Be sure to use pure pumpkin purée, not pumpkin pie mix, which contains sugar and spices. Add a walnut topping (below) to make them extra fancy.

MAKES 12 MUFFINS

1½ cups all-purpose flour

1 teaspoon baking soda

½ teaspoon baking powder

½ teaspoon salt

½ teaspoon ground cinnamon

½ teaspoon ground cloves

½ teaspoon ground nutmeg

1½ cups sugar

1 cup canned pumpkin purée

½ cup canola oil

2 large eggs

1 tablespoon finely grated orange zest

½ teaspoon vanilla extract

Preheat the oven to 350°F. Line a standard 12-cup muffin pan with paper or foil liners.

In a medium bowl, whisk together the flour, baking soda, baking powder, salt, cinnamon, cloves, and nutmeg. In a large bowl, whisk together the sugar, pumpkin, oil, eggs, orange zest, and vanilla until well combined. Add the flour mixture and whisk gently just until blended.

Divide the batter evenly among the prepared muffin cups. Bake until a wooden skewer inserted into the center of a muffin comes out clean, about 20 minutes. Remove from the oven and let cool in the pan on a wire rack for about 5 minutes, then carefully transfer them directly to the rack. Let cool completely and serve.

Walnut topping

In a small bowl, stir together 3 tablespoons firmly packed light brown sugar, 2 tablespoons all-purpose flour, and ¼ teaspoon each ground nutmeg and ground cinnamon. Add ¼ cup chopped walnuts and mix well. Add 1 tablespoon unsalted butter (at room temperature) and, using your fingertips, rub it into the mixture until blended. Right before baking, sprinkle the topping over the batter, dividing it evenly.

Apple Streusel Muffins

For these streusel-topped muffins, use apples with a crisp, firm texture. Tart ones like Granny Smith or Pippin, or sweet varieties such as Fuji or Braeburn, are all good choices. The buttery topping turns amazingly crunchy during baking.

MAKES 12 MUFFINS

8 tablespoons (1 stick) unsalted butter, at room temperature

1 pound crisp apples (see note), peeled, cored, and cut into 1-inch chunks

2 tablespoons, plus ¾ cup sugar

¾ cup all-purpose flour

¼ cup whole-wheat flour

¾ teaspoon baking powder

½ teaspoon salt

½ teaspoon ground cinnamon

¼ teaspoon baking soda

¼ teaspoon ground allspice

Pinch of ground nutmeg

2 large eggs

½ teaspoon vanilla extract

¼ cup sour cream

Cinnamon Streusel (page 134)

Preheat the oven to 350°F. Line a standard 12-cup muffin pan with paper or foil liners.

Put 2 tablespoons of the butter in a saucepan. Set the pan over medium-high heat and melt the butter. Add the apples and the 2 tablespoons sugar and cook, stirring often, until the apples are tender and soft, 5 to 7 minutes. Transfer the mixture to a bowl and let cool completely.

In a medium bowl, mix the all-purpose flour, whole-wheat flour, baking powder, salt, cinnamon, baking soda, allspice, and nutmeg. In a large bowl, using an electric mixer, beat the remaining 6 tablespoons butter and the ¾ cup sugar on medium-high speed until light and fluffy, 2 to 3 minutes. Turn off the mixer and scrape down the bowl with a rubber spatula. Add the eggs one at a time, beating well after each addition. Beat in the vanilla. Turn off the mixer and add about half of the flour mixture. Beat on low speed just until blended. Add the sour cream and beat until combined. Add the remaining flour mixture and beat just until blended. Add the apples and mix with the spatula until combined.

Prepare the nut streusel. Divide the batter evenly among the prepared muffin cups. Sprinkle the streusel evenly over the muffins. Bake until the topping is golden brown and a wooden skewer inserted into the center of a muffin comes out clean, 18 to 20 minutes. Remove the pan from the oven 0and set it on a wire rack. Let the muffins cool in the pan for 5 minutes, then transfer them directly to the rack. Serve warm or at room temperature.

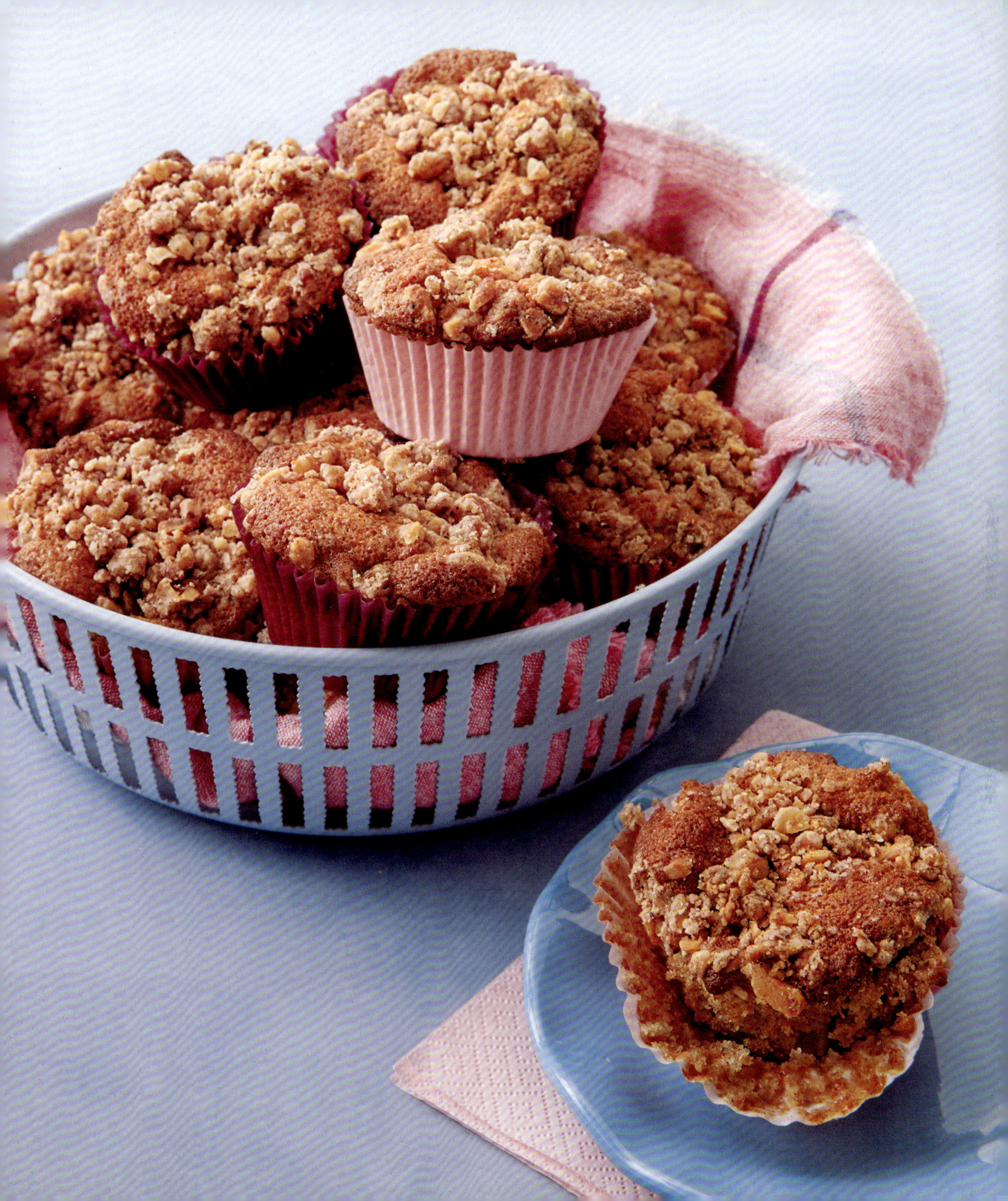

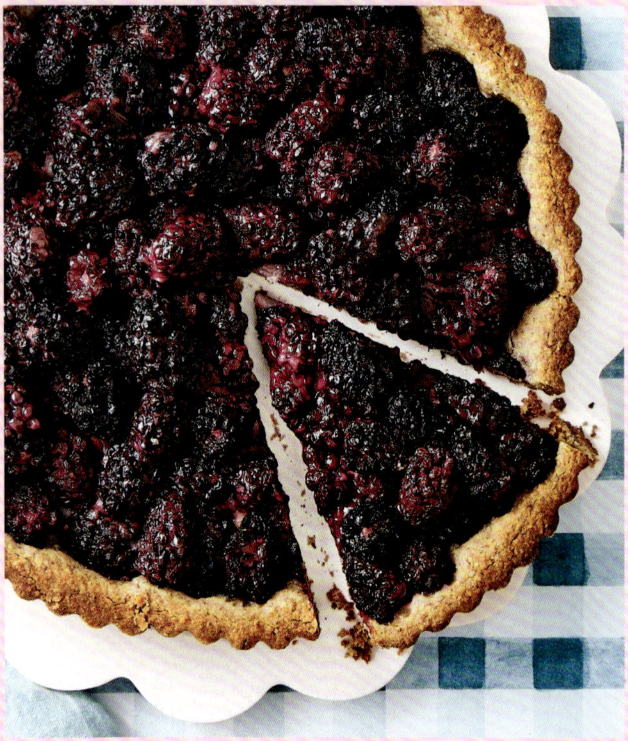
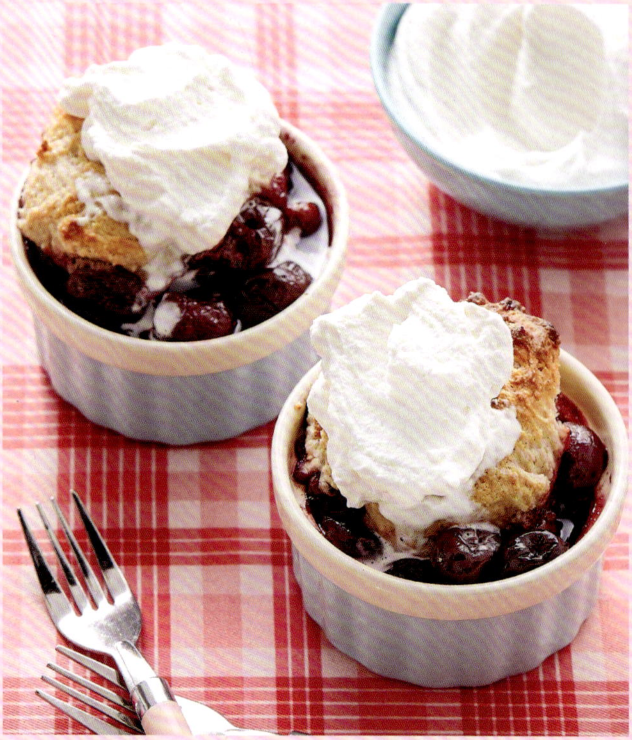
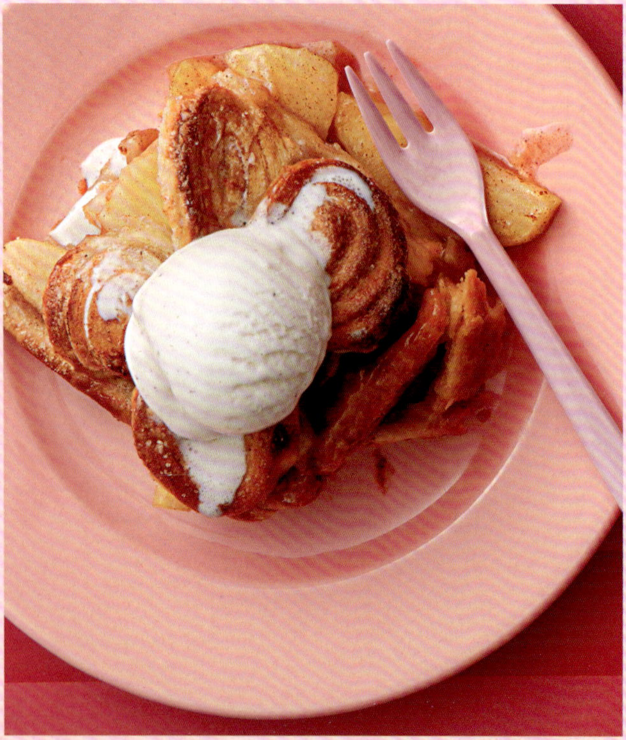
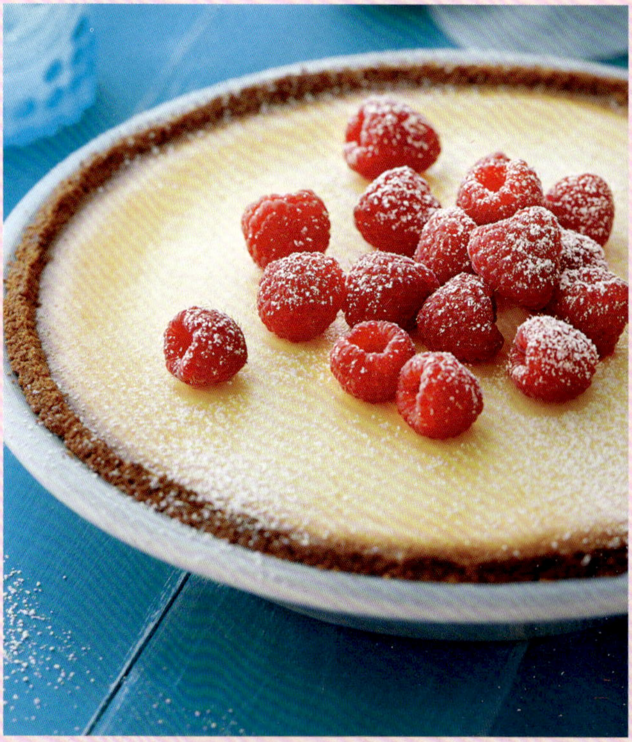

Pies & Tarts

Blackberry Slab Pie

Slab pie really is a genius dessert. It has all the elements of a traditional round pie—a flaky crust bursting with fresh fruit—but will feed a crowd, is easier to make, and is less fussy to serve. You can use any type of berry, but blackberries are always a favorite.

MAKES 8 TO 10 SERVINGS

All-purpose flour, for dusting

1 package (2 sheets) store-bought pie dough, divided into 2 disks

4 pints blackberries

1 cup sugar

¼ cup instant tapioca

2 teaspoons grated lemon zest

½ teaspoon ground cinnamon

¼ teaspoon ground allspice

¼ teaspoon salt

3 tablespoons unsalted butter, cut into small pieces

1 large egg, beaten with 1 teaspoon water

Place a rack in the lower third of the oven and preheat to 375°F.

Very lightly dust a clean work surface with flour. Lay the pie dough on the surface and lightly dust the top with flour. Using a rolling pin, roll out 1 dough disk into an 11-by-14-inch rectangle. Transfer to a 9-by-12 inch rimmed cookie sheet and fit the dough into the bottom and up the sides of the pan. Roll out the other dough disk on a piece of parchment paper into another 11-by-14-inch rectangle.

In a large bowl, gently stir together the blackberries, sugar, tapioca, lemon zest, cinnamon, allspice, and salt. Pour the filling into the crust in the pan and spread to the edges of the crust. Sprinkle the butter pieces over the top.

Using the parchment, turn the rolled-out crust upside down and lower it onto the filling, lining up the edges. Peel off the parchment. Trim the dough edges, leaving 3/4 inch of the dough extending past the sides of the cookie sheet. Fold the extra dough under itself and use your fingers to crimp the edges together.

Lightly brush the dough with the egg mixture. Using a paring knife, make about twelve 1-inch slashes in the top crust to create steam vents.

Bake until the crust is golden brown and the filling is bubbling, 45 to 50 minutes, covering the crust with aluminum foil if it browns too quickly. Remove the cookie sheet from the oven and set it atop a wire rack. Let cool completely before serving, at least 2 hours. Cut into squares and serve.

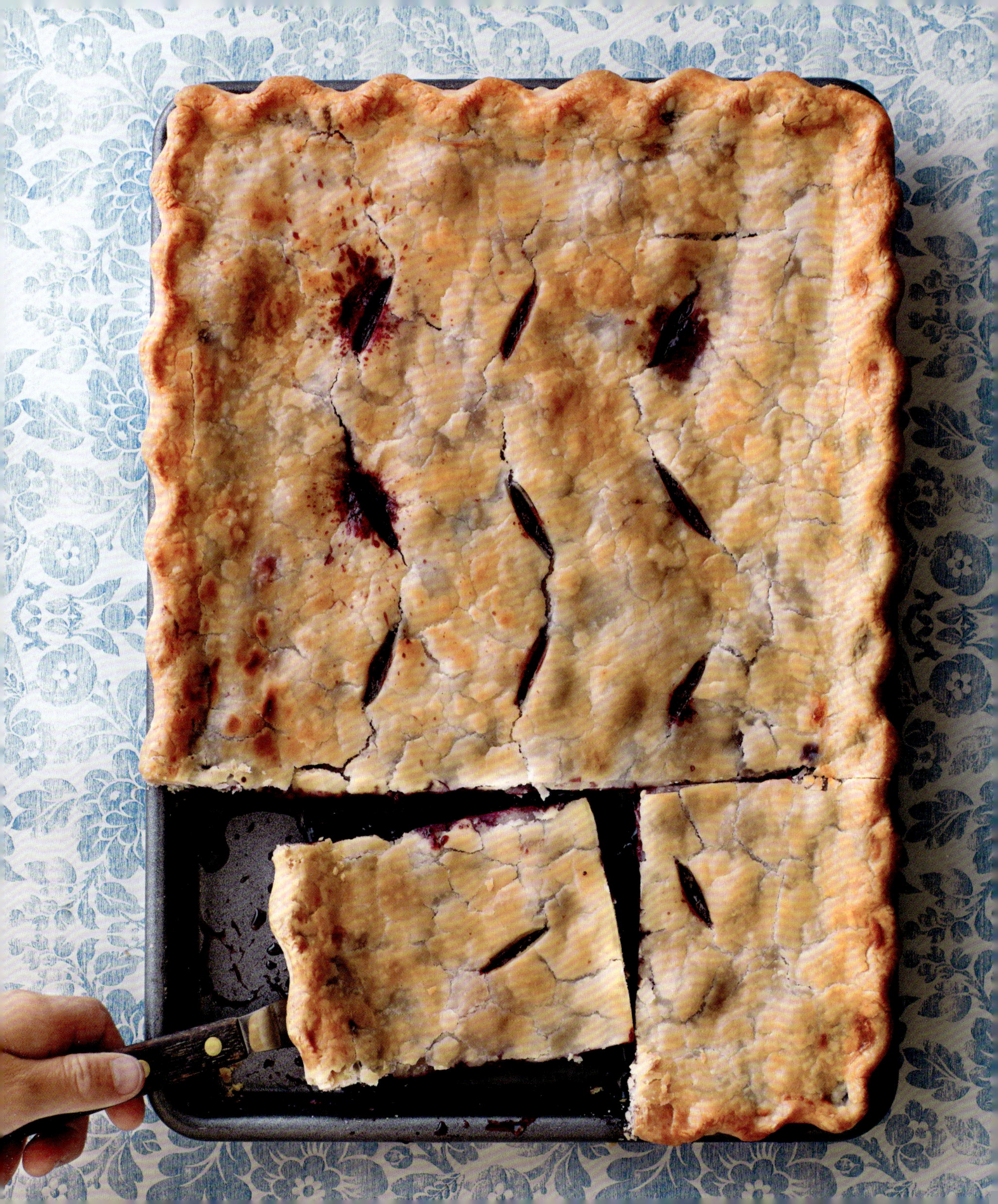

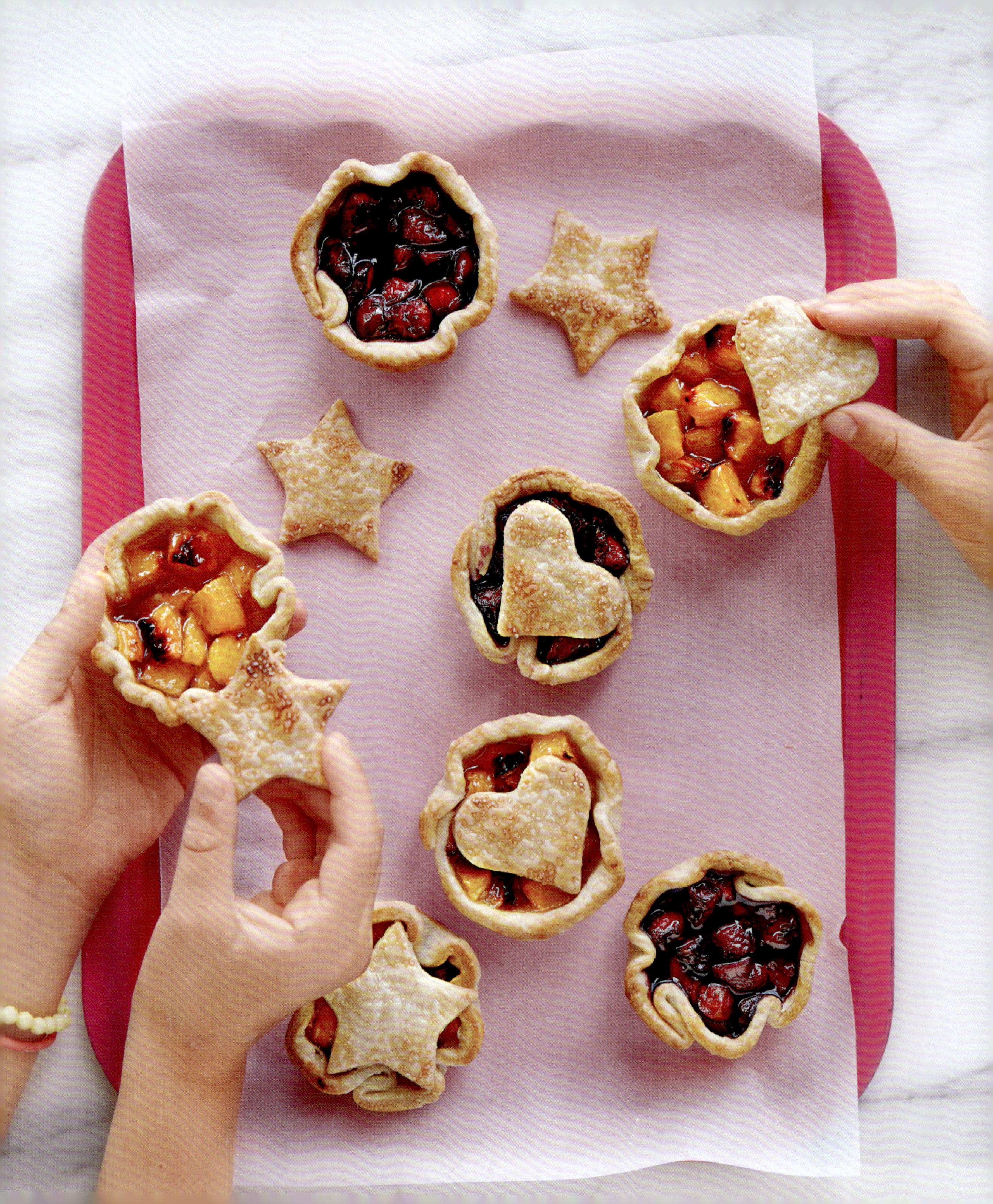

Mini Peach & Cherry Pies

Choose peaches or nectarines that are fragrant and at the peak of ripeness. They should give just slightly when gently pressed. Rock-hard stone fruit isn't as sweet, and really ripe fruits should be eaten fresh with the juices running down your chin.

MAKES 8 MINI PIES

All-purpose flour, for dusting

1 package (2 sheets) frozen store-bought pie dough, divided into 2 disks

1 to 1¼ pounds firm, ripe peaches or nectarines (about 3), or 2 cups pitted cherries, halved, or a combination of ½ pound peaches and 1 cup cherries

¼ cup granulated sugar

1 tablespoon tapioca flour

1 teaspoon fresh lemon juice

1 large egg, beaten with 1 teaspoon water

1 tablespoon raw sugar, for sprinkling

Coat a standard 12-cup muffin pan with nonstick cooking spray. Very lightly dust a clean work surface with flour. Lay the pie dough on the surface and thaw for about 10 minutes. When the dough is pliable, using a 4¼-inch round cookie or biscuit cutter, cut out 4 rounds from each piece of dough, making sure you leave some room to cut out shapes for topping the pies. You should have a total of 8 rounds. Press each round gently into a muffin cup. Refrigerate the muffin pan.

Coat a small cookie sheet lightly with cooking spray. Use a star- and/or heart-shaped cookie cutter to cut out 8 shapes from the remaining dough that are just big enough to cover the tops of the muffin cups (about 2½ inches across). (If you don't have a star- or heart-shaped cutter, you can use any shape that will fit across the muffin cup.) Place the shapes on the cookie sheet and freeze until ready to bake.

If using peaches or nectarines, fill a large saucepan three-fourths full of water. Set the pan over high heat and bring the water to a boil. Gently lower the peaches into the boiling water with a slotted spoon. Let boil for 30 seconds, then remove with the slotted spoon and transfer to a clean work surface. When they are cool enough to handle, slip off the skins, using your fingertips or a paring knife (ask an adult for help). Using a paring knife, make a cut all the way around the peach, from stem end to blossom end and back.

~ Continued on page 226 ~

> **Perfect pastry**
> *We used all-butter frozen pie dough, but you can always make your own. Roll it out to ⅛ inch thick before cutting it into shapes.*

~ *Continued from page 225* ~

Gently twist the fruit to separate the two halves and remove the pit. Cut each peach half into ¼- to ½-inch slices, then cut the slices into ½-inch pieces.

Preheat the oven to 375°F.

In a bowl, stir together the peaches (and/or cherries), granulated sugar, tapioca flour, and lemon juice until well combined. Remove the chilled pie shells from the refrigerator and divide the filling among the shells. Remove the cookie sheet with the cutout shapes from the freezer and brush each shape with the egg mixture (you will not use all of it). Sprinkle with the raw sugar.

Bake the cutouts and pies until the cutouts are golden brown and the pies are bubbly and golden brown, about 15 minutes for the cutouts and 25 to 30 minutes for the pies. Remove the cookie sheet with the cutouts from the oven and set it atop a wire rack to cool. Remove the pies from the oven and set atop a second wire rack. Place a cutout atop each pie. Let the pies cool until warm, then use a small offset spatula or butter knife to gently remove them from the pan (you may need to run the spatula or knife around the edge to loosen it). Serve warm or at room temperature.

Easy Cheesecake Pie

Who doesn't love smooth, creamy cheesecake in a crunchy graham cracker crust? Topped off with fresh, colorful berries (or other ripe summer fruit), this easy-to-make pie is perfect for a summertime party.

MAKES 8–10 SERVINGS

CRUST

15 graham crackers, broken into pieces

4 tablespoons (½ stick) unsalted butter, melted

3 tablespoons sugar

¼ teaspoon ground cinnamon

FILLING

2 (8-ounce) packages cream cheese, at room temperature

1 (14-ounce) can sweetened condensed milk

1 teaspoon finely grated lemon zest

3 tablespoons lemon juice

Mixed berries, for decorating (optional)

Preheat the oven to 350°F. Put the graham crackers in a zippered plastic bag. Press out the air and seal the bag. Use a rolling pin to crush the crackers into fine crumbs, pounding them lightly or using a gentle back-and-forth rolling motion. Measure out 1¼ cups of crumbs.

To make the crust, in a bowl, combine the graham cracker crumbs, melted butter, sugar, and cinnamon. Stir with a wooden spoon until the crumbs are evenly moistened. Pour the crumb mixture into a 9-inch glass pie dish. Using your hands, press the crumbs into an even layer into the bottom and all the way up the sides of the dish. Put the pie dish in the oven and bake until the crust is firm, 6 to 7 minutes. Ask an adult to help you remove the pie dish from the oven and place it on a wire rack. Let cool completely, about 30 minutes.

To make the filling, in a large bowl, using an electric mixer, beat the cream cheese on medium speed until smooth, 2 to 3 minutes. Turn off the mixer. Add the condensed milk and beat until smooth, about 1 minute. Turn off the mixer and scrape down the bowl with a rubber spatula. Add the lemon zest and juice and beat until the mixture is smooth, about 30 seconds. Using the rubber spatula, scrape the filling into the cooled piecrust. Spread the filling out evenly and smooth the top. Refrigerate the pie until well chilled, about 3 hours.

If you like, top the pie with mixed berries. Ask an adult to help you cut the pie into wedges and serve.

Cinnamon-Swirl Apple Pie

There's plenty of this apple pie to go around. It is baked in a large baking dish, perfect for serving a hungry crowd. The pie is even more delicious topped with scoops of vanilla ice cream. Use firm, tart baking apples, such as Granny Smith or Pippin.

MAKES ABOUT 16 SERVINGS

Slab Pie Dough (page 232)

2 tablespoons unsalted butter, at room temperature, plus butter for greasing

1 cup, plus 2 tablespoons sugar

2 teaspoons ground cinnamon

4 pounds large tart, firm apples, peeled, cored, and sliced ½ inch thick

2 tablespoons lemon juice

3 tablespoons all-purpose flour, plus flour for dusting

¼ teaspoon salt

1 large egg, lightly beaten with 1 teaspoon water

Vanilla ice cream for serving (optional)

Prepare the pie dough, divide into 2 rectangular disks, cover with plastic wrap, and chill as directed.

Butter a rimmed 10-by-15-inch baking sheet or a 9-by-13-inch baking dish.

Sprinkle a work surface with flour. Unwrap 1 dough disk and place it on the floured surface. Using a rolling pin, roll out the dough into a 12-by-16-inch rectangle. Spread the top of the dough with the butter. In a small bowl, stir together ⅓ cup of the sugar and 1 teaspoon of the cinnamon and sprinkle evenly over the butter, leaving a narrow edge uncovered on the long side farthest from you. Starting at the long side nearest to you, roll up the dough into a log (see page 230), pressing the dough to seal. Wrap in plastic wrap and refrigerate for 30 minutes.

On the floured surface, roll out the remaining dough disk into a rectangle that is 2 to 4 inches wider and longer than the baking sheet or baking dish. Fold into quarters and transfer the dough to the prepared baking sheet. Unfold the dough, fitting it into the pan. Fold over any uneven edges to make them even with the pan rim. Refrigerate for 30 minutes.

Position a rack in the lower third of the oven and preheat to 375°F.

Continued on page 231

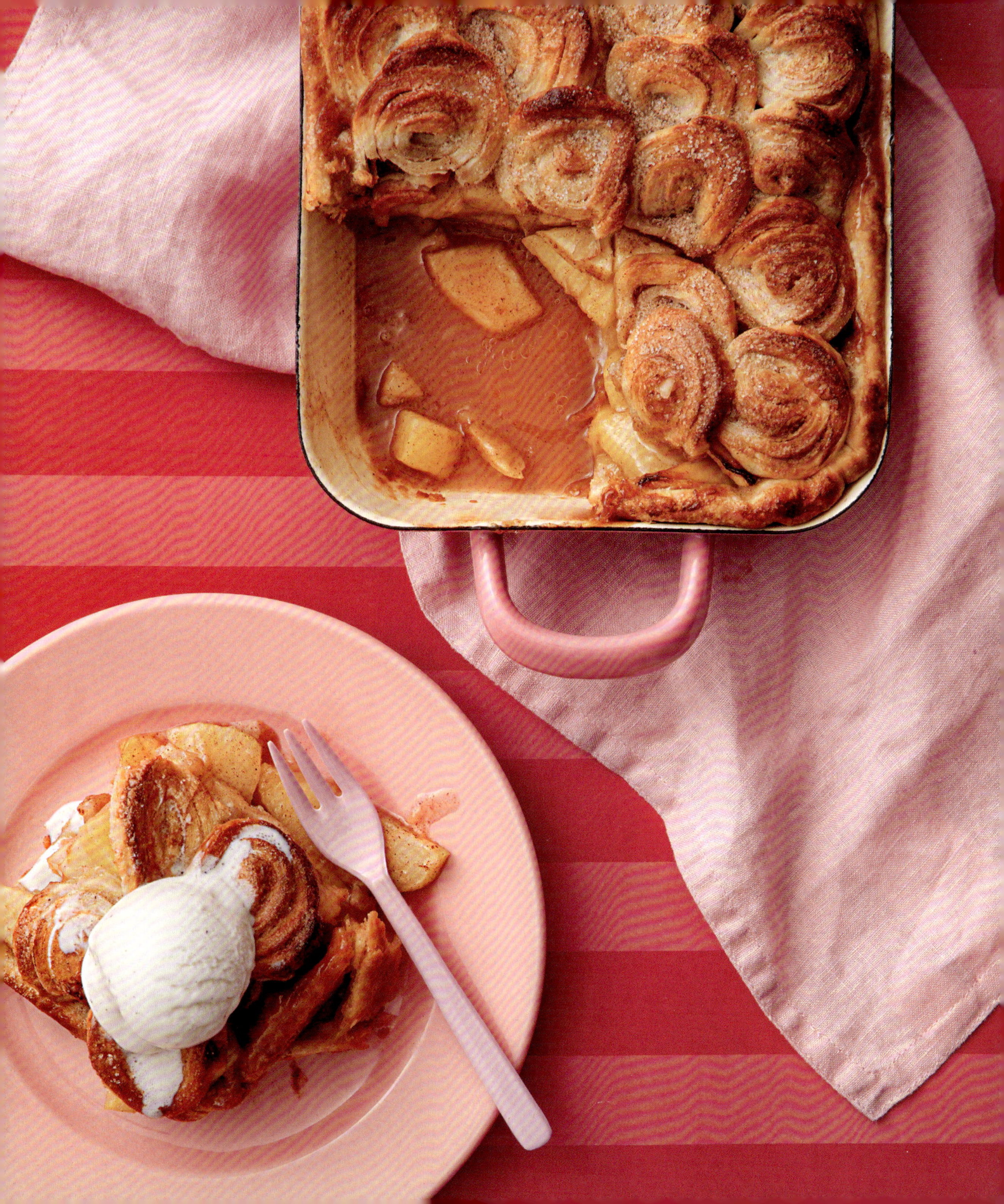

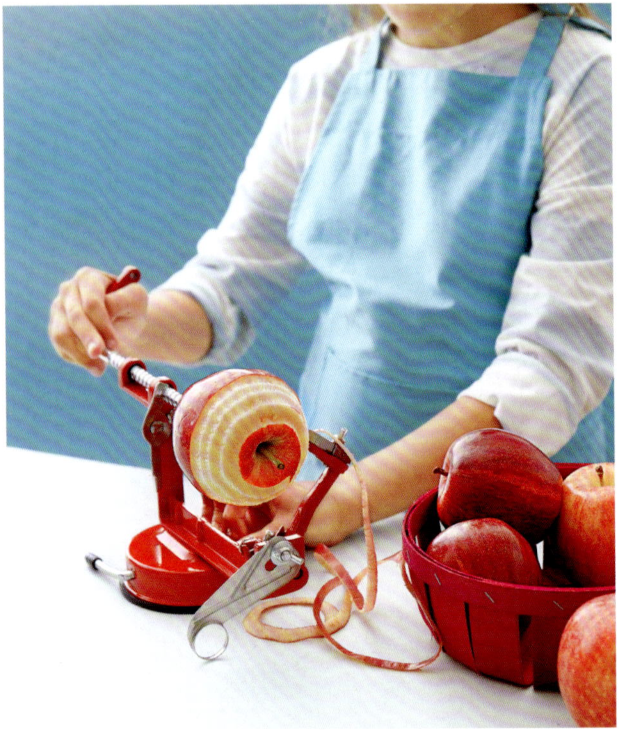
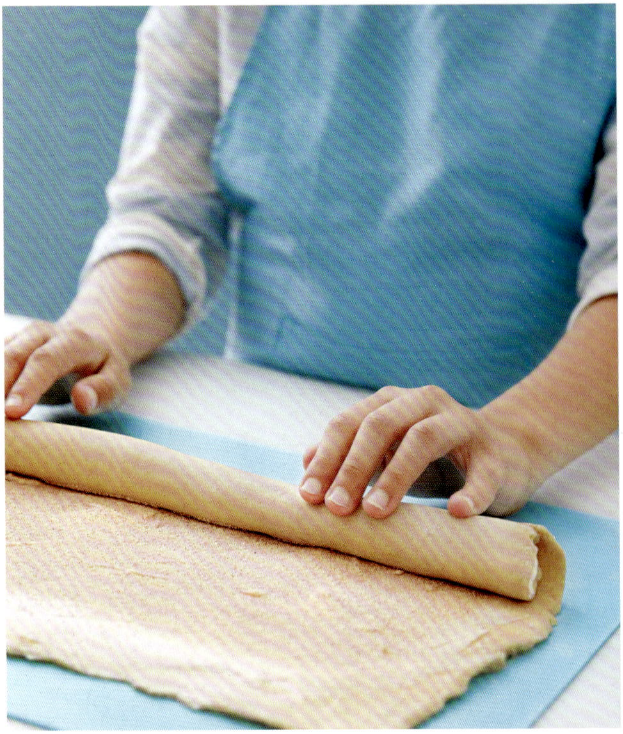
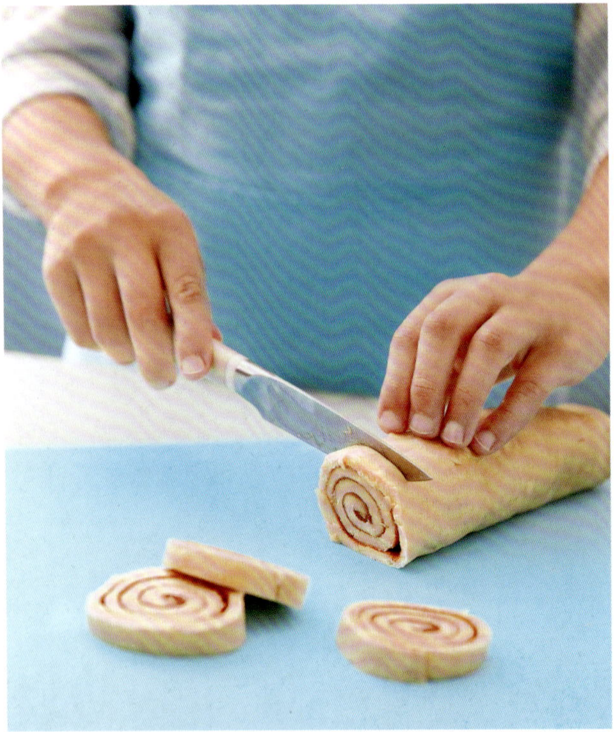
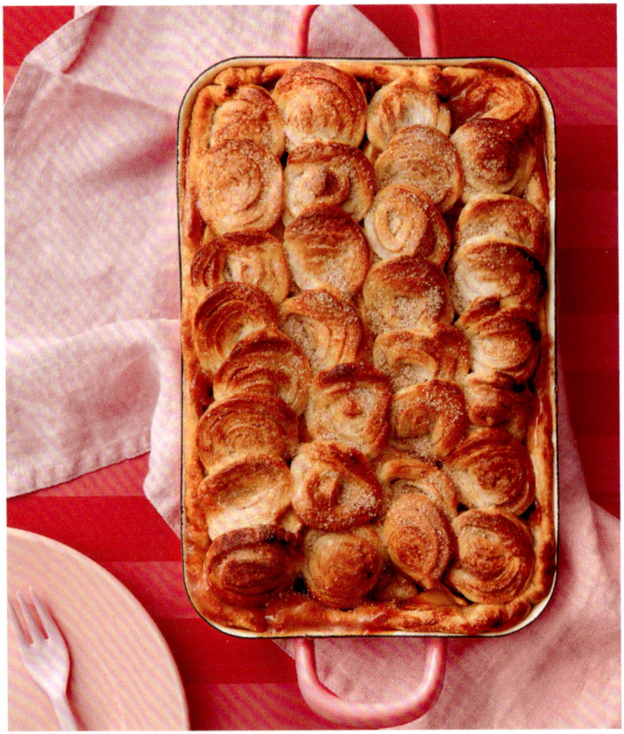

Apple prep

Peel and core apples with an old-fashioned apple peeler (shown at right), or peel them with a vegetable peeler and core them with a small knife.

~ *Continued from page 228* ~

In a large bowl, toss together the apples and lemon juice. Add ⅔ cup of the sugar, the flour, the remaining 1 teaspoon cinnamon, and the salt and toss to distribute evenly.

Remove the dough log from the refrigerator and cut it crosswise into slices ¼ to ⅜ inch thick. (You will need 32 to 40 slices.)

Pour the apples into the dough-lined baking sheet and spread evenly. Arrange the dough slices over the apple mixture, slightly overlapping them, in about 8 rows of 4 to 5 slices each. Brush the top with the egg mixture, then sprinkle evenly with the remaining 2 tablespoons sugar.

Bake until the crust is golden and the apples are tender, about 50 minutes. If the crust is browning too quickly, cover it loosely with a piece of aluminum foil until the end of baking. Remove the baking sheet from the oven and set it on a wire rack. Let cool until just slightly warm, about 45 minutes. Cut the pie into squares. Serve with vanilla ice cream, if you like.

Sweet Potato Pie

Sweet potatoes were bountiful in the South and easier to grow than pumpkins, so a tradition of making sweet potato pies grew from Southern plantations—and is now very popular everywhere. For the best results, be sure to bake this pie gently, just until the filling is set but still has a slight wobble. Serve it with a big dollop of lightly whipped cream.

MAKES 6 TO 8 SERVINGS

PIE DOUGH

1¼ cups all-purpose flour, plus flour for dusting

1 tablespoon granulated sugar (optional)

¼ teaspoon salt

½ cup (1 stick) cold unsalted butter, cut into small pieces

3 tablespoons very cold water, plus more if needed

1 large egg beaten with 1 teaspoon water

To make the dough, in a food processor, combine the flour, granulated sugar (if using), and salt. Sprinkle the butter over the top and pulse until the butter is slightly broken up but still in visible pieces. Evenly sprinkle the water over the flour mixture, then process just until the mixture starts to come together. Dump the dough into a large zippered plastic bag and press into a flat disk. Refrigerate for at least 30 minutes or up to 1 day before using, or freeze for up to 1 month.

Sprinkle a work surface with flour. Dump the dough onto the floured surface. Roll out the dough into a 12-inch round about ⅛ inch thick. Transfer the dough round to a 9-inch pie dish. Using kitchen scissors or a knife, trim the dough edges, leaving a ¾-inch overhang. Fold the overhand under itself around the rim of the dish, brush with the egg mixture, and use a fork to crimp the edges. Cover with plastic wrap and freeze for 30 minutes.

Meanwhile, preheat the oven to 350°F. Line the pie shell with aluminum foil and fill with pie weights, dried beans, or uncooked rice. Bake until the pie shell is lightly browned, about 20 minutes. Remove the pie dish from the oven and carefully remove the foil and weights. Set the dish on a wire rack and let cool completely. Keep the oven set.

Continued on page 234

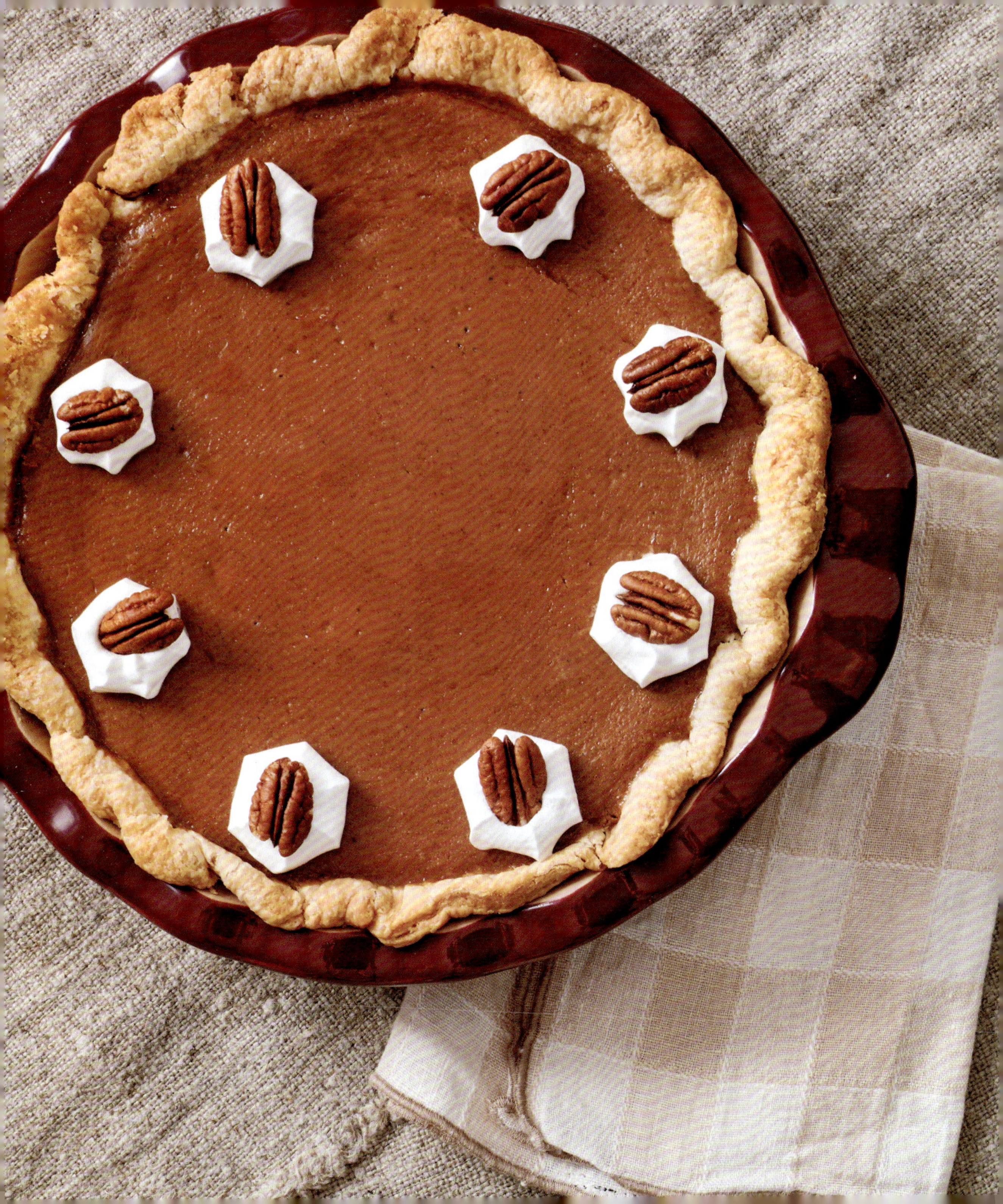

Continued from page 232

FILLING

2 cups peeled, cooked, and mashed sweet potatoes (from about 2½ pounds sweet potatoes)

1 cup firmly packed light brown sugar

4 tablespoons (½ stick) unsalted butter, melted and cooled

1 teaspoon ground cinnamon

½ teaspoon salt

¼ teaspoon ground nutmeg

1 (12-ounce) can evaporated milk

3 large eggs

1 tablespoon vanilla extract

Whipped Cream, for serving (page 128)

Pecans for decorating

To make the filling, in a food processor, blend the sweet potatoes until smooth. Add the brown sugar, melted butter, cinnamon, salt, nutmeg, evaporated milk, eggs, and vanilla and process until smooth, stopping the processor occasionally to scrape down the sides with a spatula. Pour the filling into the cooled crust.

Bake until the center is just set and the filling is golden brown, 45 to 50 minutes. If the edges of the crust are browning too quickly, cover them loosely with wide strips of aluminum foil. Remove the pie dish from the oven and set it on a wire rack. Let cool completely. Cut the pie into wedges and serve with dollops of whipped cream and pecans.

Classic Pumpkin Pie

A great pumpkin pie recipe is a must for any holiday baker. For an extra-special garnish, cut leaves or other small shapes from any excess dough, bake them alongside the pie, then decorate the top when the pie has cooled.

MAKES 8–10 SERVINGS

Pie Dough (page 232)

All-purpose flour for dusting

FILLING

1¼ cups firmly packed light brown sugar

1 tablespoon cornstarch

1½ teaspoons ground cinnamon

½ teaspoon salt

½ teaspoon ground ginger

¼ teaspoon ground nutmeg

⅛ teaspoon ground cloves

2 cups canned pumpkin purée

3 large eggs, lightly beaten

1 cup heavy cream

⅓ cup whole milk

Prepare the pie dough and chill as directed. Remove the dough disk from the refrigerator; let stand at room temperature for 5 minutes. Unwrap the dough disk and place it on a lightly floured work surface. Using a rolling pin, roll out the dough into a 12-inch round. Transfer the dough round to a 9-inch deep-dish pie dish. Using kitchen scissors or a knife, trim the dough edges, leaving a ½-inch overhang. Fold the overhang under itself around the rim of the dish and flute the dough edges, if desired.

Position a rack in the lower third of the oven and preheat to 400°F. Line the pie shell with parchment paper and fill with pie weights, dried beans, or uncooked rice. Place on a baking sheet and bake for 20 minutes. Remove the pie dish from the oven and carefully remove the parchment and weights. Continue baking until the pie shell is golden, about 5 minutes longer. Remove the pie dish from the oven and set it on a wire rack. Let cool completely.

Reduce the oven temperature to 375°F. To make the filling, in a large bowl, mix the brown sugar, cornstarch, cinnamon, salt, ginger, nutmeg, and cloves. Whisk in the pumpkin purée, eggs, cream, and milk until blended. Place the pie shell on a rimmed baking sheet and carefully pour in the filling.

Bake until the filling is set, 60 to 65 minutes. If the edges of the crust are browning too quickly, carefully cover them with strips of aluminum foil or a piecrust shield. Remove the pie dish from the oven and set it on a wire rack. Let cool for at least 2 hours before serving. Cut the pie into wedges and serve.

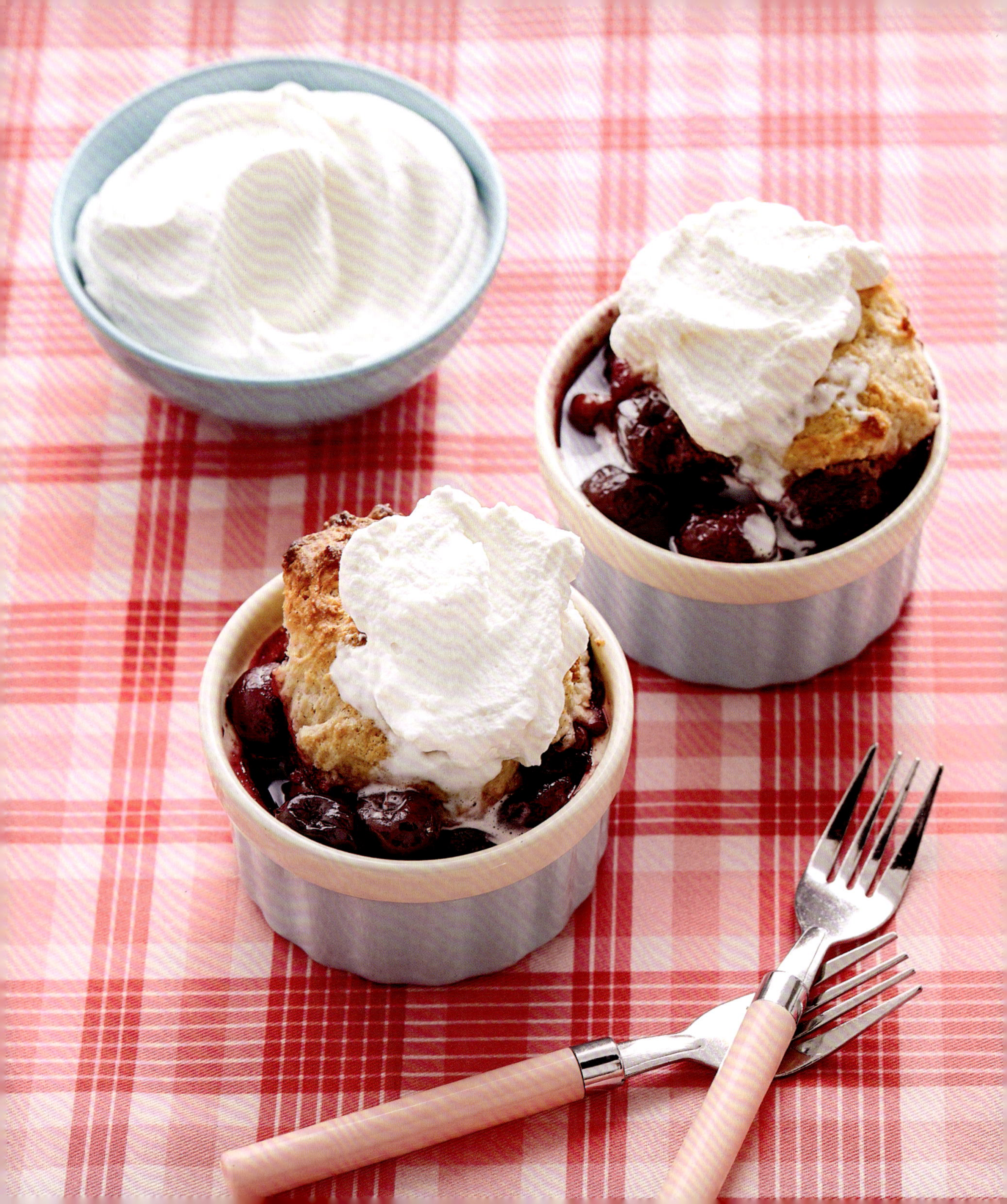

Individual Cherry Cobblers

A cobbler consists of a biscuitlike topping and a fresh fruit filling. The soft biscuit dough spreads as it bakes to cover the cherries completely, like an upside-down pie. Serve with a dollop of whipped cream or a scoop of vanilla ice cream, if you like.

MAKES 6 COBBLERS

FILLING

3 pounds fresh Bing cherries or other sweet cherries, pitted

1 tablespoon lemon juice

3 tablespoons sugar

TOPPING

⅔ cup buttermilk

1 teaspoon vanilla extract

1½ cups all-purpose flour

⅓ cup, plus 1 tablespoon sugar

1 teaspoon baking powder

½ teaspoon baking soda

½ teaspoon salt

¾ teaspoon ground cinnamon

6 tablespoons (¾ stick) cold unsalted butter, cut into ½-inch pieces

Preheat the oven to 375°F. Place six 1-cup ramekins or custard cups on a baking sheet.

To make the filling, in a large bowl, toss together the cherries, lemon juice, and sugar. Divide the mixture evenly among the ramekins. Bake for 10 minutes.

Meanwhile, make the topping: In a small bowl, stir together the buttermilk and vanilla; set aside. In a large bowl, sift together the flour, the ⅓ cup sugar, the baking powder, baking soda, salt, and ½ teaspoon of the cinnamon. Add the butter and, using a pastry blender or 2 knives, cut the butter into the flour mixture until large, coarse crumbs the size of small peas form. Pour the buttermilk mixture over the flour mixture and, using a wooden spoon, stir just until combined and a soft, sticky, evenly moistened dough forms.

Using oven mitts, remove the baking sheet from the oven. Drop the dough by heaping spoonfuls onto the hot fruit, spacing it evenly over the surface. The topping will not completely cover the fruit but will spread during baking. In a small bowl, stir together the remaining 1 tablespoon sugar and ¼ teaspoon cinnamon. Sprinkle over the dough.

Bake until the fruit filling is bubbling, the topping is browned, and a wooden skewer inserted into the topping comes out clean, 30 to 35 minutes. Using the oven mitts, remove the baking sheet from the oven and set it on a wire rack. Let cool for 15 minutes. Serve warm.

Strawberry Hand Pies

Whether you're enjoying a picnic at the park, a day at the beach, or a poolside snack, these hand pies are the perfect portable dessert. An egg wash brushed over the pies before baking creates a shiny, golden-brown sheen in the oven.

MAKES 4 HAND PIES

1 cup strawberries, sliced

2 tablespoons water

¼ cup sugar, plus sugar for sprinkling

2 tablespoons cornstarch

Pinch of salt

All-purpose flour for dusting

1 sheet frozen puff pastry, thawed

1 egg

1 tablespoon milk

In a saucepan, combine the strawberries, water, sugar, cornstarch, and salt. Set the pan over low heat and cook, stirring constantly, until the mixture is thick and jamlike, about 5 minutes. Transfer the strawberries to a bowl and cover with plastic wrap, pressing it directly onto the surface of the berries. Refrigerate until completely cool, about 1 hour.

Line a baking sheet with parchment paper. Sprinkle a work surface with flour. Place the puff pastry on the floured surface. Roll out and/or cut the pastry as needed to make an even 10-inch square. Cut the pastry into 4 equal squares. Divide the strawberry filling evenly among the squares, placing it in the center of each one. Lightly brush the edges of each square with water and fold into a triangle. Gently press the edges together with the tines of a fork to seal. Place the turnovers on the prepared baking sheet, spacing them about 2 inches apart, and refrigerate for 15 minutes.

Meanwhile, preheat the oven to 375°F.

In a cup, whisk together the egg and milk. Using a pastry brush, brush the egg wash over the tops of the pies, then sprinkle with sugar. Bake until puffed and golden brown, 25 to 35 minutes. Using oven mitts, remove the baking sheet from the oven and set it on a wire rack. Let cool for 20 minutes, then serve warm.

Maple-Pecan Pie with Shortbread Crust

If you're a fan of pecans and maple syrup, this is the pie for you. For a pretty presentation, keep the pecans whole and arrange them on top of the unbaked pie instead of stirring them into the filling.

MAKES 8–10 SERVINGS

Shortbread Crust (page 252) or store-bought pie pastry

2 cups pure maple syrup

2 large eggs, lightly beaten

¼ cup firmly packed light or dark brown sugar

2 tablespoons unsalted butter, melted and cooled

1 teaspoon vanilla extract

⅛ teaspoon salt

1½ cups pecans, coarsely chopped

Prepare and bake the shortbread crust as directed, or follow the package directions to bake a store-bought pie pastry in a 9-inch pie dish. Remove the pie dish from the oven and set it on a wire rack. Let cool. Reduce the oven temperature to 325°F.

Pour the maple syrup into a saucepan. Set the pan over medium-high heat and boil the syrup for 8 to 10 minutes (this will concentrate its flavor and texture). Remove from the heat and carefully pour the syrup into a heatproof measuring pitcher. The syrup should be reduced to 1½ cups. If necessary, return the syrup to the saucepan and continue to boil until sufficiently reduced. Let cool.

In a bowl, stir together the cooled maple syrup, eggs, brown sugar, melted butter, vanilla, and salt until well mixed. Add the pecans and stir well. Pour into the cooled crust, making sure the pecans are evenly distributed.

Bake until the center of the pie is slightly puffed and firm to the touch, 30 to 35 minutes. If the edges of the crust are browning too quickly, cover them loosely with wide strips of aluminum foil or a piecrust shield. Remove the pie dish from the oven and set it on a wire rack. Let cool until just slightly warm, about 45 minutes. Cut the pie into wedges and serve warm.

Chocolate-Raspberry Tartlets

Looking for a super-special dessert? These adorable raspberry-topped chocolate tarts are just the thing. Dust them with powdered sugar before serving if you like, though they're equally tasty without it.

MAKES 12 TARTLETS

PASTRY SHELLS

1 cup blanched almonds

3 tablespoons firmly packed light brown sugar

3 tablespoons unsalted butter, melted and cooled, plus butter for greasing

FILLING

½ cup heavy cream

5 ounces semisweet chocolate chips

2 pints fresh raspberries

Fresh mint leaves for garnish

To make the pastry shells, preheat the oven to 325°F. Grease the bottoms of twelve 3-inch tartlet pans or standard muffins cups with butter.

Spread the almonds on a rimmed baking sheet and toast in the oven, stirring once or twice, until lightly browned and fragrant, about 12 minutes. Remove the baking sheet from the oven and set it on a wire rack. Let cool.

In a food processor, combine the almonds and brown sugar. Process until finely ground. Add the melted butter and process until moist clumps form. Firmly press 1½ tablespoons of the nut mixture onto the bottom and up the sides of each prepared tartlet pan, creating an even layer. Place on a baking sheet.

Bake until the pastry shells are golden brown and firm to the touch, about 12 minutes. Remove the baking sheet from the oven and set it on a wire rack. Let cool completely. Remove the pastry shells from the pan, using the tip of a knife to loosen them if necessary. Transfer to a serving plate and set aside.

Meanwhile, make the filling: Bring the cream to a simmer in a small saucepan over medium heat. Remove from the heat. Add the chocolate chips and whisk until smooth. Let cool until thickened but still pourable, about 10 minutes.

Spoon the filling into the pastry shells, dividing it evenly. Refrigerate until the filling has thickened, about 30 minutes. Arrange the raspberries in a single layer on the tarts, dividing them evenly. Cover and refrigerate until the filling is firm, at least 2 hours or up to 2 days. Garnish with mint leaves and serve.

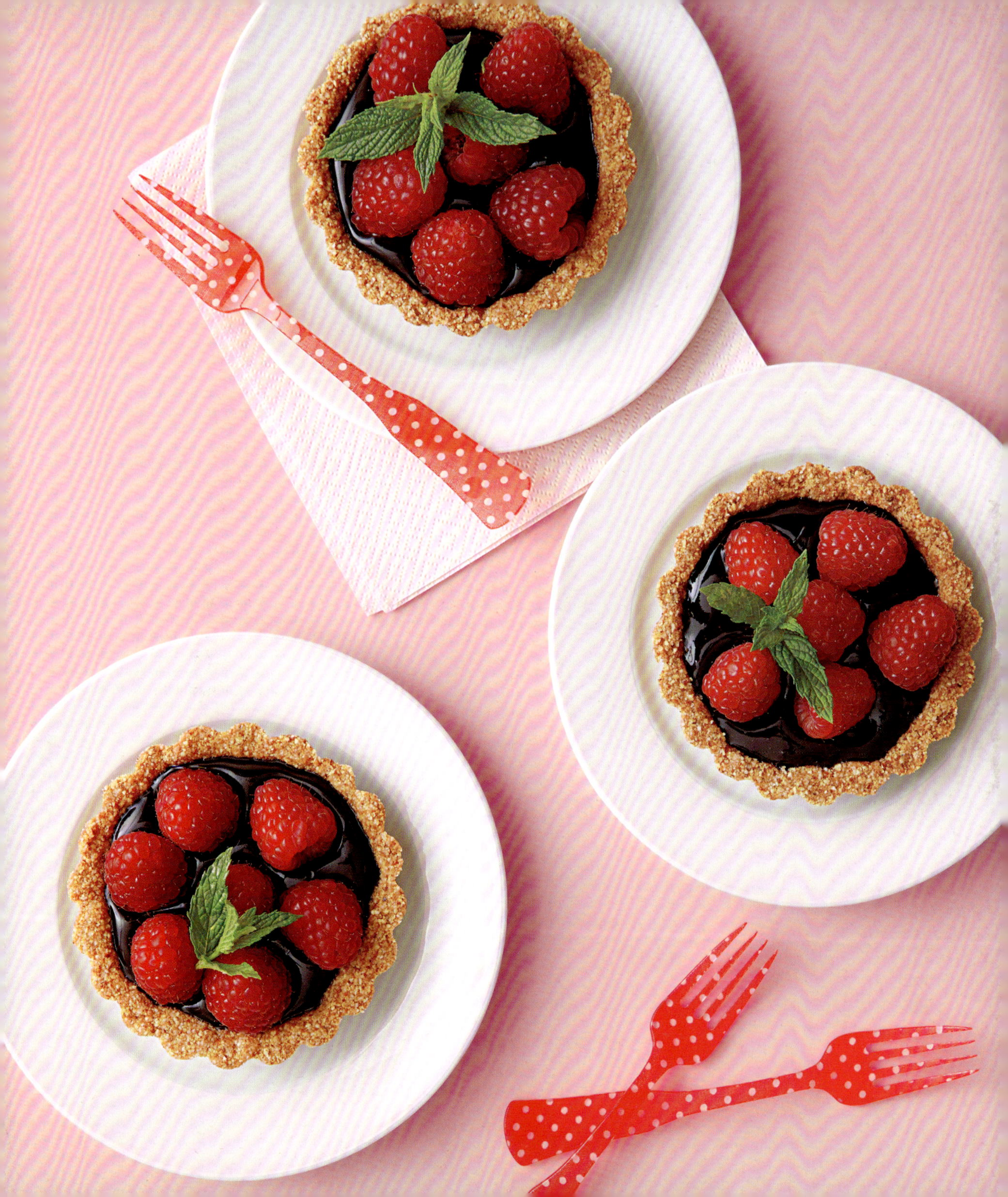

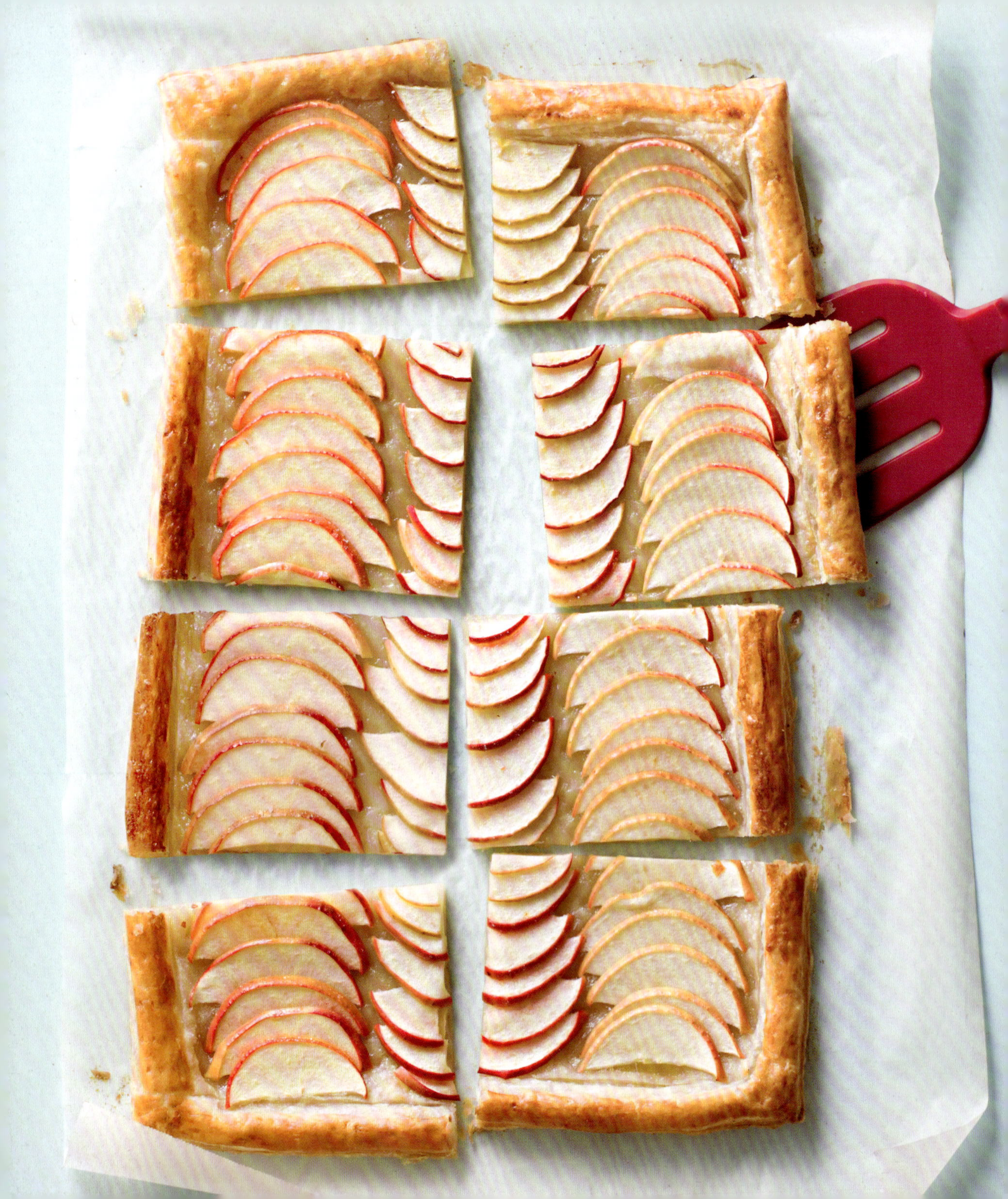

French Apple Tart

Impress your friends with this dessert that looks super fancy but uses only four ingredients and is super easy to make! The secret: frozen puff pastry, which you roll into a big rectangle before layering on the sliced apples.

MAKES 6 TO 8 SERVINGS

All-purpose flour, for dusting

1 sheet frozen puff pastry, thawed overnight in the refrigerator

2 Granny Smith, Braeburn, Fuji, or Cortland apples

¼ cup sugar

Preheat the oven to 425°F. Line a rimmed cookie sheet with parchment paper.

Very lightly dust a clean work surface with flour. Lay the puff pastry on the surface and lightly dust the top with flour. Using a rolling pin, roll out the sheet to a 10-by-15-inch rectangle about ⅛ inch thick. Place the rectangle on the prepared cookie sheet and put in the freezer to chill while you prepare the apples.

Core the apples with an apple corer or paring knife and cut them in half lengthwise. Slice each half into ¼-inch-thick half-moons.

Remove the pastry from the freezer. With a sharp paring knife, cut a 1-inch border along the edges of the puff pastry, being careful not to cut more than halfway through the pastry. Prick the pastry inside of the border all over with a fork, and then sprinkle evenly with 2 tablespoons of the sugar. Arrange the apple slices in slightly overlapping rows on the pastry inside of the border and sprinkle the apples evenly with the remaining 2 tablespoons sugar.

Bake until the pastry is golden brown and the apples are tender, 15 to 20 minutes. Remove from the oven and let cool on the cookie sheet on a wire rack. Cut into pieces and serve warm or at room temperature.

Blackberry Tart with Pecan Crust

When fresh berries are in season, they need very little sugar to enhance their natural sweetness. You can use blueberries in place of the blackberries, if you like. For a nut-free crust, omit the pecans and use 1¼ cups all-purpose flour instead.

MAKES 8 SERVINGS

CRUST

1 cup pecan halves

¾ cup all-purpose flour

3 tablespoons sugar

½ teaspoon salt

½ cup (1 stick) unsalted butter, at room temperature

1 tablespoon white vinegar

FILLING

⅓ to ½ cup sugar

2 tablespoons all-purpose flour

Dash of ground cinnamon

4 cups blackberries

Whipped cream or ice cream for serving (optional)

Preheat the oven to 375°F. Trace the bottom of a 9-inch tart pan with a removable bottom onto a sheet of parchment paper and cut out the circle with scissors. Put the paper circle in the bottom of the pan.

To make the crust, in the bowl of a food processor, grind the pecans until fine crumbs form. Transfer to a bowl. Add the flour, sugar, and salt, and stir until combined. Add the butter and, using a pastry blender or two knives, cut the butter into the nut mixture until large crumbs form. Add the vinegar and mix gently with the fork until the dough comes together.

Pour the nut mixture into the prepared tart pan and press gently with your fingers to spread it evenly across the bottom and up the sides of the pan.

To make the filling, in a large bowl, whisk together the sugar, flour, and cinnamon. Add the blackberries and stir gently to mix. Pour the berry mixture over the crust, spreading evenly. Place the pan on a cookie sheet.

Bake the tart for 40 minutes. Cover the tart loosely with aluminum foil to prevent burning (ask an adult for help if needed!), then continue to bake until the berries are bursting and the crust is deep brown, 20 to 25 minutes longer.

Using oven mitts, remove the cookie sheet from the oven and set the tart pan on a wire rack. Let cool. Remove the outer rim of the pan and place the tart on a serving plate. Cut into slices. Serve with whipped cream or ice cream, if you like.

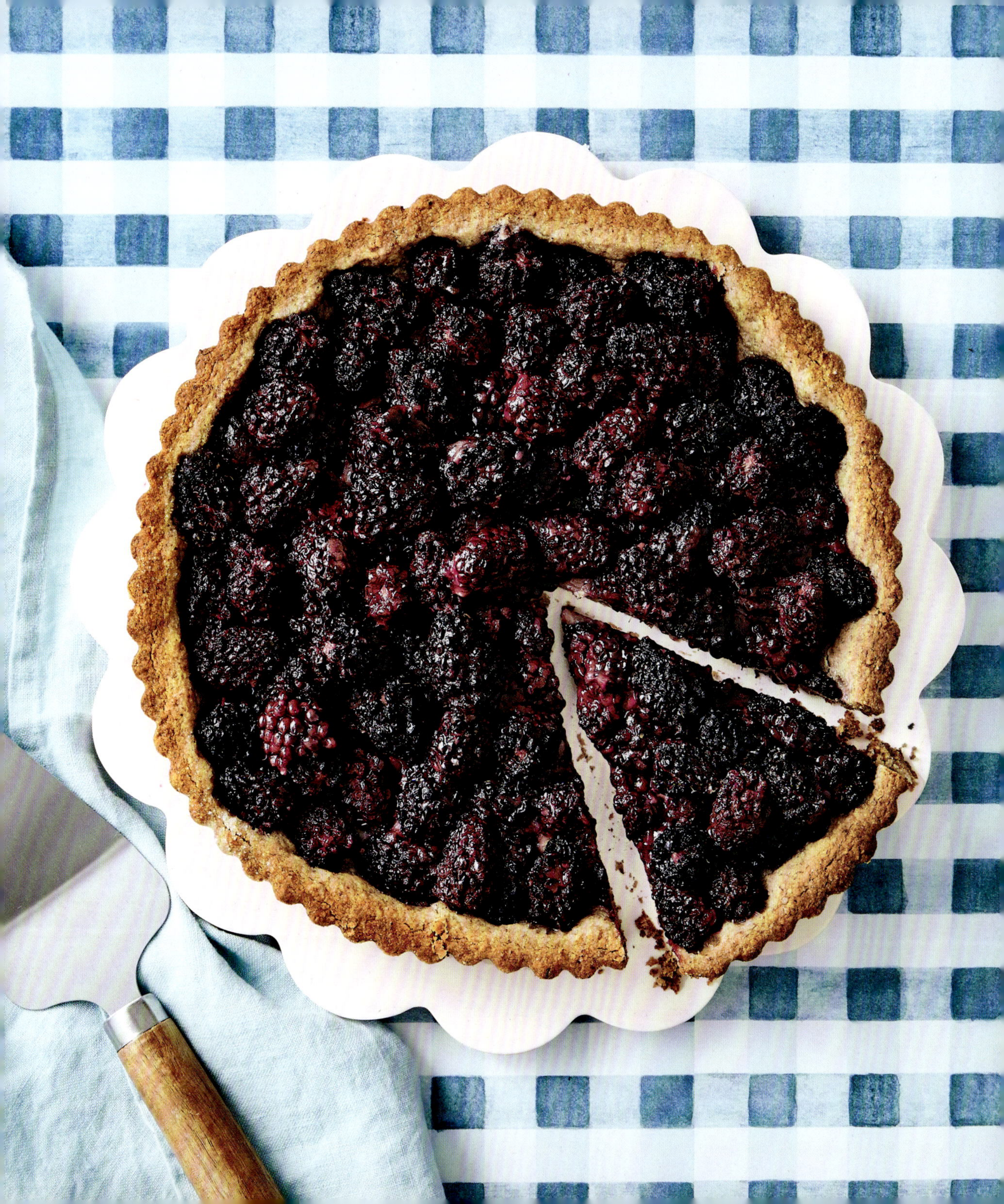

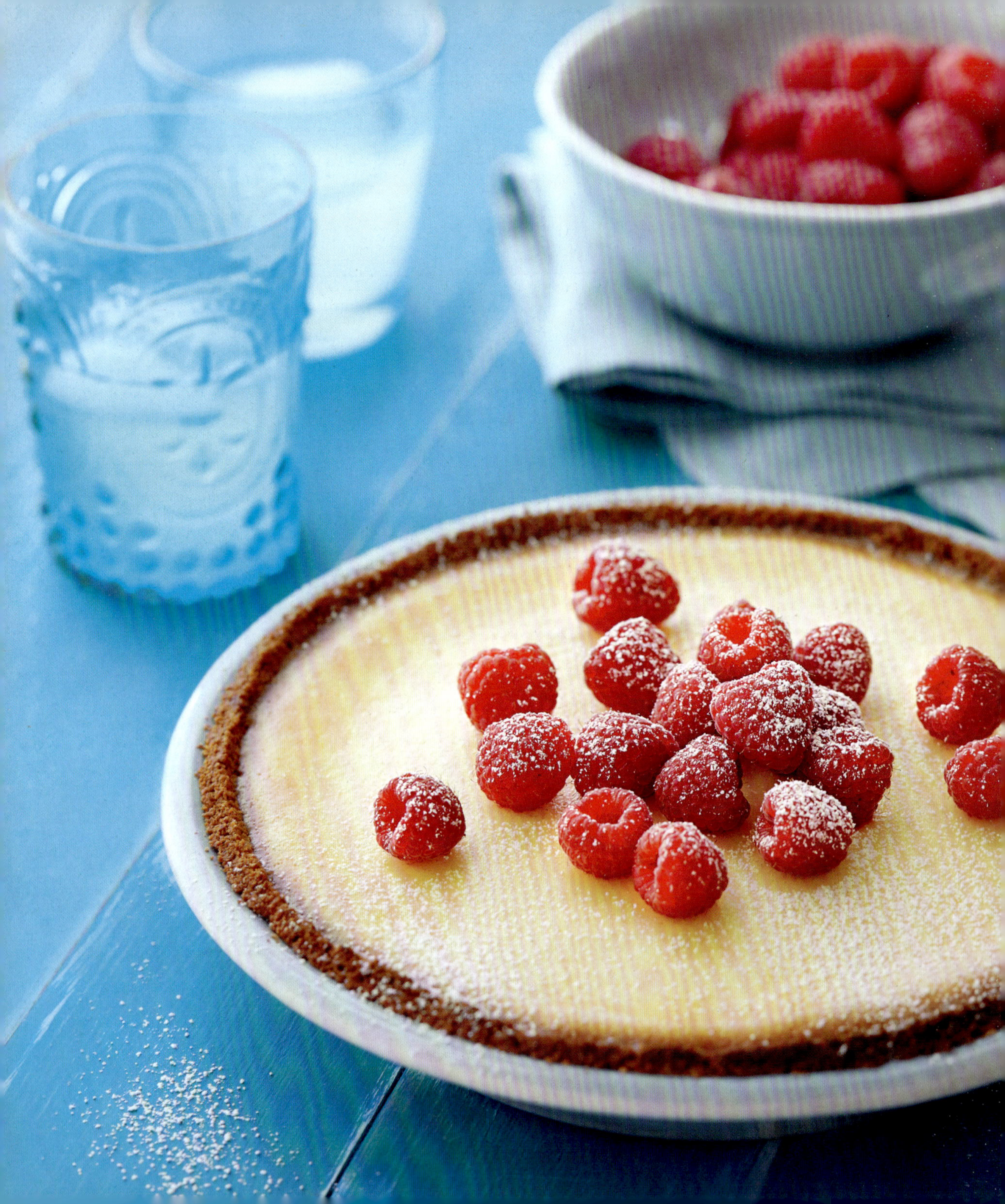

Lemon Tart with Raspberries

Lemons are great to bake with because their tart flavor keeps desserts from becoming overly sweet. Soft cream cheese, delicate raspberries, and a crunchy graham cracker crust make the perfect texture combo for every bite.

MAKES 8 SERVINGS

- 2 large eggs
- ⅔ cup granulated sugar
- 12 ounces cream cheese, at room temperature
- ½ cup sour cream
- 2 tablespoons all-purpose flour
- 2 teaspoons grated lemon zest
- Juice from 1 lemon
- 1 teaspoon vanilla extract
- 1 store-bought 9-inch graham cracker crust
- 6 ounces raspberries
- Powdered sugar, for dusting

Preheat the oven to 350°F.

Combine the eggs and granulated sugar in a food processor and process until smooth. Add the cream cheese, pulse a few times to break it up, and then process until smooth. Add the sour cream, flour, lemon zest, lemon juice, and vanilla and process just until smooth. Pour the filling into the crust and spread the top evenly.

Bake until the top looks firm and is set when you gently shake the pan, 35 to 45 minutes. Remove the pan from the oven and set it atop a wire rack. Let cool for about 1 hour. Cover with plastic wrap and refrigerate until cold, at least 3 hours or up to overnight. Spoon the raspberries on top of the tart and dust with powdered sugar just before serving. Cut into wedges and serve cold.

Pretty presentation
After baking, place the tart in a fancy pie plate to hide the aluminum shell of the store-bought crust.

Lemon Tartlets with Sugared Flowers

Did you know that some flowers are edible? They make super cool decorations for desserts—just be sure to choose blooms that are safe to eat (see the list below). Prepare the sugared flowers the day before you make the tartlets so they have time to dry.

MAKES 12 TARTLETS

FOR THE SUGARED FLOWERS

8–16 pesticide-free edible flowers, such as violet, pansy, culinary lavender, and/or rose petals

1 large egg white

Superfine sugar, for sprinkling

FOR THE LEMON CURD

1 large whole egg

4 large egg yolks

½ cup granulated sugar

⅓ cup fresh lemon juice, strained

2 tablespoons unsalted butter

12 store-bought mini tart shells, each about 1½ inches in diameter

To make the sugared flowers, gently wash the flowers under slowly running cool water and then set them on paper towels to dry, blotting them lightly with the towels if needed. The flowers must be fully dry before you begin. Line a rimmed cookie sheet with parchment paper. In a small bowl, and using a small, clean paintbrush, lightly brush the egg white mixture over the front and back of the flower. Then, holding the flower over the sugar bowl, scoop up a little sugar and sprinkle it over the top, coating the flower completely. Set the flower aside on the prepared cookie sheet. Repeat with the remaining flowers. Let the flowers dry at room temperature for 12 to 24 hours until they are stiff and dry to the touch.

Meanwhile, to make the lemon curd, fill a saucepan about one-third full of water and bring to a gentle simmer over medium-low heat. Put the whole egg, egg yolks, granulated sugar, and lemon juice into a heatproof bowl that will rest snugly on the rim of the saucepan. Place the bowl on the saucepan over (but not touching) the simmering water.

Continued on page 250

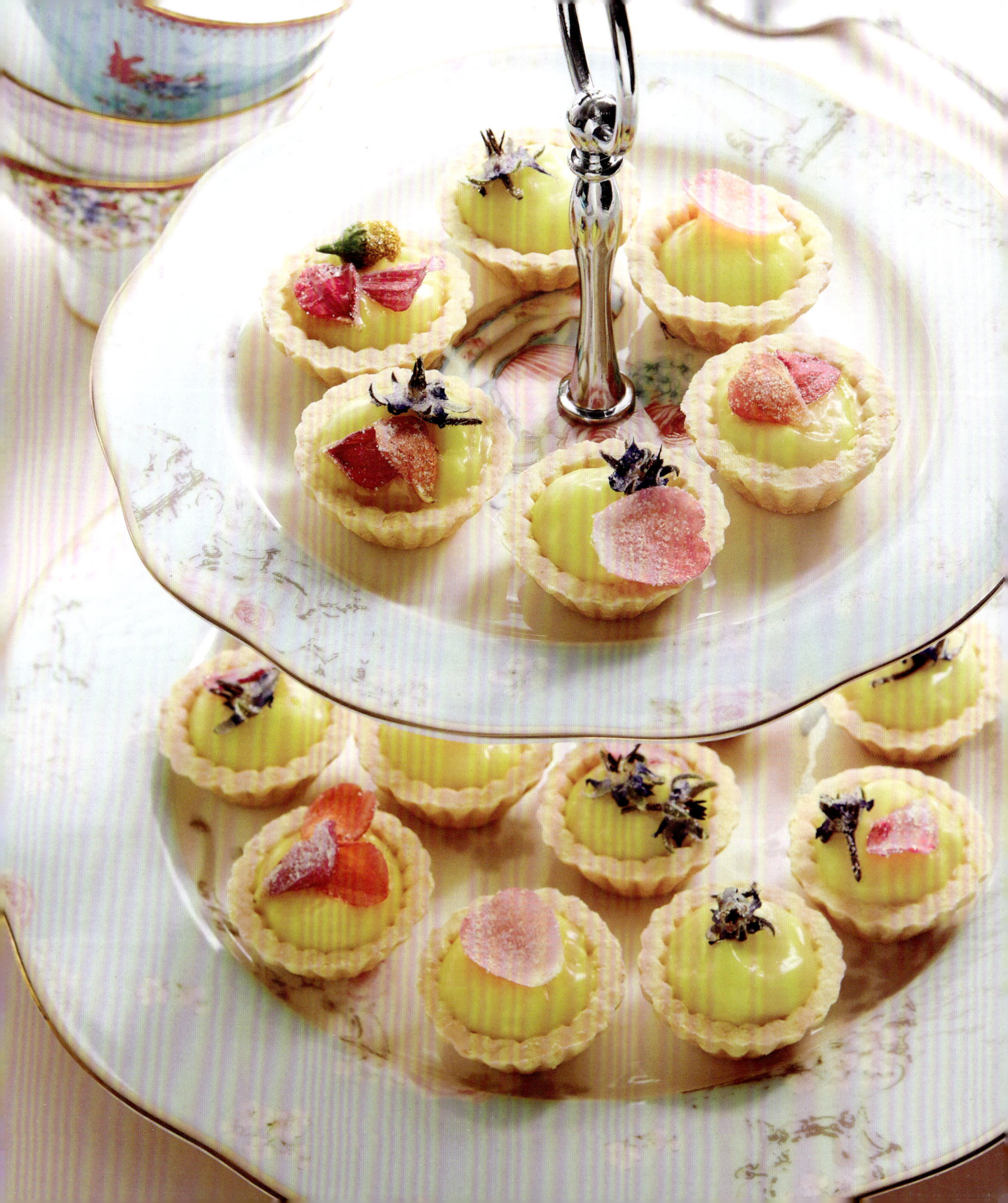

Tea party perfection
This yummy mochi treat is best served with a piping-hot cup of green tea.

~ *Continued from page 248* ~

Cook, stirring constantly with a wooden spoon or silicone spatula, until thickened, about 5 minutes. Remove from the heat, add the butter, and stir until melted and incorporated. Pour the curd through a fine-mesh sieve placed over a bowl, pressing against the curd with the back of the spoon or spatula to force as much through as possible. Cover the bowl with plastic wrap, pressing the plastic directly onto the surface of the curd (to prevent a "skin" from forming), and let cool until tepid. Refrigerate until chilled, about 1 hour, before using.

Line up the tartlet shells on a work surface. Fill each shell with about 1 tablespoon of the lemon curd, then garnish with the sugared blossoms. (You can use any leftover lemon curd as a topping for yogurt or ice cream.) Arrange the tarts on a large plate or tray and serve.

Cranberry Chess Tart

Made with a simple custardy buttermilk filling, chess pie is a classic dessert of the American South. In our modern version, it's baked in a square tart pan and bursting with sweet-tart cranberries and orange zest for a festive dessert.

MAKES 8 SERVINGS

Tart Dough (page 253)

All-purpose flour for dusting

1⅓ cups sugar

½ cup (1 stick) unsalted butter, melted and cooled

⅛ teaspoon salt

3 large eggs

¼ cup all-purpose flour

⅓ cup buttermilk

1 teaspoon cider vinegar

2 teaspoons finely grated orange zest

2 cups fresh or thawed frozen cranberries, coarsely chopped

Prepare the tart dough and chill as directed.

Unwrap the dough and place it on a lightly floured work surface. Using a rolling pin, roll out the dough into a 12-inch round about ⅛ inch thick. Transfer the dough to a 10-inch square or round tart pan, gently pressing it into the pan. Trim the dough edges, leaving a ¾-inch overhang. Fold the overhang over onto itself and pinch to create a double-thick edge. Refrigerate or freeze the dough until firm, about 30 minutes.

Preheat the oven to 400°F. Line the tart shell with parchment paper and fill with pie weights. Bake until the crust starts to look dry, about 15 minutes. Remove the tart pan from the oven and carefully remove the parchment and weights. Continue baking until the tart shell is lightly golden, about 5 minutes longer. Remove the tart pan from the oven and set it on a wire rack. Let cool completely.

In a large bowl, whisk together the sugar, melted butter, and salt. Add the eggs and beat until smooth. Stir in the flour, then stir in the buttermilk, vinegar, and orange zest, mixing well. Stir in the cranberries. Pour the mixture into the cooled tart shell, spreading it evenly.

Bake until the top of the tart is lightly golden brown and domed and the filling is firm, about 45 minutes. Remove the tart pan from the oven and set it on a wire rack. Let cool completely. Cut the tart into wedges.

Shortbread Crust

This sweet, cookie-like crust is first baked and then filled after it cools. To prevent the unbaked crust from puffing up in the oven, line the dough with foil and cover it with pie weights, dried beans, or uncooked rice—a technique known as blind baking.

MAKES ONE 9-INCH CRUST

6 tablespoons (¾ stick) unsalted butter, at room temperature

3 tablespoons granulated sugar

3 tablespoons firmly packed light brown sugar

2 large egg yolks

1¼ cups all-purpose flour

1 teaspoon salt

1 teaspoon vanilla extract

Preheat the oven to 375°F.

In a large bowl, using an electric mixer, beat the butter, granulated sugar, and brown sugar on medium speed until light and fluffy, about 3 minutes. Turn off the mixer and scrape down the bowl with a rubber spatula. Add the egg yolks, flour, salt, and vanilla and beat just until combined, about 2 minutes. Scrape down the bowl.

Transfer the dough to a 9-inch pie dish and spread evenly across the bottom and up the sides, pressing until compact. Pierce the bottom of the crust all over with a fork and freeze for 20 minutes.

Line the crust with aluminum foil and fill with pie weights. Bake until the crust is lightly browned, about 20 minutes. Remove the pie dish from the oven and carefully remove the foil and weights. Set the pie dish on a wire rack and let cool completely before filling.

Tart Dough

Unlike pie dough, tart dough includes egg, which results in a slightly cakier crust. As with pie dough, keep the butter and water cold to ensure the flakiest crust. If you prefer a larger tart, you can also use this dough to line a 9-inch tart pan.

MAKES 25 TARTLETS

1 large egg yolk

2 tablespoons very cold water

1 teaspoon vanilla extract

1¼ cups all-purpose flour

¼ cup sugar

¼ teaspoon salt

½ cup (1 stick) cold unsalted butter, cut into small pieces

In a small bowl, stir together the egg yolk, water, and vanilla. In the bowl of a food processor, combine the flour, sugar, and salt. Sprinkle the butter over the top and pulse for a few seconds, or just until the butter is broken up into the flour but still in visible pieces. Pour the egg mixture over the flour mixture and process just until the mixture starts to come together. Dump the dough into a large zippered plastic bag and press into a flat disk. Refrigerate the dough for at least 30 minutes or up to 1 day before using, or freeze for up to 1 month.

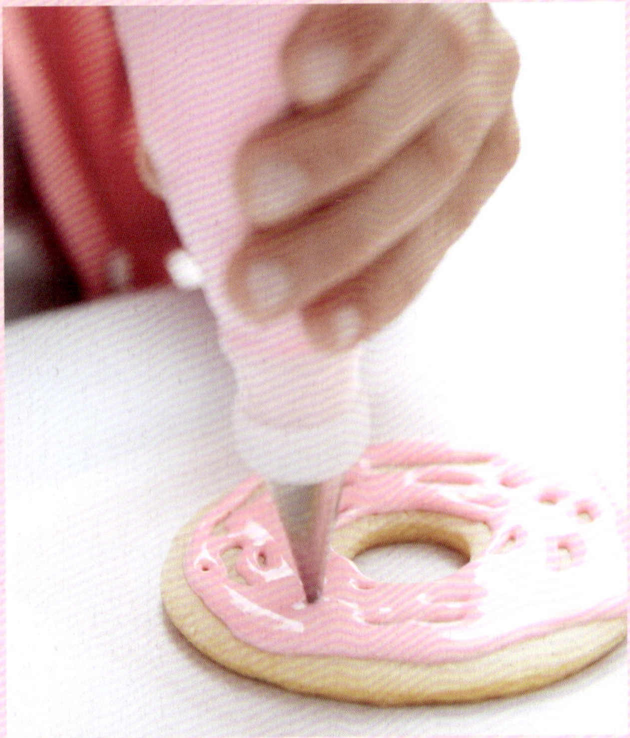
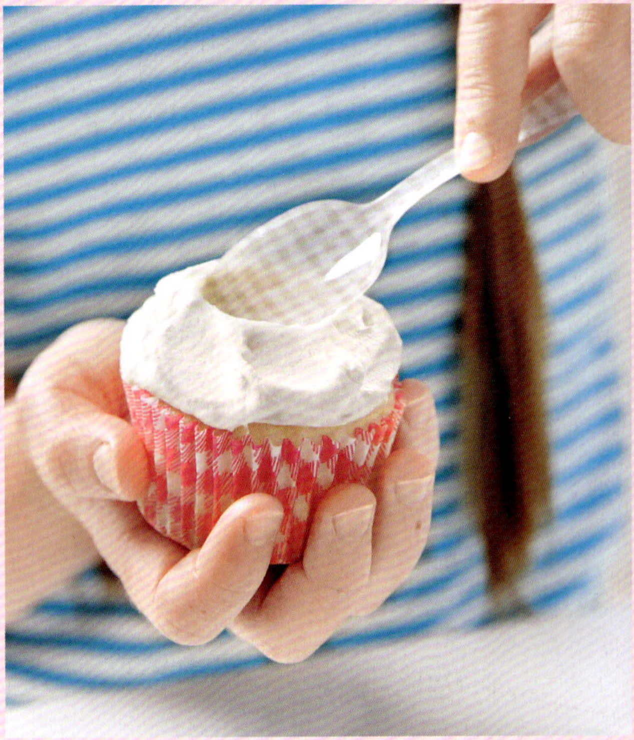
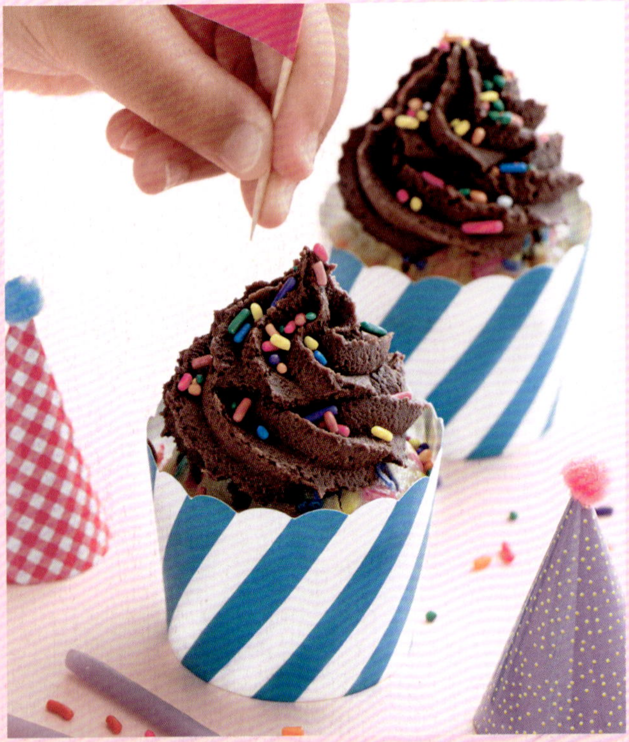
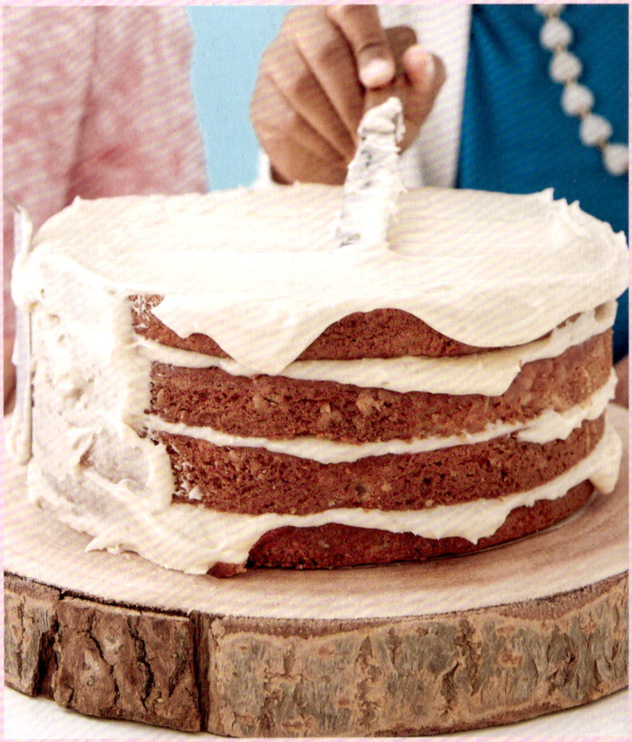

Icings & Frostings

Royal Icing

This stiff white icing, made by whipping powdered sugar with water and meringue powder, got its name after it was used to ice Queen Victoria's white wedding cake in England in the 1800s. Luckily for us, it's the perfect icing to top sugar cookies, too.

MAKES ABOUT 3 CUPS

4 cups powdered sugar

3 tablespoons meringue powder

½ cup warm water, plus more as needed

½ teaspoon vanilla extract or ¼ teaspoon almond extract (optional)

Gel paste food coloring in your favorite colors (optional)

In a large bowl, using an electric mixer, beat the sugar, meringue powder, ½ cup warm water, and vanilla (if using) on medium speed until the mixture is very thick but drizzleable, 7 to 8 minutes. To test if the consistency is correct, drizzle a spoonful of icing onto itself in the bowl; it should sit on the surface for about 5 seconds. If it is too thick, stir in additional warm water 1 teaspoon at a time with a rubber spatula.

Icing Technique: Flooding If using food coloring, divide the royal icing among small bowls, using one bowl for each color you want to make. Add just a dab or two of food coloring to each bowl and mix well; if needed, stir in more food coloring until the desired color intensity is reached.

To fill a pastry bag, firmly push a ⅛-inch round piping tip (or other desired size) down into the small hole at the bottom of the bag. Form a cuff by folding down the top one-third of the bag. Place one hand under the cuff. Using a rubber spatula, scoop icing into the bag with your other hand, no more than half full. Unfold the cuff, push the icing down toward the tip, and twist the bag closed where the icing ends. Squeeze the bag from the top when you pipe.

Pipe icing around the edge of a cookie to form a border. Using the same or a different color, pipe the icing into the center of the cookie and let it run to the border. Gently tap the cookie against the work surface to get the icing to settle into a smooth, even layer.

Continued on page 258

Pipe like a pro
Piping tips for pastry bags come in a variety of shapes and sizes—the smaller the numeral, the smaller the hole.

Handy helper
Use a large wide-rimmed glass to hold your piping bag while you fill it and to rest it in between decorating.

~ *Continued from page 256* ~

To create a design on top of the first icing layer, let dry at room temperature until slightly hardened, about 2 hours. Cover and refrigerate the unused icing until needed; stir well before use. Pipe your second design on top, then let dry at room temperature until the icing is firm, at least 6 hours or up to overnight.

Icing Technique: Swirling Place ¼ cup of royal icing into each of 3 small bowls. Add just a dab or two of food coloring to each bowl and mix well; if needed, stir in more food coloring until the desired color intensity is reached. Spoon each colored icing into a pastry bag fitted with a ¼-inch round tip.

Pipe one color of icing around the edge of a cookie to form a border, then pipe icing into the center of the cookie and let it run to the border. Gently tap the cookie a couple of times against the work surface to get the icing to settle into a smooth, even layer.

While the icing is still wet, pipe horizontal parallel lines of one or both of the other colors across the cookie. Lightly drag the tip of a toothpick from top to bottom through the lines. Wipe the toothpick clean, then drag it through the lines in the opposite direction, from the bottom to the top, spaced about ½ inch from the first swirl. Continue dragging the toothpick through the lines, moving in opposite directions and wiping the toothpick clean between each pass. Let the icing dry until firm, at least 6 hours or up to overnight.

White Chocolate Frosting

Creamy, fluffy, and smooth—this frosting is first-rate when it comes to topping cakes and cupcakes. For best results, have all the ingredients at about the same temperature when blending. To add pizzazz, beat in a few drops of food coloring at the end of mixing.

MAKES ABOUT 2½ CUPS

4 ounces white chocolate, finely chopped

½ cup (1 stick) unsalted butter, at room temperature

2½ cups powdered sugar

3 tablespoons whole milk

½ teaspoon vanilla extract

Pinch of salt

Put the white chocolate in a small microwave-safe bowl. Microwave on high for 25 seconds, stir, then microwave in 15-second intervals, stirring at each interval, just until the chocolate is melted and smooth. Let cool for about 10 minutes.

In a large bowl, using an electric mixer, beat the butter on medium speed until light and fluffy, about 2 minutes. Turn off the mixer and scrape down the bowl with a rubber spatula. Add the powdered sugar, milk, vanilla, and salt and beat on medium speed until combined, then add the white chocolate and beat until combined. Turn off the mixer and scrape down the bowl. Beat on medium-high speed until the frosting is fluffy and smooth, about 5 minutes. Use right away, or store in an airtight container in the refrigerator for up to 2 days. Stir vigorously just before using.

Variation

White Chocolate–Peppermint Frosting
Add ½ teaspoon peppermint extract in place of the vanilla extract.

Fluffy Vanilla Frosting

This versatile frosting is delicious paired with almost any cupcake in this book. And it's a great base for flavor variations such as mint, white chocolate, raspberry, and coconut; see variations below.

MAKES ABOUT 2 CUPS

½ cup (1 stick) unsalted butter, at room temperature

2½ cups powdered sugar

3 tablespoons whole milk

1 teaspoon vanilla extract

Pinch of salt

In a large bowl, using an electric mixer, beat the butter on medium speed until light and fluffy, about 2 minutes. Turn off the mixer. Add the powdered sugar, milk, vanilla, and salt. Mix on low speed just until combined. Stop the mixer and scrape down the bowl with a rubber spatula. Beat on medium-high speed until the frosting is airy and smooth, about 5 minutes.

Fluffy Mint Frosting: Add ½ teaspoon peppermint extract along with the sugar, milk, vanilla, and salt.

Fluffy Coconut Frosting: Add 1 teaspoon coconut extract along with the sugar, milk, vanilla, and salt.

Fluffy Raspberry Frosting: Follow the recipe for Fluffy Vanilla Frosting. Place 1 cup raspberries into a fine-mesh strainer. Holding the strainer over the bowl of frosting, press the raspberries with a rubber spatula to extract as much juice as you can; discard the seeds and pulp. Gently fold the raspberry juices into the frosting with the rubber spatula until no streaks remain.

Fluffy White Chocolate Frosting: Place 4 ounces white chocolate, finely chopped, in a small microwave-safe bowl. Microwave on high power, stirring every 20 seconds, just until the chocolate is melted and smooth. Let the white chocolate cool slightly. Follow the recipe for Fluffy Vanilla Frosting, add the melted white chocolate, then beat on medium-high speed until well combined.

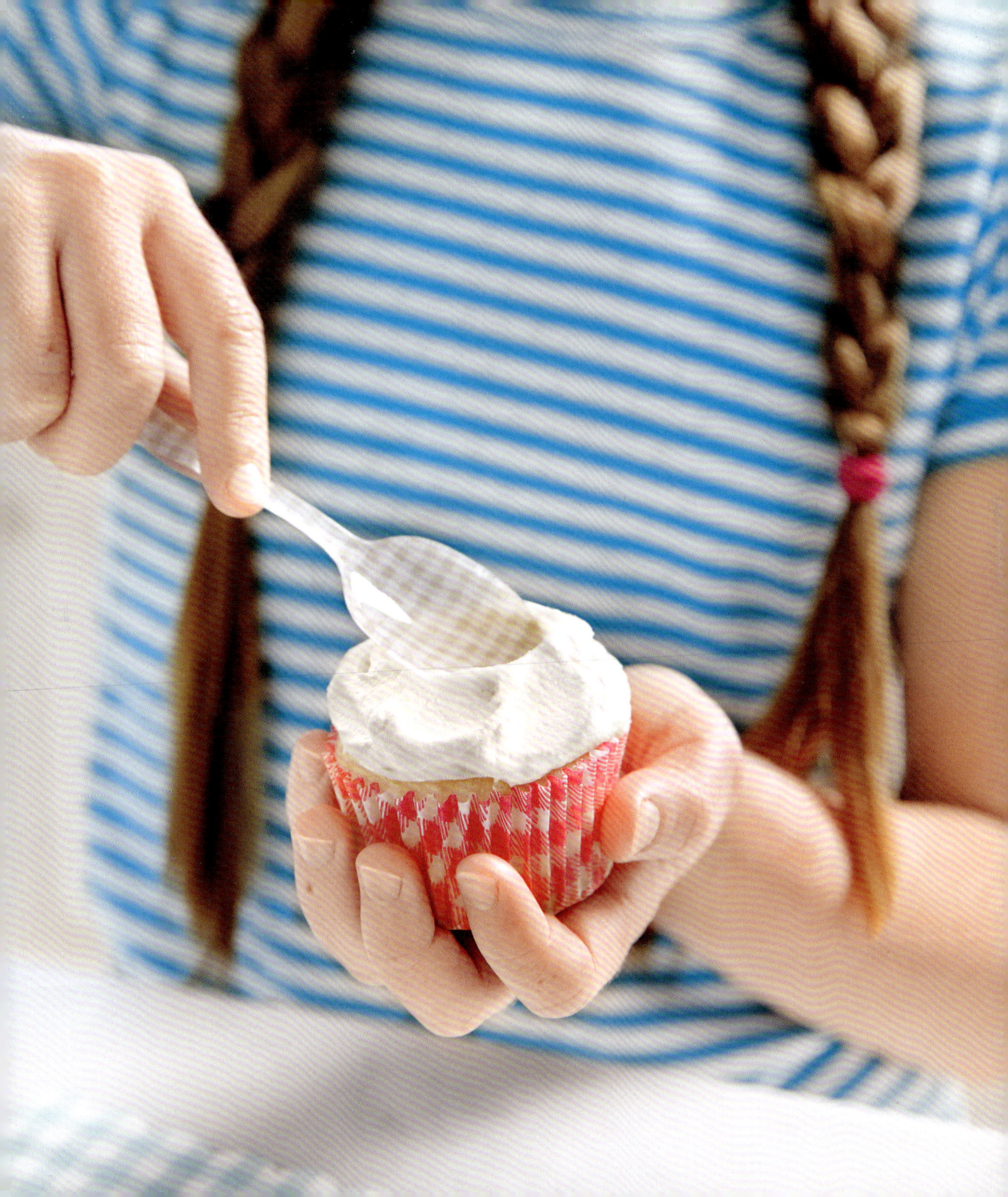

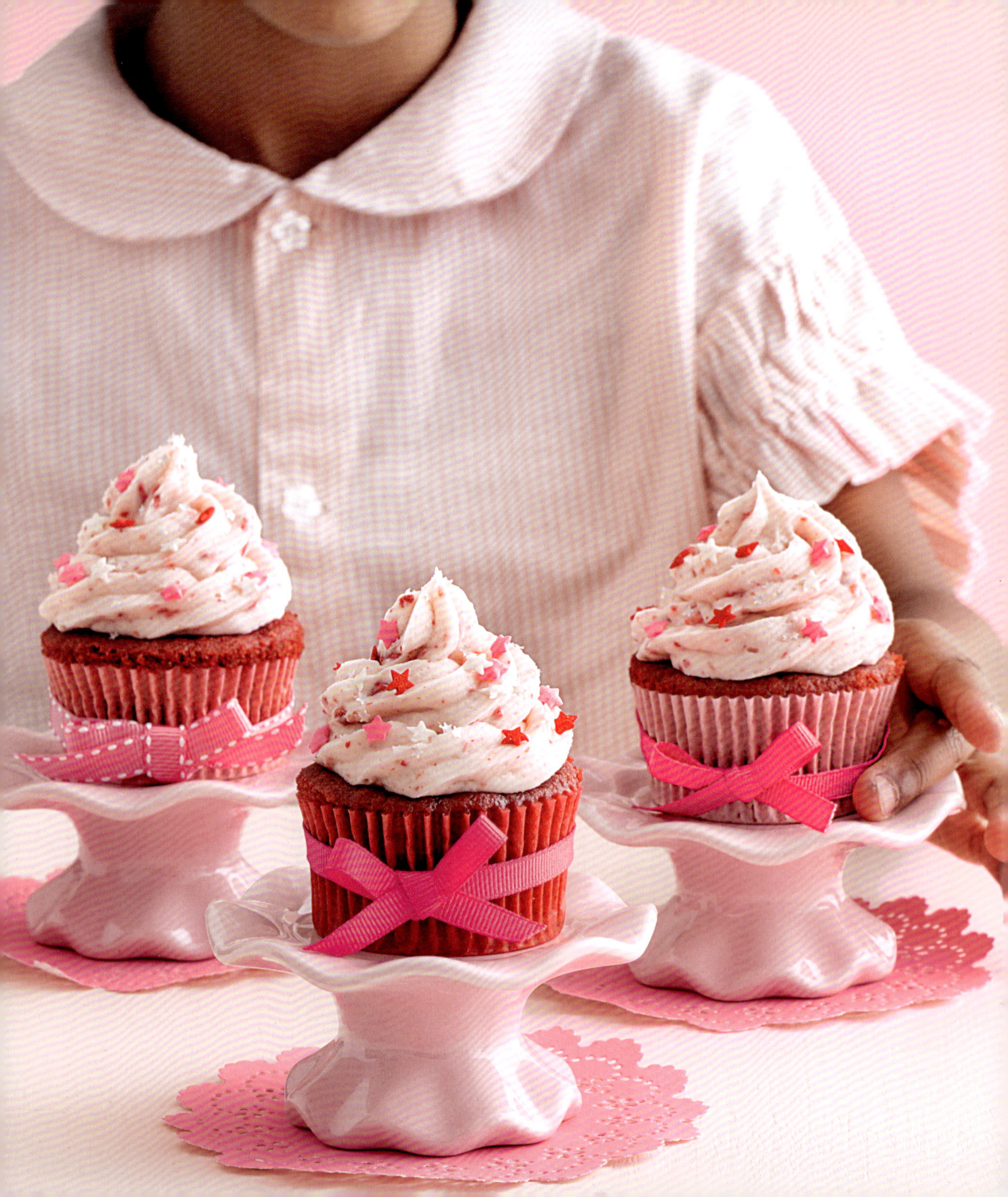

Cream Cheese Frosting

Sweet and slightly tangy, cream cheese frosting pairs well with many different types of cupcakes; see variations below. If you will be piping this frosting instead of spreading it, double the amount of powdered sugar to make it easier to work with in the piping bag.

MAKES ABOUT 1½ CUPS

1 (8-ounce) package cream cheese, at room temperature

6 tablespoons (¾ stick) unsalted butter, at room temperature

1 teaspoon vanilla extract

1 cup powdered sugar (plus 1 cup if you will be using a piping bag)

In a large bowl, using an electric mixer, beat the cream cheese, butter, and vanilla on medium-high speed until light and fluffy, about 2 minutes. Turn off the mixer and scrape down the bowl with a rubber spatula. Add about half of the powdered sugar and mix on low speed until well blended. Turn off the mixer, add the remaining sugar, and beat on medium speed until smooth. The frosting should be spreadable; if it is too soft, cover the bowl and refrigerate it for about 15 minutes.

Frosting Variations

Honey–Cream Cheese Frosting: Add 3 tablespoons honey with the cream cheese, butter, and vanilla.

Coconut–Cream Cheese Frosting: Add 1½ teaspoons coconut extract with the cream cheese, butter, and vanilla.

Strawberry–Cream Cheese Frosting: Place ½ cup freeze-dried strawberries in a quart-size zipper-lock bag and seal the bag. Using a rolling pin or wooden spoon, crush the strawberries to a fine powder. Follow the recipe for Cream Cheese Frosting, then turn off the mixer. Add the strawberry powder and mix on low speed until well combined.

Blackberry–Cream Cheese Frosting: Follow the recipe for Cream Cheese Frosting, then turn off the mixer. Add ½ cup blackberry jam and mix on low speed until well combined.

Chocolate Frosting

This rich and buttery chocolate frosting is so delicious you'll want to eat it from the bowl. No one will notice if you sneak a spoonful or two, but try to save most of it for frosting your cupcakes!

MAKES ABOUT 3 CUPS

3½ cups powdered sugar

1 cup unsweetened cocoa powder

½ cup (1 stick) unsalted butter, cut into 8 pieces, at room temperature

1 teaspoon vanilla extract

Pinch of salt

1 cup heavy cream, plus more as needed

Sift the powdered sugar and cocoa into a large bowl. Add the butter. Using an electric mixer, beat the mixture on low speed just until crumbly. Add the vanilla and salt and beat until combined. Turn off the mixer. Add the cream and beat on medium speed until the frosting is smooth, about 1 minute. The frosting should be smooth and spreadable; if it is too thick, beat in more cream 1 teaspoon at a time until it reaches the proper consistency.

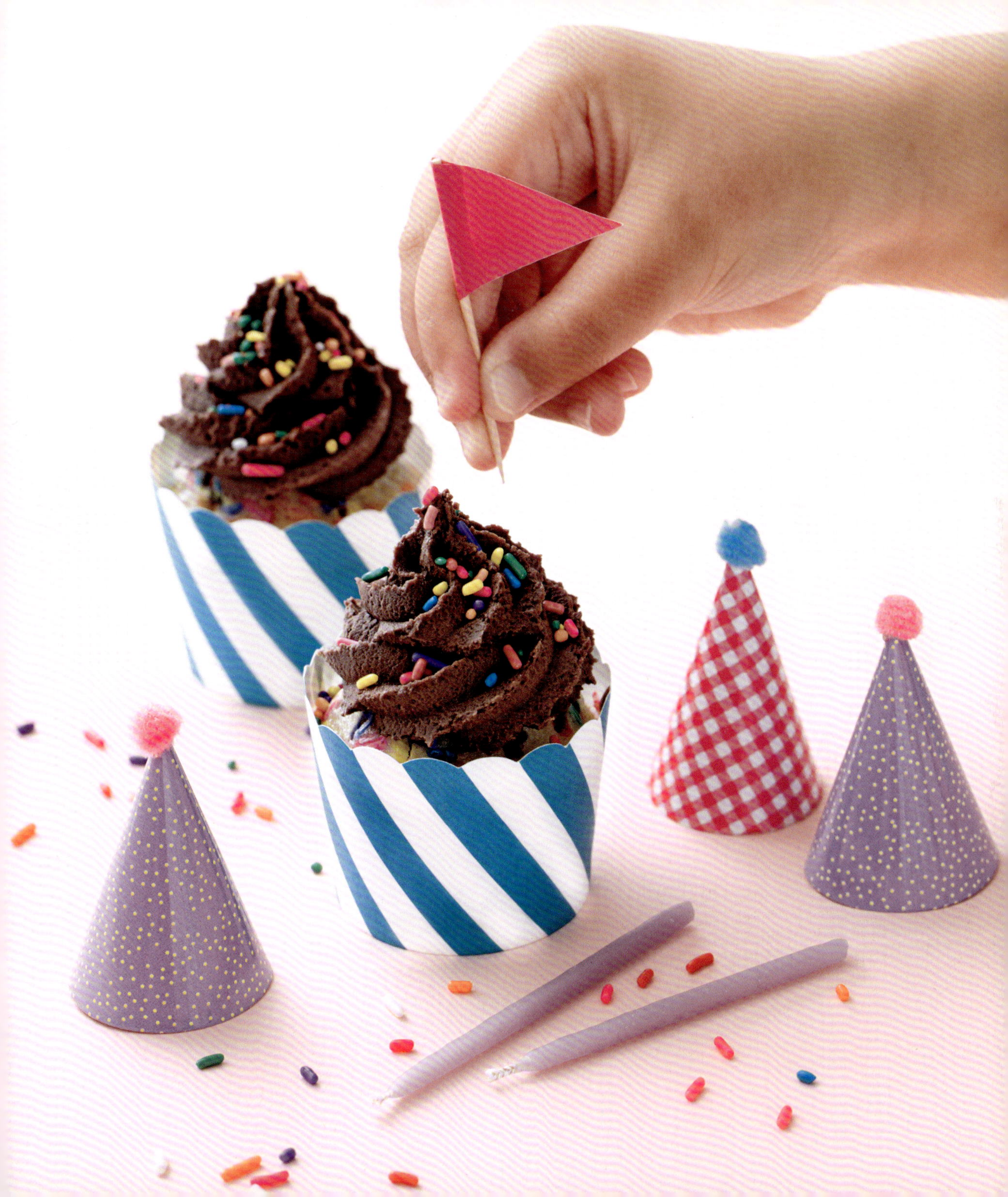

Peanut Butter Frosting

If you thought peanut butter couldn't get any better, try this super-simple frosting. For really rich, extra-nutty flavor, use natural or old-fashioned peanut butter, but make sure to stir it well before measuring because the oil naturally separates to the top.

MAKES ABOUT 1½ CUPS

6 tablespoons (¾ stick) unsalted butter, at room temperature

¾ cup powdered sugar

¾ cup smooth peanut butter

¼ cup heavy cream

In a large bowl, using an electric mixer, beat the butter, powdered sugar, peanut butter, and cream on medium-low speed until smooth and combined, about 2 minutes. Turn off the mixer and scrape down the bowl with a rubber spatula as needed.

Rich Chocolate Glaze

This smooth, shiny, very chocolaty glaze can be used as a filling or as a topping. Let the glaze cool a bit before you use it; it should be warm if used for a filling, or cooled to room temperature if used as a topping, otherwise it'll be too thin to coat the cupcakes.

MAKES ABOUT 1¾ CUPS

1 cup heavy cream

1 tablespoon light corn syrup

Pinch of salt

8 ounces semisweet chocolate, chopped

In a medium saucepan, combine the cream, corn syrup, and salt. Set the pan over medium-high heat and bring to a simmer, stirring occasionally. Remove the pan from the heat, add the chocolate, and let stand for about 3 minutes.

Using a wooden spoon, stir until the chocolate is completely melted and the mixture is smooth. Let cool until warm if using the glaze as a filling; let cool to room temperature if using as a topping.

(The cooled glaze can be refrigerated in an airtight container for up to 3 days. Before using, soften the glaze by gently heating it in a heatproof bowl set over, but not touching, simmering water in a saucepan.)

Vanilla & Lemon Glazes

Vanilla Glaze: In a small bowl, whisk together 1 cup powdered sugar, 2 tablespoons whole milk, and 1 teaspoon vanilla extract until smooth; the glaze should be spreadable but not runny. If it is too thick, whisk in additional milk a few drops at a time; if it is too thin, whisk in additional sugar 1 teaspoon at a time.

Lemon Glaze: Substitute fresh lemon juice for the milk and 2 teaspoons grated lemon zest for the vanilla.

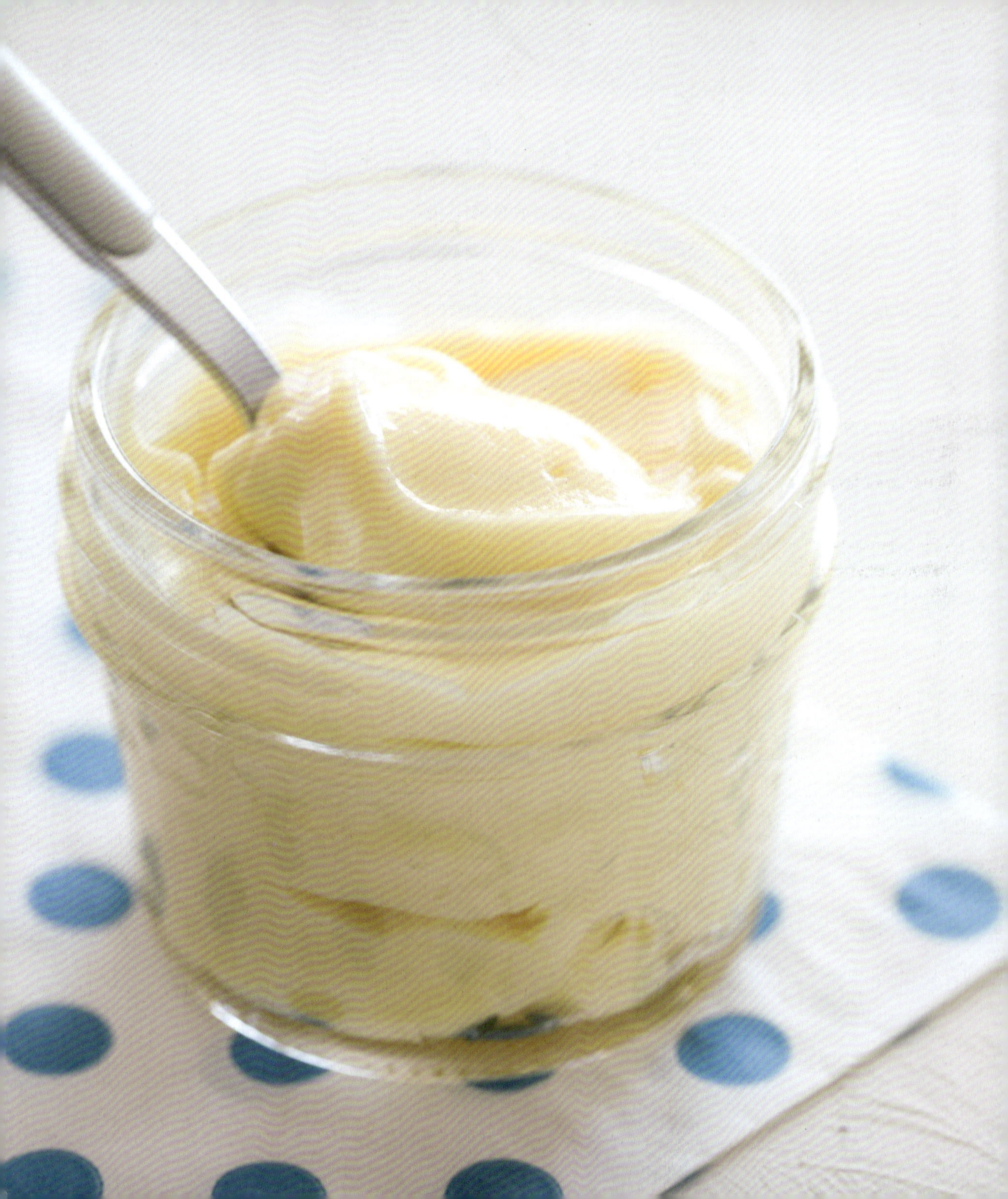

Vanilla Custard

This creamy cupcake filling is so yummy that you'll want to eat it with a spoon. It's also great spread between layers of cake or piped into cream puffs. Straining after cooking removes any lumps so that it's sure to be silky and smooth.

MAKES ABOUT 2½ CUPS

4 large egg yolks
½ cup sugar
¼ cup cornstarch
¼ teaspoon salt
2 cups whole milk
1½ teaspoons vanilla extract

In a medium bowl, whisk the egg yolks and set aside.

In a medium saucepan, whisk together the sugar, cornstarch, and salt. Slowly whisk in the milk and vanilla. Set the pan over medium heat and bring the mixture to a simmer, stirring occasionally to start but constantly as the mixture comes close to a simmer and thickens. Remove the pan from the heat.

While whisking constantly, add about one-third of the hot thickened milk mixture to the egg yolks. Now whisk the egg yolk mixture into the hot milk mixture in the saucepan. Set the pan over medium heat and cook, stirring constantly, until the pastry cream reaches a simmer and thickens, about 4 minutes. Continue to cook, whisking constantly, for about 1 minute longer. The custard should be thick enough to coat the back of a spoon. Remove from the heat.

Set a medium-mesh strainer over a medium bowl and pour the pastry cream into the strainer. Using a rubber spatula, stir and push the pastry cream through the strainer, then scrape the bottom of the strainer to collect as much of the pastry cream as you can. Press a piece of plastic wrap directly against the surface of the pastry cream to prevent a skin from forming. Let cool for 15 minutes.

(The custard can be stored in the refrigerator in an airtight container for up to 2 days.)

Caramel Drizzle

A drizzle of thick, rich caramel makes even the simplest cupcakes look and taste special. Sugar becomes very hot and sticky when made into caramel, so ask an adult for help. Watch the sugar as it cooks because once it starts to turn brown, it darkens very quickly.

MAKES ABOUT 2½ CUPS

1½ cups sugar
1¼ cups heavy cream
Pinch of salt

Place the sugar in a heavy-bottomed, high-sided medium saucepan and set the pan over medium-high heat. Cook the sugar until it begins to melt around the edges, about 5 minutes. Stir with a clean wooden spoon and continue to cook until the sugar is melted and has turned golden brown in color, about 3 minutes longer.

Carefully pour the cream down the inside of the pan in a slow, steady stream—be very careful because the mixture will bubble and spatter! Continue to cook over medium heat, stirring constantly, until the caramel is completely smooth. Remove the pan from the heat and stir in the salt. Pour the caramel into a small heatproof bowl and let cool completely.

(The caramel can be refrigerated in an airtight container for up to 1 week; bring to room temperature before using.)

Crumb Topping

This buttery, crumbly topping turns irresistibly crunchy during baking. Use it to jazz up vanilla, yellow, or even gingerbread cupcakes. It's also good atop muffins.

MAKES ABOUT 2 CUPS

- 1¼ cups all-purpose flour
- ½ cup firmly packed light brown sugar
- 1½ teaspoons ground cinnamon
- ¼ teaspoon salt
- ¾ cup (1½ sticks) unsalted butter, at room temperature

In a medium bowl, whisk together the flour, brown sugar, cinnamon, and salt. Add the butter and, using a fork, mash it into the flour mixture until large, moist crumbs form.

Better butter
Be gentle when using a fork to incorporate the softened butter into the topping. Only mix until large crumbs form.

Whipped Honey Frosting

A little honey goes a long way in this fluffy frosting, giving it a unique taste and sweet appeal. The frosting should be soft and spreadable. If it's too thick, stir in a little extra cream until you have achieved the consistency you want.

MAKES ABOUT 2½ CUPS

1 cup (2 sticks) unsalted butter, at room temperature

⅓ cup honey

¼ teaspoon salt

4 cups powdered sugar

3 tablespoons heavy cream, plus more as needed

2 teaspoons vanilla extract

In a large bowl, using an electric mixer, beat the butter, honey, and salt on medium-high speed until light and fluffy, about 2 minutes. Turn off the mixer and scrape down the bowl with a rubber spatula. Sift 2 cups of the powdered sugar into the bowl and beat on low speed until the sugar is incorporated. Raise the speed to medium-high and beat until smooth, about 3 minutes. Sift the remaining 2 cups powdered sugar into the bowl, add the cream and vanilla, and beat on low speed until incorporated. Turn off the mixer and scrape down the bowl. Beat on medium-high speed until the frosting is fluffy and smooth, about 5 minutes. The frosting should be easily spreadable; if not, stir in a little more cream, 1 tablespoon at a time, until the desired consistency is reached. Use right away, or store in an airtight container in the refrigerator for up to 2 days. Stir vigorously just before using.

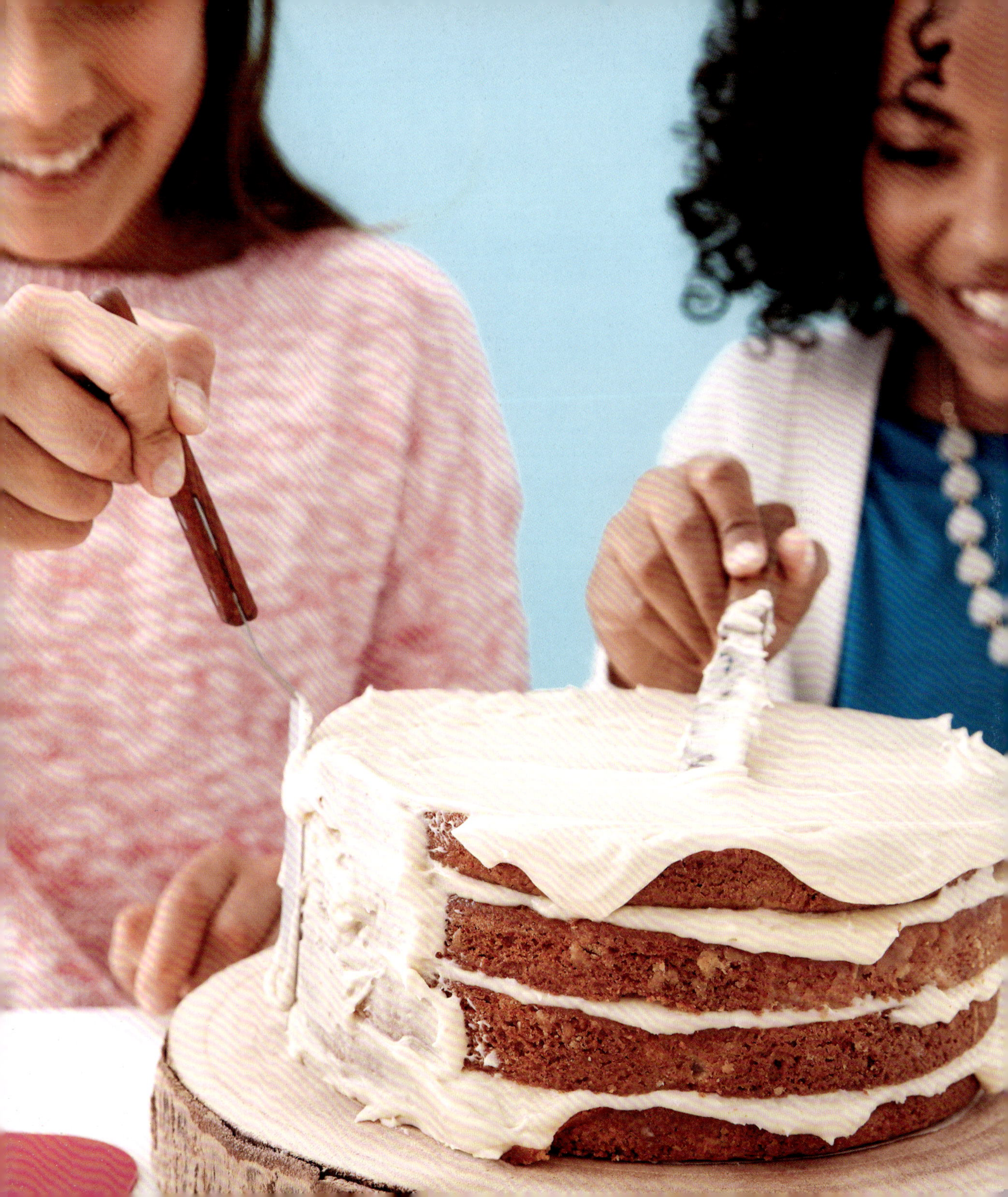

Index

A

Almond butter
    Nut, Seed & Fruit Granola Bars, 95
Almond flour
    Colorful Macarons, 75–76
    Peppermint Swirl Macarons, 69–70
Almonds
    Baked Nectarines with Cinnamon Streusel, 134
    Chocolate-Drizzled Almond Florentines, 63
    Chocolate-Raspberry Tartlets, 240
    Kitchen Sink Cookies, 32
Apples
    Apple Galettes, 196
    Apple Streusel Muffins, 218
    Cinnamon-Swirl Apple Pie, 228–31
    French Apple Tart, 243
    Frosted Apple Cake, 119–21
Applesauce
    Spiced Apple & Honey Cake, 122–24
    Spiced Applesauce Muffins, 209
Appliances, 10
Apricots and apricot jam
    Apricot Puff-Pastry Twists, 205
    Nut, Seed & Fruit Granola Bars, 95
Aprons, 9

B

Baked Nectarines with Cinnamon Streusel, 134
Baking tips and hints
    baking tips, 10
    basic baking tools, 9
    help from adults, 10, 11
    safety tips, 11
Banana-Chocolate Cream Pie Cupcakes, 165–66

Bars. See also Blondies; Brownies
    Caramel-Glazed Blondies, 86
    Lemon-Blackberry Crumb Bars, 92
    Lemony Berry Bars, 96
    Nut, Seed & Fruit Granola Bars, 95
    Ooey-Gooey Layer Bars, 90
    Sugar Cookie Bars, 89
Berries. See also specific berries
    Mixed Berry Shortcake, 127–28
Bite-Sized Chocolate Chip Scones, 200
Blackberries and blackberry jam
    Blackberry–Cream Cheese Frosting, 263
    Blackberry Slab Pie, 222
    Blackberry Tart with Pecan Crust, 244
    Lemon-Blackberry Crumb Bars, 92
Black Forest Cake, 110–11
Blondies, Caramel-Glazed, 86
Blueberries
    Blueberry Turnovers, 194
    Mini Blueberry-Oat Muffins, 215
    Vanilla-Glazed "Toaster" Pastries, 193
Brownies
    Chocolate–Peanut Butter Brownies, 99
    Crispy Rice and Chocolate Layer Brownies, 100–103
    Frosted Chocolate Brownies, 93
Butter, room temperature, 10
Butterfly Cupcakes, 181

C

Cakes. See also Cupcakes
    Black Forest Cake, 110–11
    Chocolate Chip Cookie Birthday Cake, 115

Chocolate-Dipped Vanilla Madeleines, 140
Chocolate Ice Box Cake, 129–30
Chocolate Madeleines, 139
Cranberry Upside-Down Cake, 133
Frosted Apple Cake, 119–21
Golden Layer Cake with Chocolate Frosting, 106–9
Honey Madeleines, 136
Mixed Berry Shortcake, 127–28
Orange Madeleines, 138
Pink Orange Cake, 116–18
Southern Tea Cakes, 125
Spiced Apple & Honey Cake, 122–24
Tres Leches Cakes, 112
Caramel
    Caramel Drizzle, 270
    Caramel-Glazed Blondies, 86
Cheesecake Pie, Easy, 227
Cherries
    Black Forest Cake, 110–11
    Individual Cherry Cobblers, 237
    Mini Peach & Cherry Pies, 225–26
    Vanilla-Glazed "Toaster" Pastries, 193
Chess Tart, Cranberry, 251
Chewy White Chocolate Coconut Cookies, 53
Chocolate. See also White chocolate
    Bite-Sized Chocolate Chip Scones, 200
    Black Forest Cake, 110–11
    Chocolate-Banana Cream Pie Cupcakes, 165–66
    Chocolate Chip Cookie Birthday Cake, 115
    Chocolate Chip Cookie Sandwiches, 26
    Chocolate Cookies, 129–30

Chocolate-Covered Mint Wafers, 54–56
Chocolate Crinkle Cookies, 29
Chocolate-Dipped Butter Cookie Triangles, 45
Chocolate-Dipped Vanilla Madeleines, 140
Chocolate-Drizzled Almond Florentines, 63
Chocolate Éclair Cupcakes, 166
Chocolate-Filled Vanilla Sandwich Cookies, 57
Chocolate Frosting, 264
Chocolate Ice Box Cake, 129–30
Chocolate Madeleines, 139
Chocolate–Peanut Butter Brownies, 99
Chocolate-Raspberry Tartlets, 240
Cookies 'n' Cream Cupcakes, 174
Cosmos Doughnuts, 206–8
Crispy Rice and Chocolate Layer Brownies, 100–103
Cupcake Cones, 183
Devil's Food Cupcakes, 144
Frosted Chocolate Brownies, 93
Golden Layer Cake with Chocolate Frosting, 106–9
Homemade Oreos, 33
Hot Chocolate Cookies, 36
Ice Cream Sandwiches, 79
Kitchen Sink Cookies, 32
Milk-and-Cookie Cups, 49–50
Moon Pies, 80–82
Ooey-Gooey Layer Bars, 90
Rich Chocolate Glaze, 267
S'mores Cupcakes, 159
Triple-Chocolate-Chunk Cookies, 42
Triple Chocolate Cupcakes, 180

Cinnamon
  Baked Nectarines with Cinnamon Streusel, 134
  Cinnamon Rolls with Cream Cheese Icing, 191–92
  Cinnamon-Sugar Donut Holes, 203–4
  Cinnamon-Swirl Apple Pie, 228–31
  Snickerdoodles, 19
  Sugar-and-Spice Popovers, 188
Classic Peanut Butter Cookies, 62
Classic Pumpkin Pie, 235
Cobblers, Individual Cherry, 237
Coconut
  Chewy White Chocolate Coconut Cookies, 53
  Coconut–Cream Cheese Frosting, 263
  Fluffy Coconut Frosting, 260
  Kitchen Sink Cookies, 32
  Ooey-Gooey Layer Bars, 90
  Snowball Cupcakes, 148
  Toasted Coconut Cupcakes, 169
Coffee Cake Muffins, 211
Colorful Macarons, 75–76
Cones, Cupcake, 183
Confetti Cookies, 46
Confetti Donut Holes, 204
Cookie cutters, 9
Cookies
  Chewy White Chocolate Coconut Cookies, 53
  Chocolate Chip Cookie Sandwiches, 26
  Chocolate Cookies, 129–30
  Chocolate-Covered Mint Wafers, 54–56
  Chocolate Crinkle Cookies, 29
  Chocolate-Dipped Butter Cookie Triangles, 45

Chocolate-Drizzled Almond Florentines, 63
Chocolate-Filled Vanilla Sandwich Cookies, 57
Classic Peanut Butter Cookies, 62
Colorful Macarons, 75–76
Confetti Cookies, 46
Donut Cookies, 64
Elephant Ears, 20
Flower Cookie Pops, 73–74
Fortune Cookies, 23
Galaxy Cookies, 39
Gingerbread Cookies, 83
Graham Cookies, 80
Homemade Oreos, 33
Hot Chocolate Cookies, 36
Ice Cream Sandwiches, 79
Kitchen Sink Cookies, 32
Lemon Crinkle Cookies, 35
Milk-and-Cookie Cups, 49–50
Moon Pies, 80–82
Peppermint Swirl Macarons, 69–70
Pinwheel Icebox Cookies, 17–18
Raspberry Jam Heart Cookies, 30
Snickerdoodles, 19
Southern Tea Cakes, 125
Sugar Cookie Cutouts, 59–60
Thumbprint Cookies, 14
Triple-Chocolate-Chunk Cookies, 42
Cookie sheets, 9
Cookies 'n' Cream Cupcakes, 174
Cosmos Doughnuts, 206–8
Cranberries
  Cranberry Chess Tart, 251
  Cranberry-Oat Muffins, 216
  Cranberry Upside-Down Cake, 133
Cream, Whipped, 127–28, 129–30

Cream cheese
    Blackberry–Cream Cheese Frosting, 263
    Cinnamon Rolls with Cream Cheese Icing, 191–92
    Coconut–Cream Cheese Frosting, 263
    Cream Cheese Frosting, 263
    Easy Cheesecake Pie, 227
    Frosted Apple Cake, 119–21
    Honey–Cream Cheese Frosting, 263
    Lemon Tart with Raspberries, 247
    Strawberry–Cream Cheese Frosting, 263
    Sugar Cookie Bars, 89
Crispy Rice and Chocolate Layer Brownies, 100–103
Crumb Topping, 271
Crumpets, 197
Cupcakes
    Butterfly Cupcakes, 181
    Chocolate-Banana Cream Pie Cupcakes, 165–66
    Chocolate Éclair Cupcakes, 166
    Cookies 'n' Cream Cupcakes, 174
    Cupcake Cones, 183
    Devil's Food Cupcakes, 144
    Gingerbread Cupcakes, 177
    Iced Lemon Drizzle Cupcakes, 184
    PB & J Cupcakes, 156
    Pink Velvet Cupcakes, 170
    Pumpkin Cupcakes, 160
    Rainbow Cupcakes, 178
    Red Velvet Cupcakes, 155
    S'mores Cupcakes, 159
    Snowball Cupcakes, 148
    Snow White Cupcakes, 173
    Strawberries & Cream Cupcakes, 147
    Strawberry Cupcakes, 163–64
    Sweet Lemony Cupcakes, 151
    Toasted Coconut Cupcakes, 169
    Triple Chocolate Cupcakes, 180
    White Chocolate & Raspberry Cupcakes, 152
    Yellow Cupcakes, 157
Custard, Vanilla, 269

D

Devil's Food Cupcakes, 144
Donut Cookies, 64
Donut Holes
    Cinnamon-Sugar Donut Holes, 203–4
    Confetti Donut Holes, 204
    Powdered-Sugar Donut Holes, 204
Doughnuts, Cosmos, 206–8
Drizzle, Caramel, 270

E

Easy Cheesecake Pie, 227
Eggs, room temperature, 10
Electric mixer, 9
Elephant Ears, 20

F

Florentines, Chocolate-Drizzled Almond, 63
Flower Cookie Pops, 73–74
Flowers, Sugared, Lemon Tartlets with, 248–50
Fluffy Coconut Frosting, 260
Fluffy Mint Frosting, 260
Fluffy Raspberry Frosting, 260
Fluffy Vanilla Frosting, 260
Fluffy White Chocolate Frosting, 260
Fortune Cookies, 23
French Apple Tart, 243
Frosted Apple Cake, 119–21
Frosted Chocolate Brownies, 93
Frostings
    Blackberry–Cream Cheese Frosting, 263
    Chocolate Frosting, 264
    Coconut–Cream Cheese Frosting, 263
    Cream Cheese Frosting, 263
    Fluffy Coconut Frosting, 260
    Fluffy Mint Frosting, 260
    Fluffy Raspberry Frosting, 260
    Fluffy Vanilla Frosting, 260
    Fluffy White Chocolate Frosting, 260
    Honey–Cream Cheese Frosting, 263
    Peanut Butter Frosting, 266
    Strawberry–Cream Cheese Frosting, 263
    Whipped Honey Frosting, 272
    White Chocolate Frosting, 259
    White Chocolate–Peppermint Frosting, 259
Fruit. *See also* specific fruits
    Nut, Seed & Fruit Granola Bars, 95

G

Galaxy Cookies, 39
Galettes, Apple, 196
Gingerbread Cookies, 83
Gingerbread Cupcakes, 177
Glazes
    Lemon Glaze, 267
    Rich Chocolate Glaze, 267
    Vanilla Glaze, 267
Golden Layer Cake with Chocolate Frosting, 106–9
Graham crackers
    Easy Cheesecake Pie, 227
    Graham Cookies, 80
    Ooey-Gooey Layer Bars, 90

S'mores Cupcakes, 159
Granola Bars, Nut, Seed & Fruit, 95

H

Hand Pies, Strawberry, 238
Homemade Oreos, 33
Honey
    Honey–Cream Cheese Frosting, 263
    Honey Madeleines, 136
    Spiced Apple & Honey Cake, 122–24
    Whipped Honey Frosting, 272
Hot Chocolate Cookies, 36

I

Ice Box Cake, Chocolate, 129–30
Icebox Cookies, Pinwheel, 17–18
Ice Cream Sandwiches, 79
Ice cream scoop, 9
Iced Lemon Drizzle Cupcakes, 184
Icings
    Royal Icing, 256–58
    Vanilla Icing, 60
Icing spatulas, 9
Icing techniques
    flooding, 256–58
    swirling, 258
Individual Cherry Cobblers, 237

J

Jams, fruit
    Apricot Puff-Pastry Twists, 205
    Blackberry–Cream Cheese Frosting, 263
    Butterfly Cupcakes, 181
    Coffee Cake Muffins, 211
    Jam Twists, 199
    Lemony Berry Bars, 96

PB & J Cupcakes, 156
Raspberry Jam Heart Cookies, 30
Strawberries & Cream Cupcakes, 147
Strawberry Cupcakes, 163–64
Strawberry Jam Muffins, 212
Thumbprint Cookies, 14

K

Kitchen Sink Cookies, 32

L

Lemon
    Iced Lemon Drizzle Cupcakes, 184
    Lemon-Blackberry Crumb Bars, 92
    Lemon Crinkle Cookies, 35
    Lemon Glaze, 267
    Lemon Tartlets with Sugared Flowers, 248–50
    Lemon Tart with Raspberries, 247
    Lemony Berry Bars, 96
    Southern Tea Cakes, 125
    Sweet Lemony Cupcakes, 151

M

Macarons
    Colorful Macarons, 75–76
    Peppermint Swirl Macarons, 69–70
Madeleine pans, 9
Madeleines
    Chocolate-Dipped Vanilla Madeleines, 140
    Chocolate Madeleines, 139
    Honey Madeleines, 136
    Orange Madeleines, 138
Maple-Pecan Pie with Shortbread Crust, 239

Marshmallow crème
    Moon Pies, 80–82
Marshmallows
    Crispy Rice and Chocolate Layer Brownies, 100–103
    Hot Chocolate Cookies, 36
    Rainbow Cupcakes, 178
    S'mores Cupcakes, 159
Measuring cups and spoons, 9
Milk-and-Cookie Cups, 49–50
Mini Blueberry-Oat Muffins, 215
Mini Peach & Cherry Pies, 225–26
Mint
    Chocolate-Covered Mint Wafers, 54–56
    Fluffy Mint Frosting, 260
    Peppermint Swirl Macarons, 69–70
Mixed Berry Shortcake, 127–28
Molasses
    Gingerbread Cookies, 83
    Gingerbread Cupcakes, 177
Moon Pies, 80–82
Muffin pans, 9
Muffins
    Apple Streusel Muffins, 218
    Coffee Cake Muffins, 211
    Cranberry-Oat Muffins, 216
    Mini Blueberry-Oat Muffins, 215
    Pumpkin Spice Muffins, 217
    Spiced Applesauce Muffins, 209
    Strawberry Jam Muffins, 212

N

Nectarines, Baked, with Cinnamon Streusel, 134
Nuts. *See* Almonds; Pecans; Walnuts

O

Oats
- Cranberry-Oat Muffins, 216
- Kitchen Sink Cookies, 32
- Mini Blueberry-Oat Muffins, 215
- Nut, Seed & Fruit Granola Bars, 95
- Ooey-Gooey Layer Bars, 90

Ooey-Gooey Layer Bars, 90

Oranges
- Orange Madeleines, 138
- Pink Orange Cake, 116–18

Oreos, Homemade, 33
Oven mitts, 9
Ovens, 10

P

Parchment paper, 9

Pastries
- Apple Galettes, 196
- Apricot Puff-Pastry Twists, 205
- Blueberry Turnovers, 194
- Jam Twists, 199
- Vanilla-Glazed "Toaster" Pastries, 193

PB & J Cupcakes, 156
Peach & Cherry Pies, Mini, 225–26

Peanut butter
- Chocolate–Peanut Butter Brownies, 99
- Classic Peanut Butter Cookies, 62
- Crispy Rice and Chocolate Layer Brownies, 100–103
- Nut, Seed & Fruit Granola Bars, 95
- PB & J Cupcakes, 156
- Peanut Butter Frosting, 266

Pecans
- Blackberry Tart with Pecan Crust, 244
- Maple-Pecan Pie with Shortbread Crust, 239
- Ooey-Gooey Layer Bars, 90
- Sweet Potato Pie, 232–34

Peppermint Swirl Macarons, 69–70

Pies
- Blackberry Slab Pie, 222
- Cinnamon-Swirl Apple Pie, 228–31
- Classic Pumpkin Pie, 235
- Easy Cheesecake Pie, 227
- Maple-Pecan Pie with Shortbread Crust, 239
- Mini Peach & Cherry Pies, 225–26
- Strawberry Hand Pies, 238
- Sweet Potato Pie, 232–34

Pink Orange Cake, 116–18
Pink Velvet Cupcakes, 170
Pinwheel Icebox Cookies, 17–18
Piping bag, 9
Popovers, Sugar-and-Spice, 188
Powdered-Sugar Donut Holes, 204

Puff pastry
- Apricot Puff-Pastry Twists, 205
- Blueberry Turnovers, 194
- Elephant Ears, 20
- French Apple Tart, 243
- Jam Twists, 199
- Strawberry Hand Pies, 238
- Vanilla-Glazed "Toaster" Pastries, 193

Pumpkin
- Classic Pumpkin Pie, 235
- Pumpkin Cupcakes, 160
- Pumpkin Spice Muffins, 217

R

Rainbow Cupcakes, 178

Raspberries
- Chocolate-Raspberry Tartlets, 240
- Fluffy Raspberry Frosting, 260
- Lemon Tart with Raspberries, 247
- Mixed Berry Shortcake, 127–28
- White Chocolate & Raspberry Cupcakes, 152

Raspberry jam
- Butterfly Cupcakes, 181
- Lemony Berry Bars, 96
- Raspberry Jam Heart Cookies, 30
- Thumbprint Cookies, 14

Red Velvet Cupcakes, 155
Rich Chocolate Glaze, 267
Rolls, Cinnamon, with Cream Cheese Icing, 191–92
Royal Icing, 256–58
Rubber spatula, 9

S

Sandwich cookies
- Chocolate Chip Cookie Sandwiches, 26
- Chocolate-Filled Vanilla Sandwich Cookies, 57
- Colorful Macarons, 75–76
- Homemade Oreos, 33
- Ice Cream Sandwiches, 79
- Moon Pies, 80–82
- Peppermint Swirl Macarons, 69–70

Scones, Bite-Sized Chocolate Chip, 200
Seed, Nut & Fruit Granola Bars, 95
Shortbread Crust, 252
Shortcake, Mixed Berry, 127–28
Slab Pie, Blackberry, 222
S'mores Cupcakes, 159
Snickerdoodles, 19
Snowball Cupcakes, 148
Snow White Cupcakes, 173
Southern Tea Cakes, 125
Spatulas, 9

Spiced Apple & Honey Cake, 122–24
Spiced Applesauce Muffins, 209
Sprinkles
    Black Forest Cake, 110–11
    Chocolate-Dipped Butter Cookie Triangles, 45
    Confetti Cookies, 46
    Confetti Donut Holes, 204
    Cupcake Cones, 183
    Donut Cookies, 64
    Golden Layer Cake with Chocolate Frosting, 106–9
    Sugar Cookie Bars, 89
Strawberries
    Chocolate Chip Cookie Birthday Cake, 115
    Mixed Berry Shortcake, 127–28
    Pink Velvet Cupcakes, 170
    Strawberries & Cream Cupcakes, 147
    Strawberry–Cream Cheese Frosting, 263
    Strawberry Cupcakes, 163–64
    Strawberry Hand Pies, 238
Strawberry jam
    Butterfly Cupcakes, 181
    Strawberries & Cream Cupcakes, 147
    Strawberry Cupcakes, 163–64
    Strawberry Jam Muffins, 212
Streusel
    Apple Streusel Muffins, 218
    Baked Nectarines with Cinnamon Streusel, 134
    Crumb Topping, 271
Sugar-and-Spice Popovers, 188
Sugar Cookie Bars, 89
Sugar Cookie Cutouts, 59–60
Sweet Lemony Cupcakes, 151
Sweet Potato Pie, 232–34

T

Tart Dough, 253
Tarts
    Blackberry Tart with Pecan Crust, 244
    Chocolate-Raspberry Tartlets, 240
    Cranberry Chess Tart, 251
    French Apple Tart, 243
    Lemon Tartlets with Sugared Flowers, 248–50
    Lemon Tart with Raspberries, 247
Thumbprint Cookies, 14
Toasted Coconut Cupcakes, 169
"Toaster" Pastries, Vanilla-Glazed, 193
Tools, 9
Topping, Crumb, 271
Tres Leches Cakes, 112
Triple-Chocolate-Chunk Cookies, 42
Triple Chocolate Cupcakes, 180
Turnovers, Blueberry, 194

V

Vanilla
    Chocolate-Dipped Vanilla Madeleines, 140
    Chocolate-Filled Vanilla Sandwich Cookies, 57
    Fluffy Vanilla Frosting, 260
    Vanilla Custard, 269
    Vanilla Glaze, 267
    Vanilla-Glazed "Toaster" Pastries, 193
    Vanilla Icing, 60

W

Walnuts
    Frosted Apple Cake, 119–21
    Ooey-Gooey Layer Bars, 90
    Pumpkin Spice Muffins, 217
Whipped Cream, 127–28, 129–30
Whipped Honey Frosting, 272
White chocolate
    Chewy White Chocolate Coconut Cookies, 53
    Fluffy White Chocolate Frosting, 260
    Triple-Chocolate-Chunk Cookies, 42
    Triple Chocolate Cupcakes, 180
    White Chocolate Frosting, 259
    White Chocolate & Raspberry Cupcakes, 152
    White Chocolate–Peppermint Frosting, 259

Y

Yellow Cupcakes, 157

weldonowen

an imprint of Insight Editions
P.O. Box 3088
San Rafael, CA 94912
www.weldonowen.com

CEO Raoul Goff
VP Publisher Roger Shaw
Associate Publisher Amy Marr
Editorial Director Katie Killebrew
Editorial Assistant Kayla Belser
VP Creative Chrissy Kwasnik
Design Manager Megan Sinead Bingham
VP Manufacturing Alix Nicholaeff
Sr. Production Manager Joshua Smith

Photograher Nicole Hill Gerulat
Food Stylists Tara Bench, Karen Evans, Robyn Valrik
Prop Stylists Veronica Olson, Leigh Noe
Hair & Makeup Kathy Hill

Conceived and produced by Weldon Owen International.

Copyright © 2023 Weldon Owen and American Girl

All rights reserved, including the right of reproduction in whole or in part in any form.

All American Girl marks are owned and used under license from American Girl.

Printed and bound in China

10 9 8 7 6 5 4 3 2 1

Library of Congress Cataloging in Publication data is available

ISBN 13: 979-8-88674-088-2

ACKNOWLEDGMENTS

Weldon Owen wishes to thank: Kelly Booth, Marisa Kwek, Kim Laidlaw, Rachel Markowitz, Alexis Mersel, and Elizabeth Parson

A VERY SPECIAL THANK YOU TO

Models: Avenlie Fullmer, Sophia Jarque, Jane Robinson, Evie Gerulat, Ruby Robinson, Lucy Smith, Naledi Sefolosha, Eav Nielsen, Ellee Arnell, Kaia Sperry, Noelle Gehman

ROOTS of PEACE   REPLANTED PAPER

Insight Editions, in association with Roots of Peace, will plant two trees for each tree used in the manufacturing of this book. Roots of Peace is an internationally renowned humanitarian organization dedicated to eradicating land mines worldwide and converting war-torn lands into productive farms and wildlife habitats. Roots of Peace will plant two million fruit and nut trees in Afghanistan and provide farmers there with the skills and support necessary for sustainable land use.